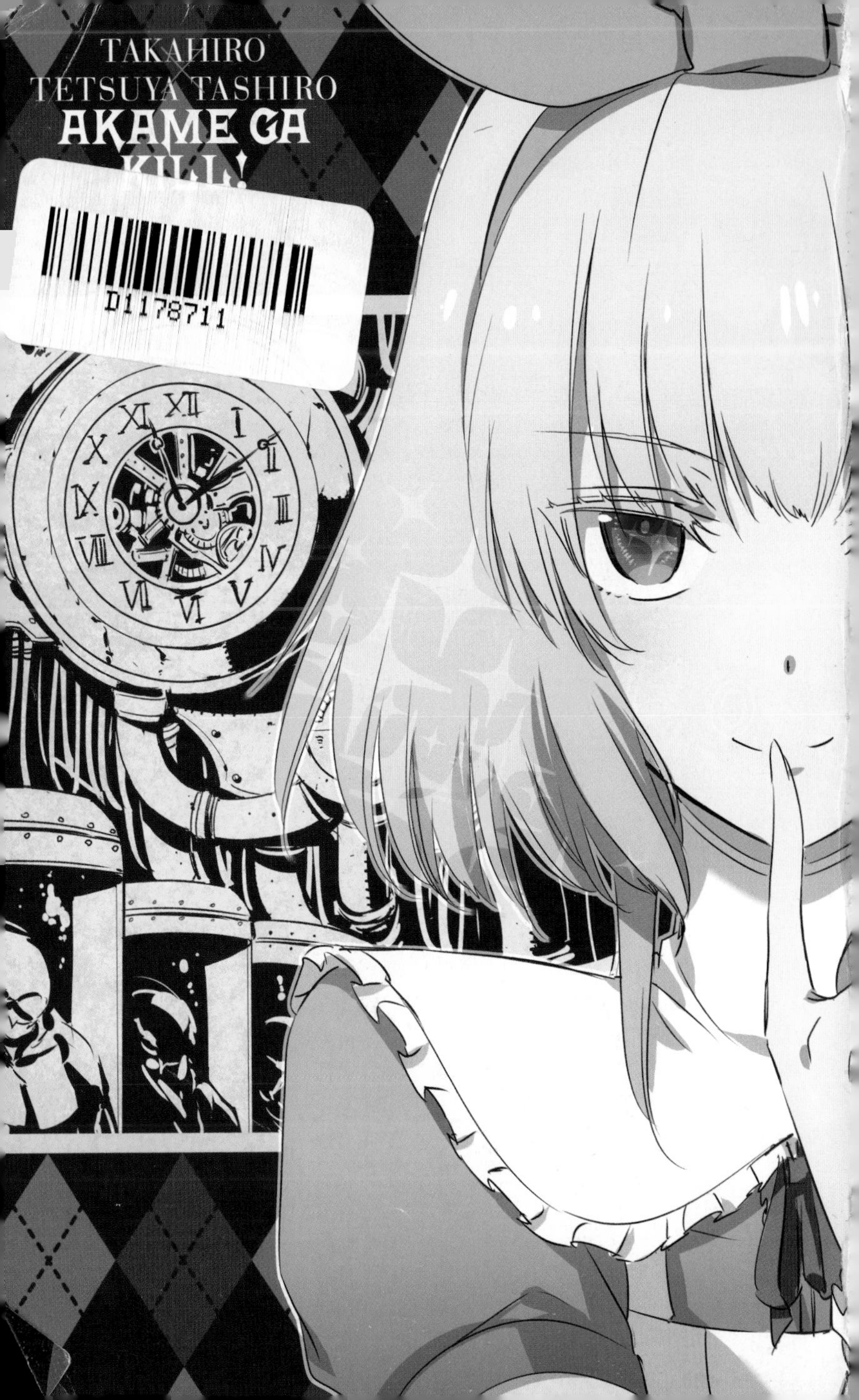
TAKAHIRO
TETSUYA TASHIRO
AKAME GA
KILL!

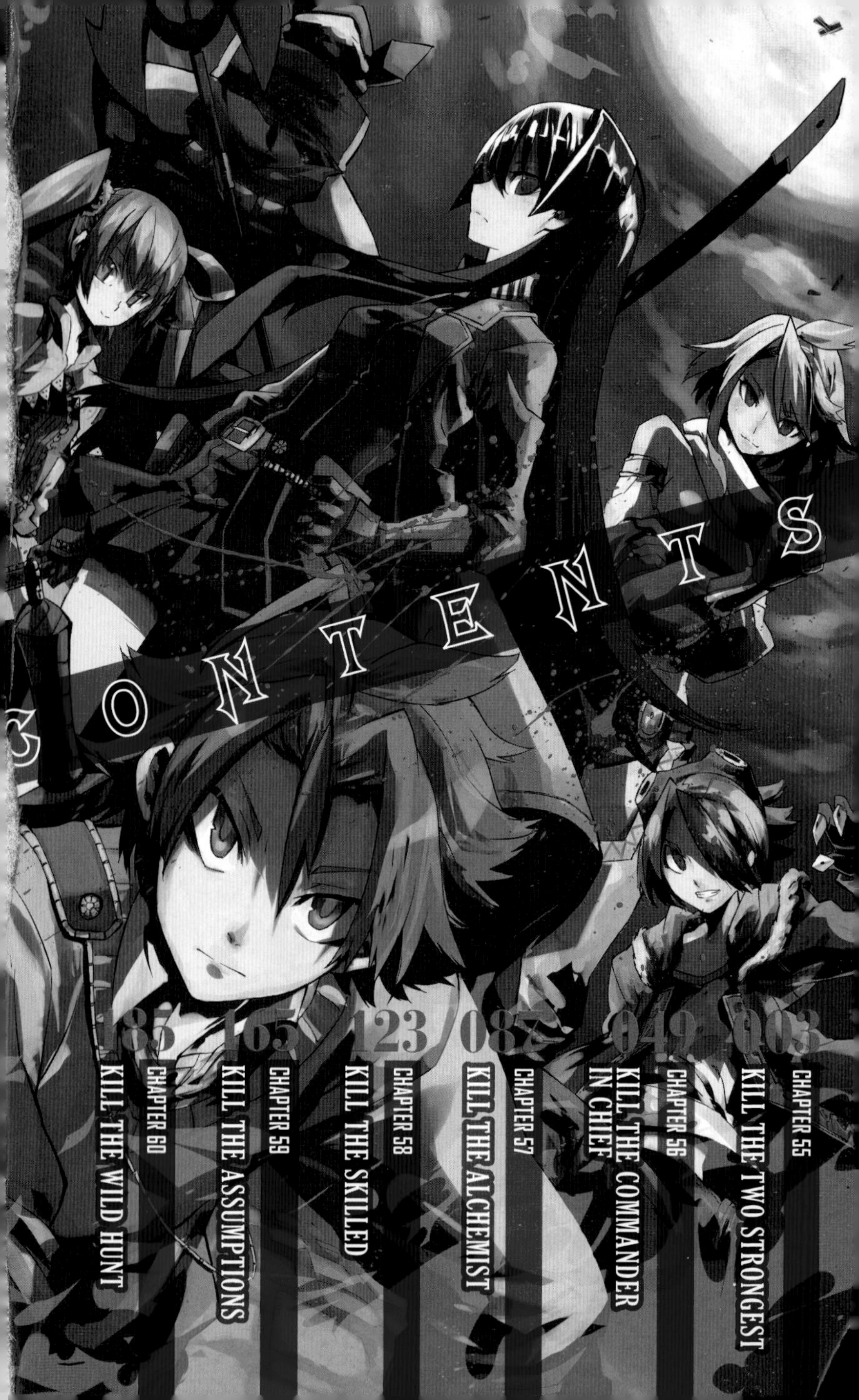

CONTENTS

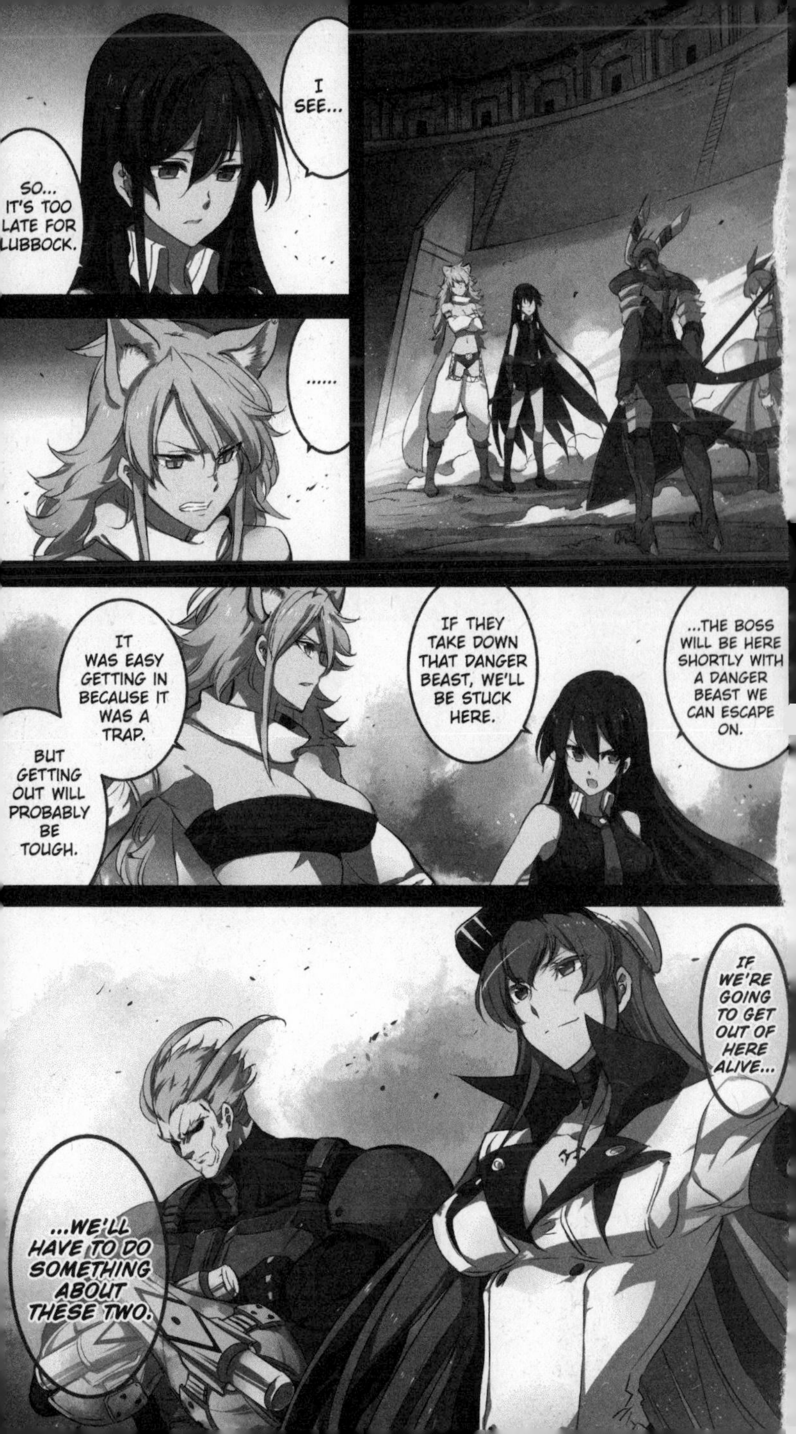
I SEE...
SO... IT'S TOO LATE FOR LUBBOCK.
......
...THE BOSS WILL BE HERE SHORTLY WITH A DANGER BEAST WE CAN ESCAPE ON.
IF THEY TAKE DOWN THAT DANGER BEAST, WE'LL BE STUCK HERE.
IT WAS EASY GETTING IN BECAUSE IT WAS A TRAP.
BUT GETTING OUT WILL PROBABLY BE TOUGH.
IF WE'RE GOING TO GET OUT OF HERE ALIVE...
...WE'LL HAVE TO DO SOMETHING ABOUT THESE TWO.

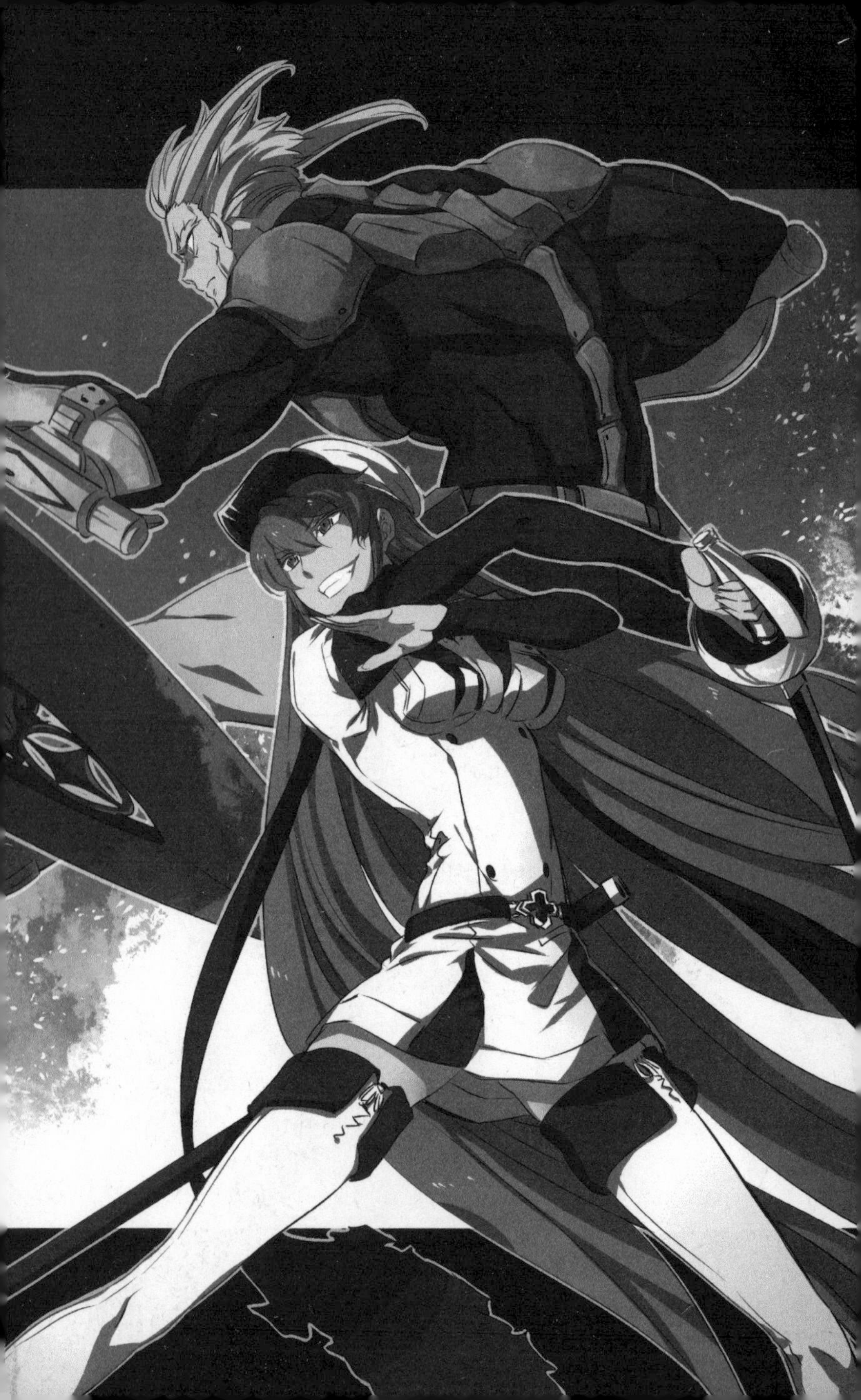

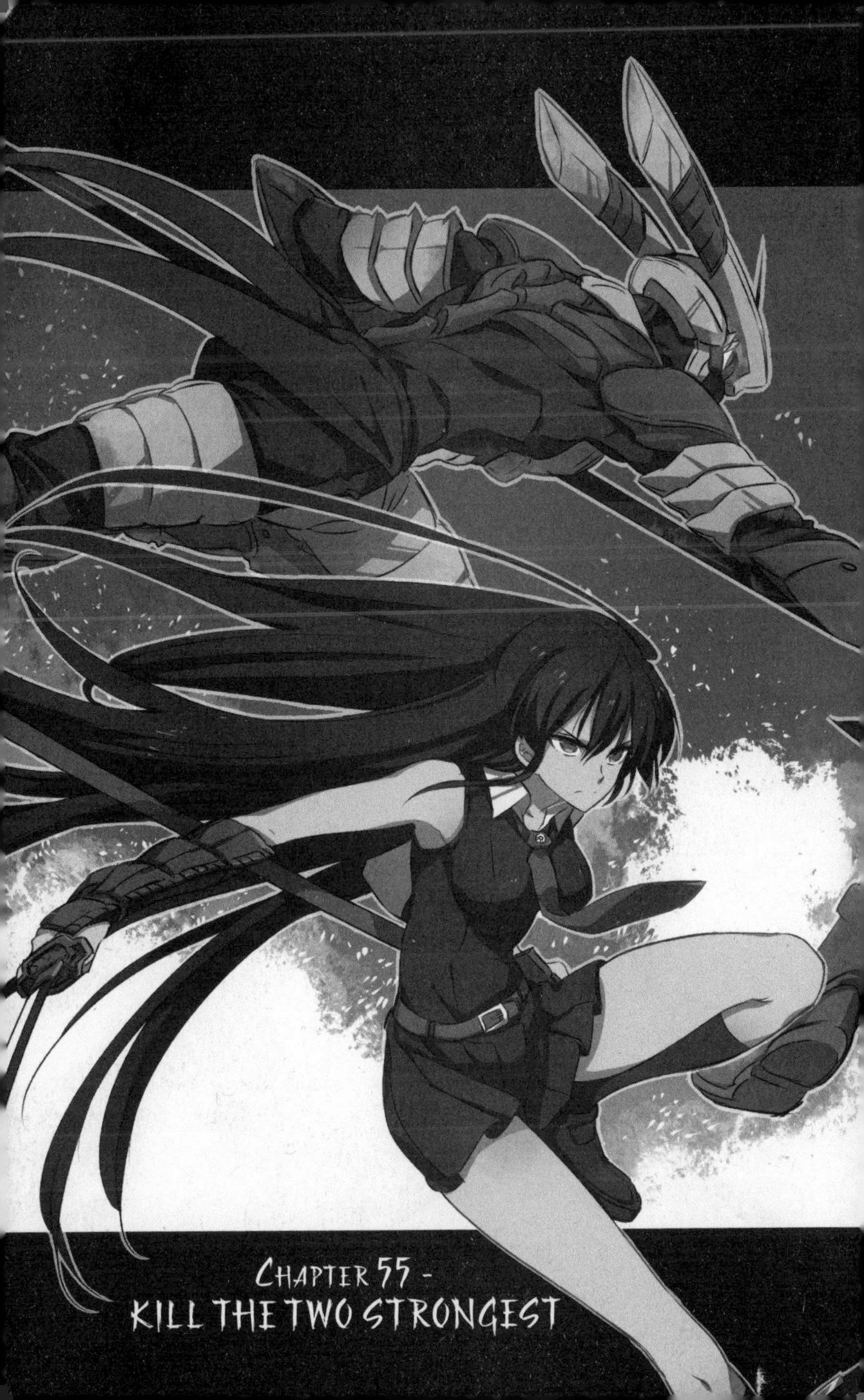

Chapter 55 - Kill the Two Strongest

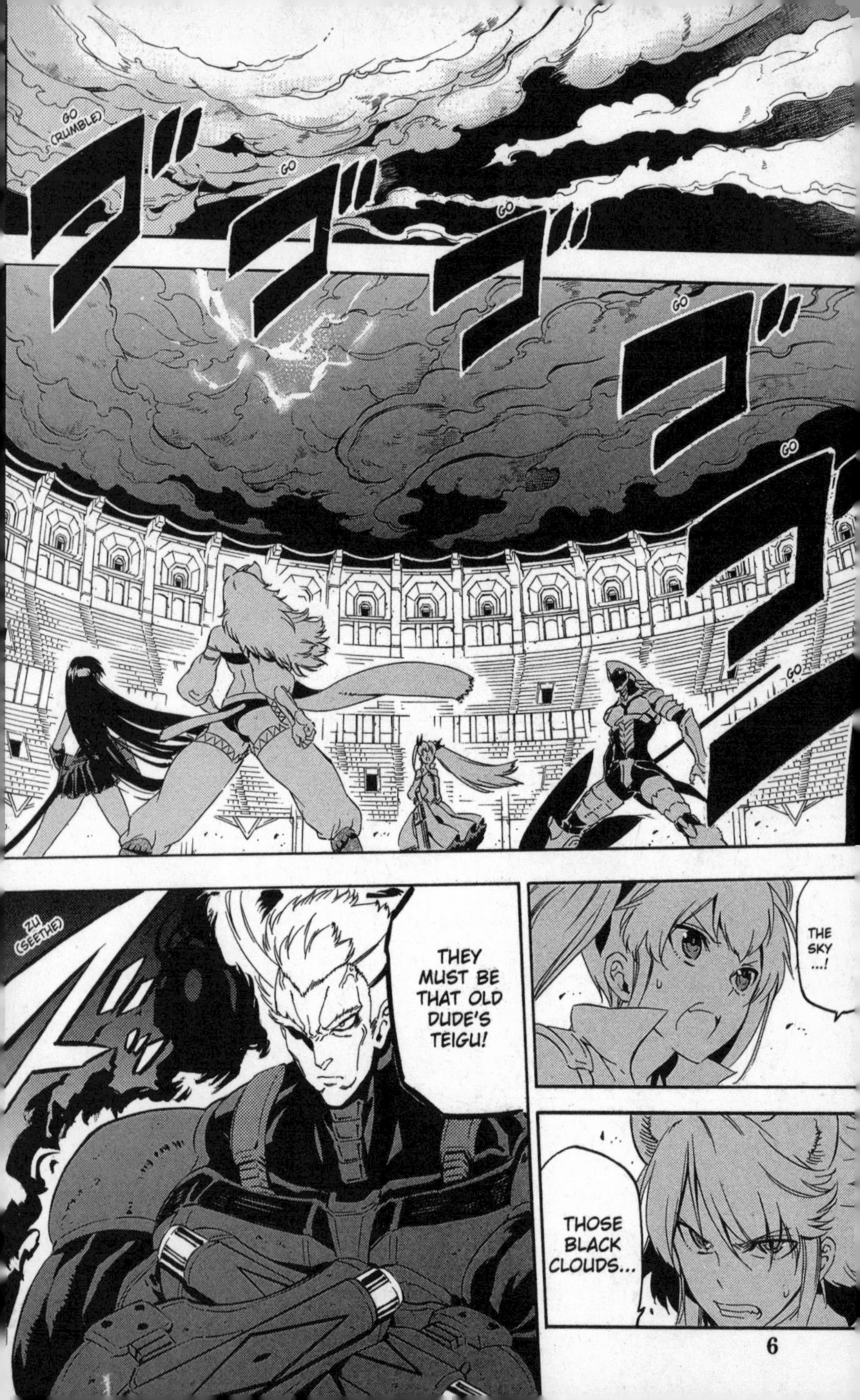
GO (RUMBLE)
GO
GO
GO
GO
GO
THE SKY ...!
THOSE BLACK CLOUDS...
ZU (SEETHE)
THEY MUST BE THAT OLD DUDE'S TEIGU!

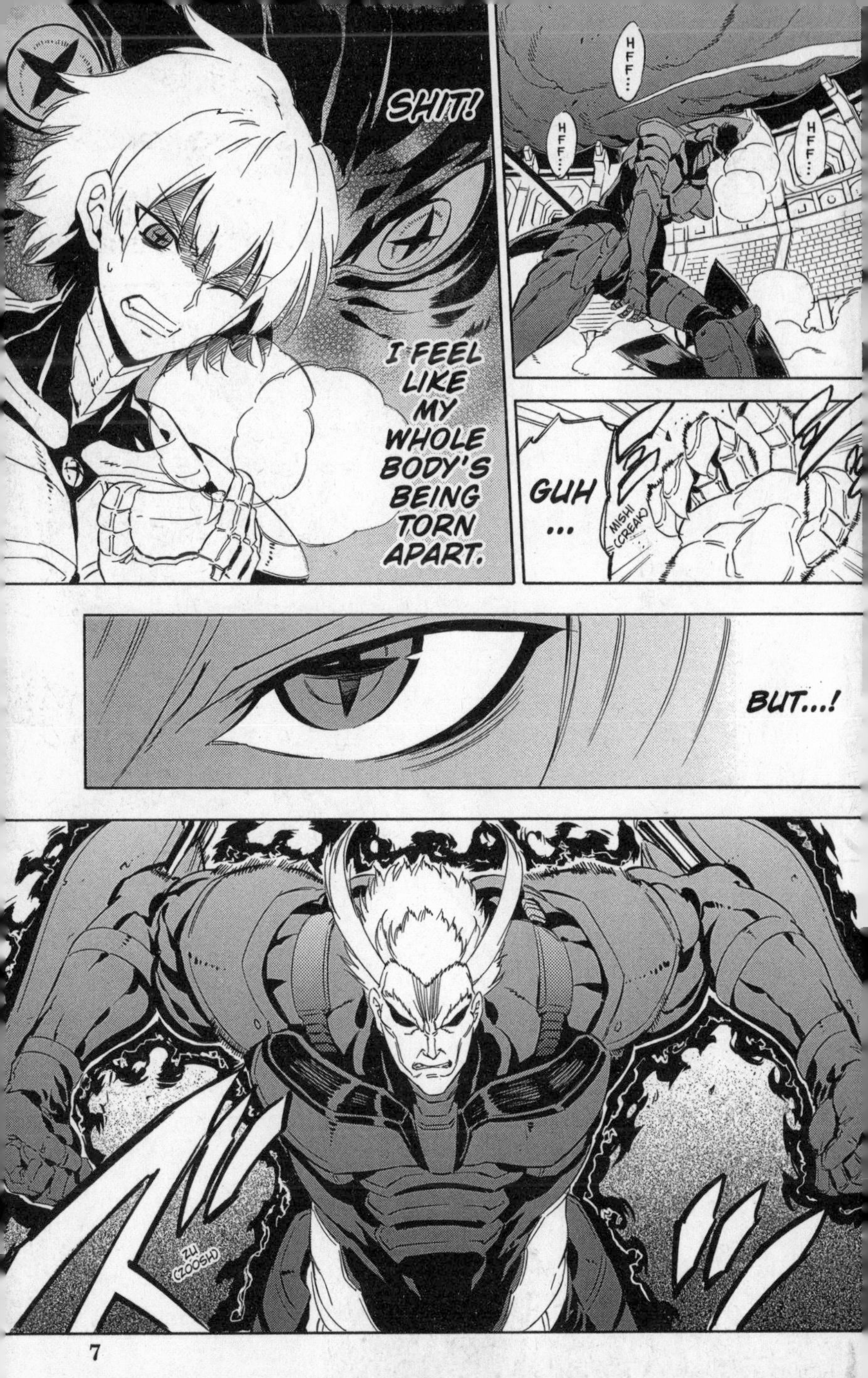
HFF...
HFF...
HFF...
GUH...
MISHI (CREAK)
SHIT!
I FEEL LIKE MY WHOLE BODY'S BEING TORN APART.
BUT...!
ZU (ZOOSH)

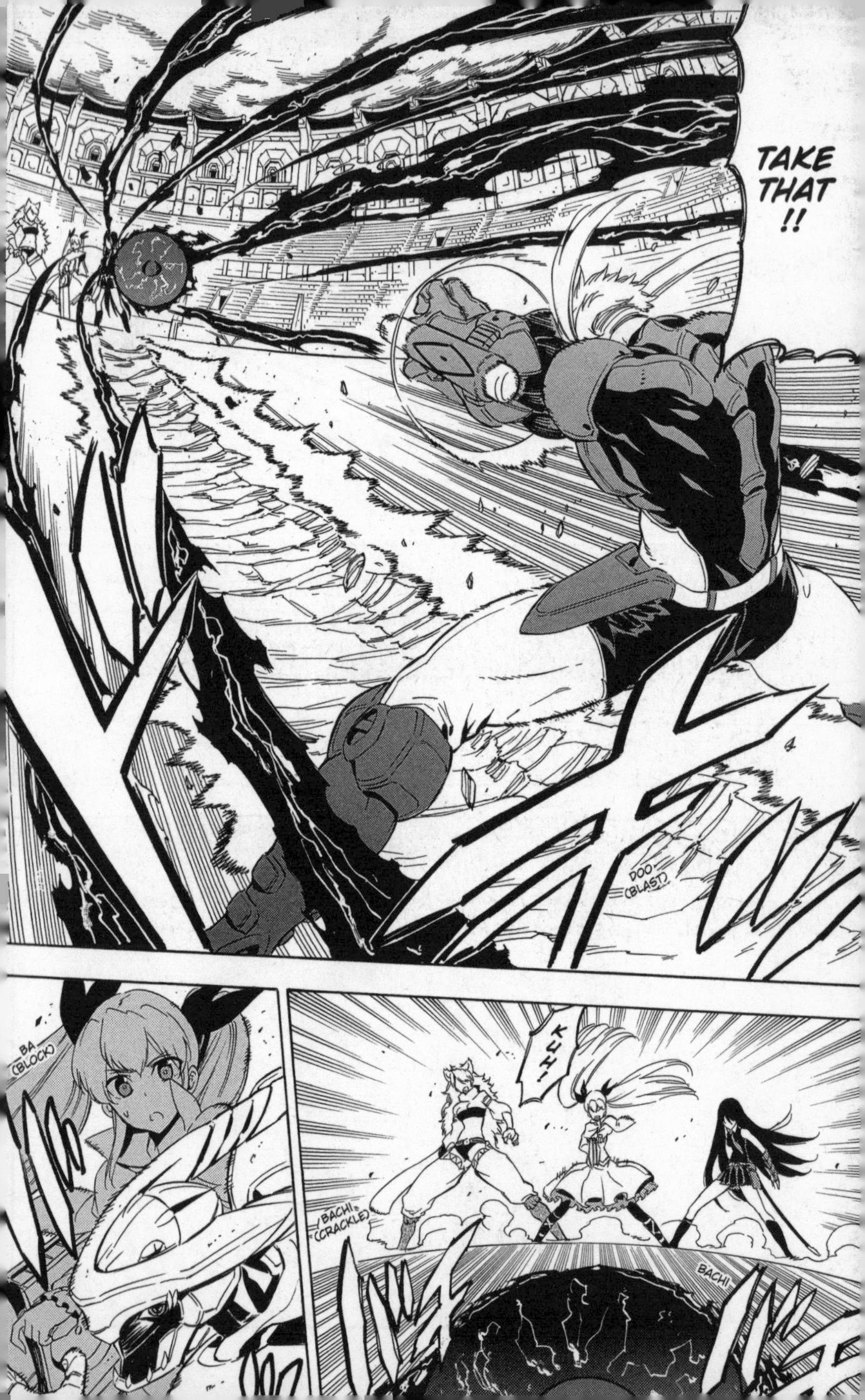
TAKE THAT!!
DOO (BLAST)
KUH!
BACHI
BACHI (CRACKLE)
BA (BLOCK)

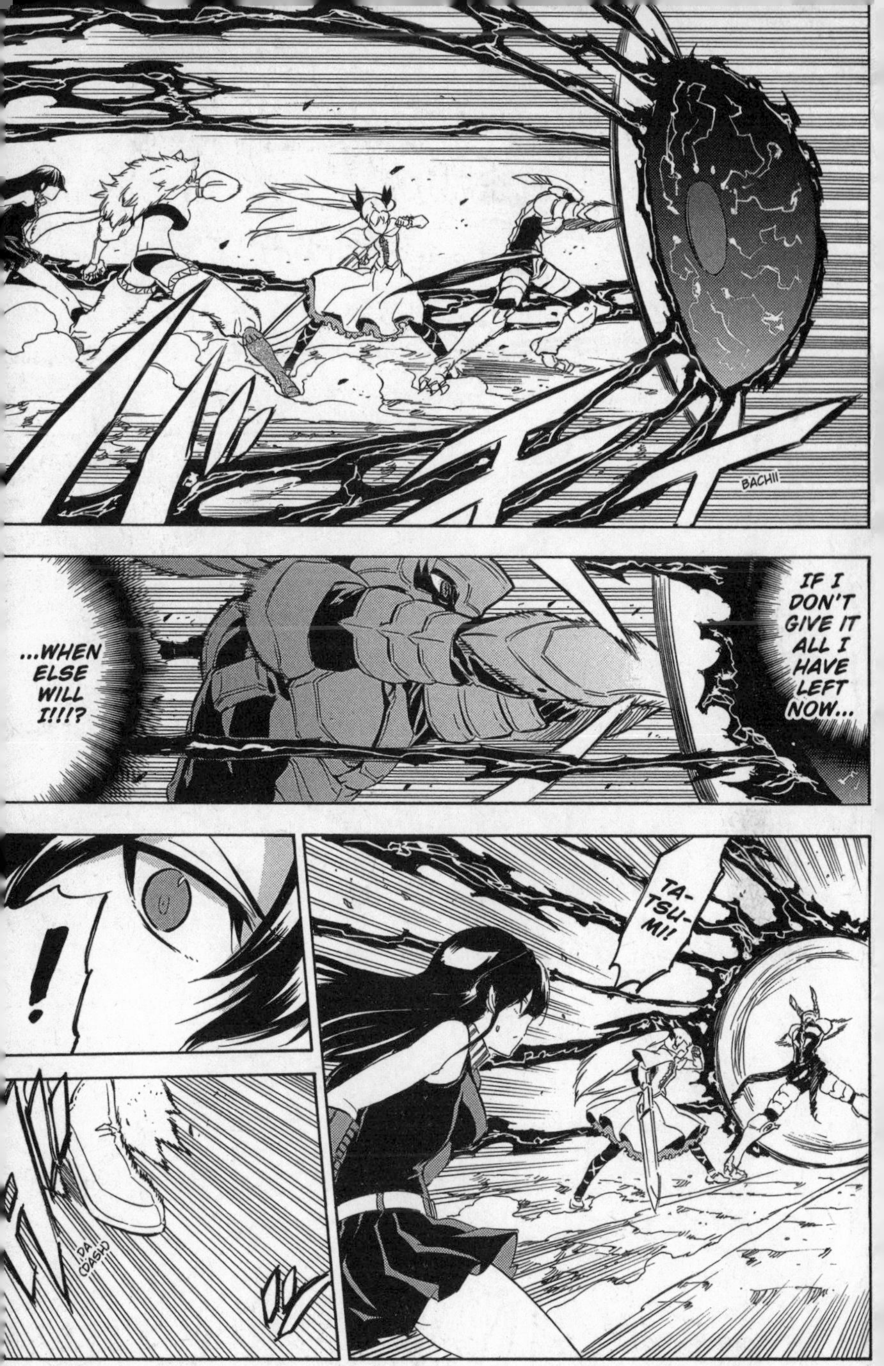
BACHII
IF I DON'T GIVE IT ALL I HAVE LEFT NOW...
...WHEN ELSE WILL I!!!?
TA-TSU-MI!!
!
DA DASH

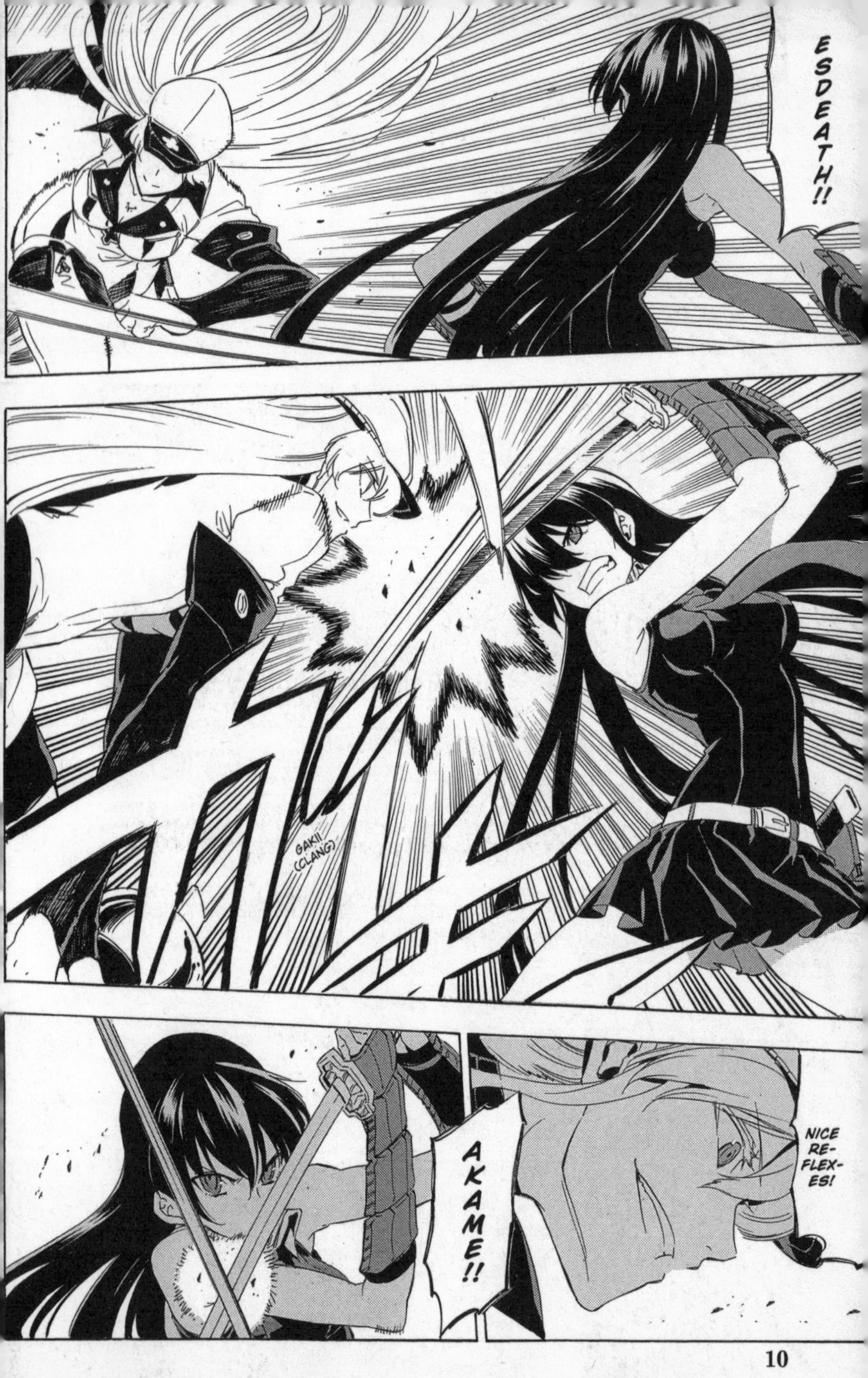
ESDEATH!!
GAKI! (CLANG)
NICE REFLEXES!
AKAME!!

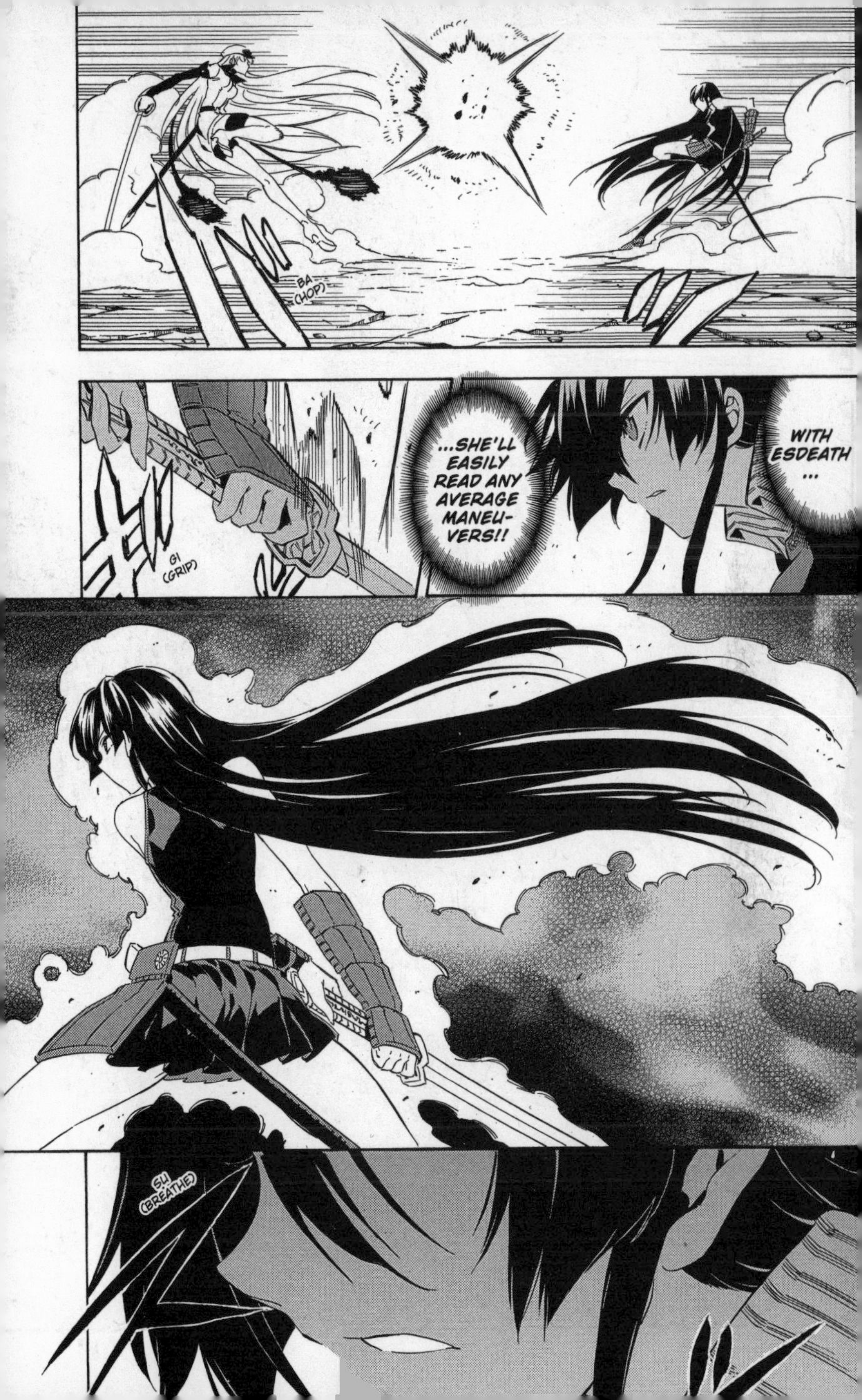
BA (HOP)
WITH ESDEATH...
...SHE'LL EASILY READ ANY AVERAGE MANEU-VERS!!
GI (GRIP)
SU (BREATHE)

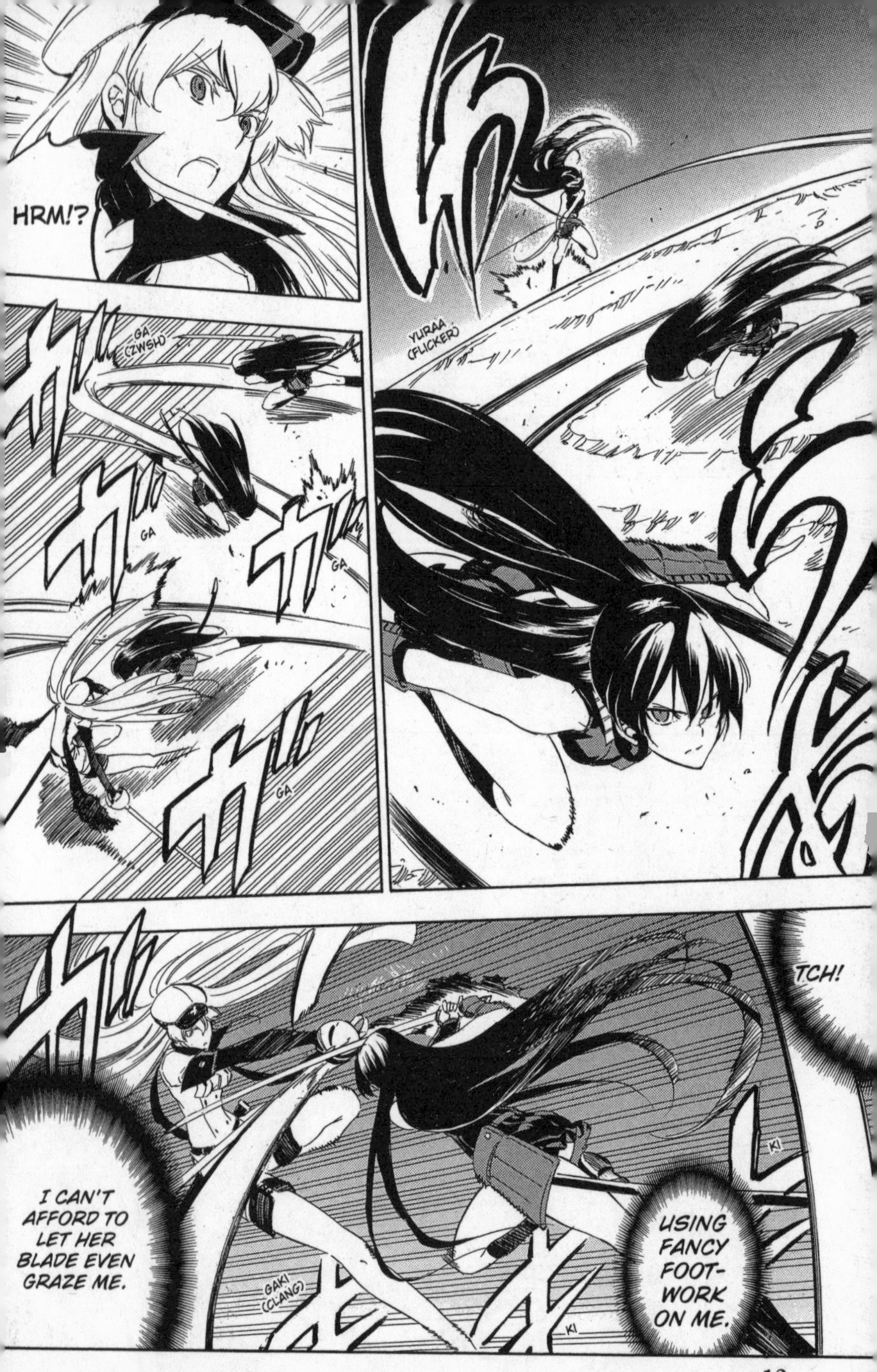
YURAA (FLICKER)
HRM!?
GA (ZWSH)
GA
GA
GA
TCH!
USING FANCY FOOT-WORK ON ME.
KI
KI
GAKI (CLANG)
I CAN'T AFFORD TO LET HER BLADE EVEN GRAZE ME.

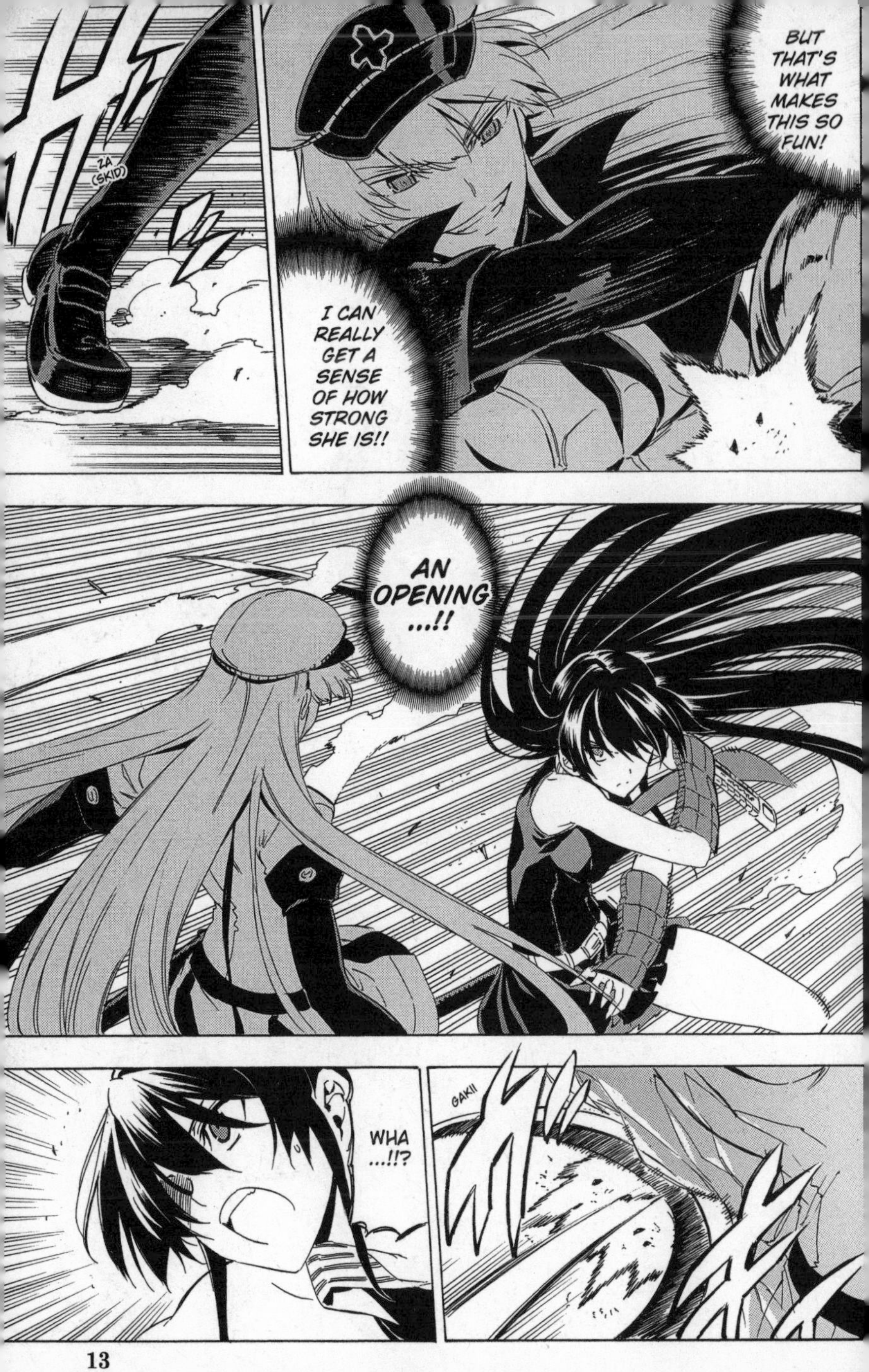
I CAN REALLY GET A SENSE OF HOW STRONG SHE IS!!
BUT THAT'S WHAT MAKES THIS SO FUN!
ZA (SKID)
AN OPENING ...!!
GAKI
WHA ...!!?

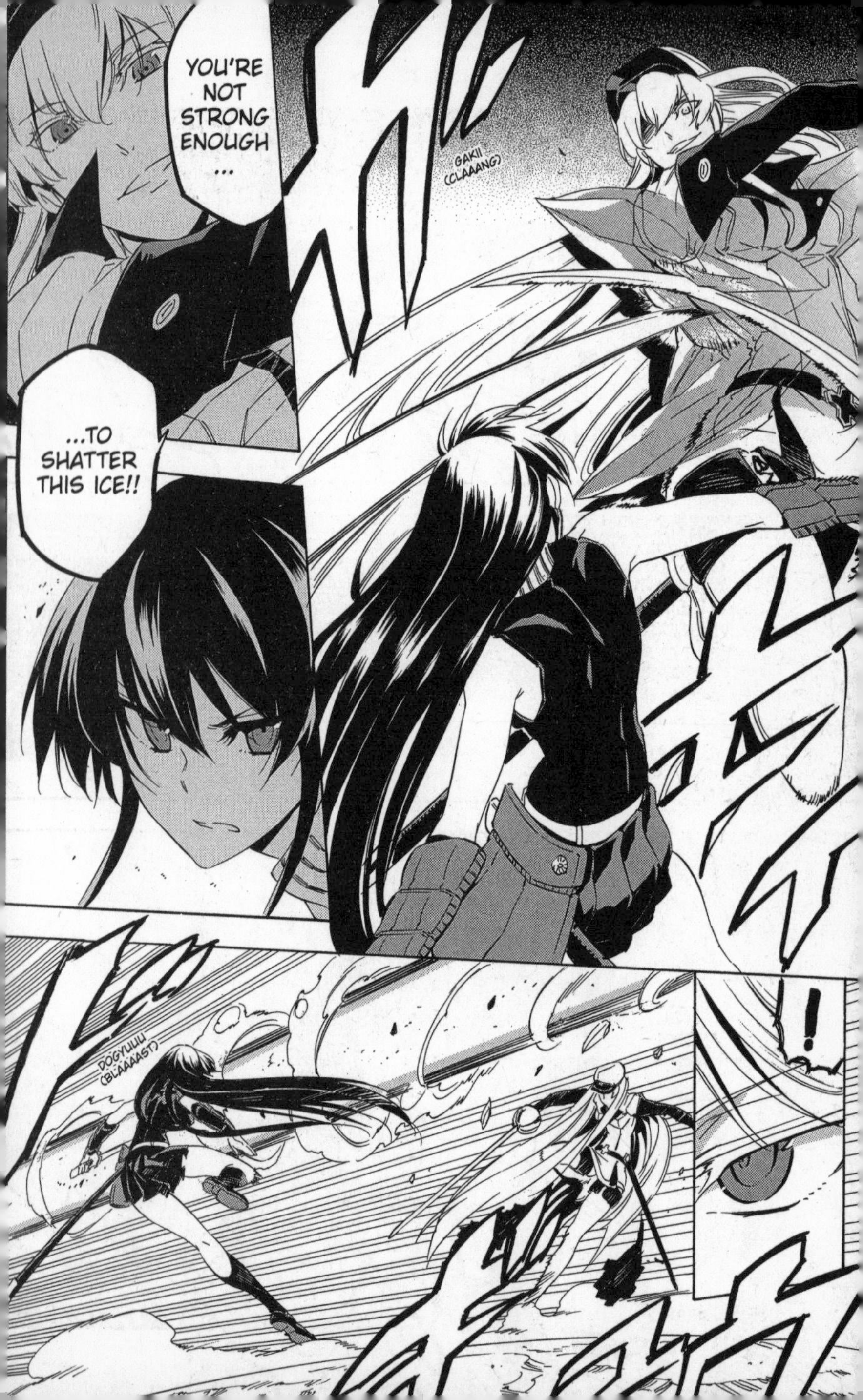
GAKII (CLAAANG)
YOU'RE NOT STRONG ENOUGH ...
...TO SHATTER THIS ICE!!
!
DOGYUUU (BLAAAAST)

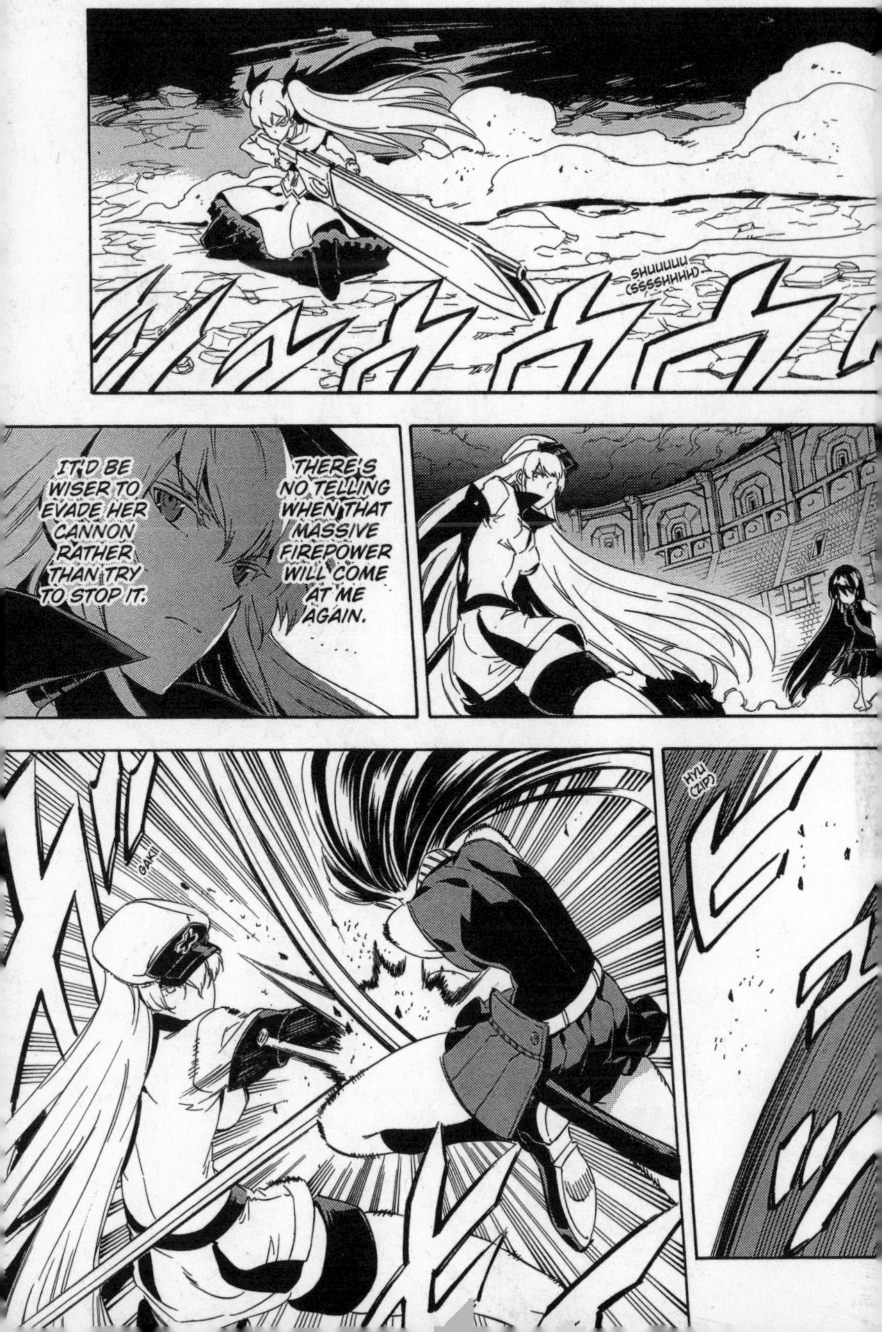
SHUUUUU (SSSSHHHH)
THERE'S NO TELLING WHEN THAT MASSIVE FIREPOWER WILL COME AT ME AGAIN.
IT'D BE WISER TO EVADE HER CANNON RATHER THAN TRY TO STOP IT.
HYU (ZIP)
GAKI

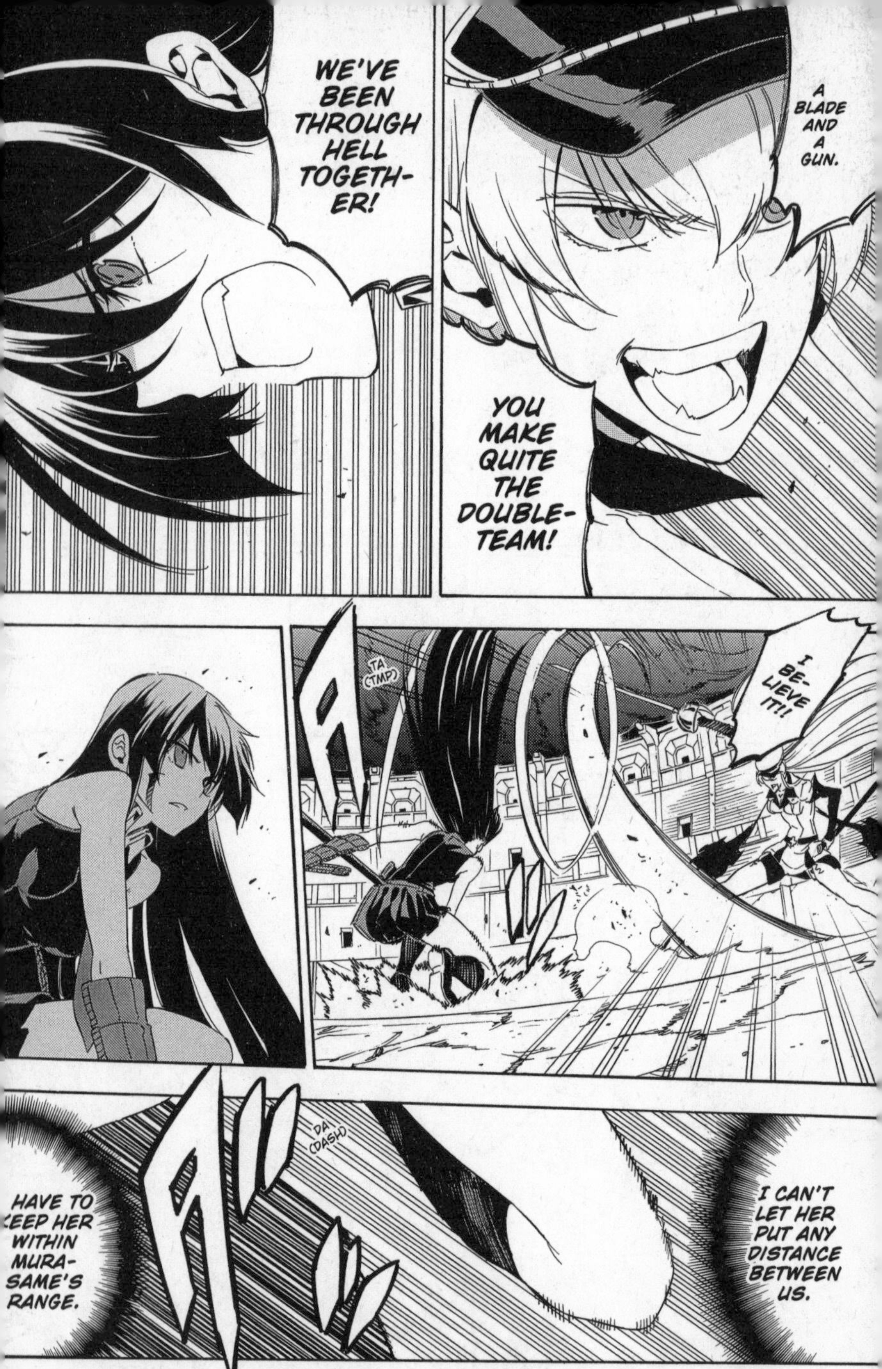
A BLADE AND A GUN.
YOU MAKE QUITE THE DOUBLE-TEAM!
WE'VE BEEN THROUGH HELL TOGETHER!
I BELIEVE IT!!
TA (TMP)
I CAN'T LET HER PUT ANY DISTANCE BETWEEN US.
DA (DASH)
HAVE TO EEP HER WITHIN MURASAME'S RANGE.

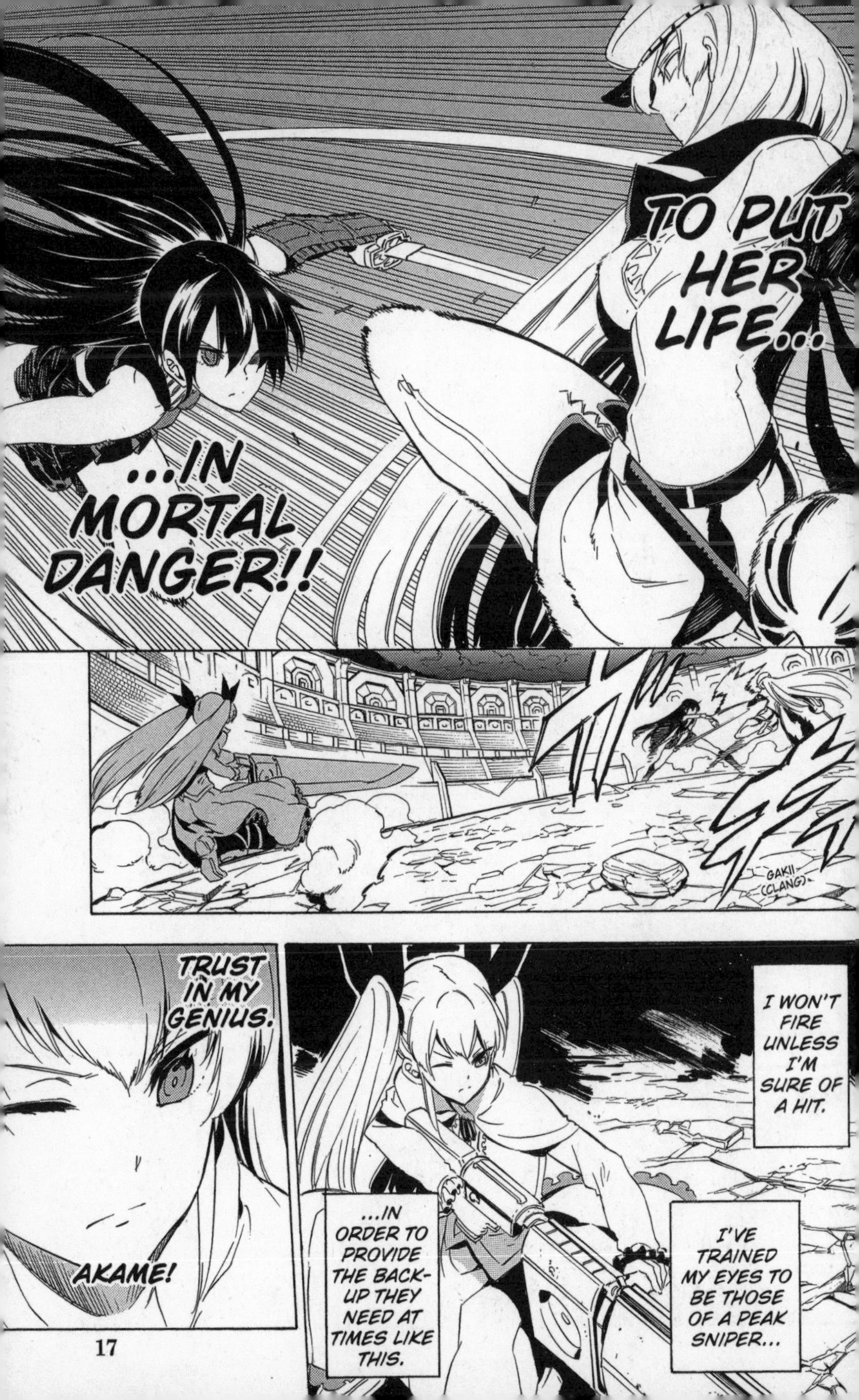
TO PUT HER LIFE...
...IN MORTAL DANGER!!
GAKII (CLANG)
I WON'T FIRE UNLESS I'M SURE OF A HIT.
I'VE TRAINED MY EYES TO BE THOSE OF A PEAK SNIPER...
...IN ORDER TO PROVIDE THE BACK-UP THEY NEED AT TIMES LIKE THIS.
TRUST IN MY GENIUS.
AKAME!

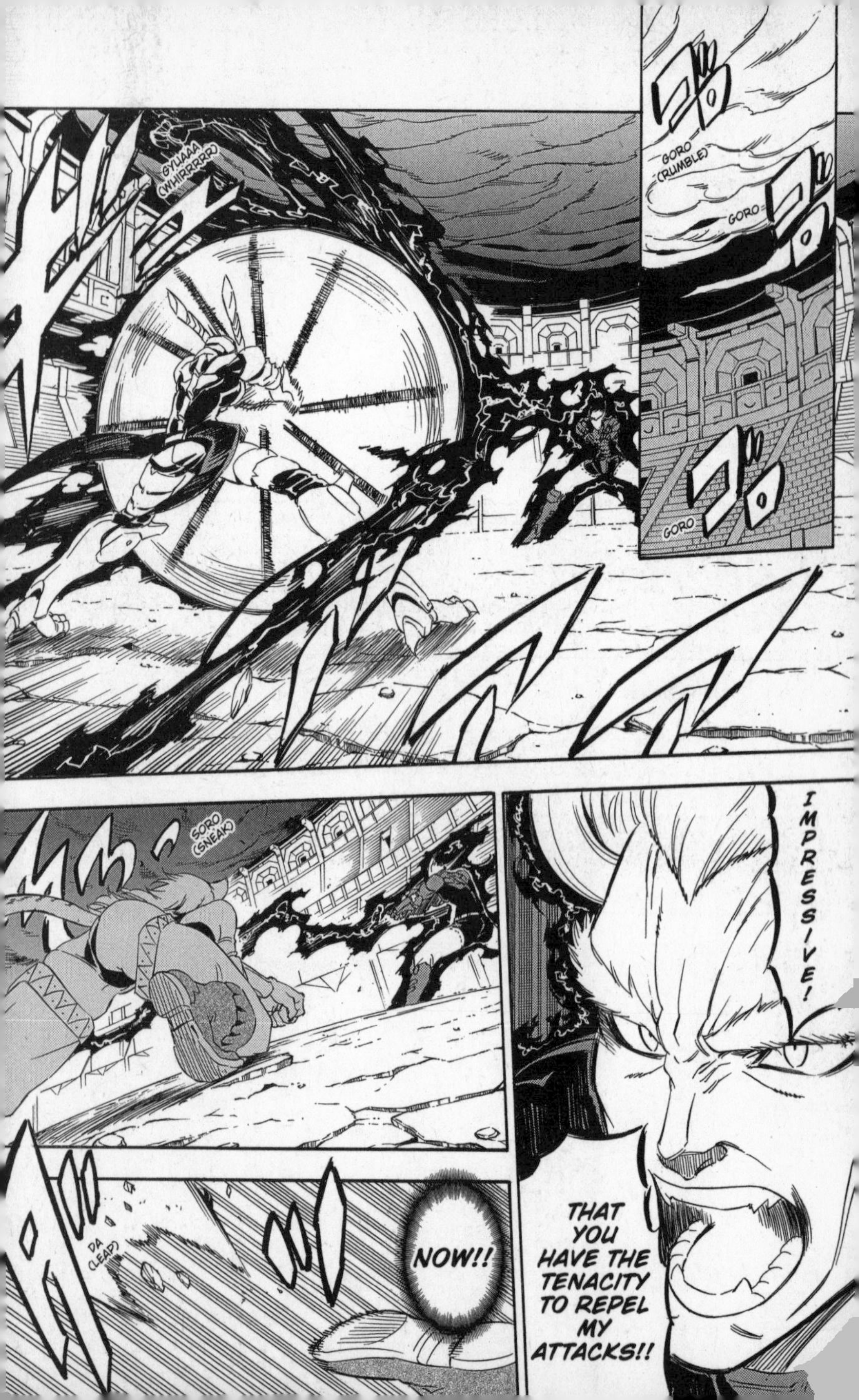
GORO (RUMBLE)
GORO
GORO
GYUAAA (WHIRRRRR)
IMPRESSIVE!
SORO (SNEAK)
THAT YOU HAVE THE TENACITY TO REPEL MY ATTACKS!!
NOW!!
DA (LEAP)

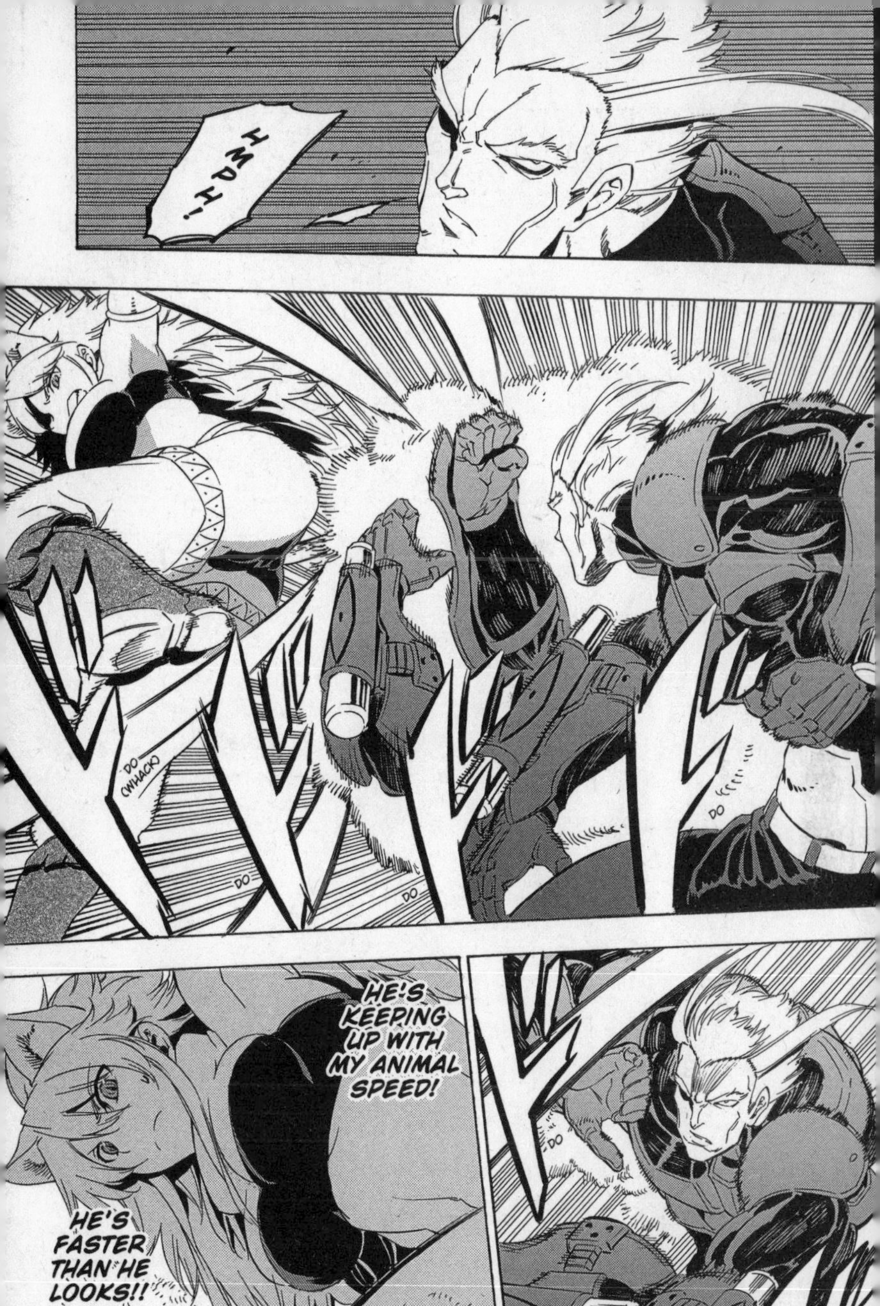
HMPH!
DO (WHACK)
DO
DO
DO
DO
DO
HE'S KEEPING UP WITH MY ANIMAL SPEED!
HE'S FASTER THAN HE LOOKS!!

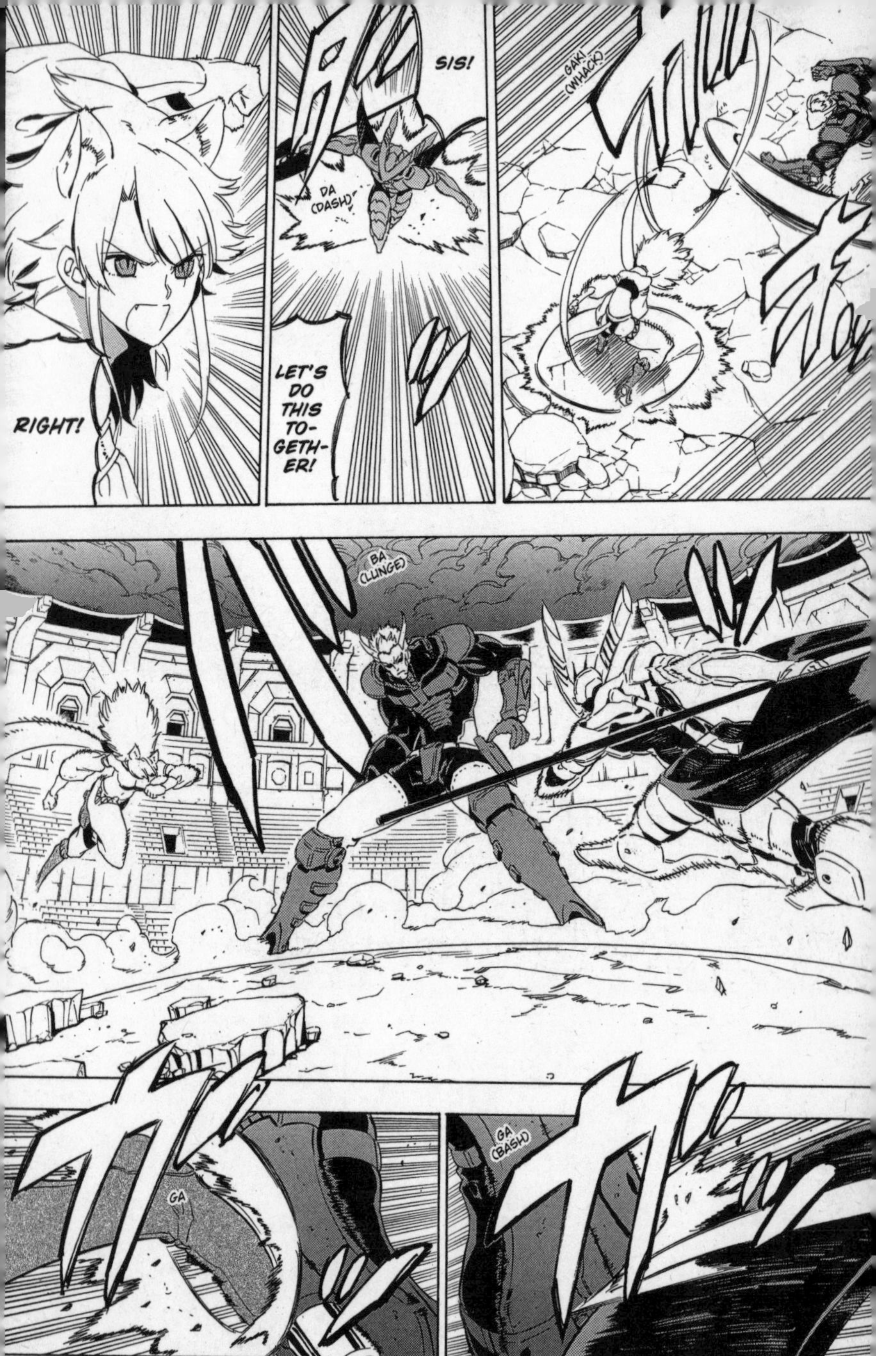
SIS!
RIGHT!
DA (DASH)
LET'S DO THIS TO-GETH-ER!
GAKI (WHACK)
BA (LUNGE)
GA (BASH)
GA

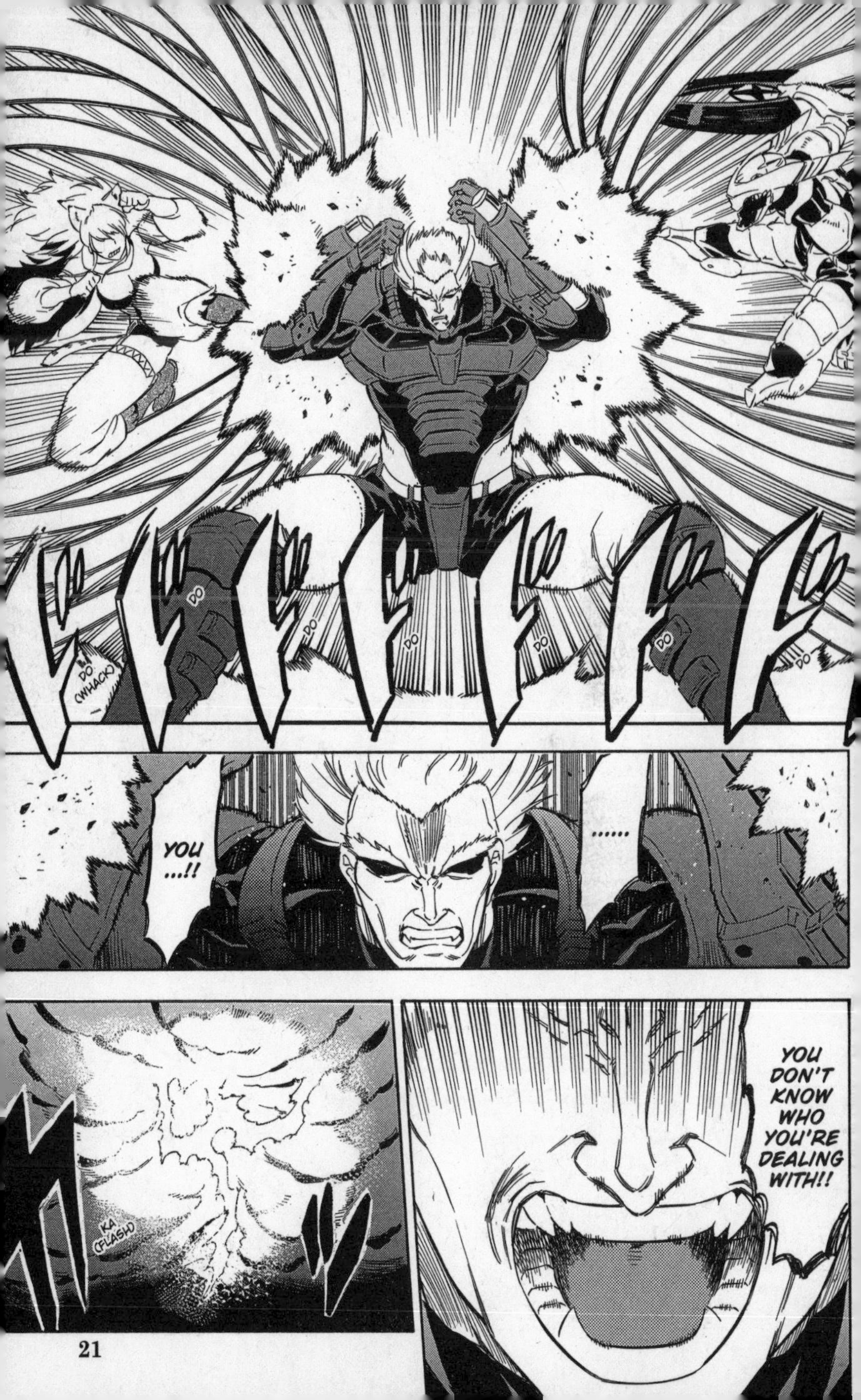
DO (WHACK)
DO
DO
DO
DO
DO
DO
......
YOU ...!!
YOU DON'T KNOW WHO YOU'RE DEALING WITH!!
KA (FLASH)

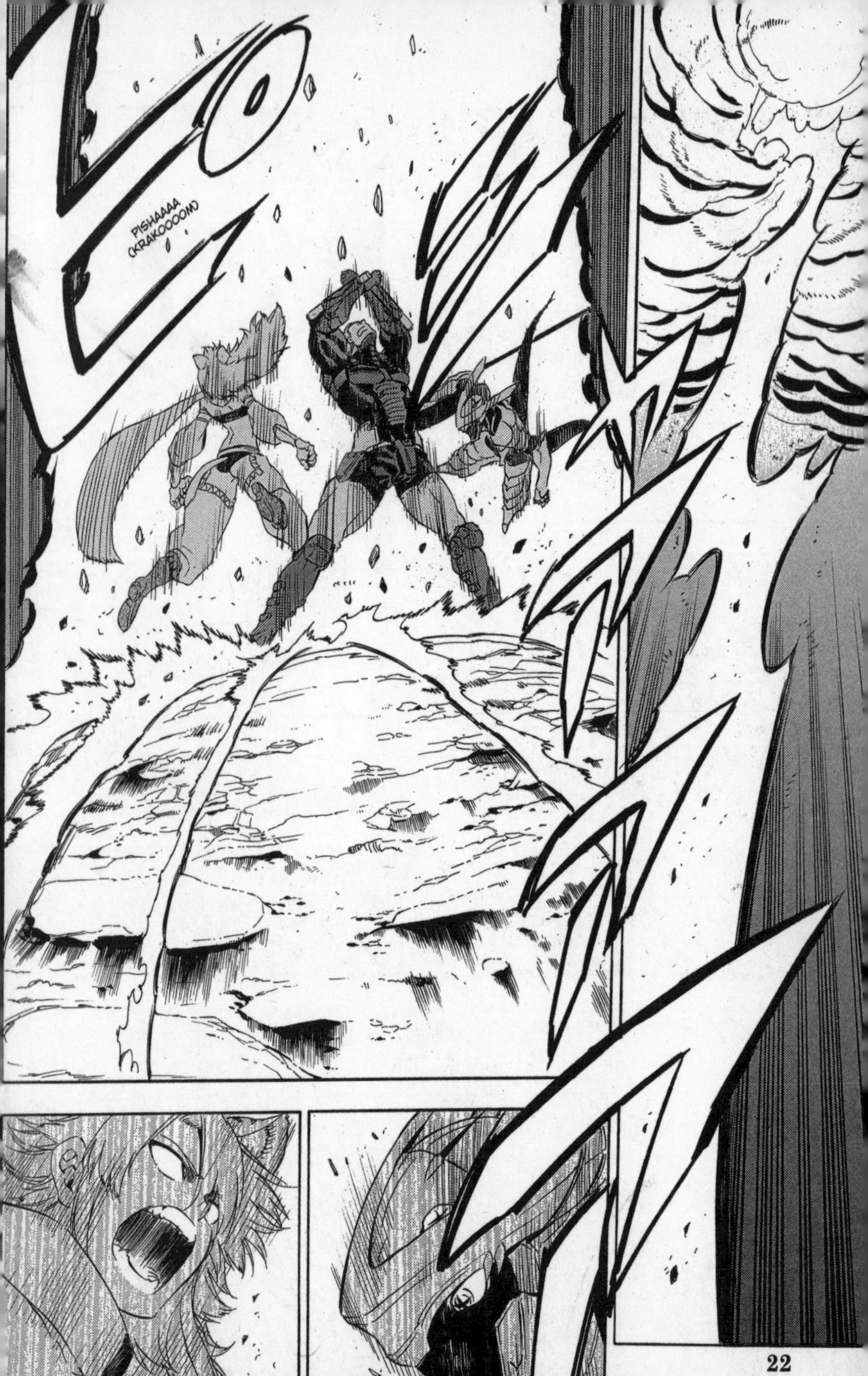
PISHAAAA
(KRAKOOOOM)

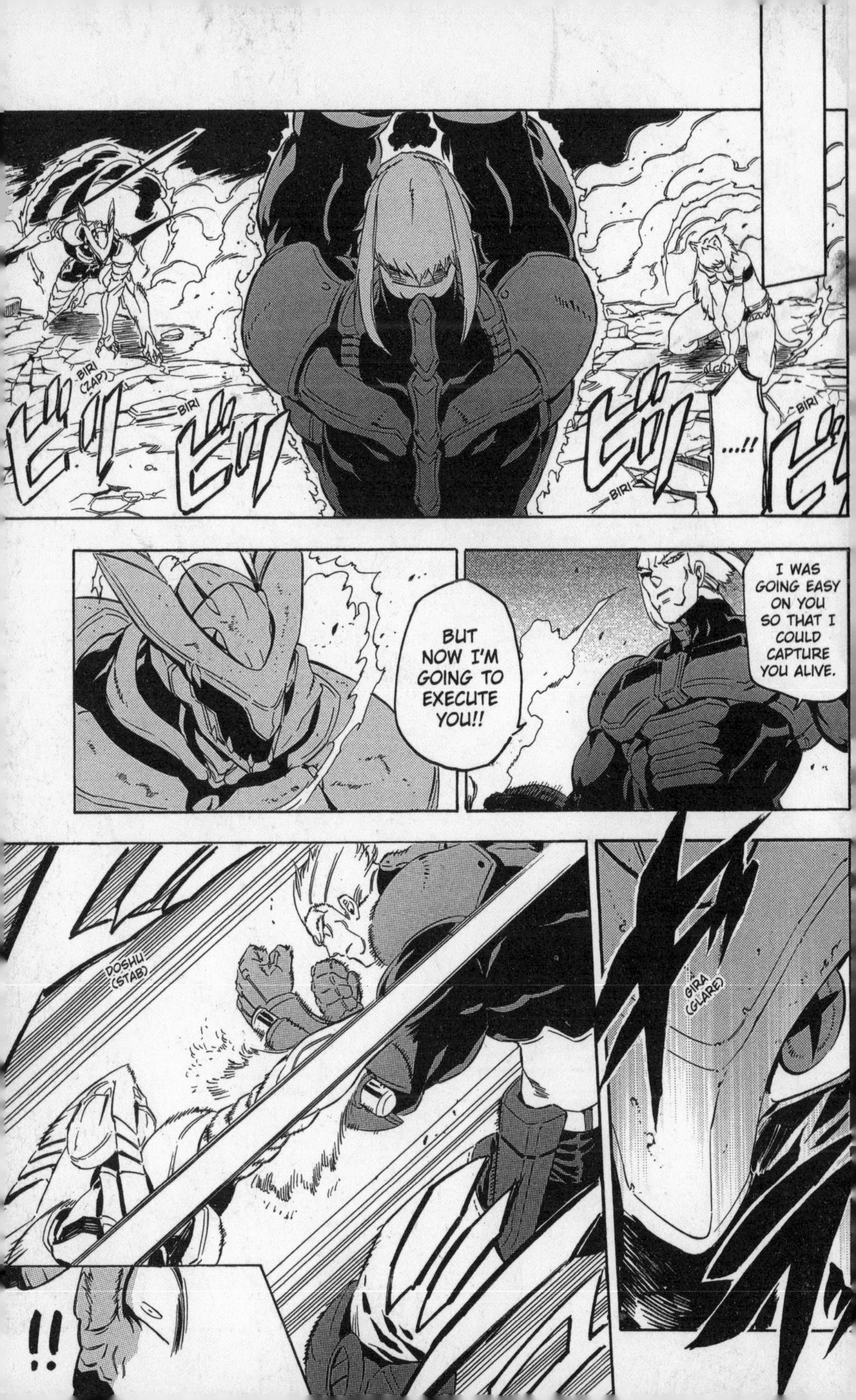
BIRI
...!!
BIRI
BIRI
BIRI (ZAP)
I WAS GOING EASY ON YOU SO THAT I COULD CAPTURE YOU ALIVE.
BUT NOW I'M GOING TO EXECUTE YOU!!
GIRA (GLARE)
DOSHU (STAB)
!!

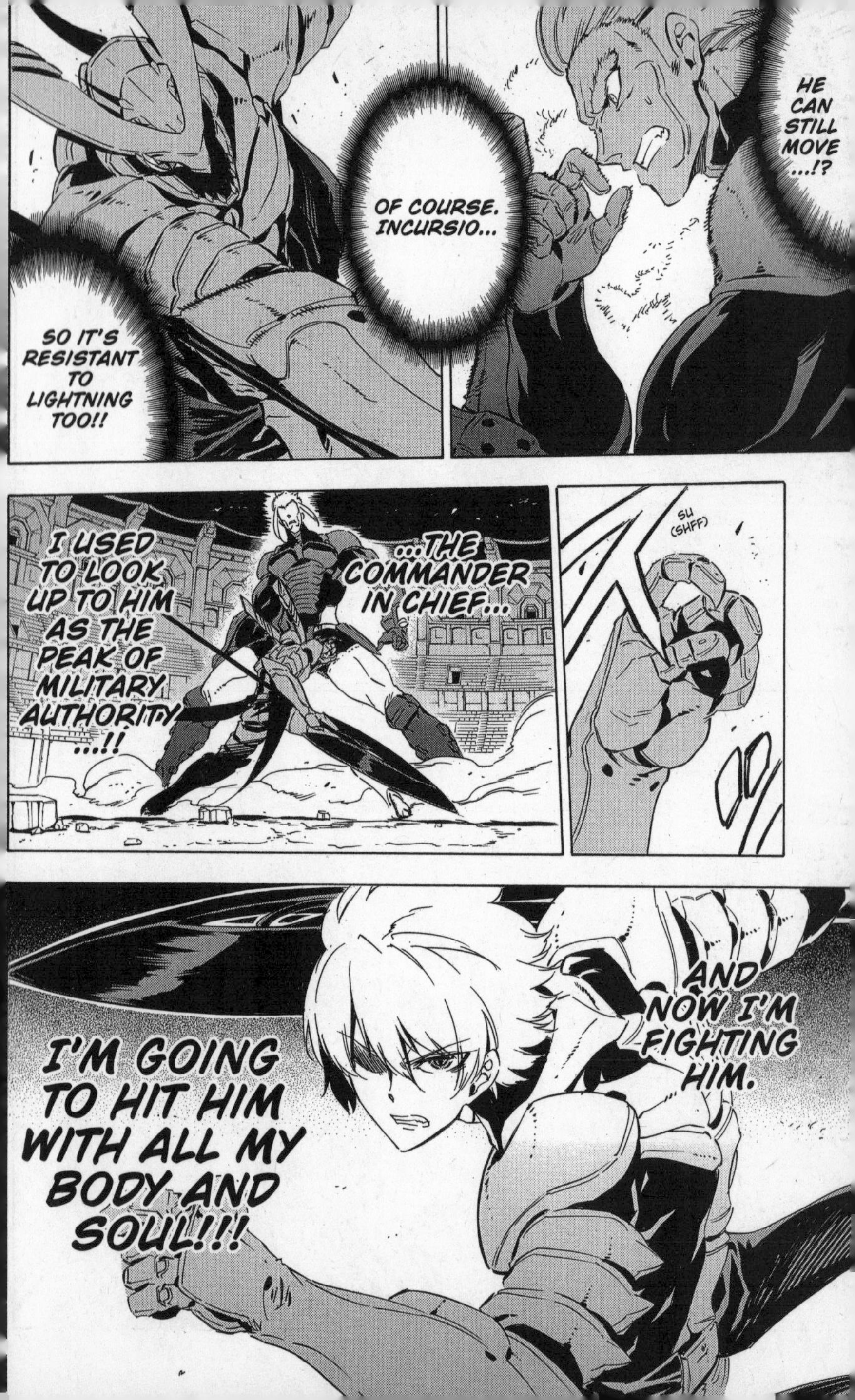
HE CAN STILL MOVE ...!?
OF COURSE. INCURSIO...
SO IT'S RESISTANT TO LIGHTNING TOO!!
SU (SHFF)
...THE COMMANDER IN CHIEF...
I USED TO LOOK UP TO HIM AS THE PEAK OF MILITARY AUTHORITY ...!!
AND NOW I'M FIGHTING HIM.
I'M GOING TO HIT HIM WITH ALL MY BODY AND SOUL!!!

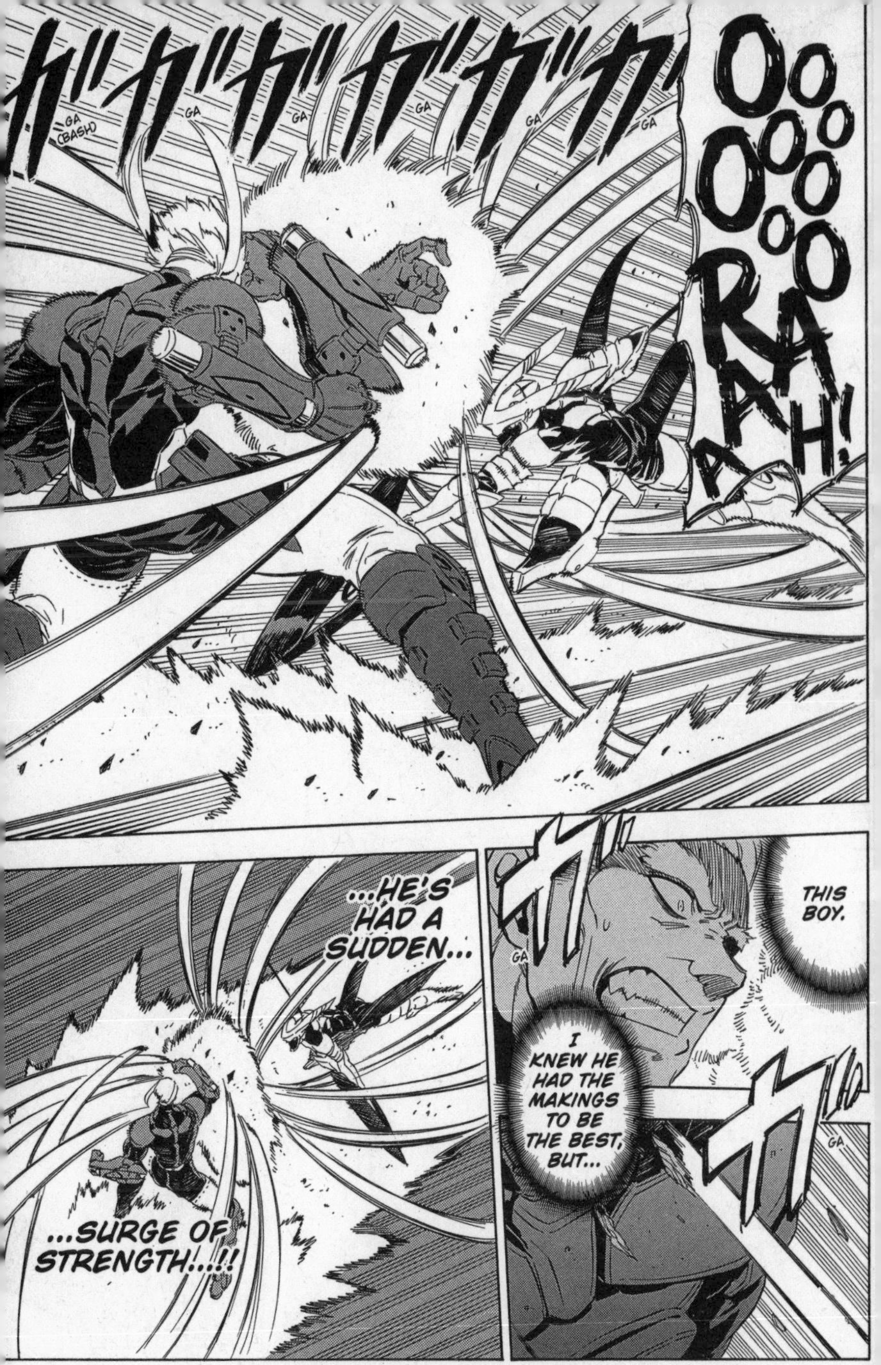
GA (BASH)
GA
GA
GA
GA
GA
OOOOOOOORAAH!
THIS BOY.
I KNEW HE HAD THE MAKINGS TO BE THE BEST, BUT...
GA
GA
...HE'S HAD A SUDDEN...
...SURGE OF STRENGTH...!!

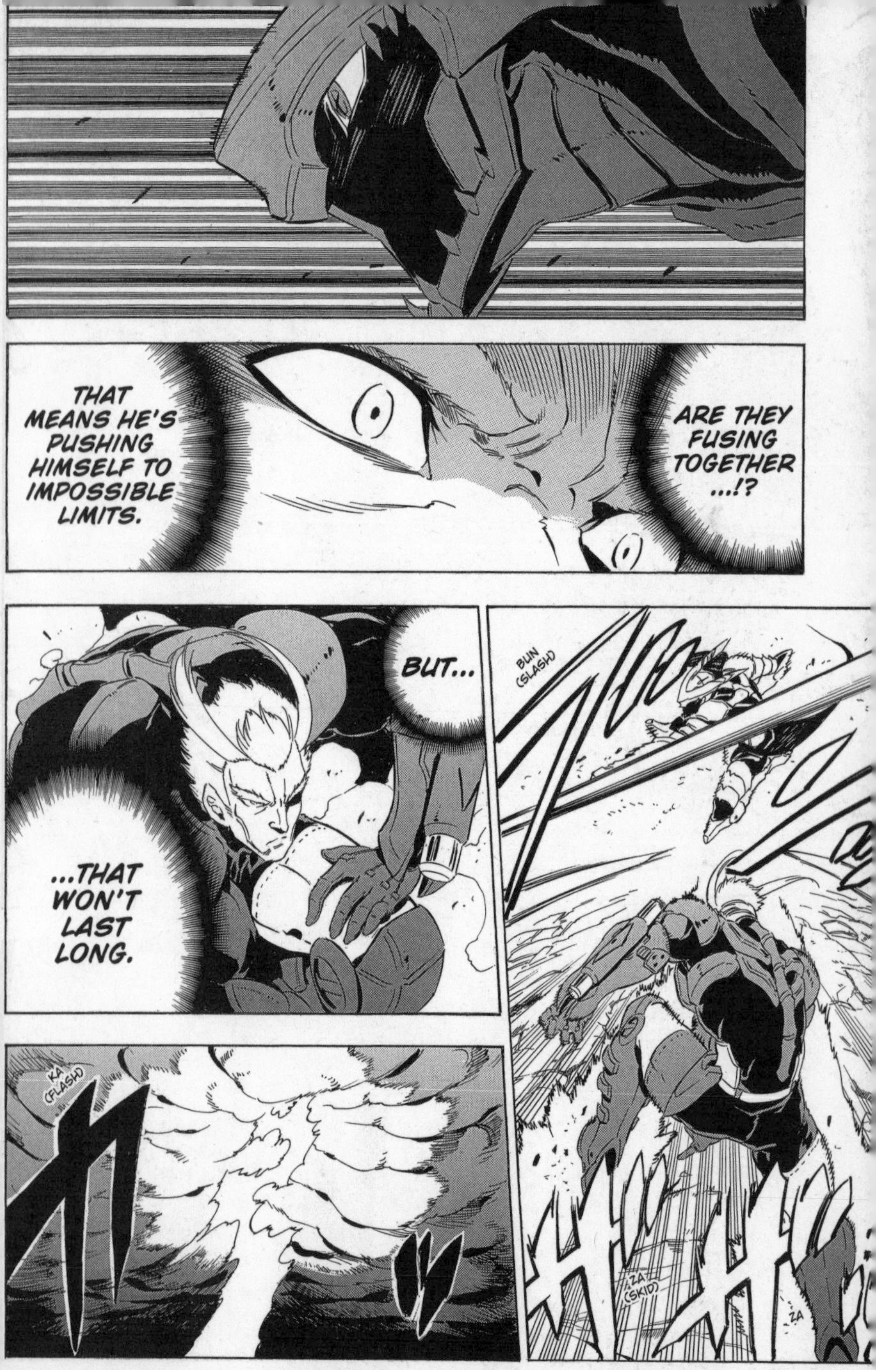
THAT MEANS HE'S PUSHING HIMSELF TO IMPOSSIBLE LIMITS.
ARE THEY FUSING TOGETHER ...!?
BUN (SLASH)
BUT...
...THAT WON'T LAST LONG.
KA (FLASH)
ZA (SKID)
ZA

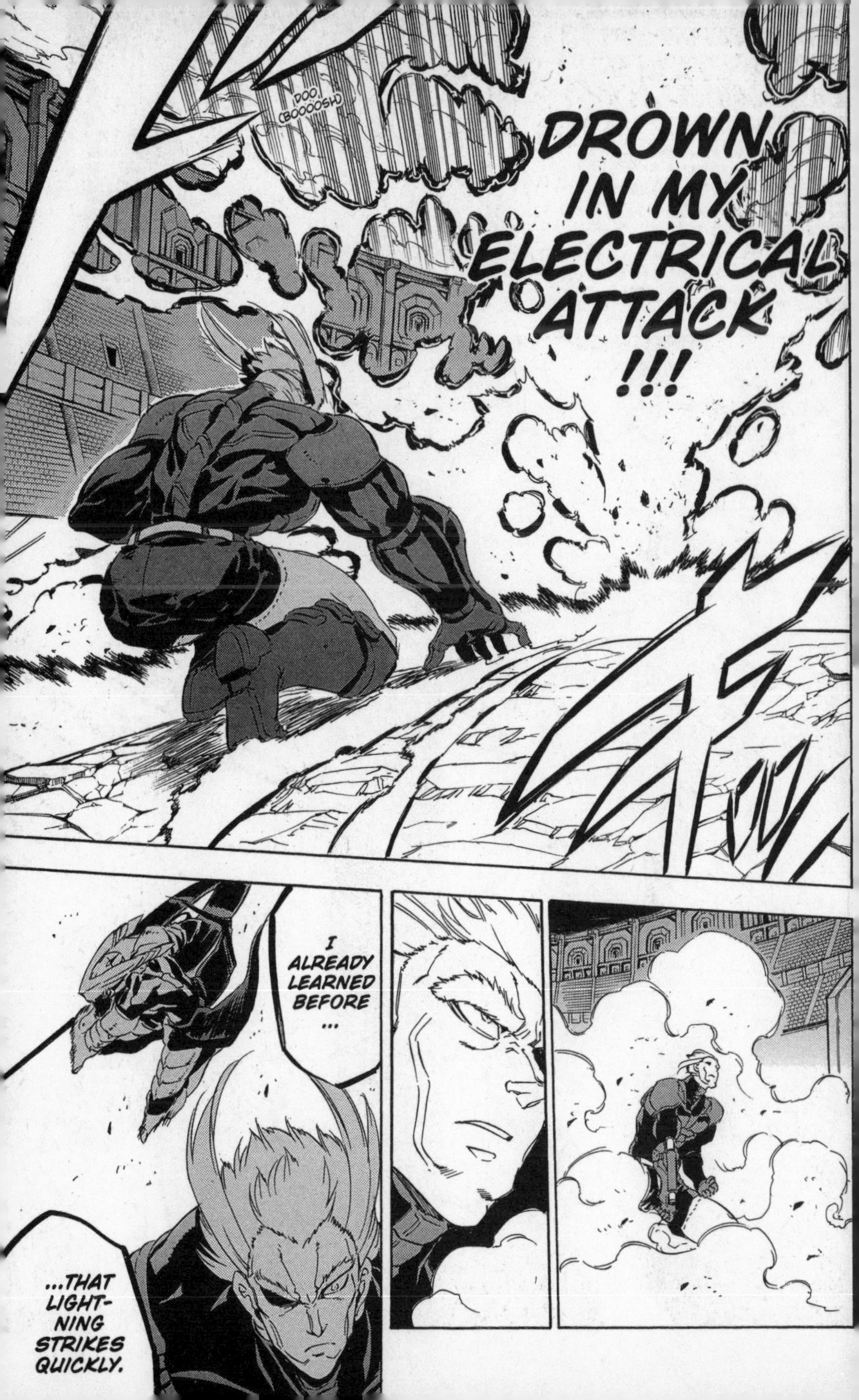
(DOO... BOOOOOSH)
DROWN IN MY ELECTRICAL ATTACK!!!
I ALREADY LEARNED BEFORE...
...THAT LIGHTNING STRIKES QUICKLY.

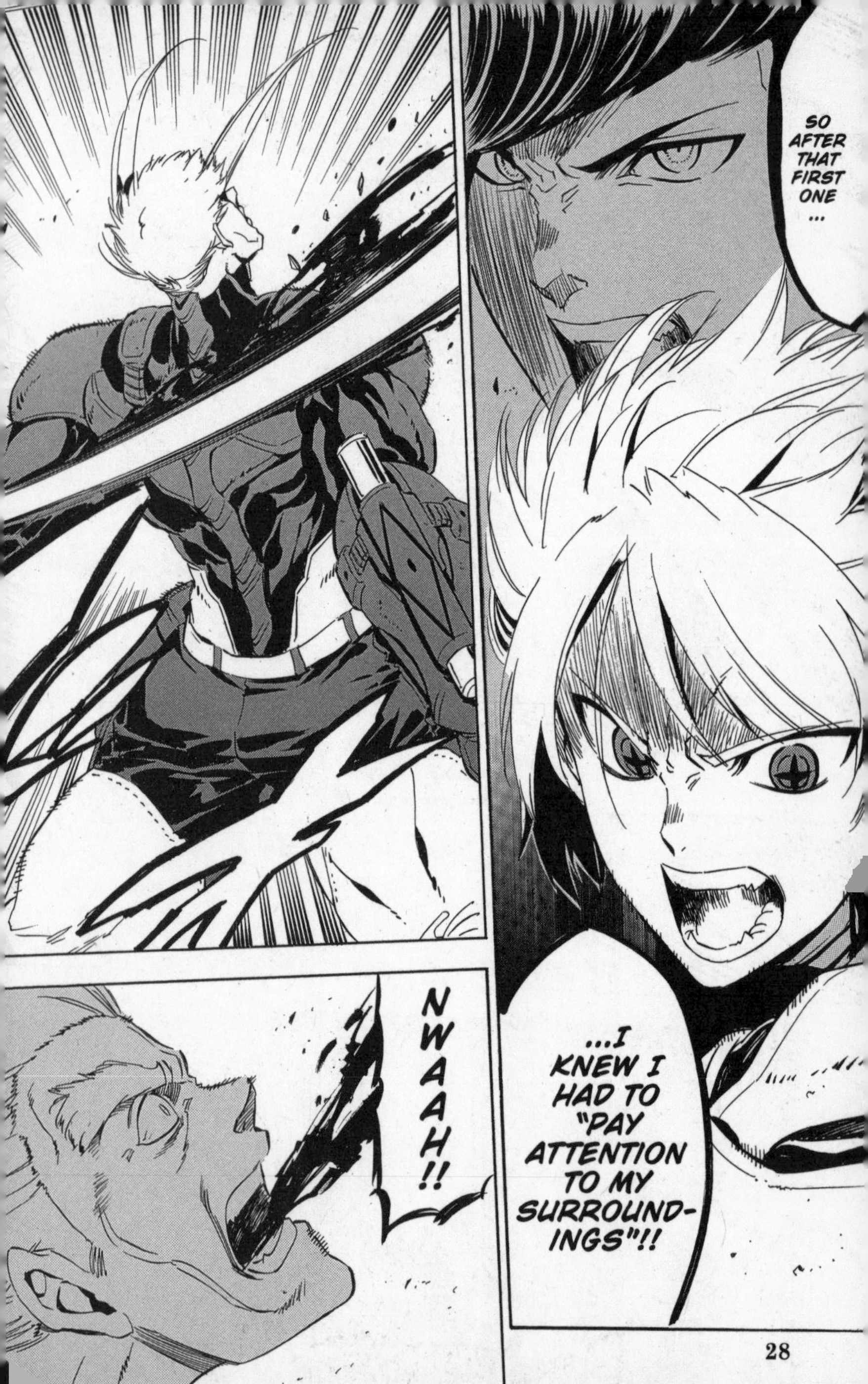
SO AFTER THAT FIRST ONE ...
...I KNEW I HAD TO "PAY ATTENTION TO MY SURROUND-INGS"!!
NWAAAH!!

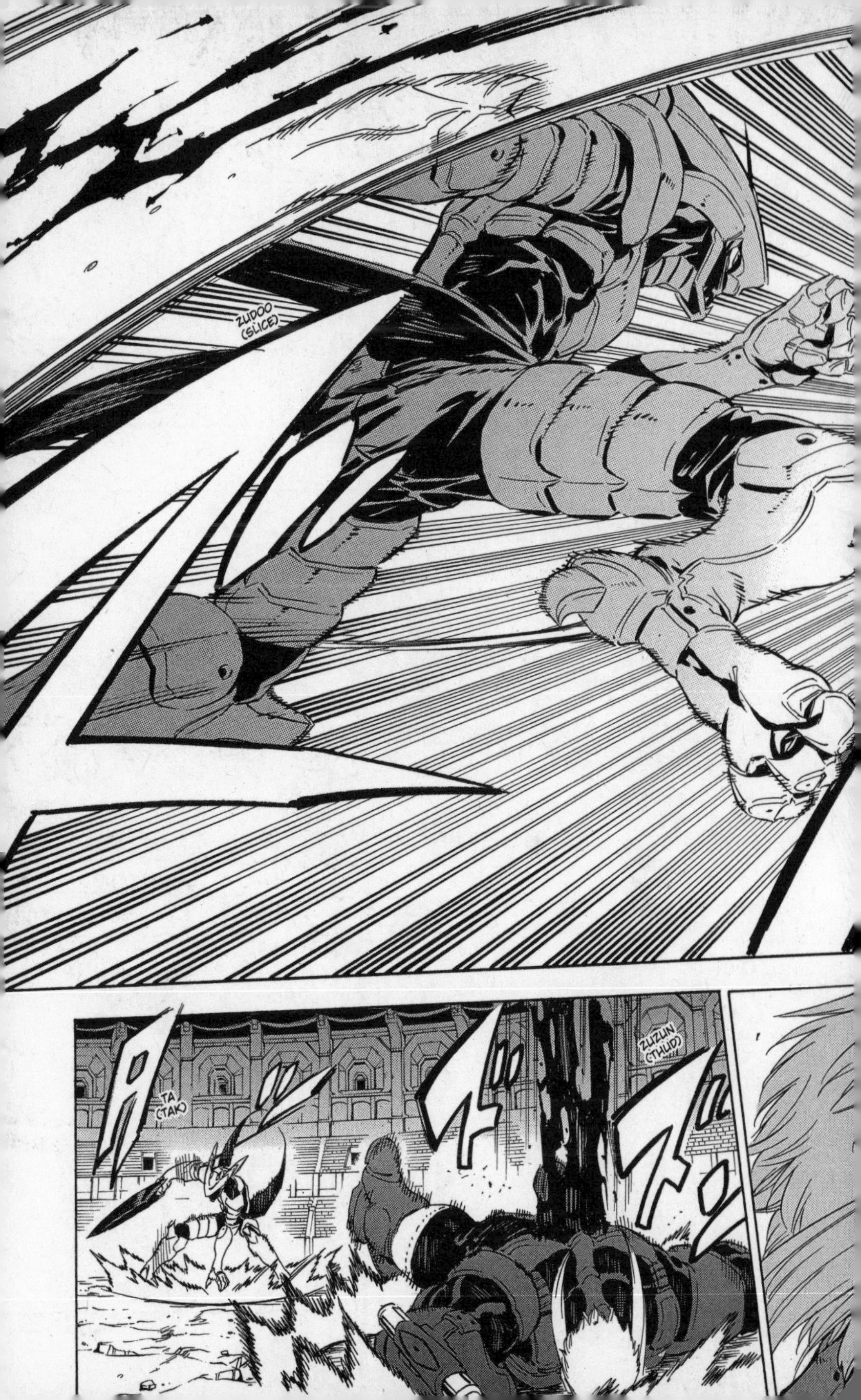
ZUDOO (SLICE)
ZUZUN (THUD)
TA (TAK)

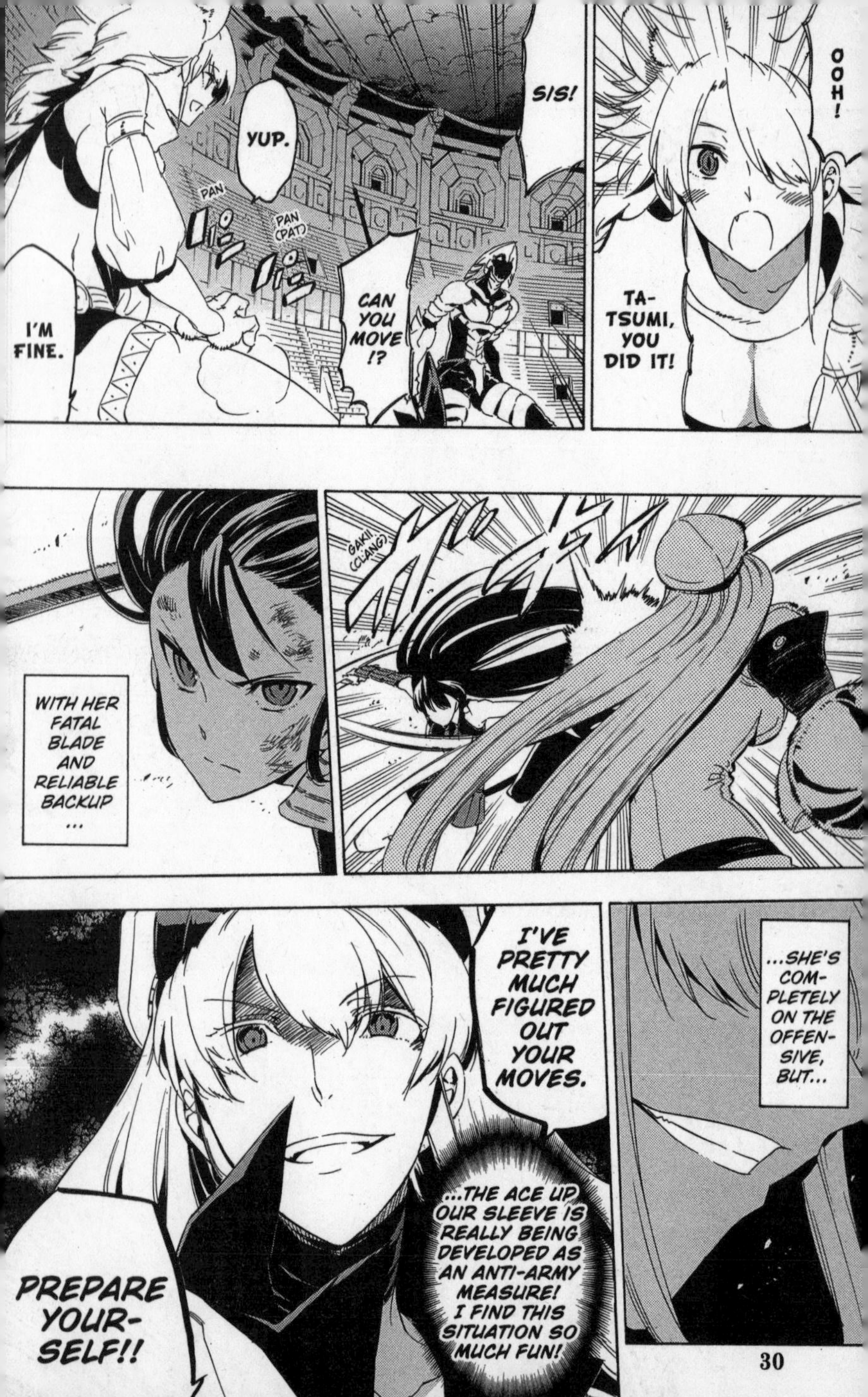
OOH!
TA-TSUMI, YOU DID IT!
SIS!
CAN YOU MOVE!?
YUP.
PAN
PAN (PAT)
I'M FINE.
GAKI! (CLANG)
WITH HER FATAL BLADE AND RELIABLE BACKUP...
...SHE'S COMPLETELY ON THE OFFENSIVE, BUT...
I'VE PRETTY MUCH FIGURED OUT YOUR MOVES.
...THE ACE UP OUR SLEEVE IS REALLY BEING DEVELOPED AS AN ANTI-ARMY MEASURE! I FIND THIS SITUATION SO MUCH FUN!
PREPARE YOURSELF!!

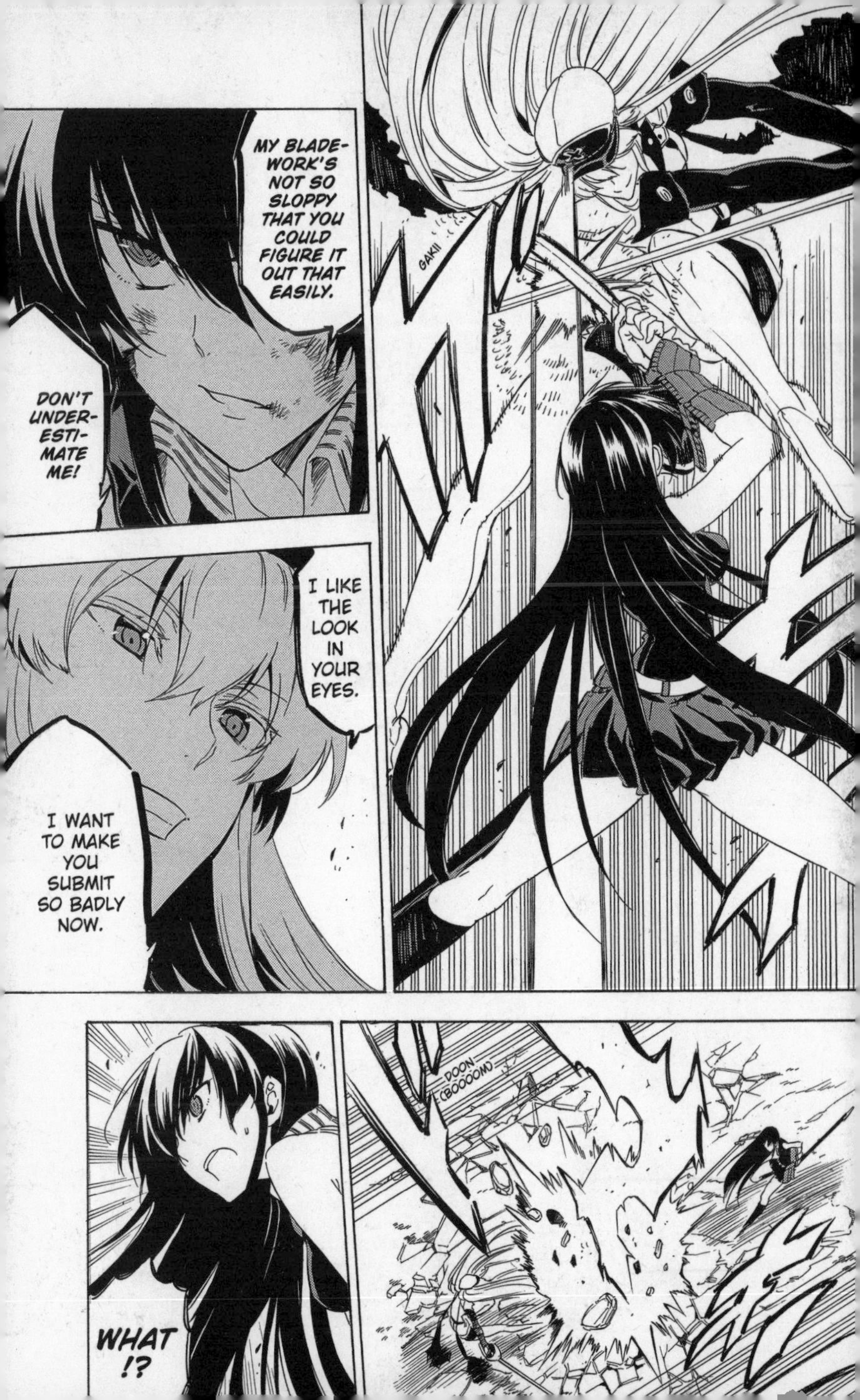
GAKII
MY BLADE-WORK'S NOT SO SLOPPY THAT YOU COULD FIGURE IT OUT THAT EASILY.
DON'T UNDER-ESTI-MATE ME!
I LIKE THE LOOK IN YOUR EYES.
I WANT TO MAKE YOU SUBMIT SO BADLY NOW.
DOON (BOOOOM)
WHAT !?

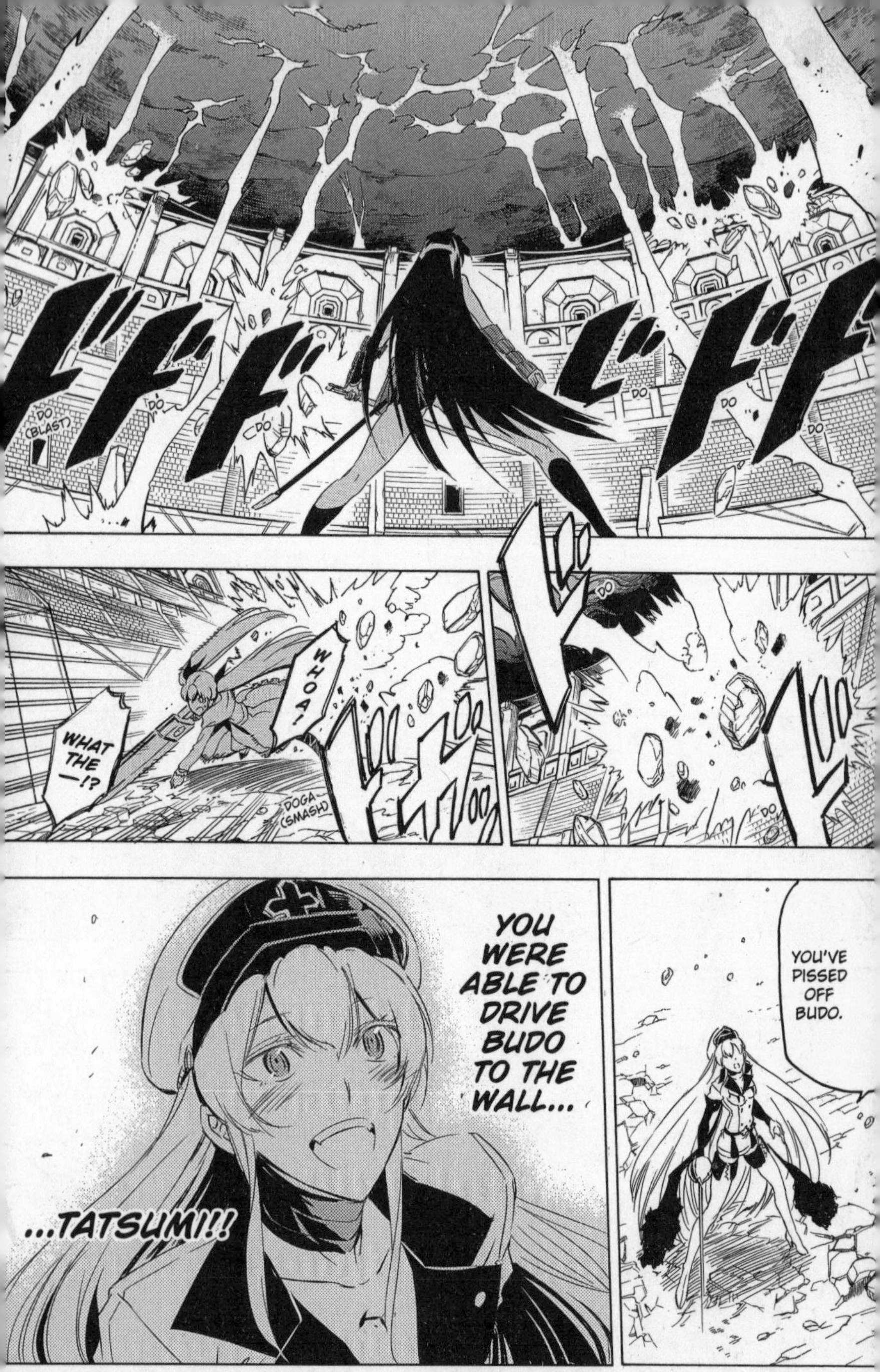
DO
DO
DO
DO
DO
DO (BLAST)
DO
DO
DOGA (SMASH)
WHOA!
WHAT THE—!?
YOU'VE PISSED OFF BUDO.
YOU WERE ABLE TO DRIVE BUDO TO THE WALL...
...TATSUMI!!

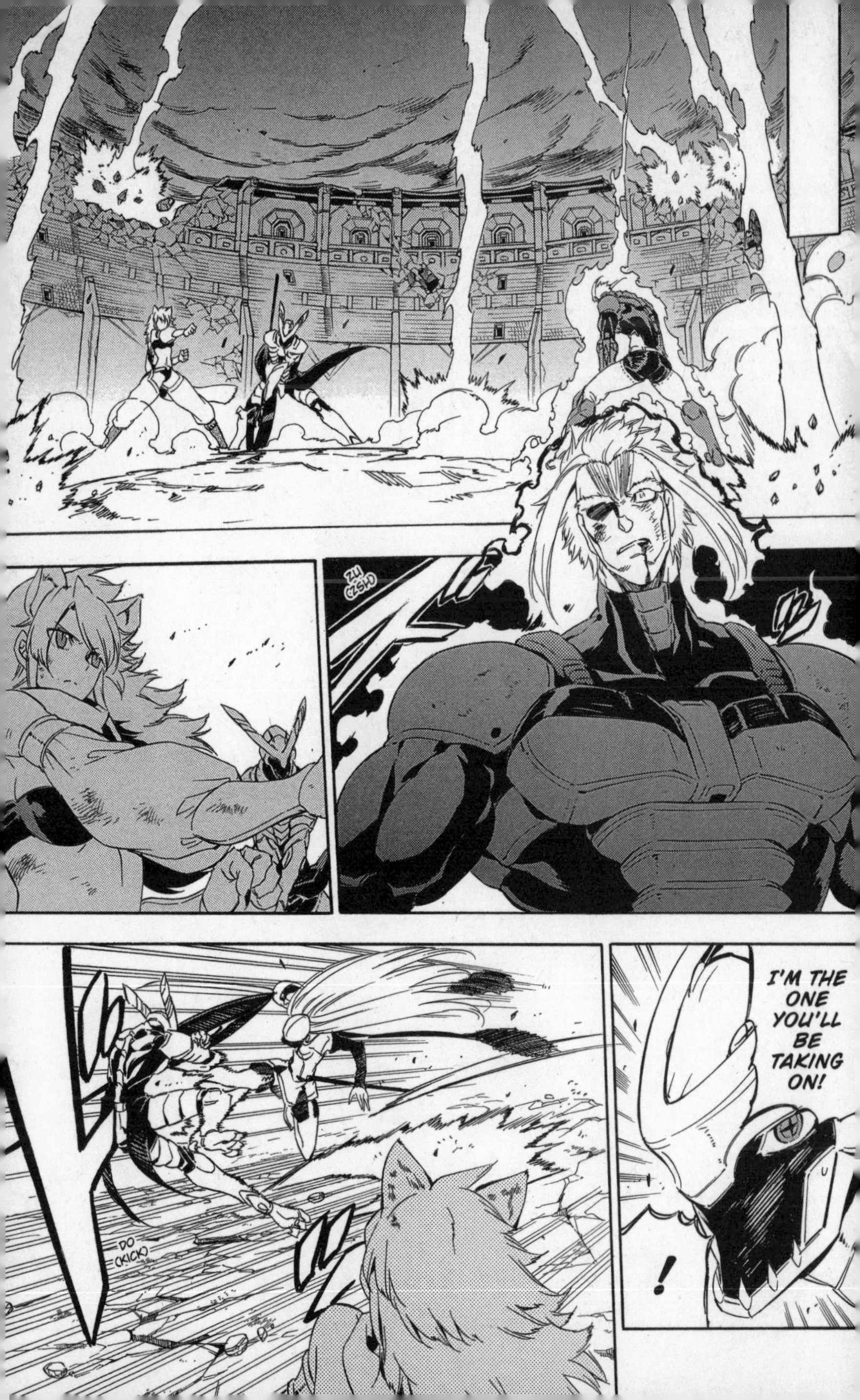
ZU
(ZSH)
I'M THE ONE YOU'LL BE TAKING ON!
!
DO
(KICK)

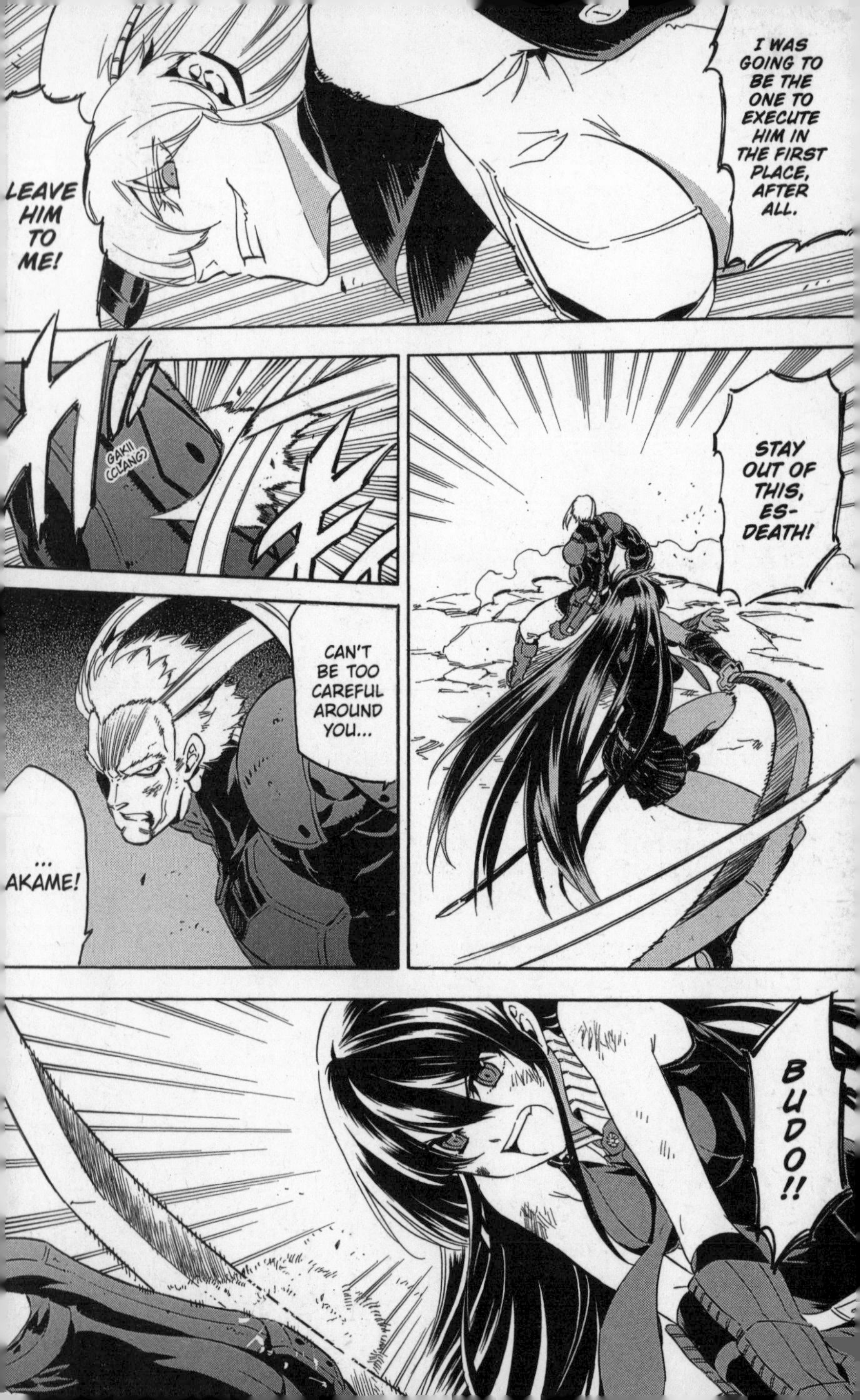
I WAS GOING TO BE THE ONE TO EXECUTE HIM IN THE FIRST PLACE, AFTER ALL.
LEAVE HIM TO ME!
STAY OUT OF THIS, ES-DEATH!
GAKII (CLANG)
CAN'T BE TOO CAREFUL AROUND YOU...
...AKAME!
BUDO!!

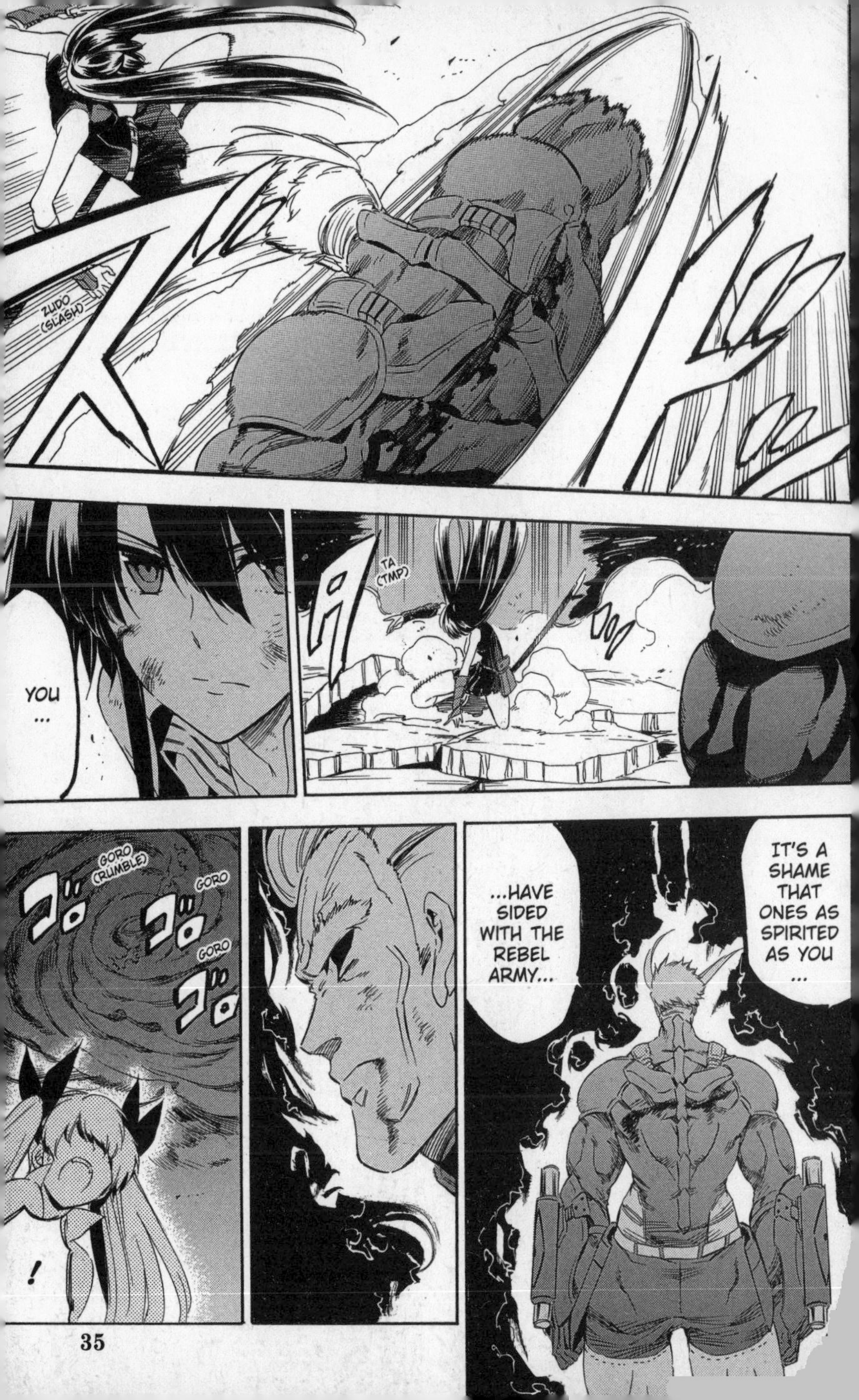
ZUDO (SLASH)
TA (TMP)
YOU ...
IT'S A SHAME THAT ONES AS SPIRITED AS YOU ...
...HAVE SIDED WITH THE REBEL ARMY...
GORO (RUMBLE)
GORO
GORO
!

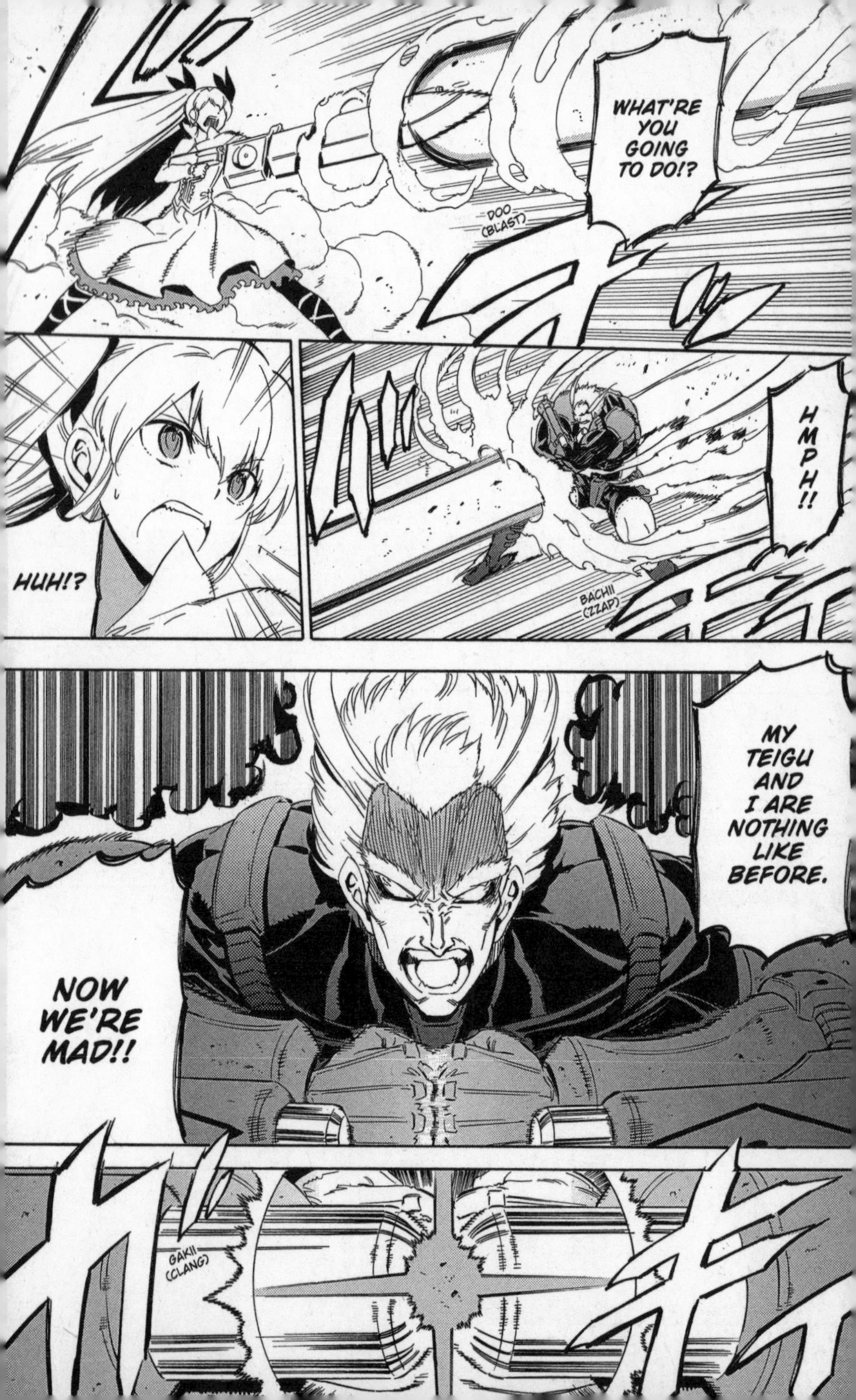
WHAT'RE YOU GOING TO DO!?
DOO (BLAST)
HMPH!!
BACHII (ZZAP)
HUH!?
MY TEIGU AND I ARE NOTHING LIKE BEFORE.
NOW WE'RE MAD!!
GAKII (CLANG)

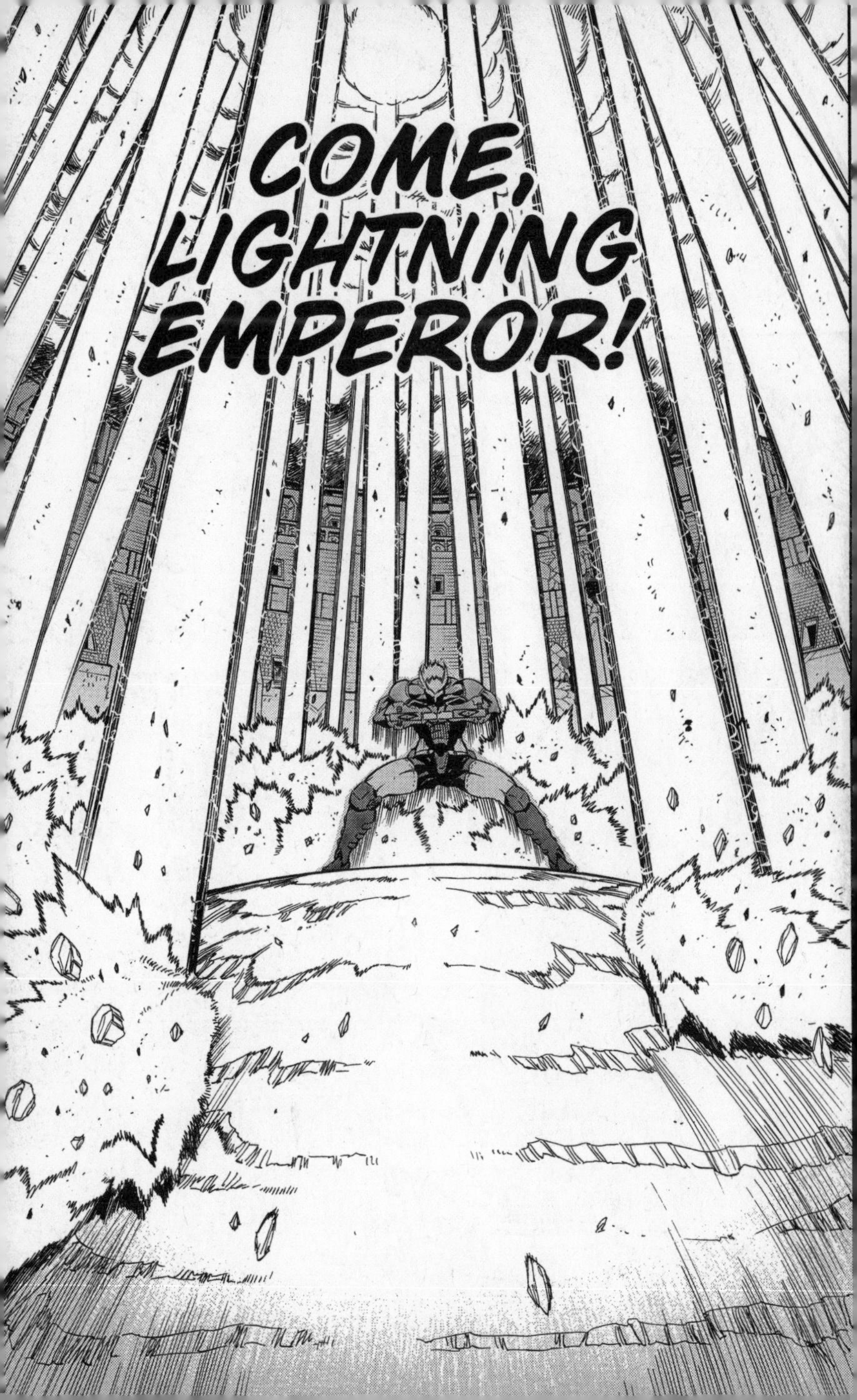
COME, LIGHTNING EMPEROR!

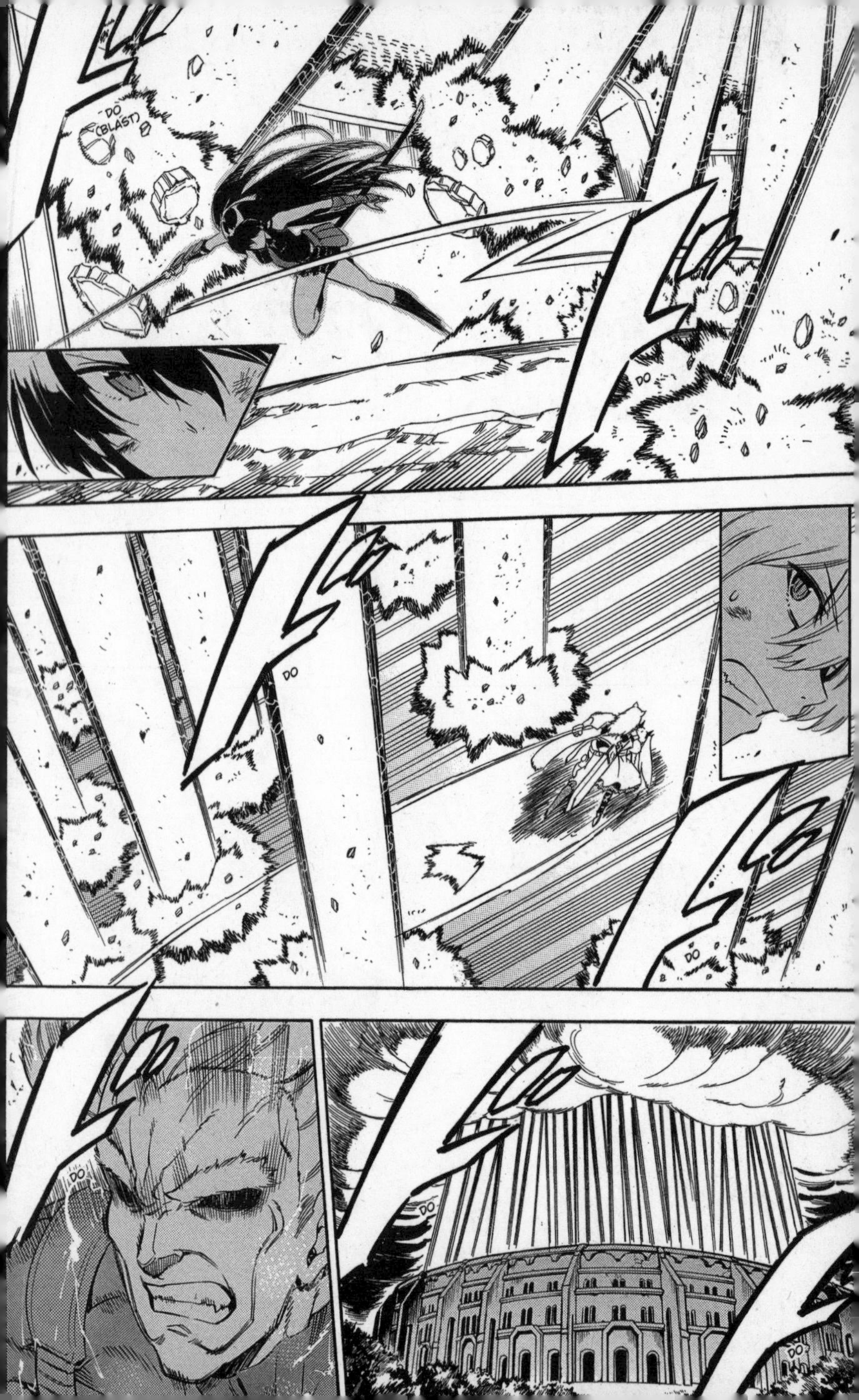
DO
(BLAST)
DO
DO
DO
DO
DO
DO

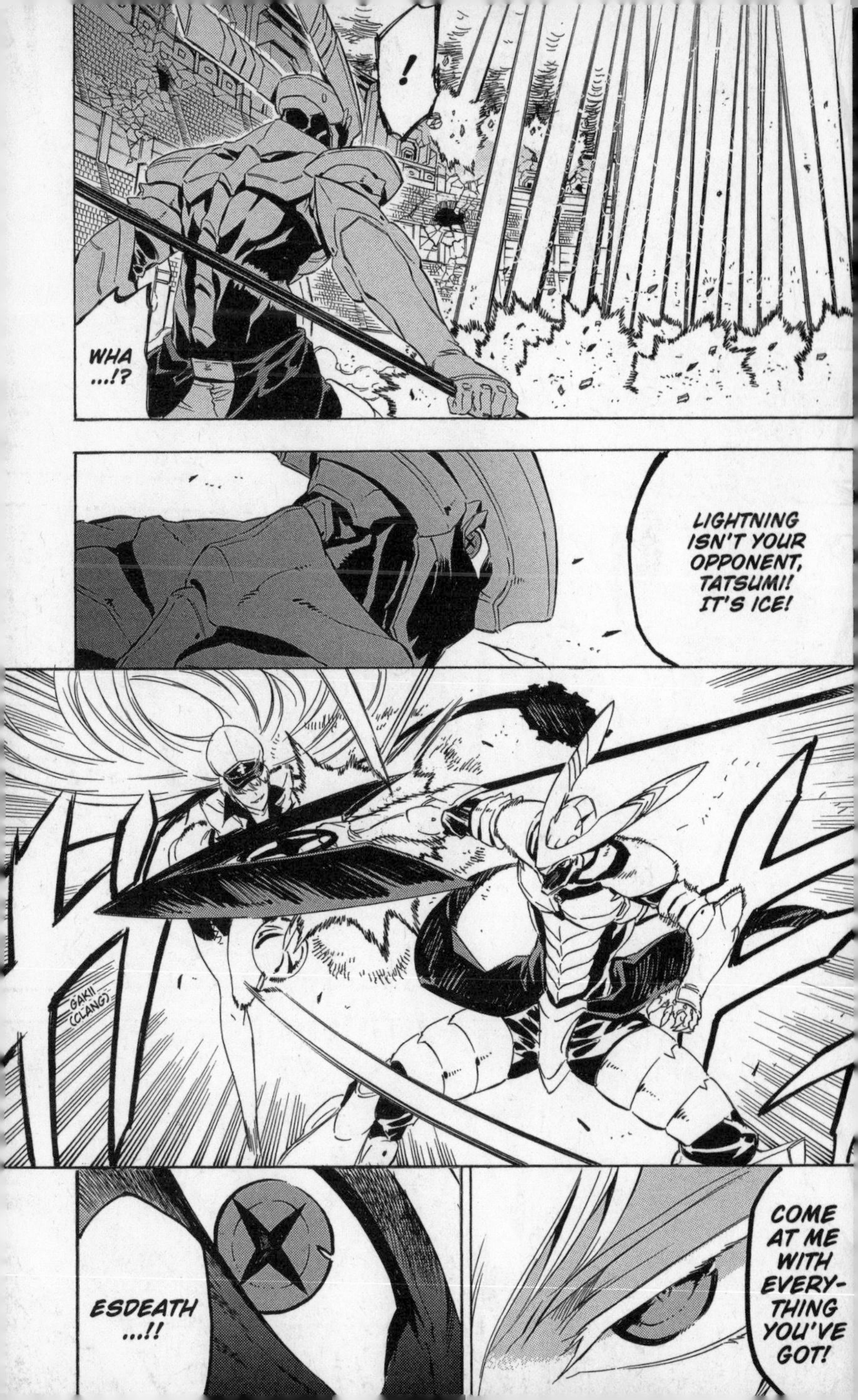
!
WHA ...!?
...
LIGHTNING ISN'T YOUR OPPONENT, TATSUMI! IT'S ICE!
GAKI (CLANG)
COME AT ME WITH EVERY-THING YOU'VE GOT!
ESDEATH ...!!

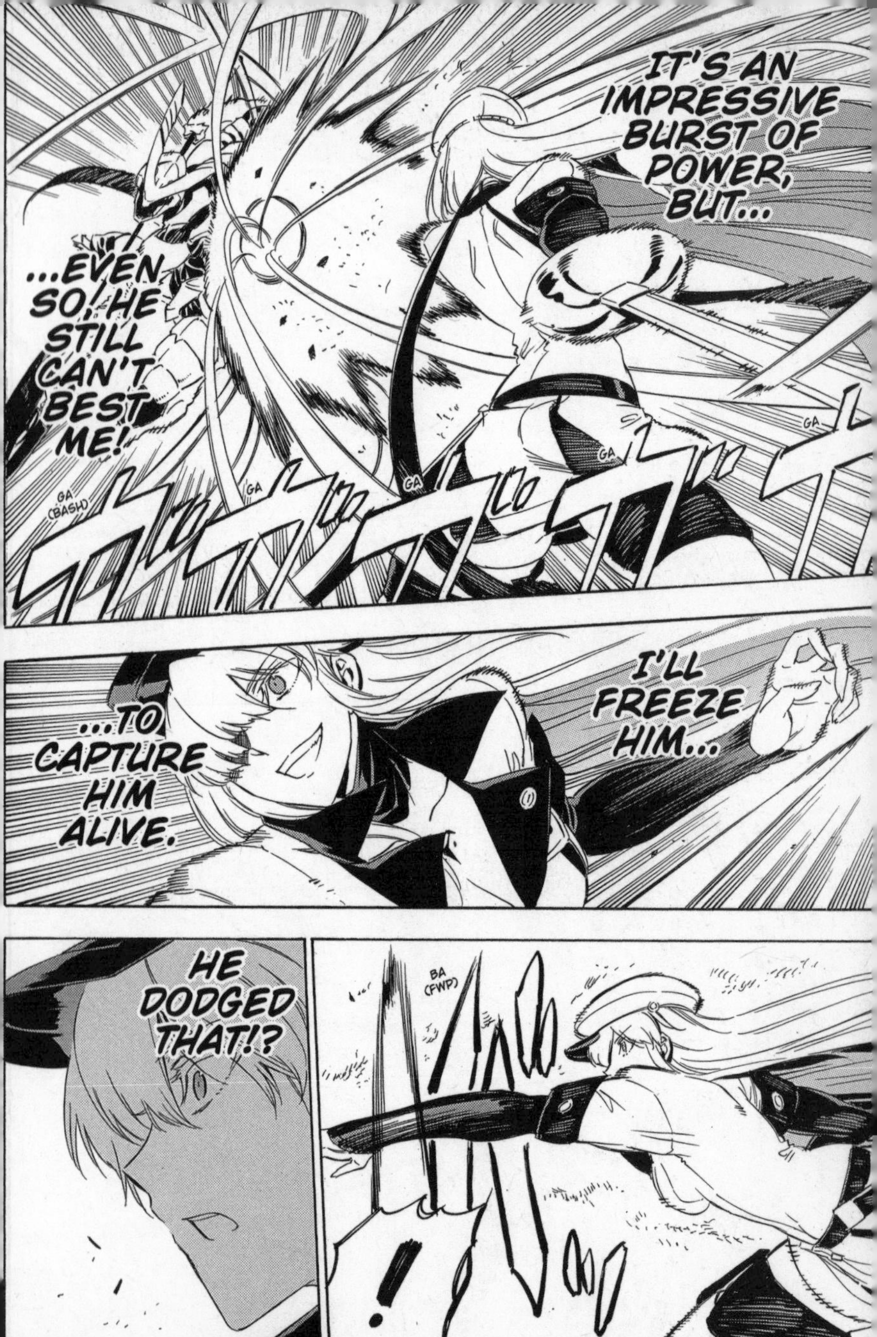
IT'S AN IMPRESSIVE BURST OF POWER, BUT...
...EVEN SO, HE STILL CAN'T BEST ME!
GA
GA
GA
GA
GA (BASH)
I'LL FREEZE HIM...
...TO CAPTURE HIM ALIVE.
BA (FWP)
HE DODGED THAT!?

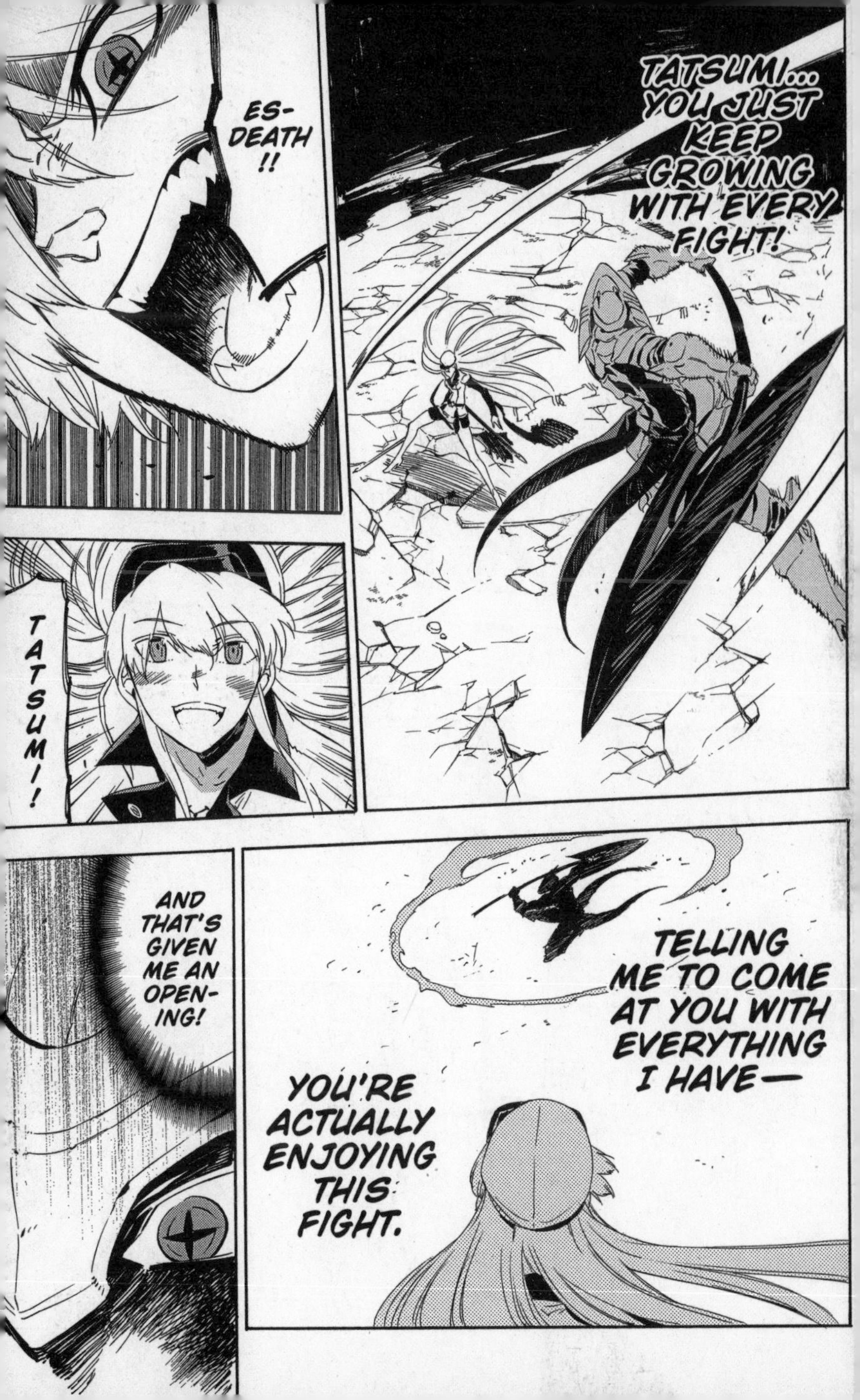
TATSUMI... YOU JUST KEEP GROWING WITH EVERY FIGHT!
ES-DEATH!!
TATSUMI!
TELLING ME TO COME AT YOU WITH EVERYTHING I HAVE—
YOU'RE ACTUALLY ENJOYING THIS FIGHT.
AND THAT'S GIVEN ME AN OPENING!

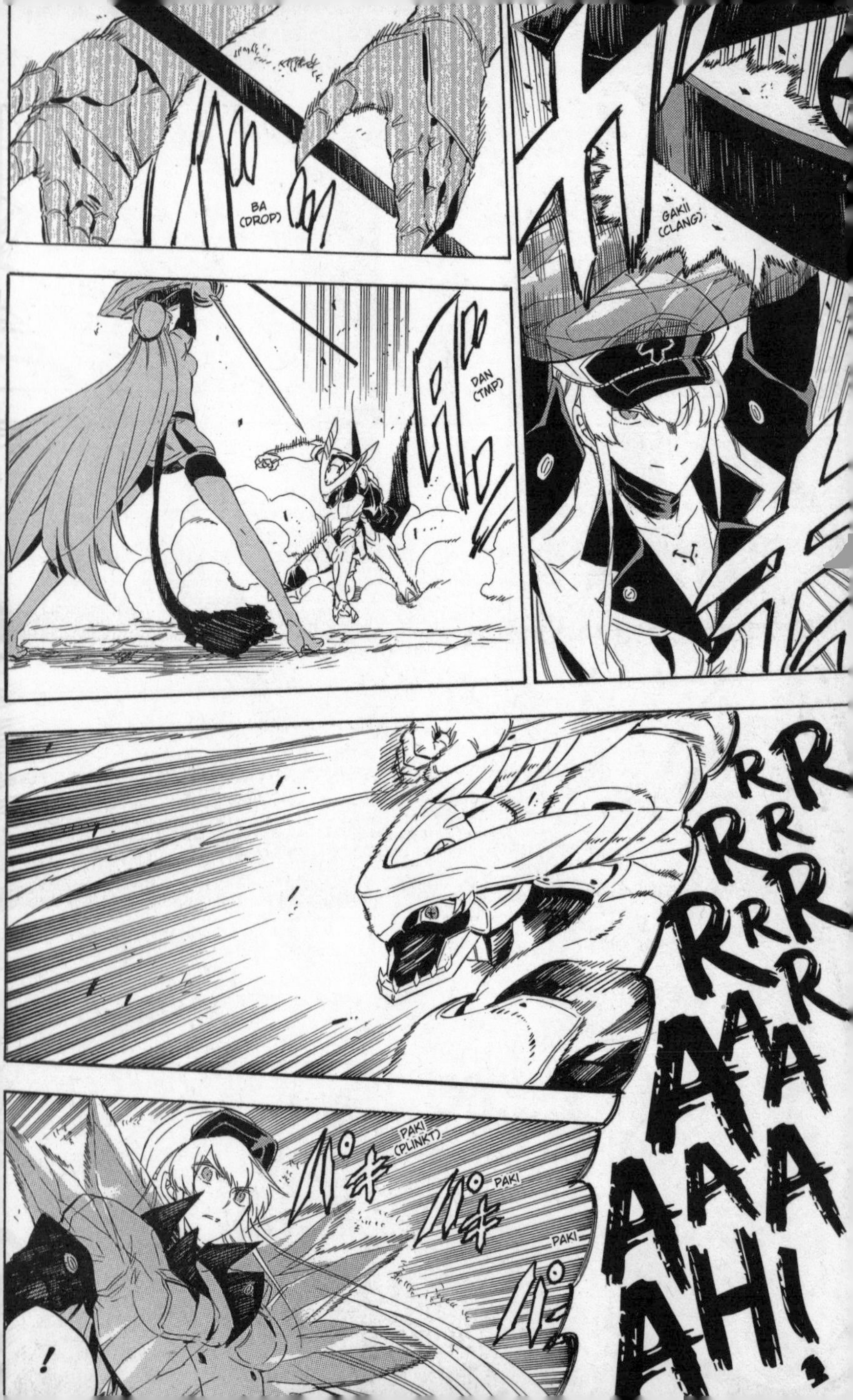
GAKII (CLANG)
BA (DROP)
DAN (TMP)
RRRRRRRRRAAAAAAAAAAAAH!
PAKI (PLINKT)
PAKI
PAKI
!

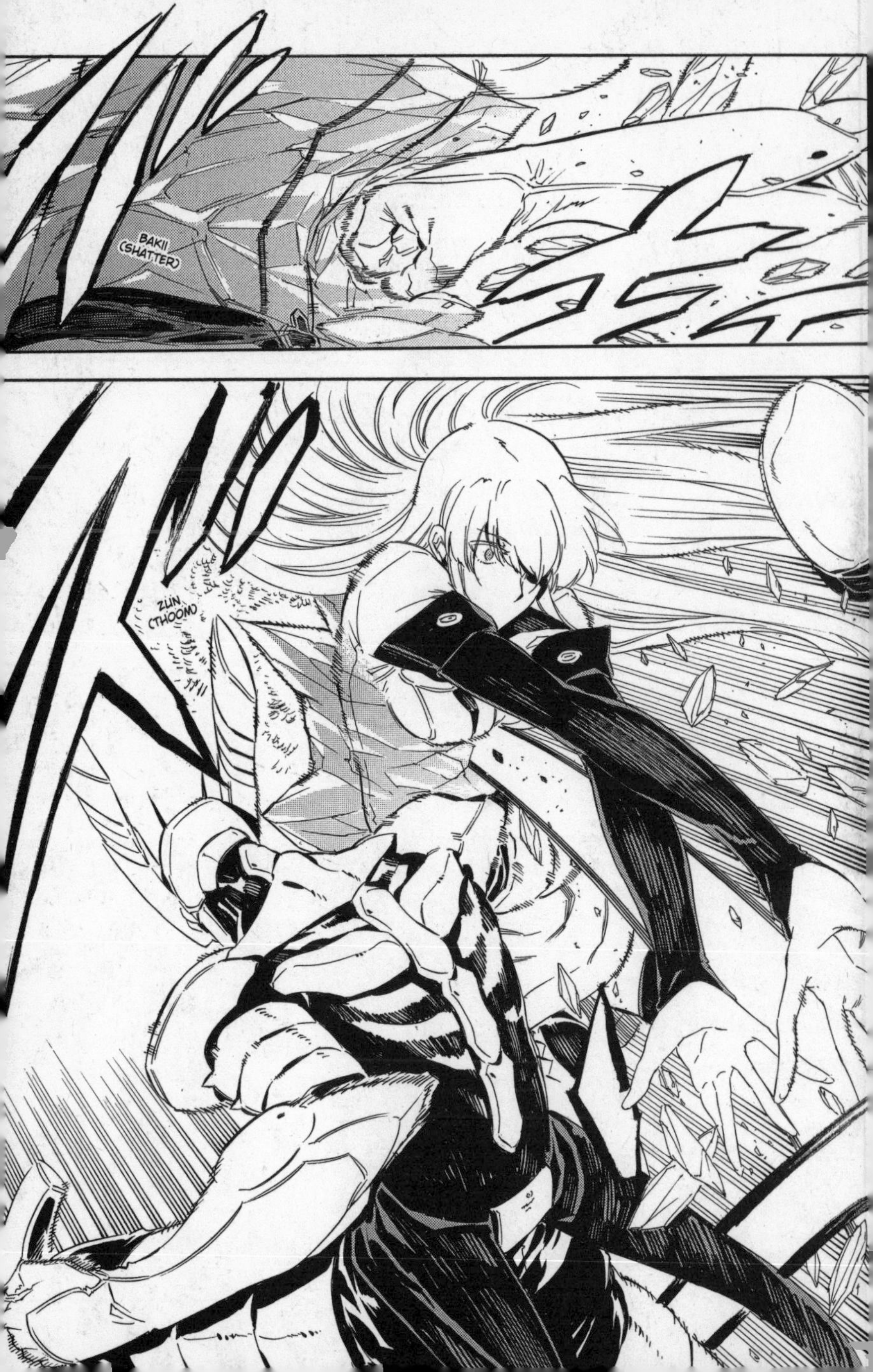
BAKII
(SHATTER)
ZUN
(THOOM)

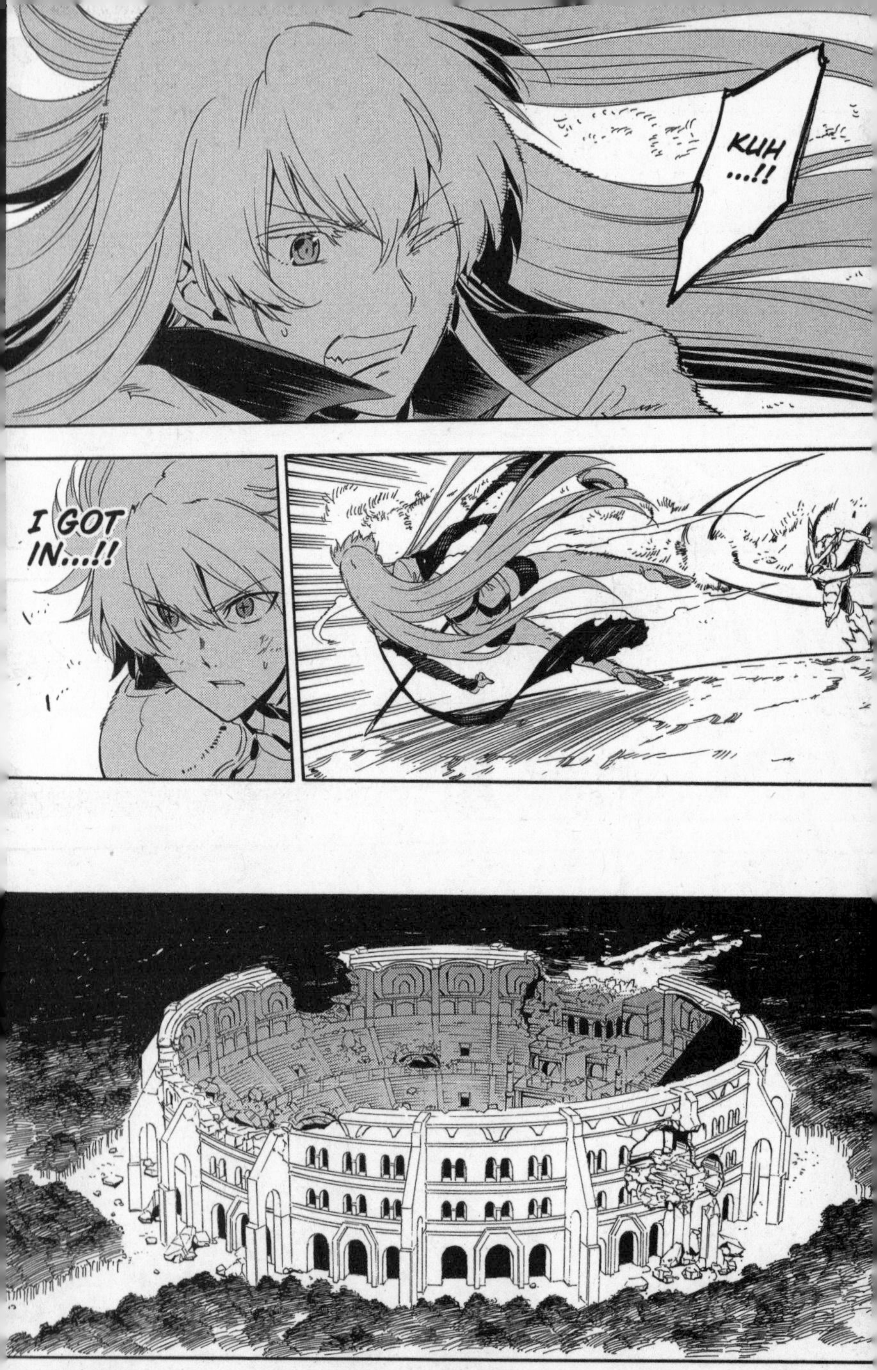
KUH ...!!
I GOT IN...!!

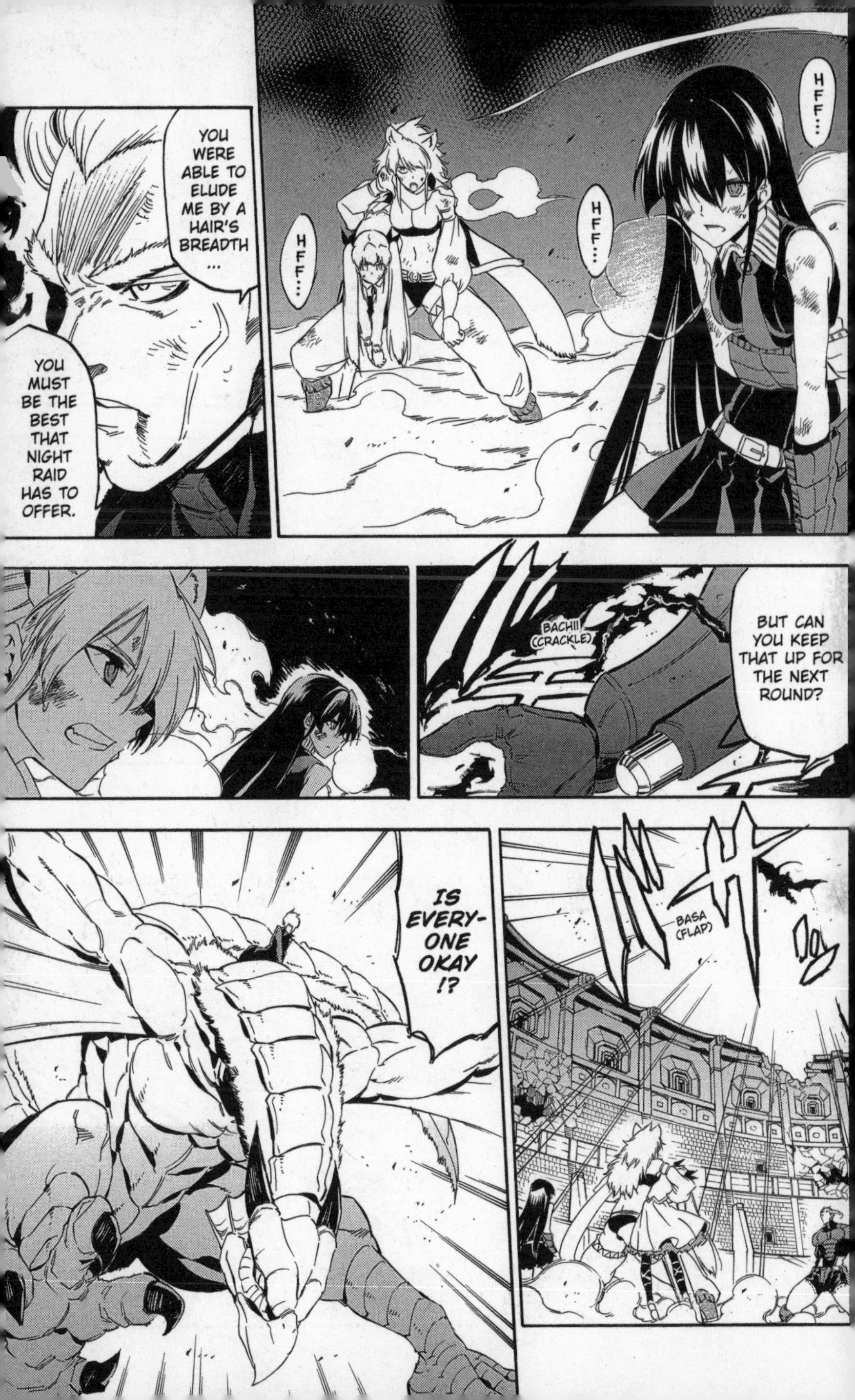
HFF...
HFF...
HFF...
YOU WERE ABLE TO ELUDE ME BY A HAIR'S BREADTH ...
YOU MUST BE THE BEST THAT NIGHT RAID HAS TO OFFER.
BUT CAN YOU KEEP THAT UP FOR THE NEXT ROUND?
BACHII (CRACKLE)
BASA (FLAP)
IS EVERY-ONE OKAY !?

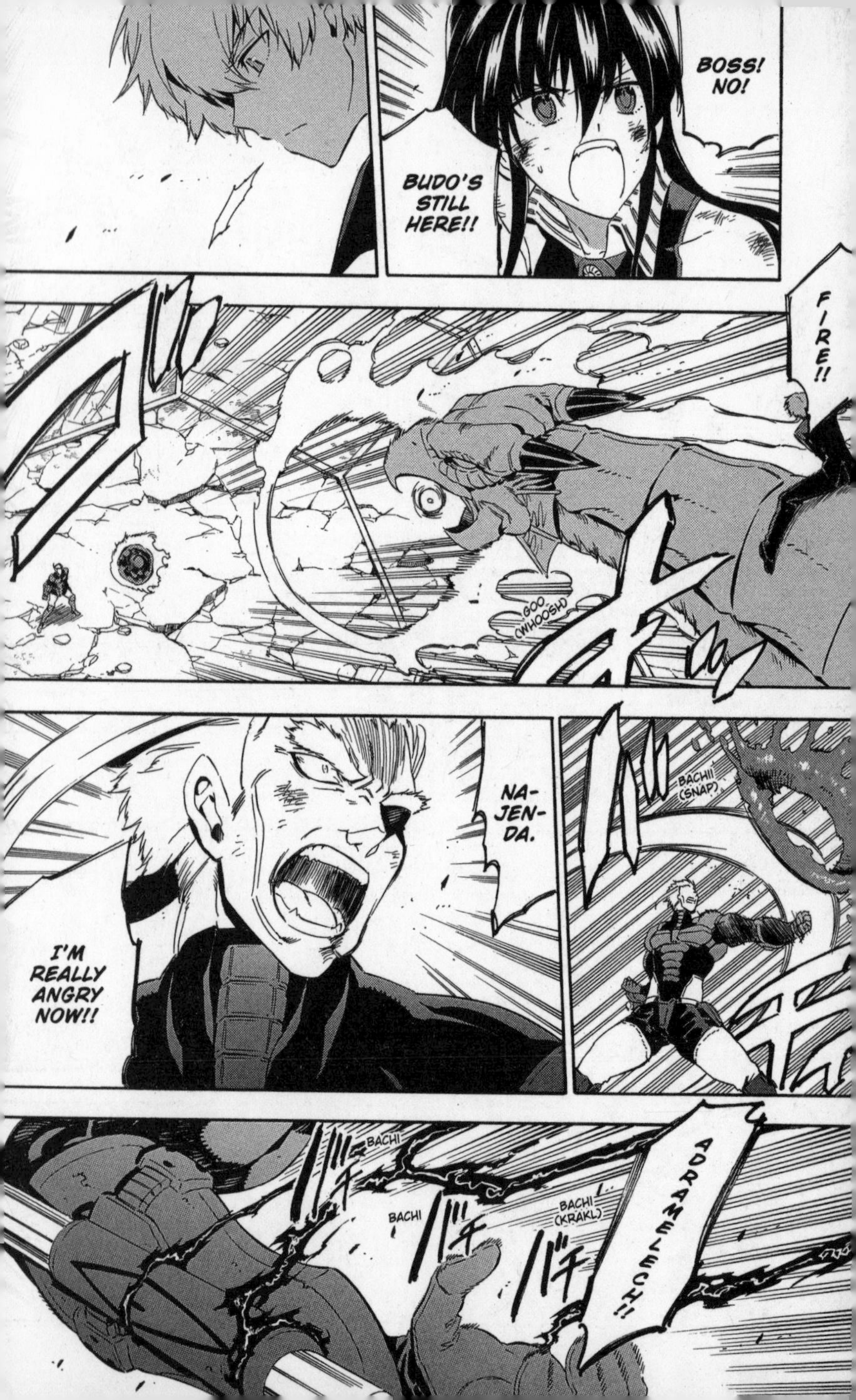
BOSS! NO!
BUDO'S STILL HERE!!
FIRE!!
GOO (WHOOSH)
BACHII (SNAP)
NA-JEN-DA.
I'M REALLY ANGRY NOW!!
ADRAMELECH!!
BACHI (KRAKL)
BACHI
BACHI

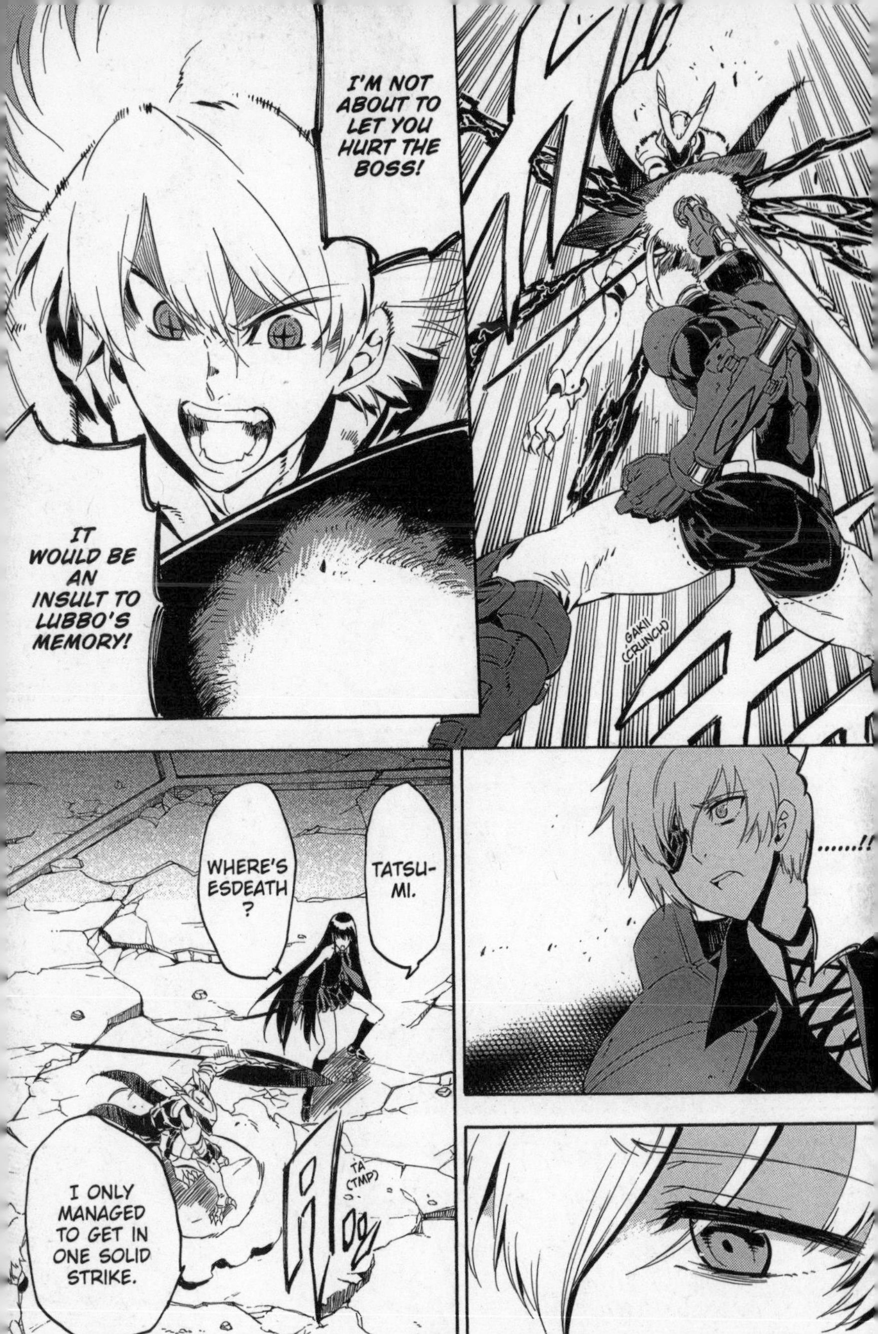
GAKII (CRUNCH)
I'M NOT ABOUT TO LET YOU HURT THE BOSS!
IT WOULD BE AN INSULT TO LUBBO'S MEMORY!
......!!
TATSUMI.
WHERE'S ESDEATH?
TA (TMP)
I ONLY MANAGED TO GET IN ONE SOLID STRIKE.

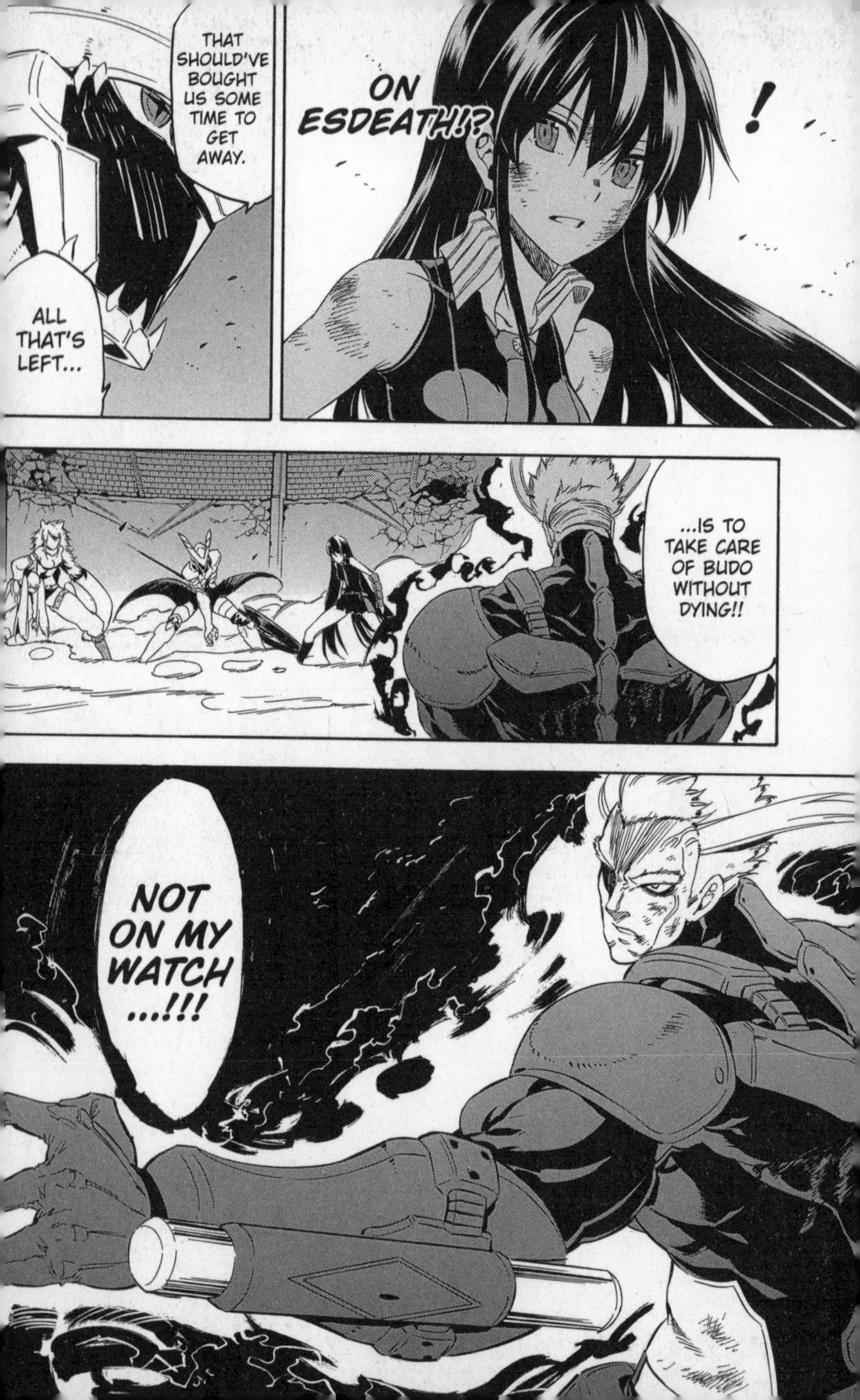
ON ESDEATH!?
!
THAT SHOULD'VE BOUGHT US SOME TIME TO GET AWAY.
ALL THAT'S LEFT...
...IS TO TAKE CARE OF BUDO WITHOUT DYING!!
NOT ON MY WATCH ...!!!

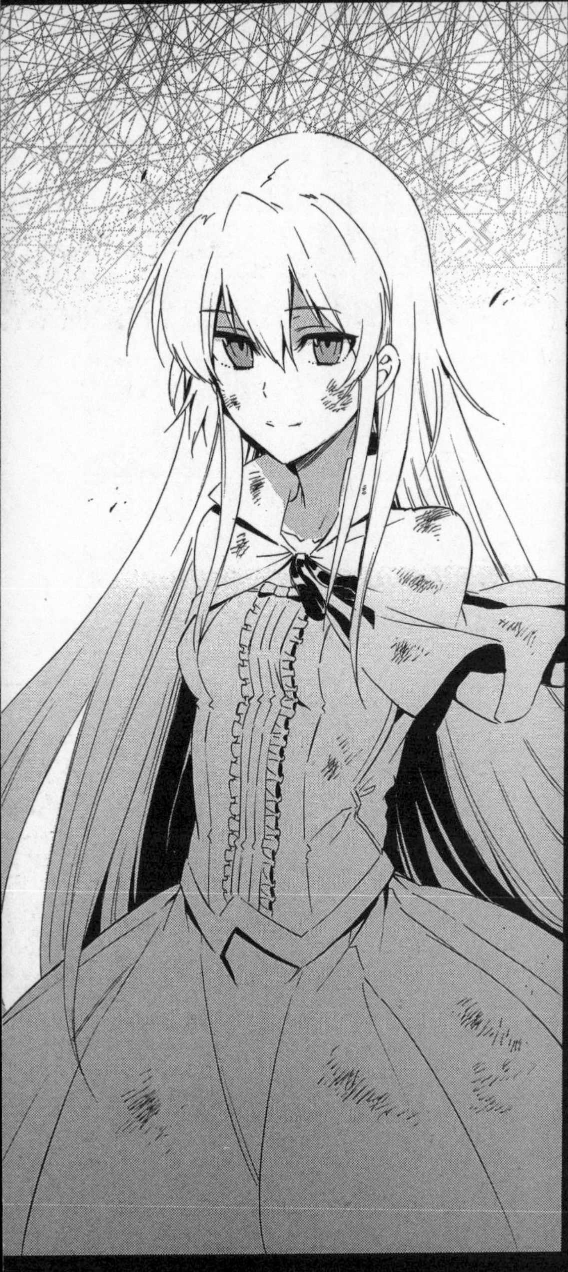

Chapter 56 - Kill the Commander in Chief

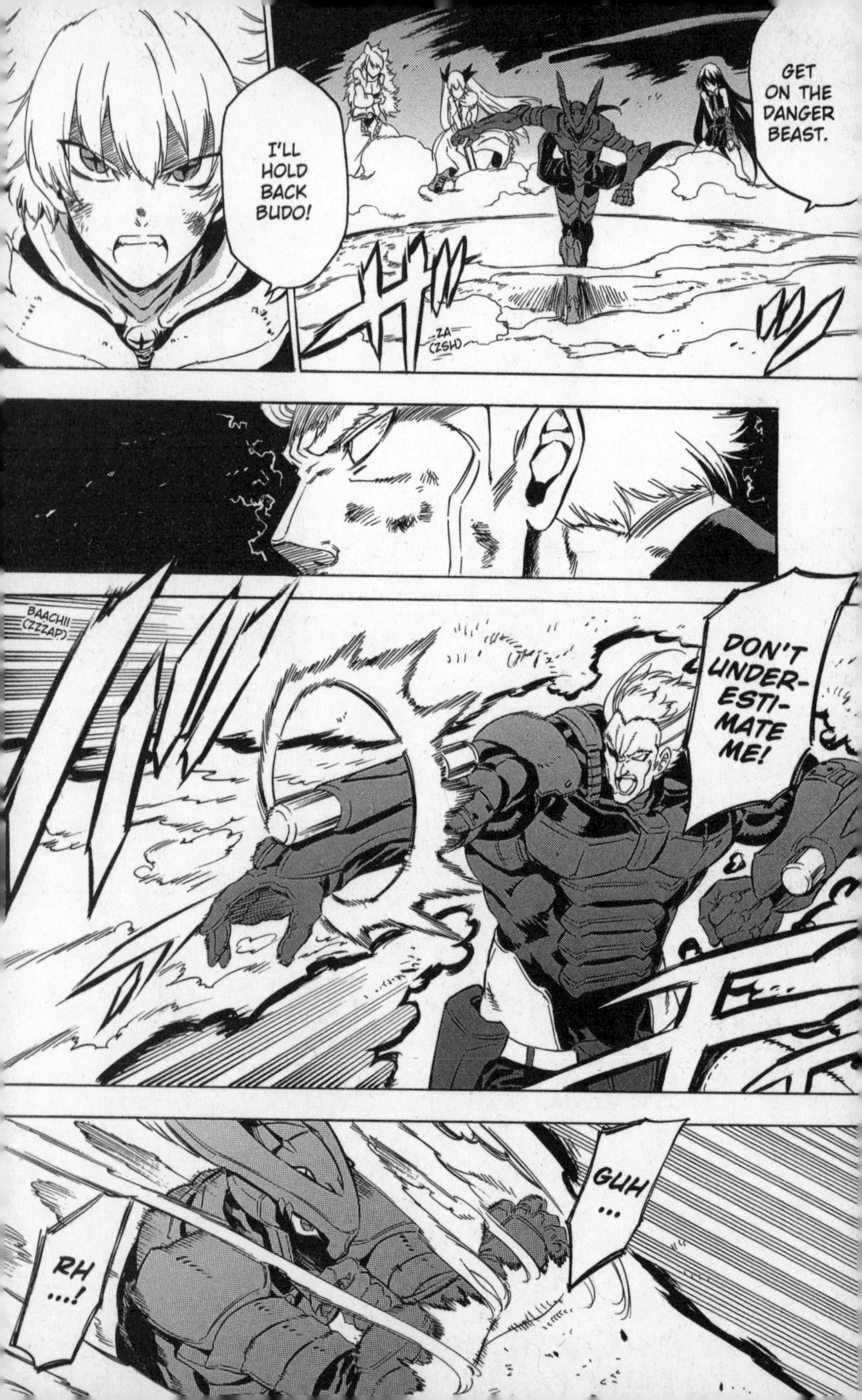

GET ON THE DANGER BEAST.
I'LL HOLD BACK BUDO!
ZA (ZSH)
DON'T UNDER-ESTI-MATE ME!
BAACHII (ZZZAP)
GUH ...
RH ...!

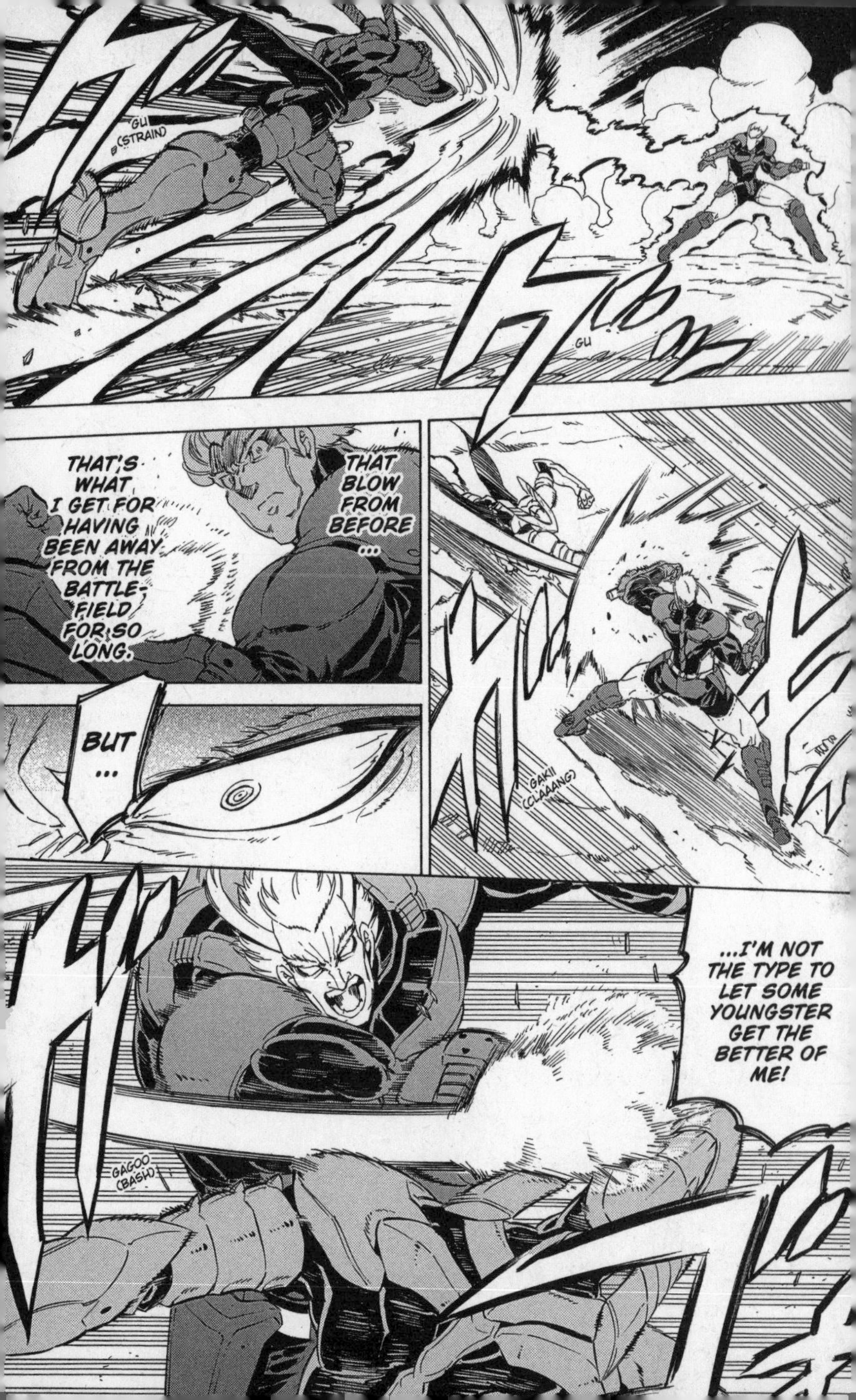
GU
GU (STRAIND)
GAKII (CLAAANG)
THAT BLOW FROM BEFORE...
THAT'S WHAT I GET FOR HAVING BEEN AWAY FROM THE BATTLE-FIELD FOR SO LONG.
BUT...
...I'M NOT THE TYPE TO LET SOME YOUNGSTER GET THE BETTER OF ME!
GAGOO (BASH)

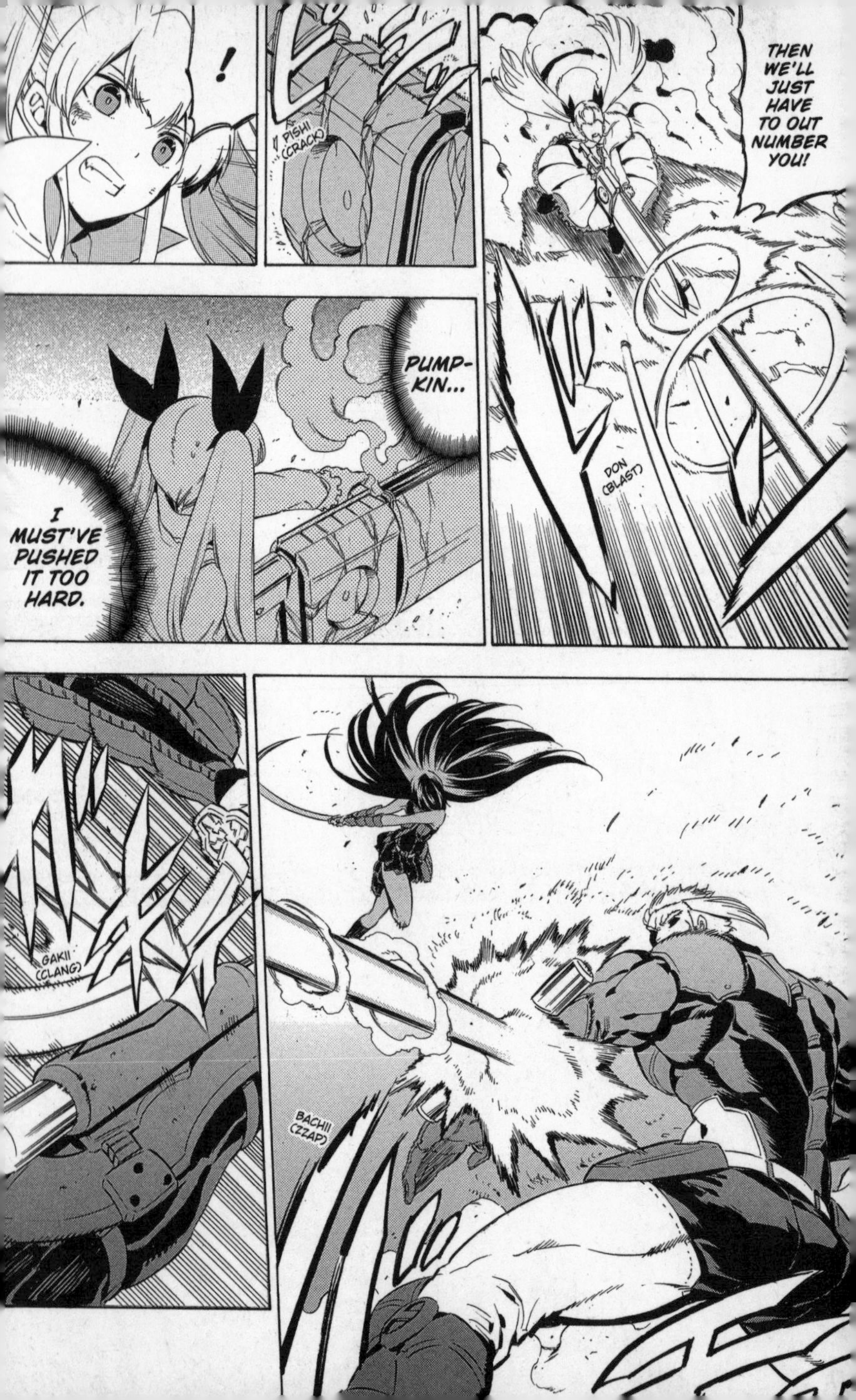
!
PISHI (CRACK)
THEN WE'LL JUST HAVE TO OUT NUMBER YOU!
DON (BLAST)
PUMP-KIN...
I MUST'VE PUSHED IT TOO HARD.
GAKII (CLANG)
BACHII (ZZAP)

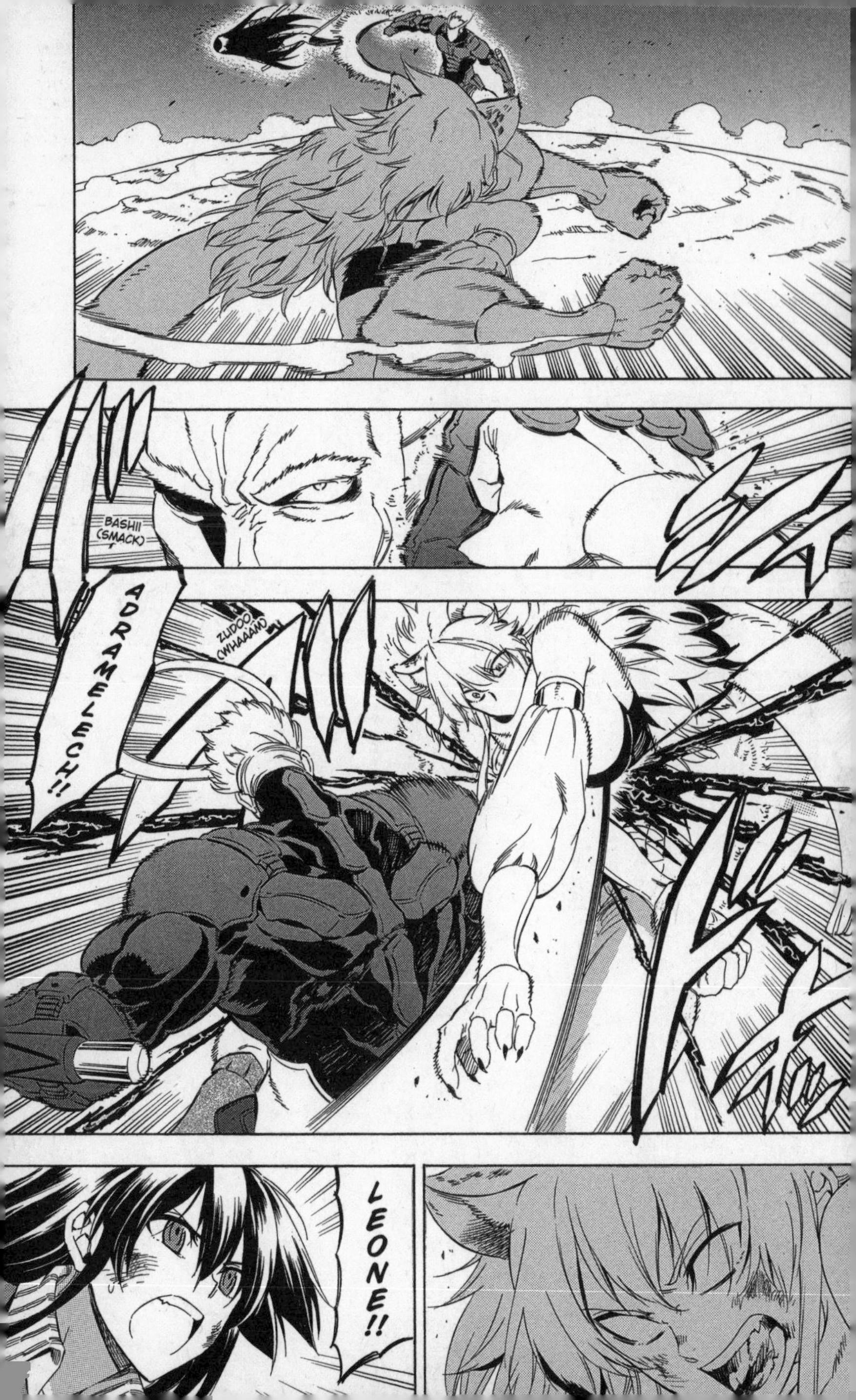
BASHII (SMACK)
ZUDOO (WHAAAM)
ADRAMELECH!!
LEONE!!

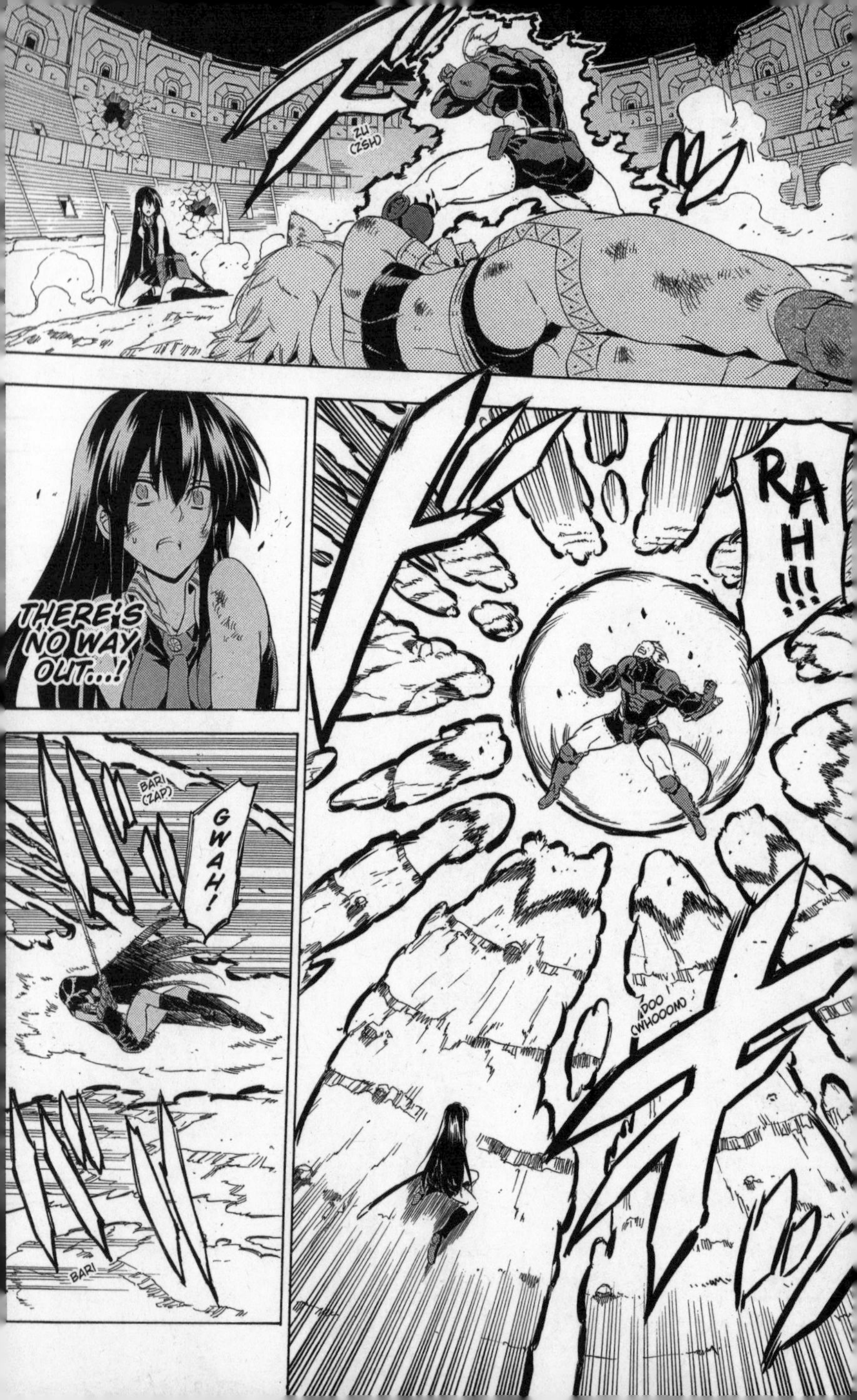
ZU (ZSHD)
THERE'S NO WAY OUT...!
RAH!!!
BARI (ZAP)
GWAH!
DOO (WHOOOM)
BARI

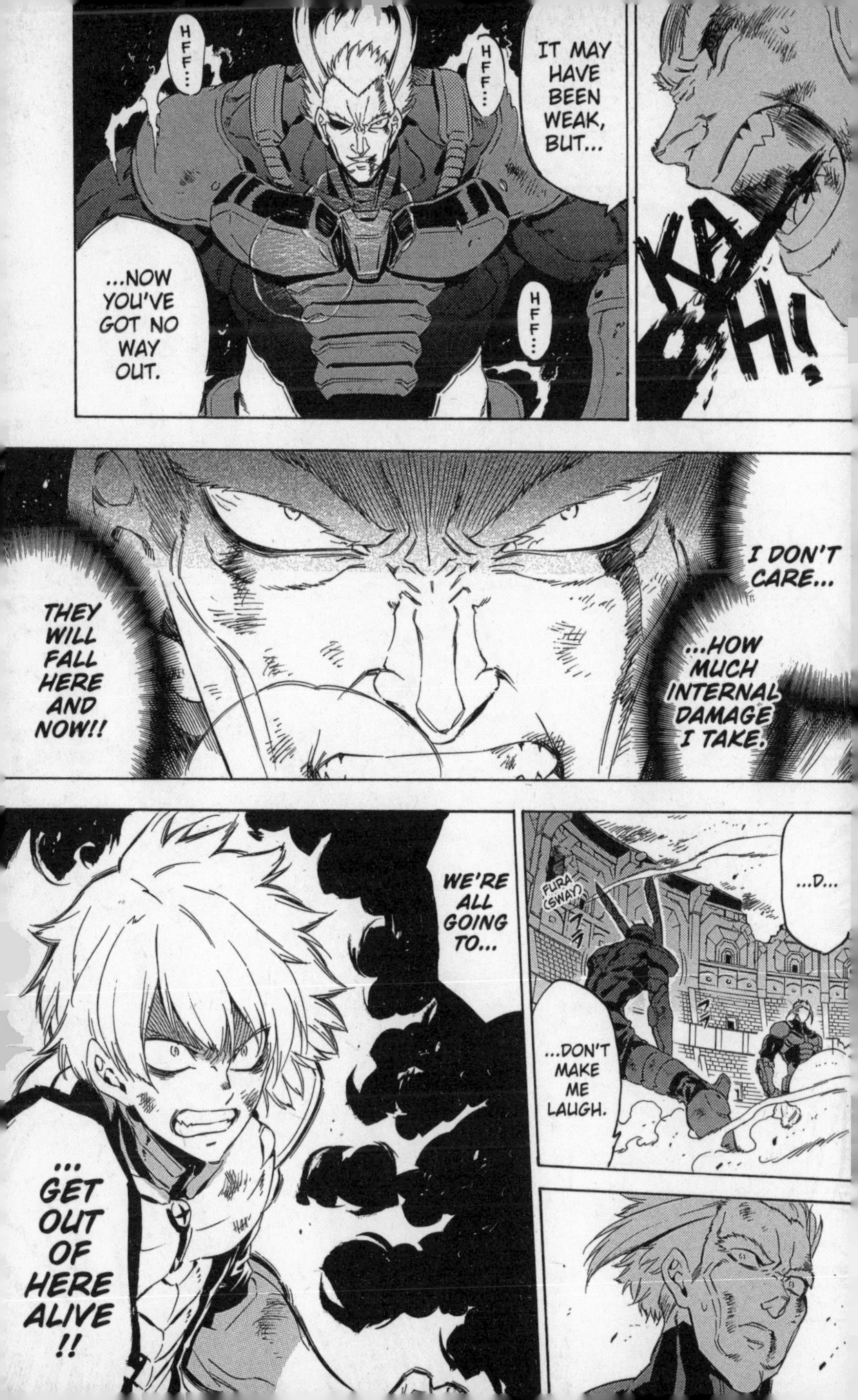
IT MAY HAVE BEEN WEAK, BUT...
HFF...
HFF...
...NOW YOU'VE GOT NO WAY OUT.
HFF...
I DON'T CARE...
...HOW MUCH INTERNAL DAMAGE I TAKE.
THEY WILL FALL HERE AND NOW!!
...D...
FURA (SWAY)
...DON'T MAKE ME LAUGH.
WE'RE ALL GOING TO...
...GET OUT OF HERE ALIVE!!

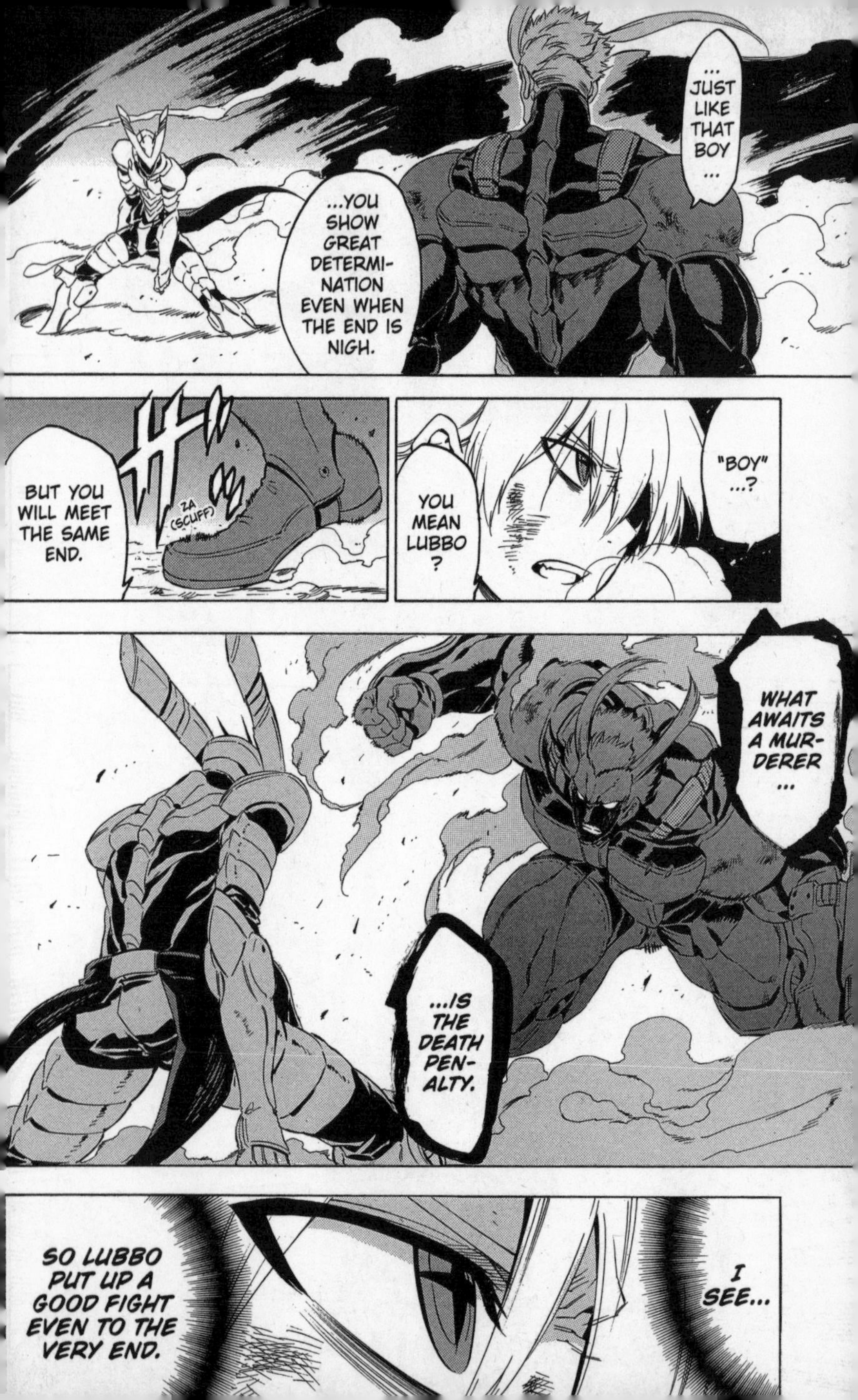
...JUST LIKE THAT BOY...
...YOU SHOW GREAT DETERMINATION EVEN WHEN THE END IS NIGH.
"BOY"...?
YOU MEAN LUBBO?
ZA (SCUFF)
BUT YOU WILL MEET THE SAME END.
WHAT AWAITS A MURDERER...
...IS THE DEATH PENALTY.
I SEE...
SO LUBBO PUT UP A GOOD FIGHT EVEN TO THE VERY END.

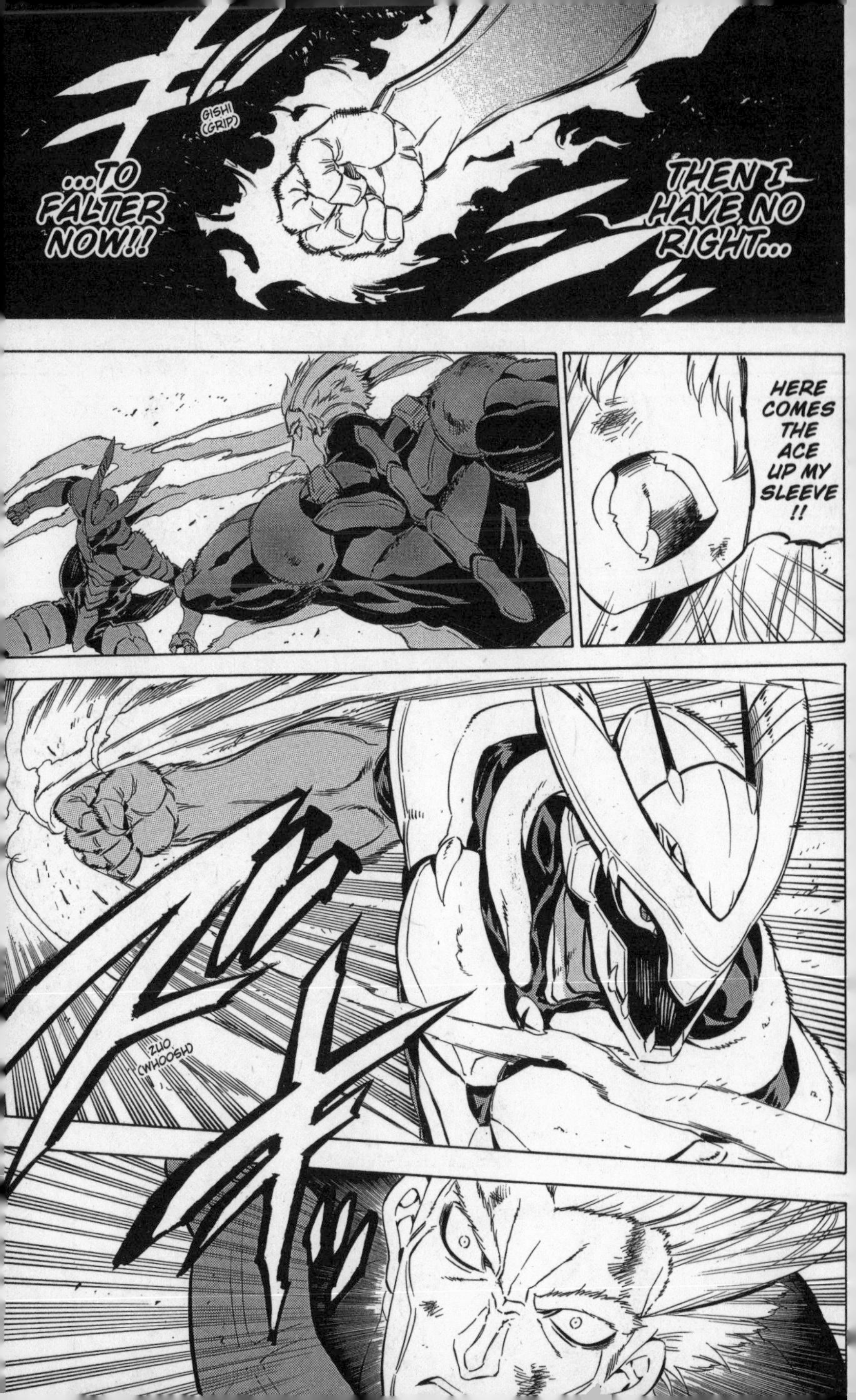
THEN I HAVE NO RIGHT...
GISHI (GRIP)
...TO FALTER NOW!!
HERE COMES THE ACE UP MY SLEEVE !!
ZUO (WHOOSH)

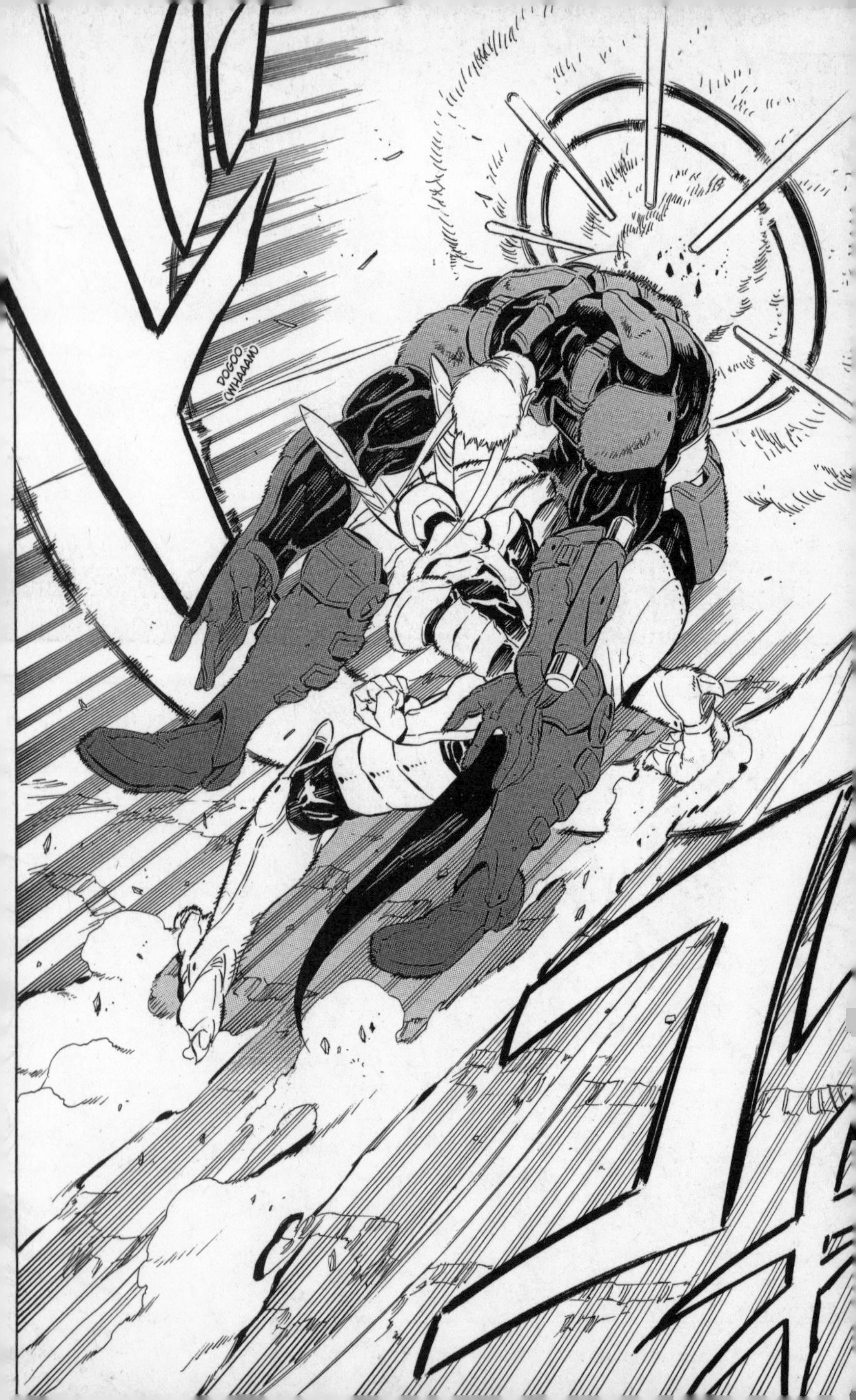
DOGOO
(WHAAAM)

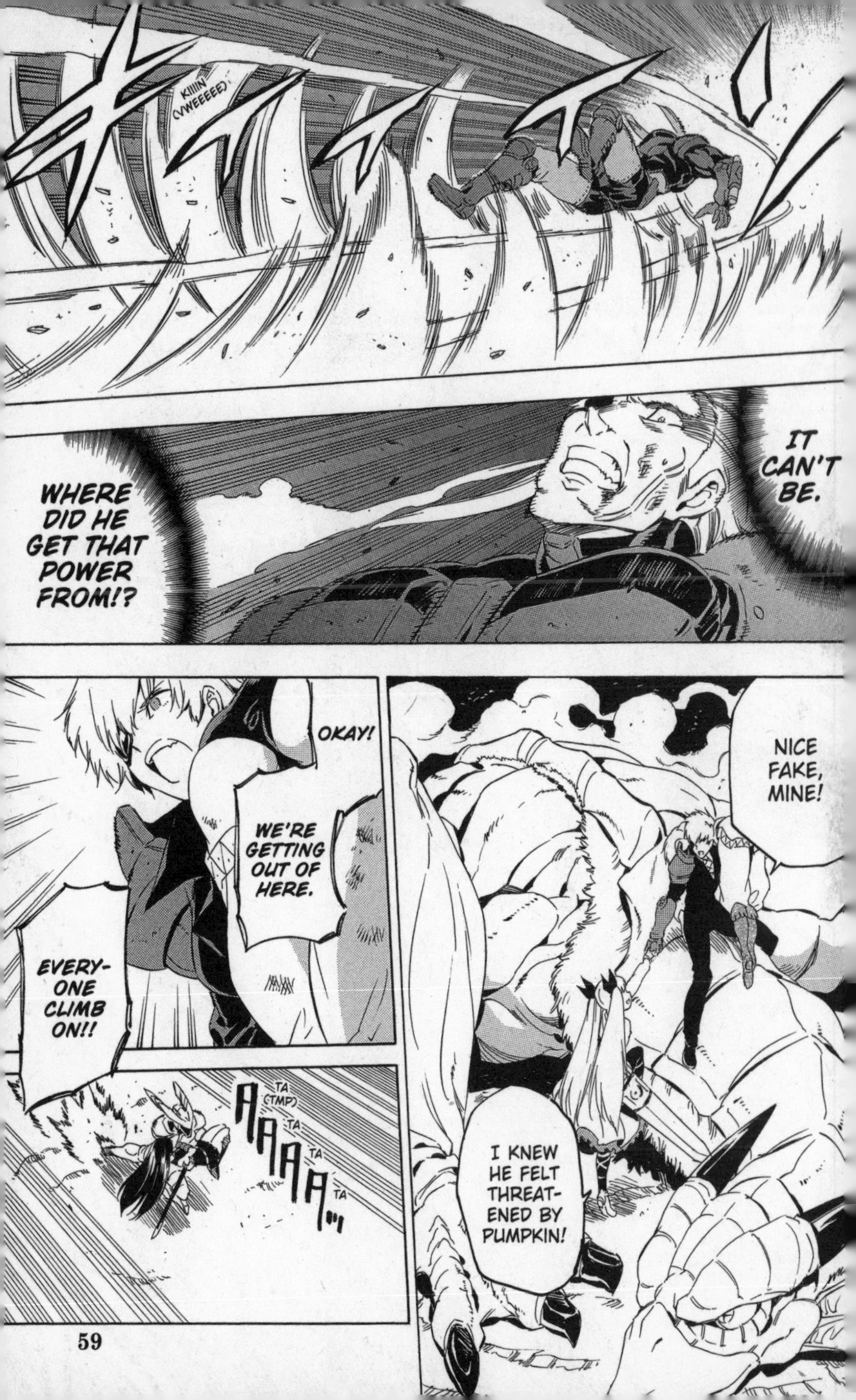
KIIIIN (VWEEEEE)
IT CAN'T BE.
WHERE DID HE GET THAT POWER FROM!?
NICE FAKE, MINE!
I KNEW HE FELT THREAT-ENED BY PUMPKIN!
OKAY!
WE'RE GETTING OUT OF HERE.
EVERY-ONE CLIMB ON!!
TA (TMP) TA TA TA

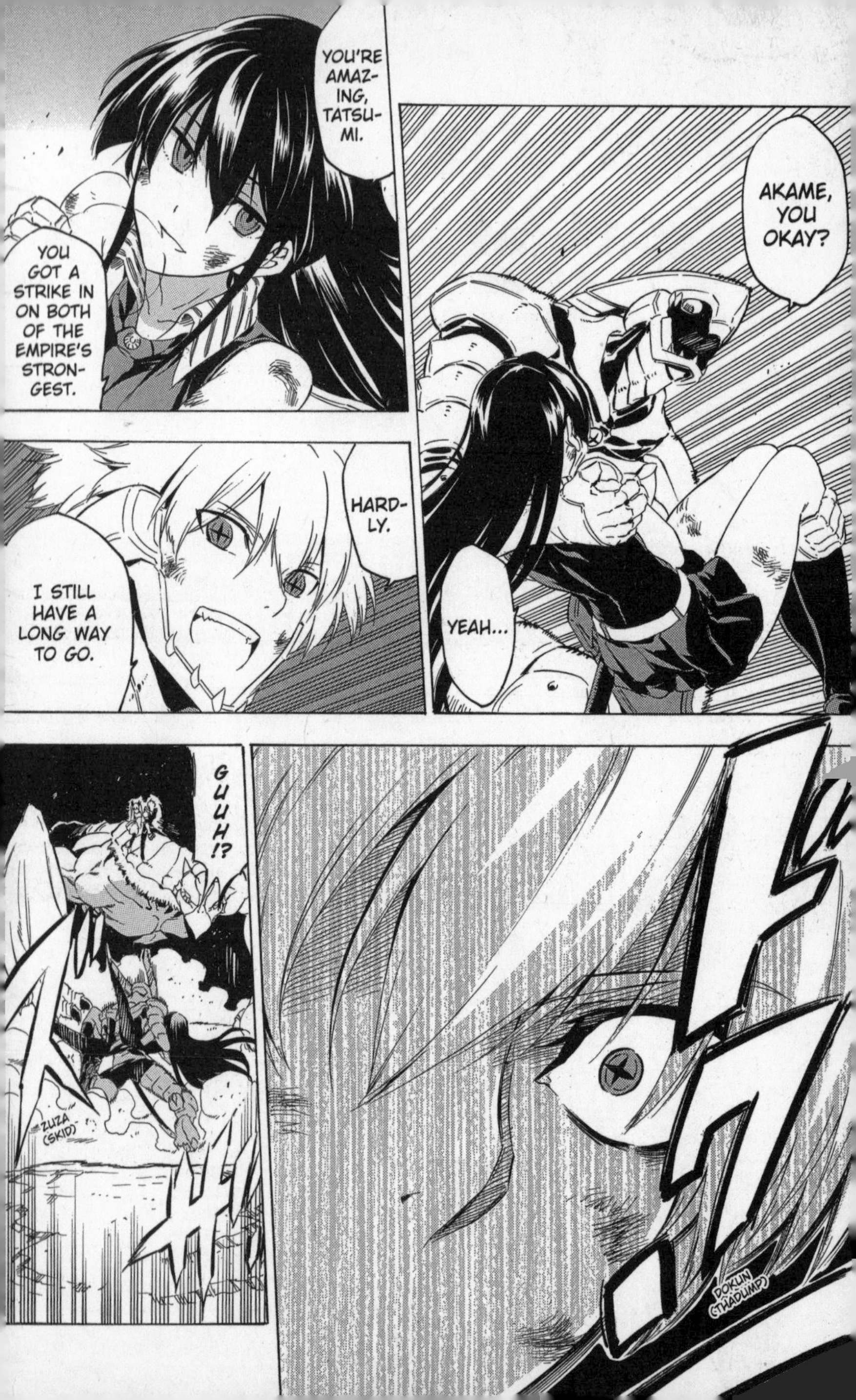
AKAME, YOU OKAY?
YEAH...
YOU'RE AMAZ-ING, TATSU-MI.
YOU GOT A STRIKE IN ON BOTH OF THE EMPIRE'S STRON-GEST.
HARD-LY.
I STILL HAVE A LONG WAY TO GO.
DOKUN (THADUMP)
GUUH!?
ZUZA (SKID)

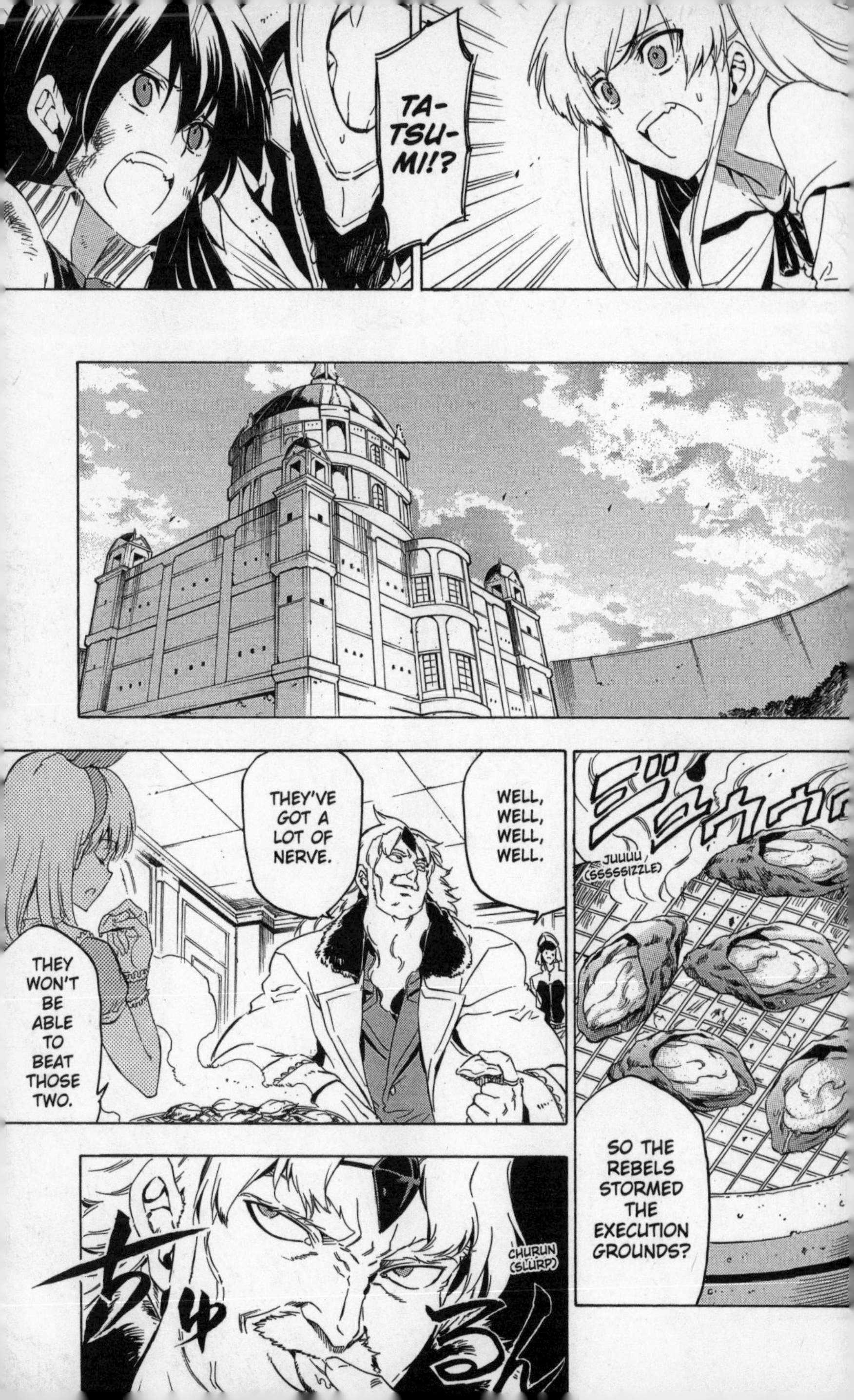
TA-TSU-MI!?
JUUUU (SSSSSIZZLE)
SO THE REBELS STORMED THE EXECUTION GROUNDS?
WELL, WELL, WELL, WELL.
THEY'VE GOT A LOT OF NERVE.
THEY WON'T BE ABLE TO BEAT THOSE TWO.
CHURUN (SLURP)

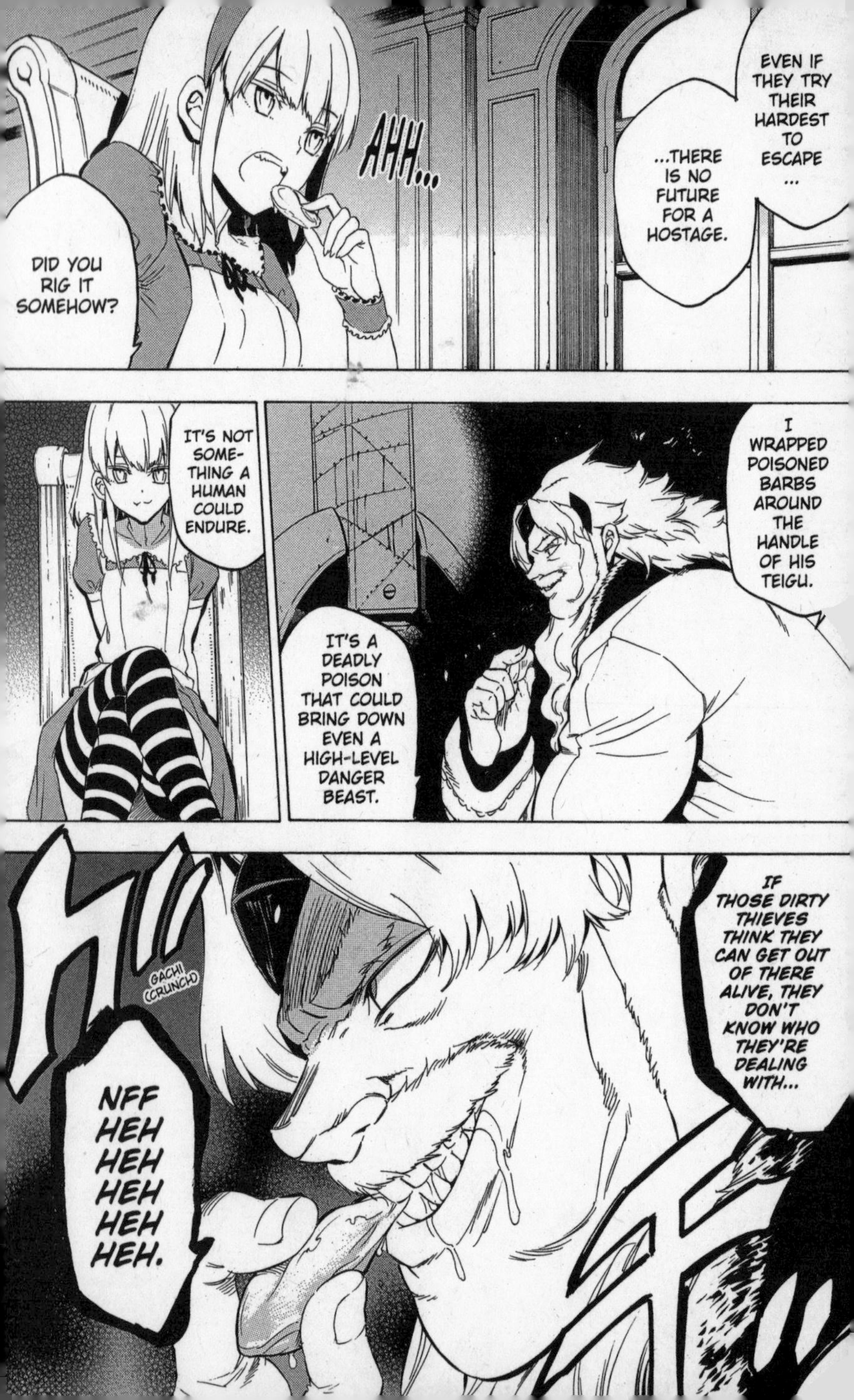
EVEN IF THEY TRY THEIR HARDEST TO ESCAPE ...
...THERE IS NO FUTURE FOR A HOSTAGE.
AHH...
DID YOU RIG IT SOMEHOW?
I WRAPPED POISONED BARBS AROUND THE HANDLE OF HIS TEIGU.
IT'S A DEADLY POISON THAT COULD BRING DOWN EVEN A HIGH-LEVEL DANGER BEAST.
IT'S NOT SOME-THING A HUMAN COULD ENDURE.
IF THOSE DIRTY THIEVES THINK THEY CAN GET OUT OF THERE ALIVE, THEY DON'T KNOW WHO THEY'RE DEALING WITH...
GACHI (CRUNCH)
NFF HEH HEH HEH HEH HEH.

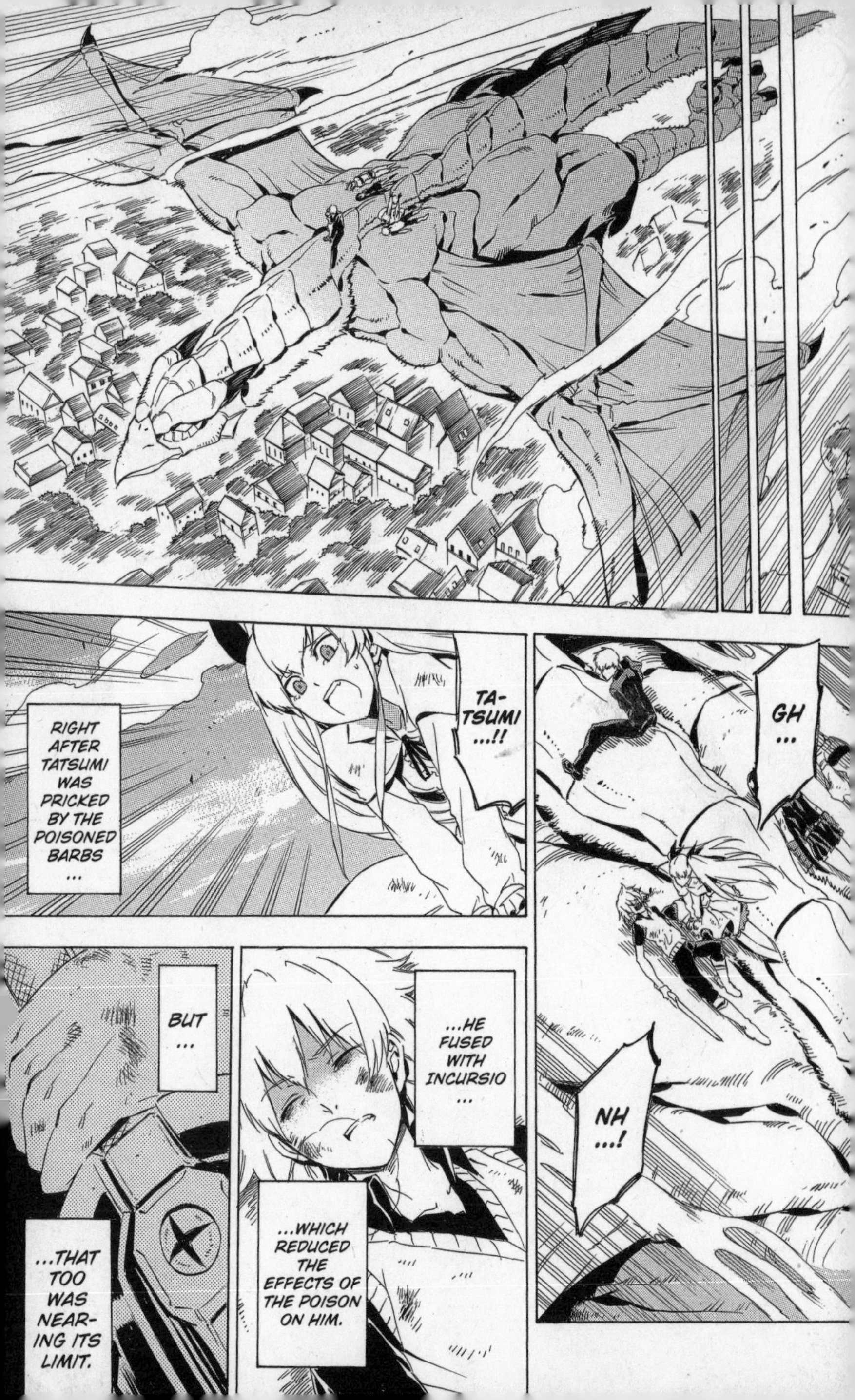
GH ...
NH ...!
TA-TSUMI ...!!
RIGHT AFTER TATSUMI WAS PRICKED BY THE POISONED BARBS ...
...HE FUSED WITH INCURSIO ...
...WHICH REDUCED THE EFFECTS OF THE POISON ON HIM.
BUT ...
...THAT TOO WAS NEARING ITS LIMIT.

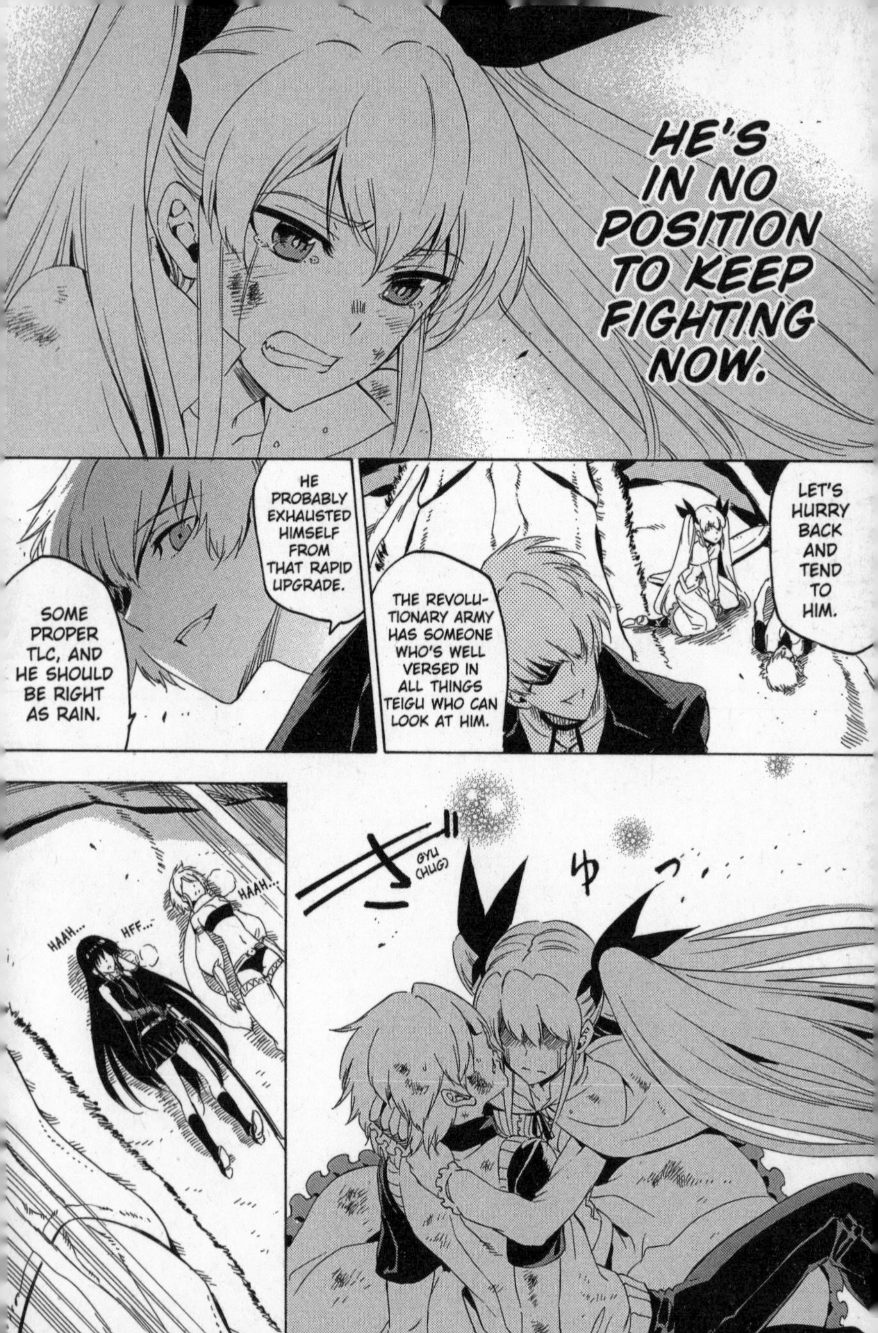
HE'S IN NO POSITION TO KEEP FIGHTING NOW.
LET'S HURRY BACK AND TEND TO HIM.
THE REVOLUTIONARY ARMY HAS SOMEONE WHO'S WELL VERSED IN ALL THINGS TEIGU WHO CAN LOOK AT HIM.
HE PROBABLY EXHAUSTED HIMSELF FROM THAT RAPID UPGRADE.
SOME PROPER TLC, AND HE SHOULD BE RIGHT AS RAIN.
GYU (HUG)
HAAH...
HAAH...
HFF...

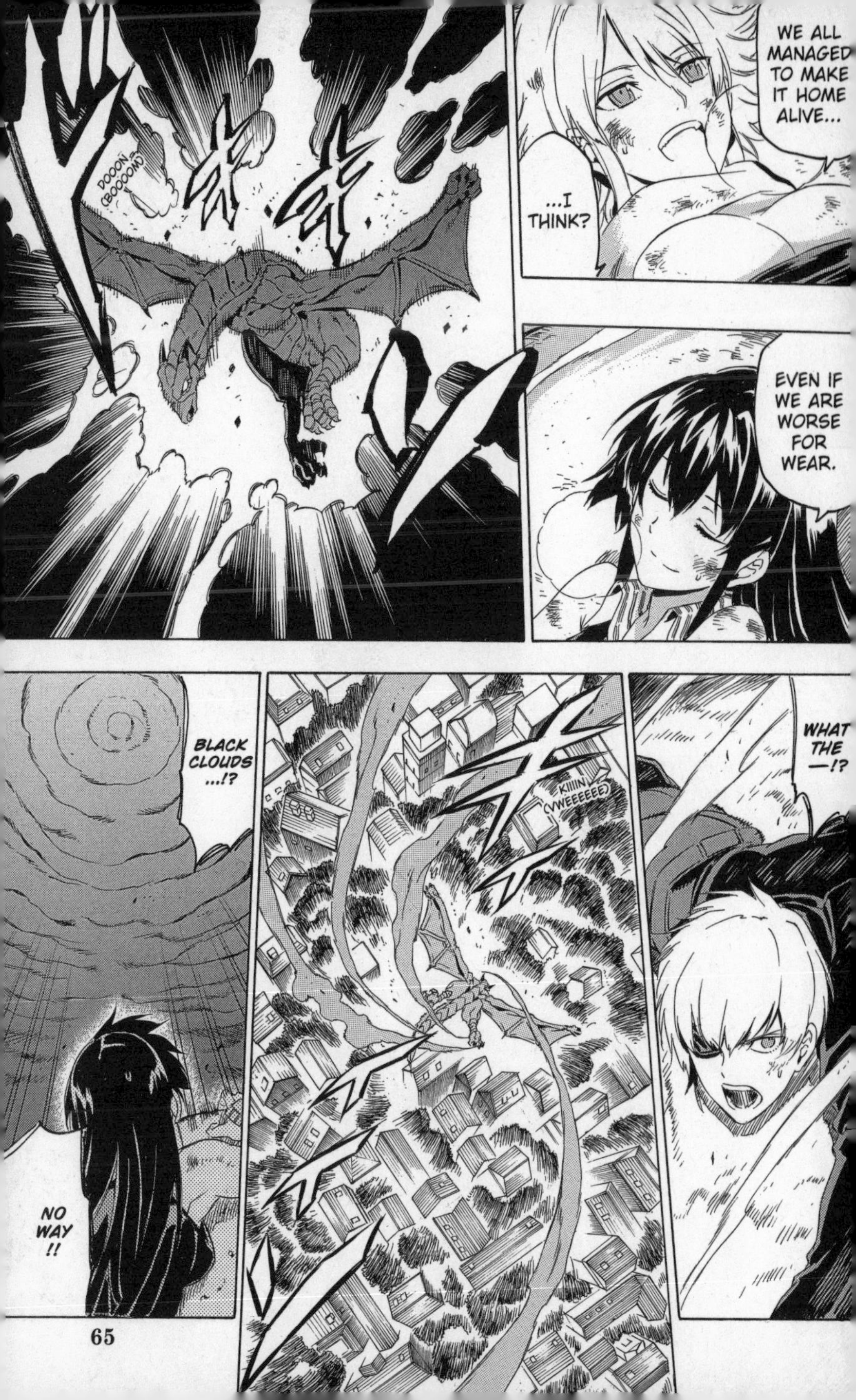
WE ALL MANAGED TO MAKE IT HOME ALIVE...
...I THINK?
EVEN IF WE ARE WORSE FOR WEAR.
DOOON (BOOOOM)
WHAT THE—!?
KIIIN (VWEEEEEE)
BLACK CLOUDS ...!?
NO WAY !!

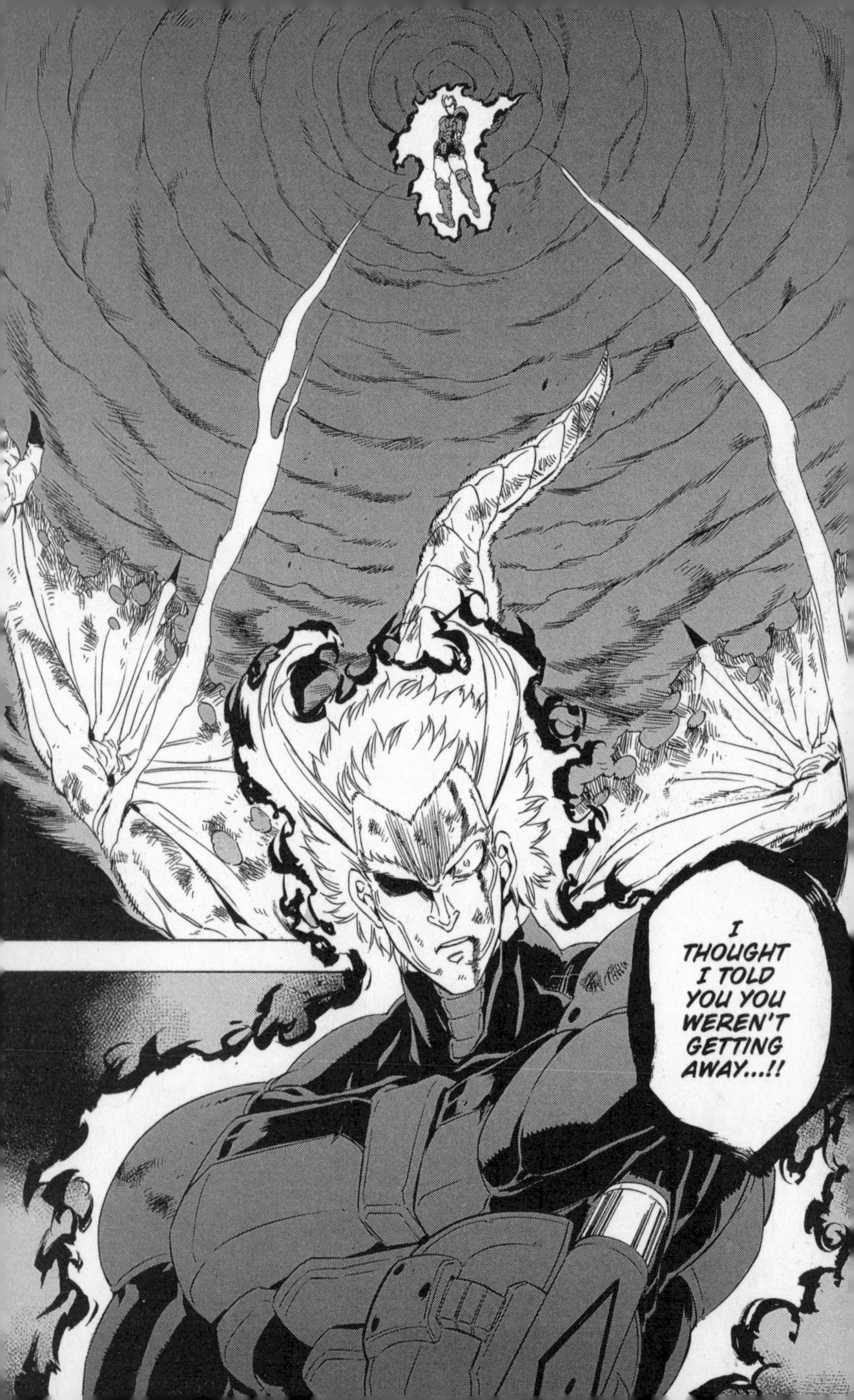
I THOUGHT I TOLD YOU YOU WEREN'T GETTING AWAY...!!

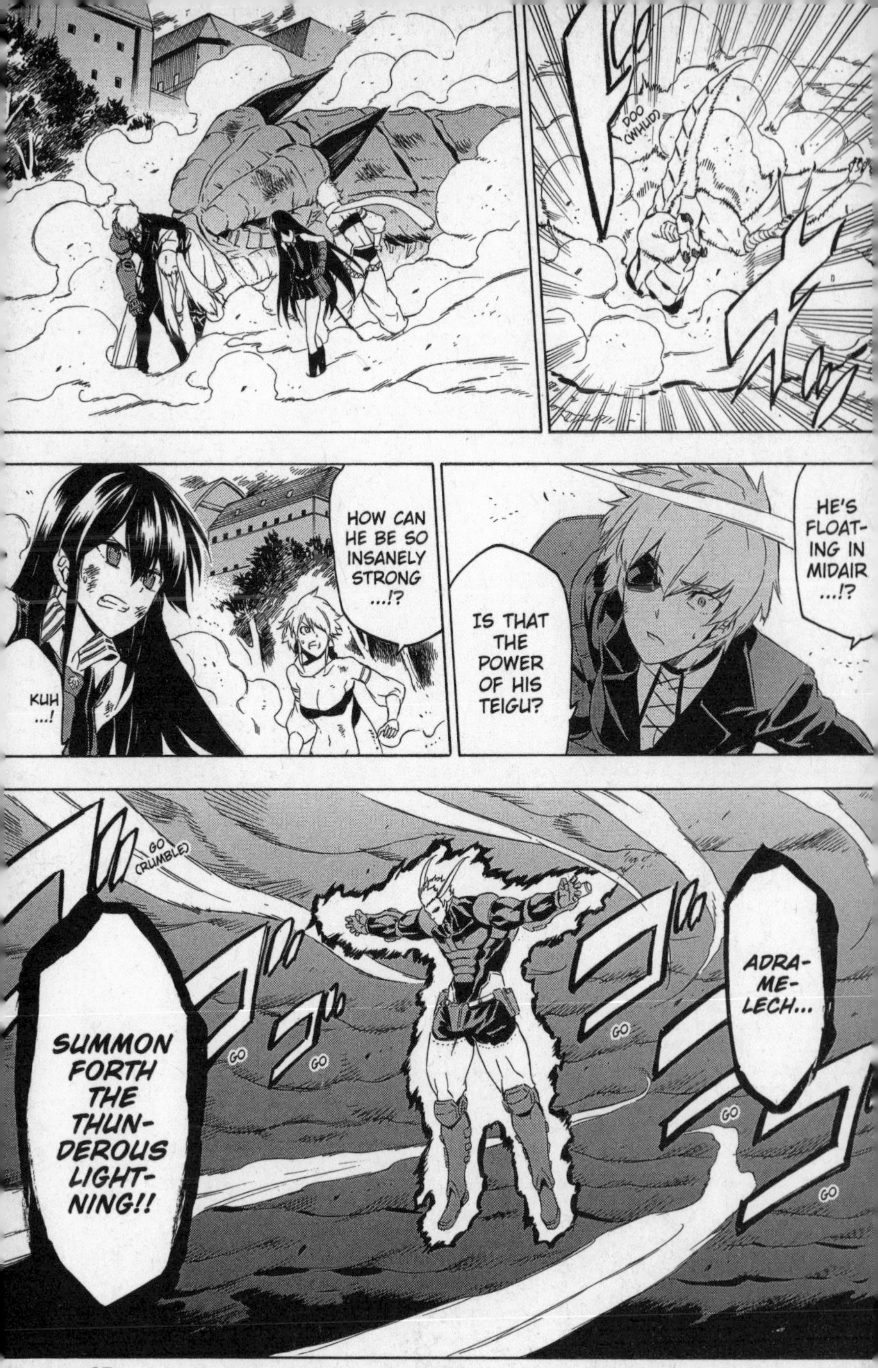
DOO (WHUD)
HE'S FLOATING IN MIDAIR ...!?
IS THAT THE POWER OF HIS TEIGU?
HOW CAN HE BE SO INSANELY STRONG ...!?
KUH ...!
GO (RUMBLE)
ADRAMELECH...
SUMMON FORTH THE THUNDEROUS LIGHTNING!!
GO
GO
GO
GO
GO

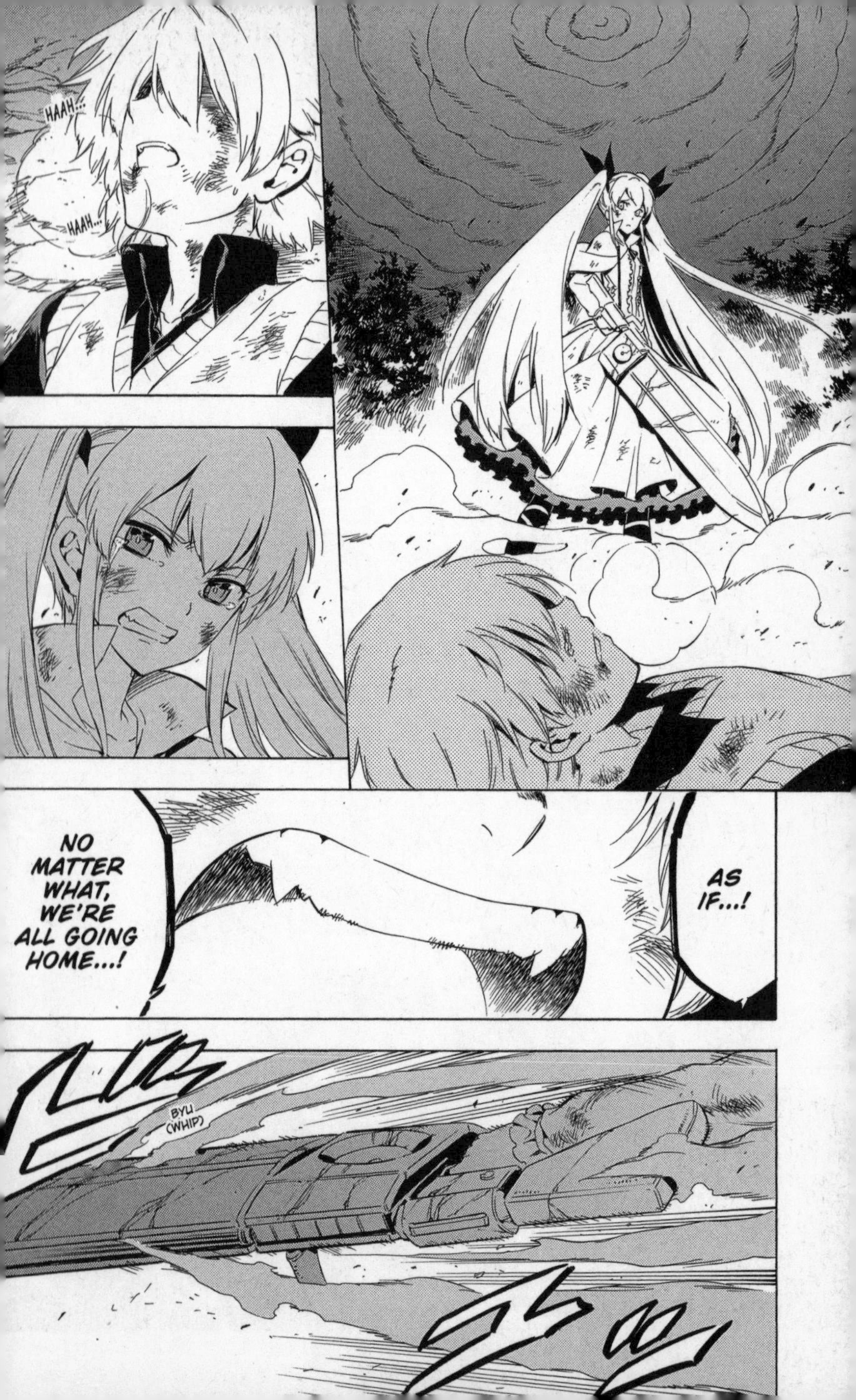
HAAH...
HAAH...
AS IF...!
NO MATTER WHAT, WE'RE ALL GOING HOME...!
BYU (WHIP)

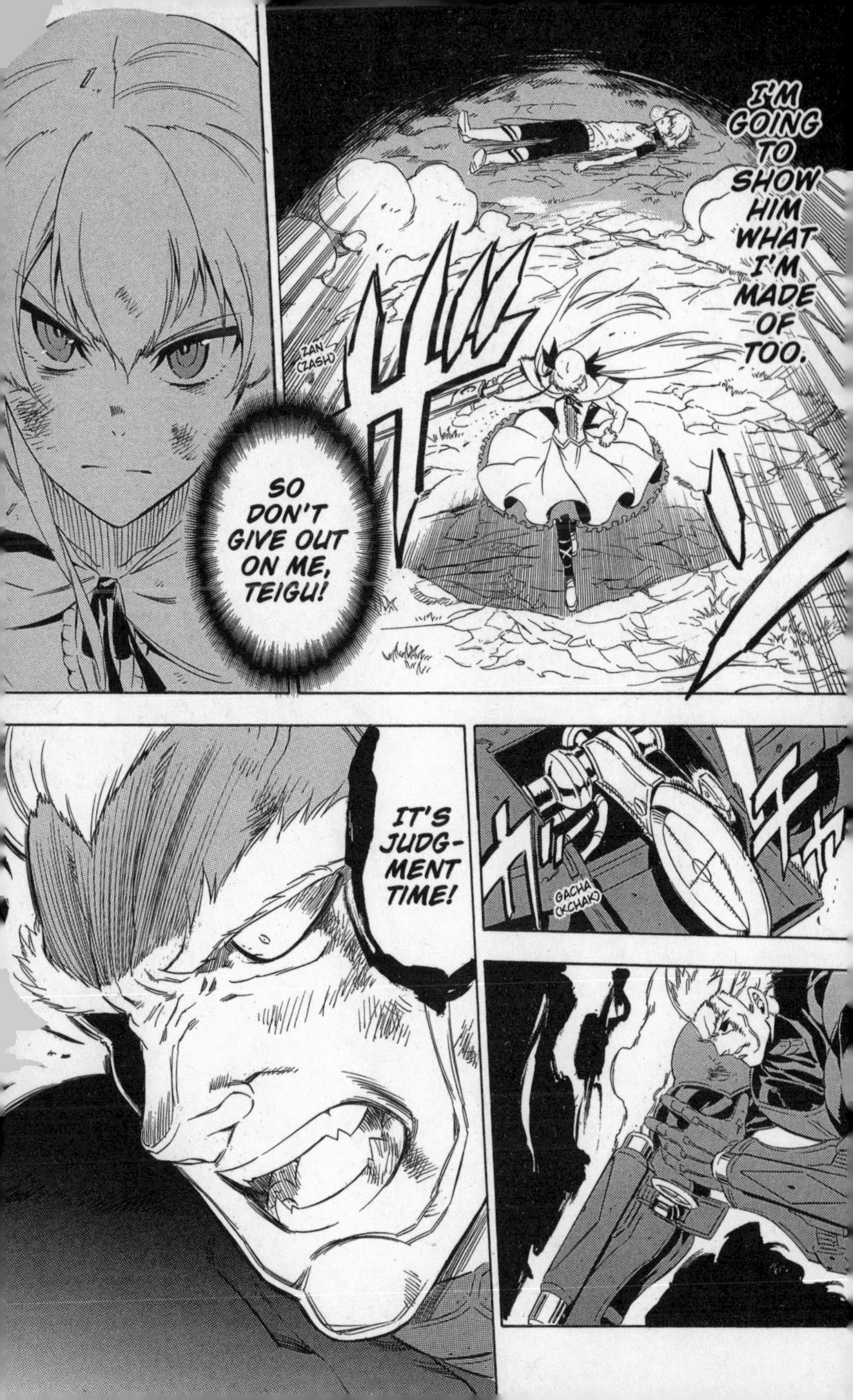
I'M GOING TO SHOW HIM WHAT I'M MADE OF TOO.
ZAN (ZASH)
SO DON'T GIVE OUT ON ME, TEIGU!
GACHA (KCHAK)
IT'S JUDG-MENT TIME!

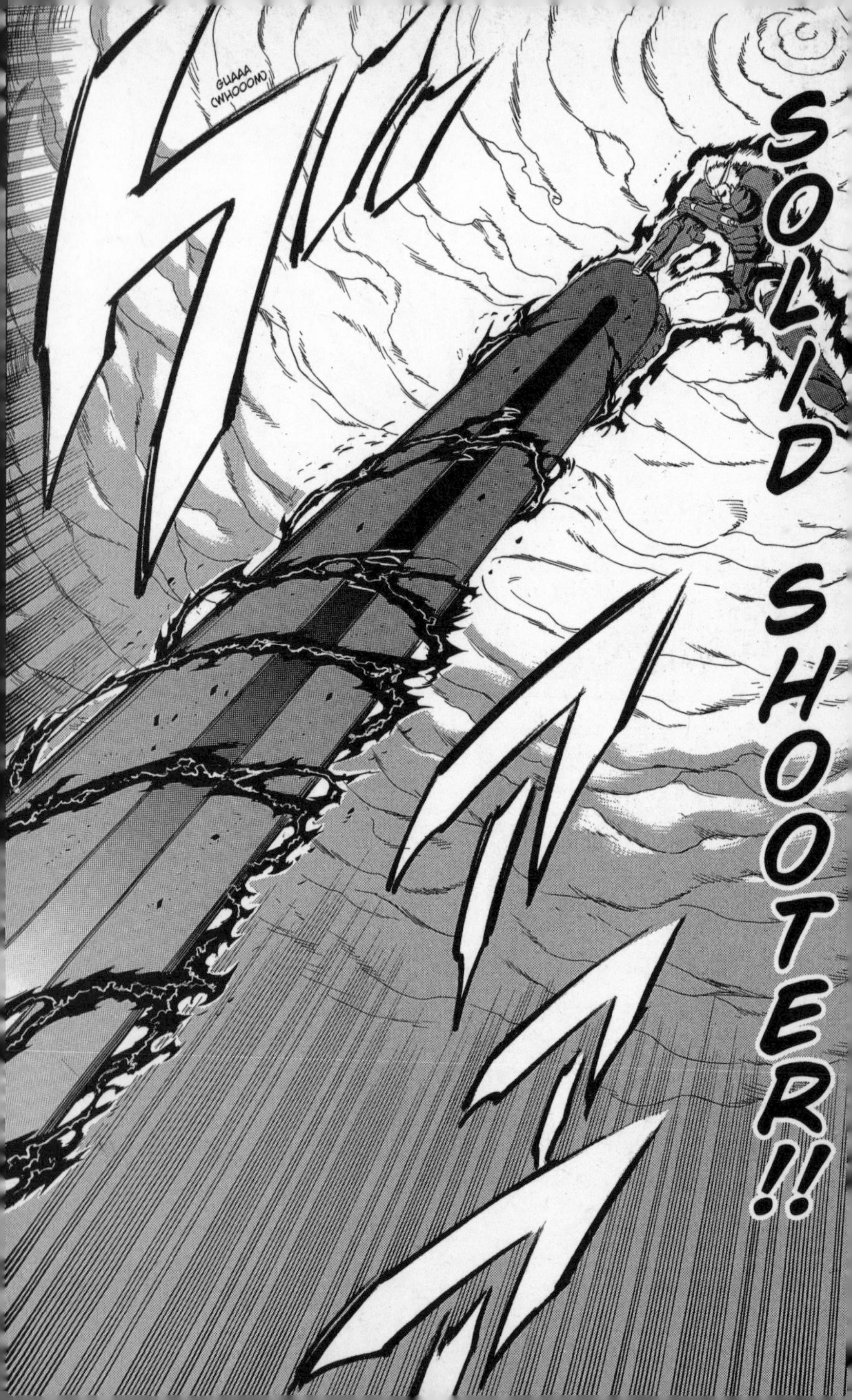
SOLID SHOOTER!!
GUAAA (WHOOOM)

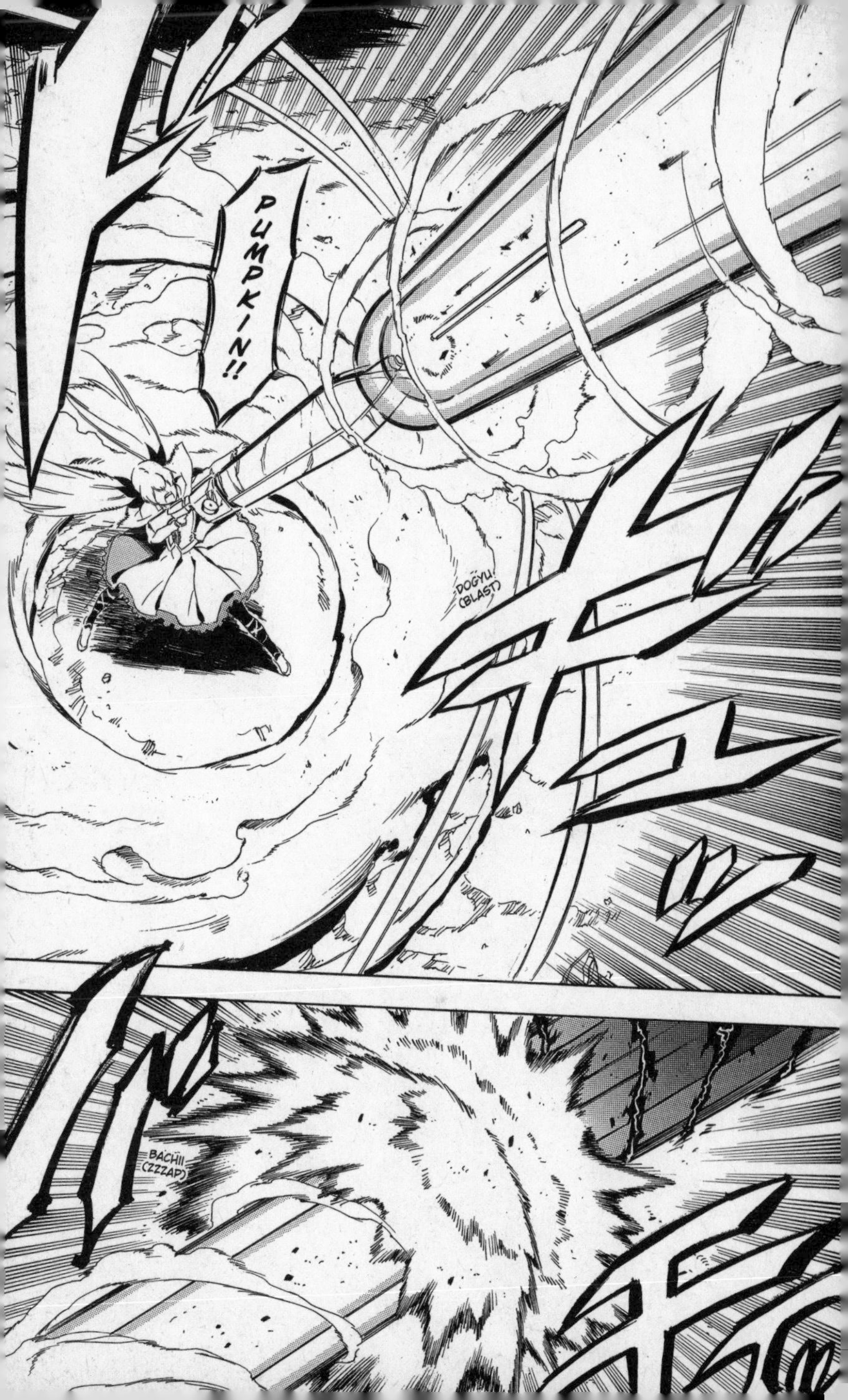
PUMPKIN!!
DOGYU (BLAST)
BACHII (ZZZAP)

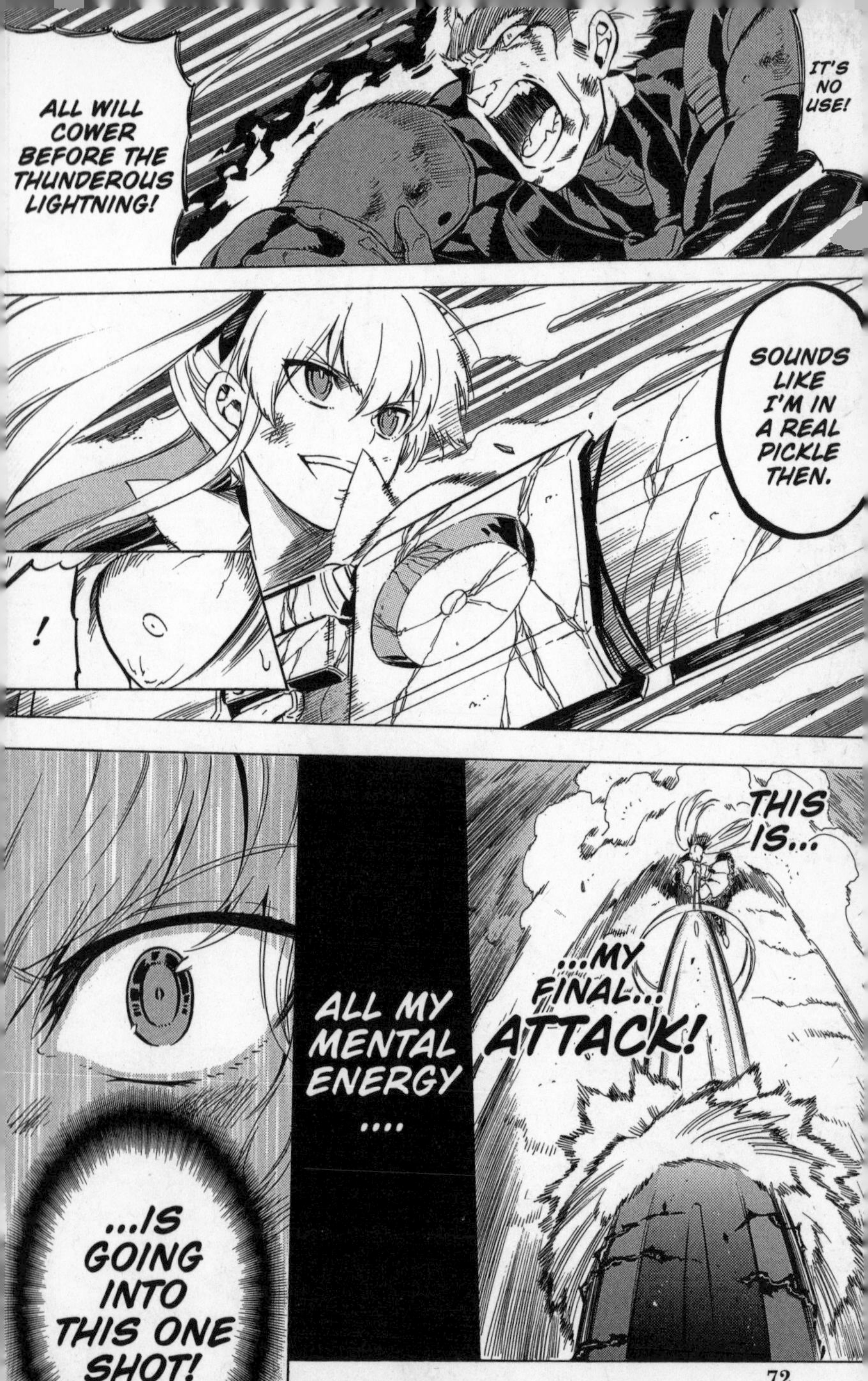
IT'S NO USE!
ALL WILL COWER BEFORE THE THUNDEROUS LIGHTNING!
SOUNDS LIKE I'M IN A REAL PICKLE THEN.
!
THIS IS...
...MY FINAL... ATTACK!
ALL MY MENTAL ENERGY ....
...IS GOING INTO THIS ONE SHOT!

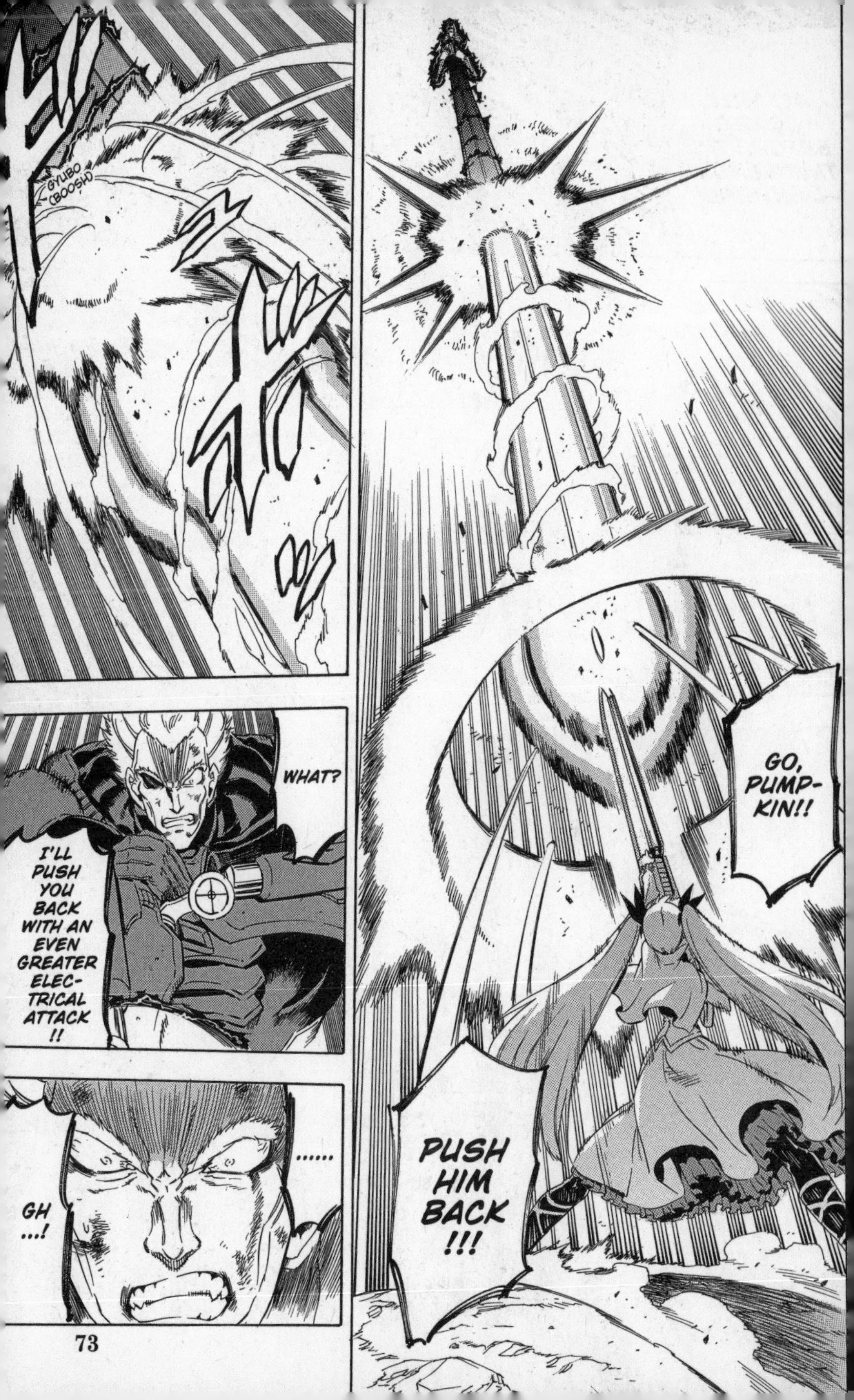
GO, PUMPKIN!!
PUSH HIM BACK !!!
GYUBO (BOOSH)
WHAT?
I'LL PUSH YOU BACK WITH AN EVEN GREATER ELECTRICAL ATTACK !!
......
GH ...!

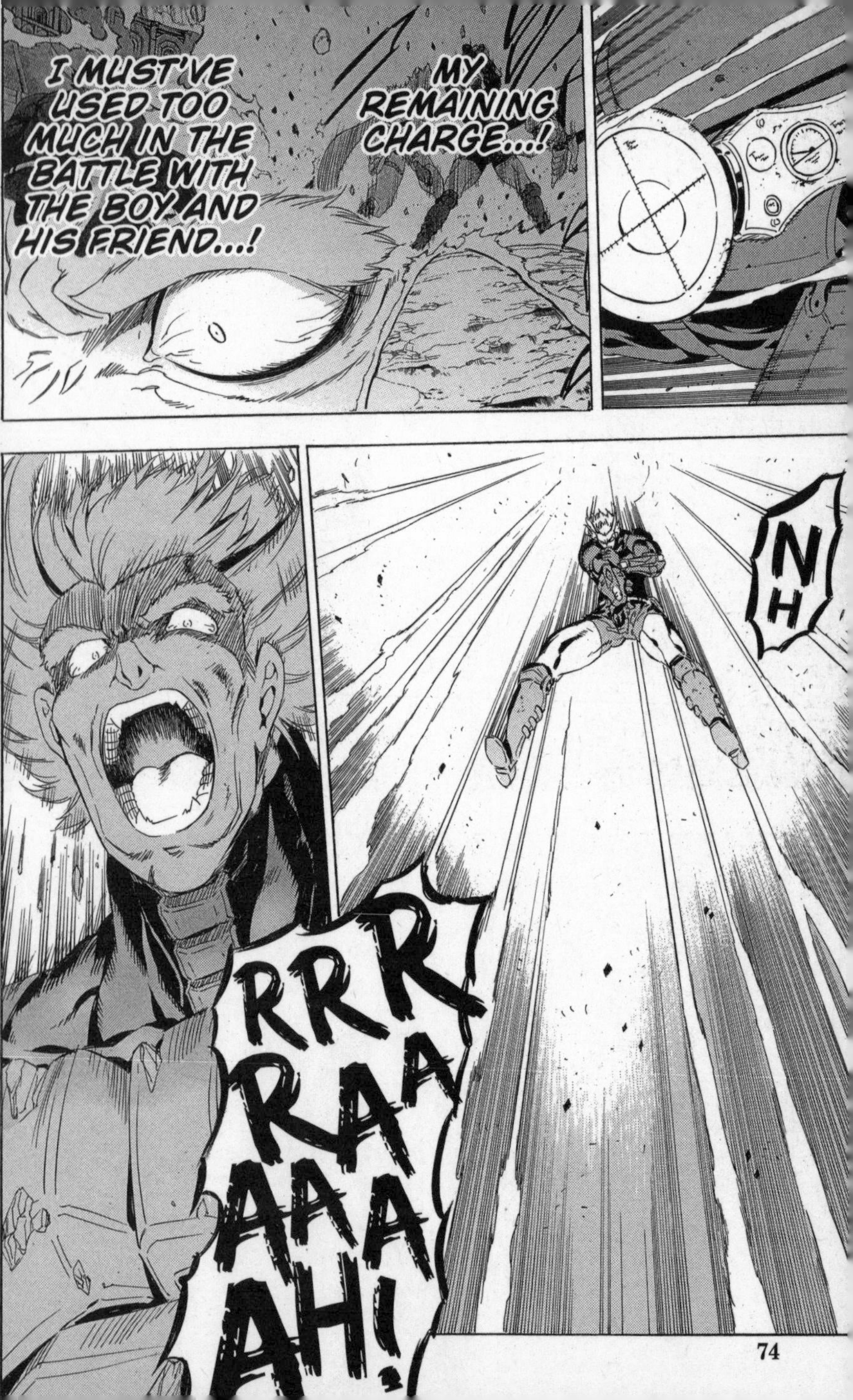
MY REMAINING CHARGE...!
I MUST'VE USED TOO MUCH IN THE BATTLE WITH THE BOY AND HIS FRIEND...!
NH
RRRRAAAAAAAH!

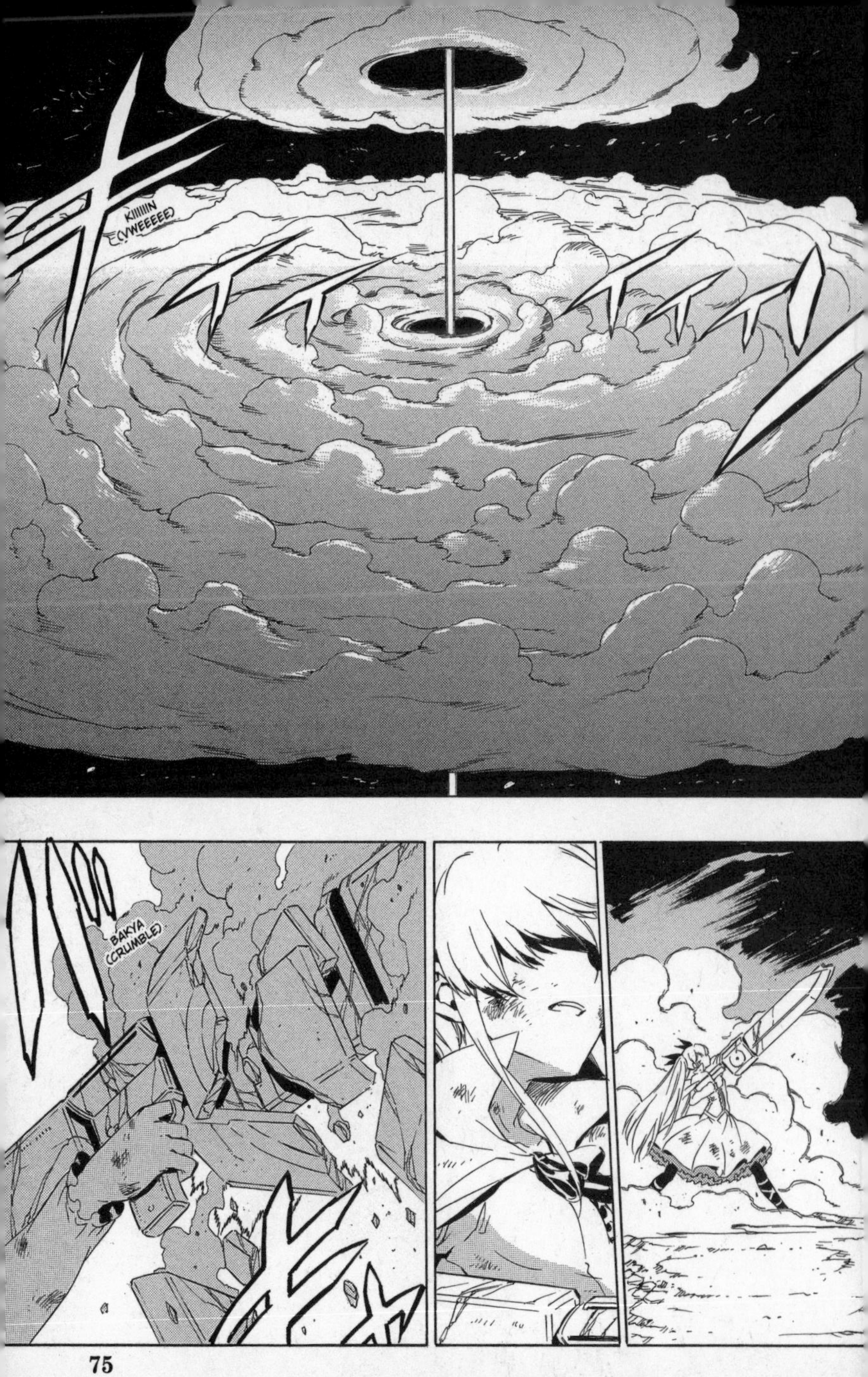
KIIIIIIN
(VWEEEEE)
BAKYA
(CRUMBLE)

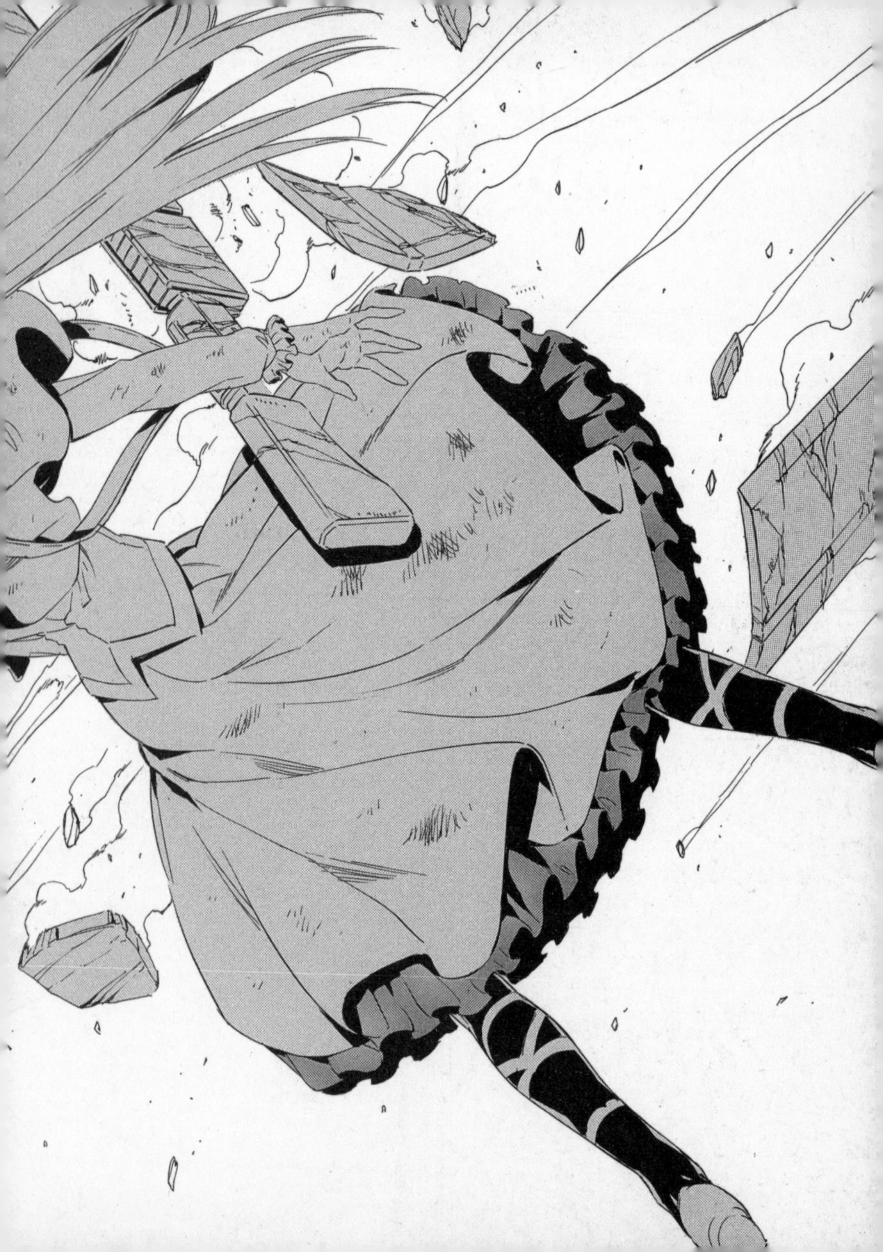

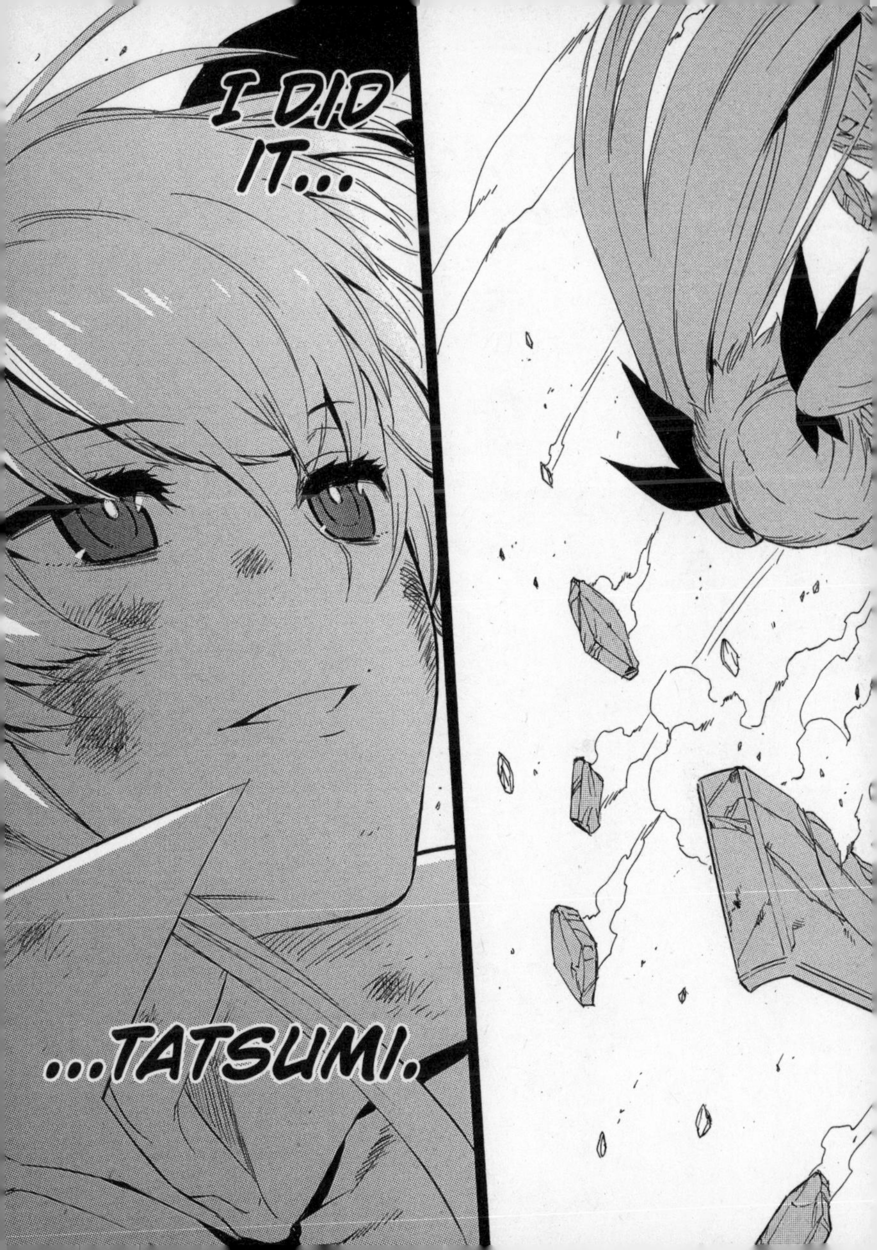
I DID IT...
...TATSUMI.

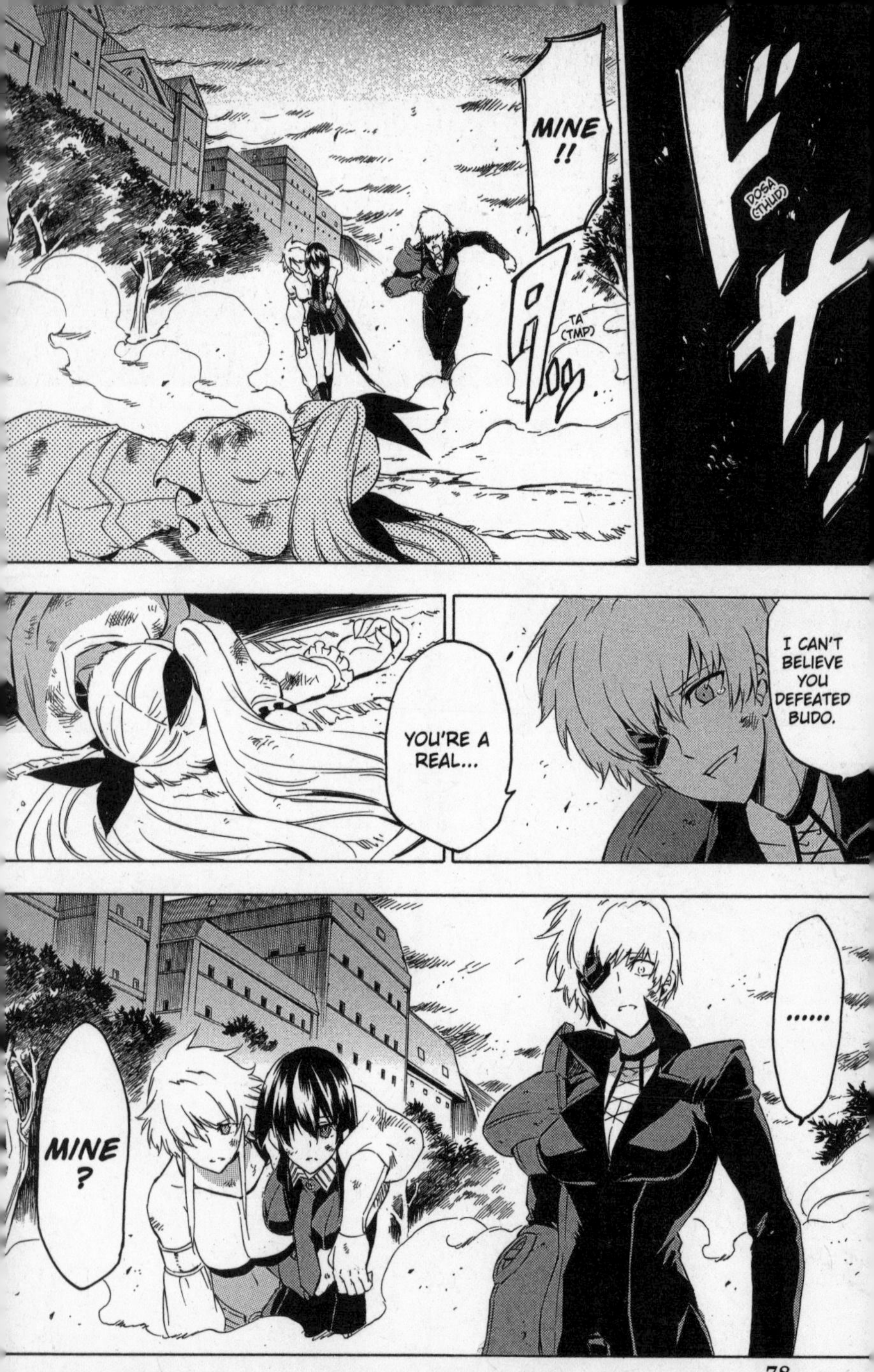
DOGA (THUD)
MINE !!
TA (TMP)
I CAN'T BELIEVE YOU DEFEATED BUDO.
YOU'RE A REAL...
......
MINE ?

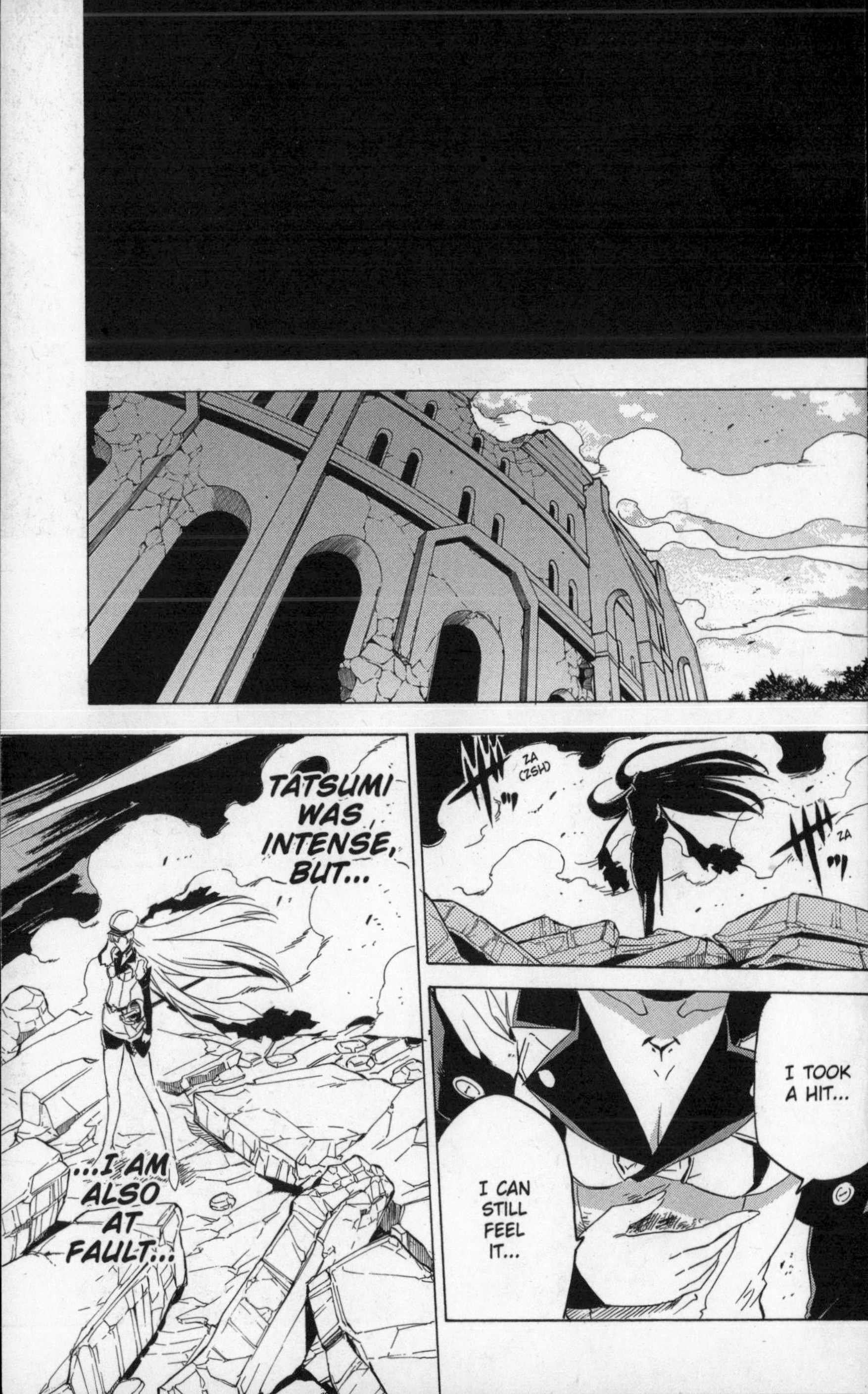
ZA (ZSH)
ZA
I TOOK A HIT...
I CAN STILL FEEL IT...
TATSUMI WAS INTENSE, BUT...
...I AM ALSO AT FAULT...

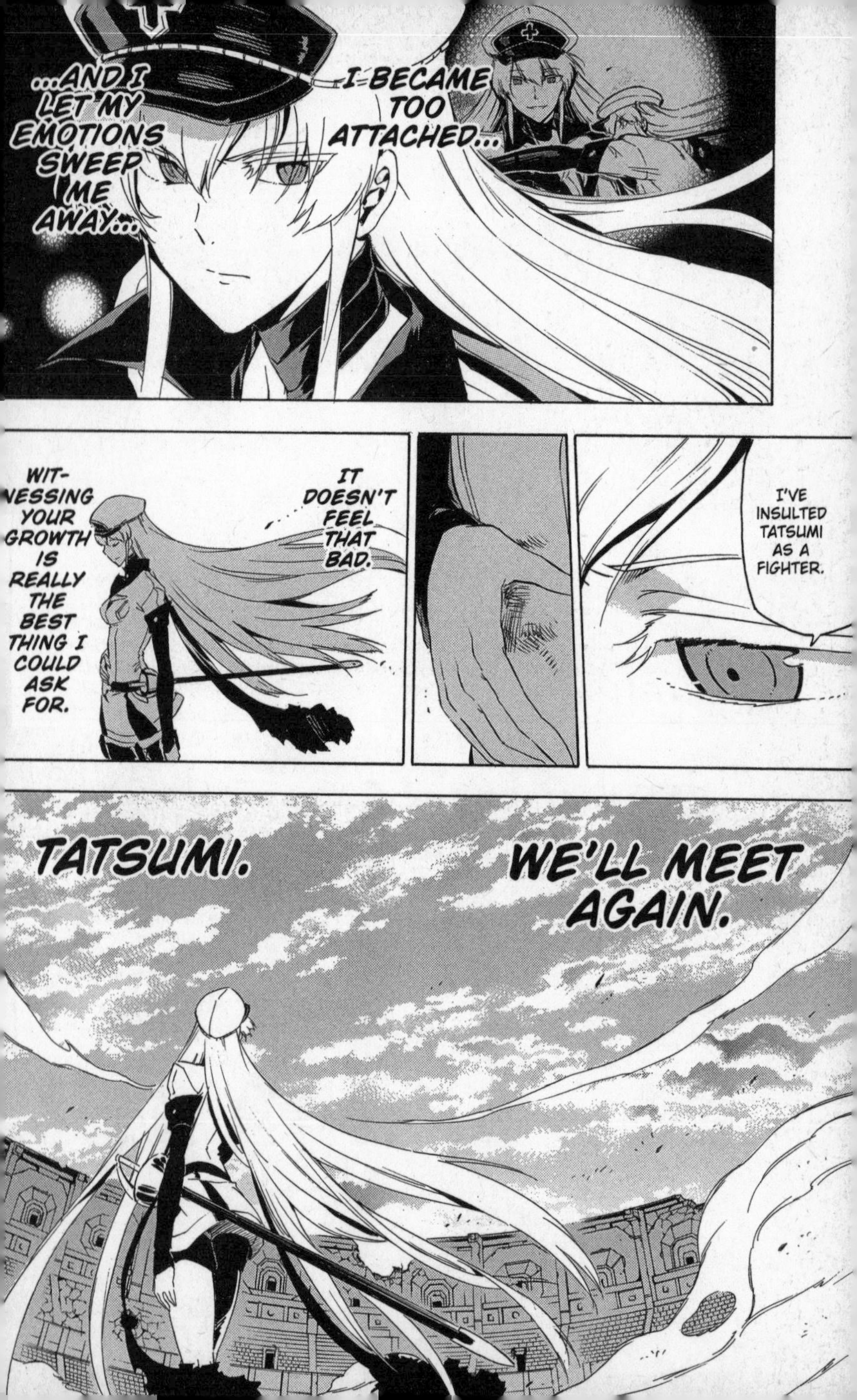
I BECAME TOO ATTACHED...
...AND I LET MY EMOTIONS SWEEP ME AWAY...
I'VE INSULTED TATSUMI AS A FIGHTER.
IT DOESN'T FEEL THAT BAD.
WIT-NESSING YOUR GROWTH IS REALLY THE BEST THING I COULD ASK FOR.
TATSUMI.
WE'LL MEET AGAIN.

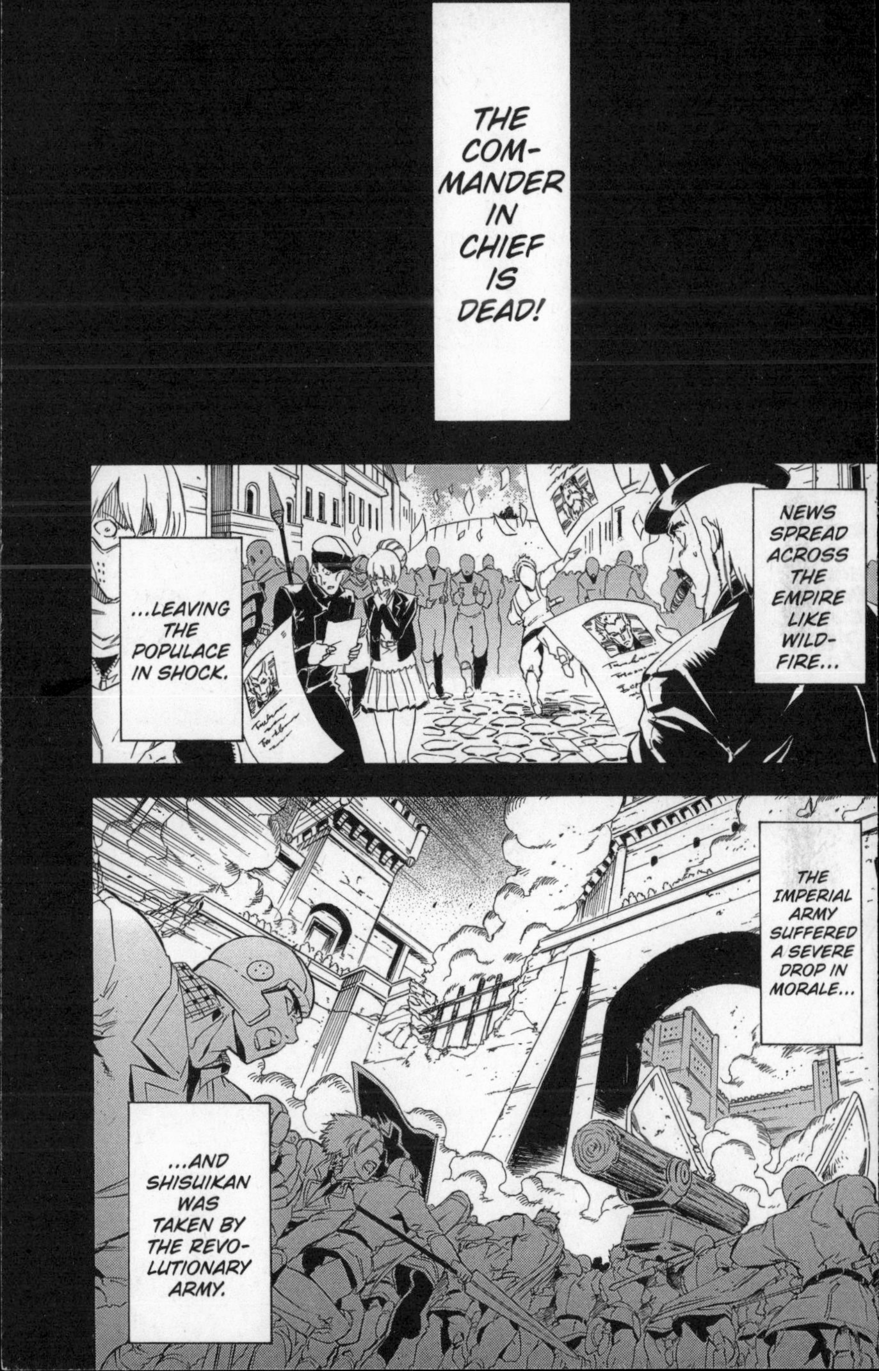
THE COM-MANDER IN CHIEF IS DEAD!
NEWS SPREAD ACROSS THE EMPIRE LIKE WILD-FIRE...
...LEAVING THE POPULACE IN SHOCK.
THE IMPERIAL ARMY SUFFERED A SEVERE DROP IN MORALE...
...AND SHISUIKAN WAS TAKEN BY THE REVO-LUTIONARY ARMY.

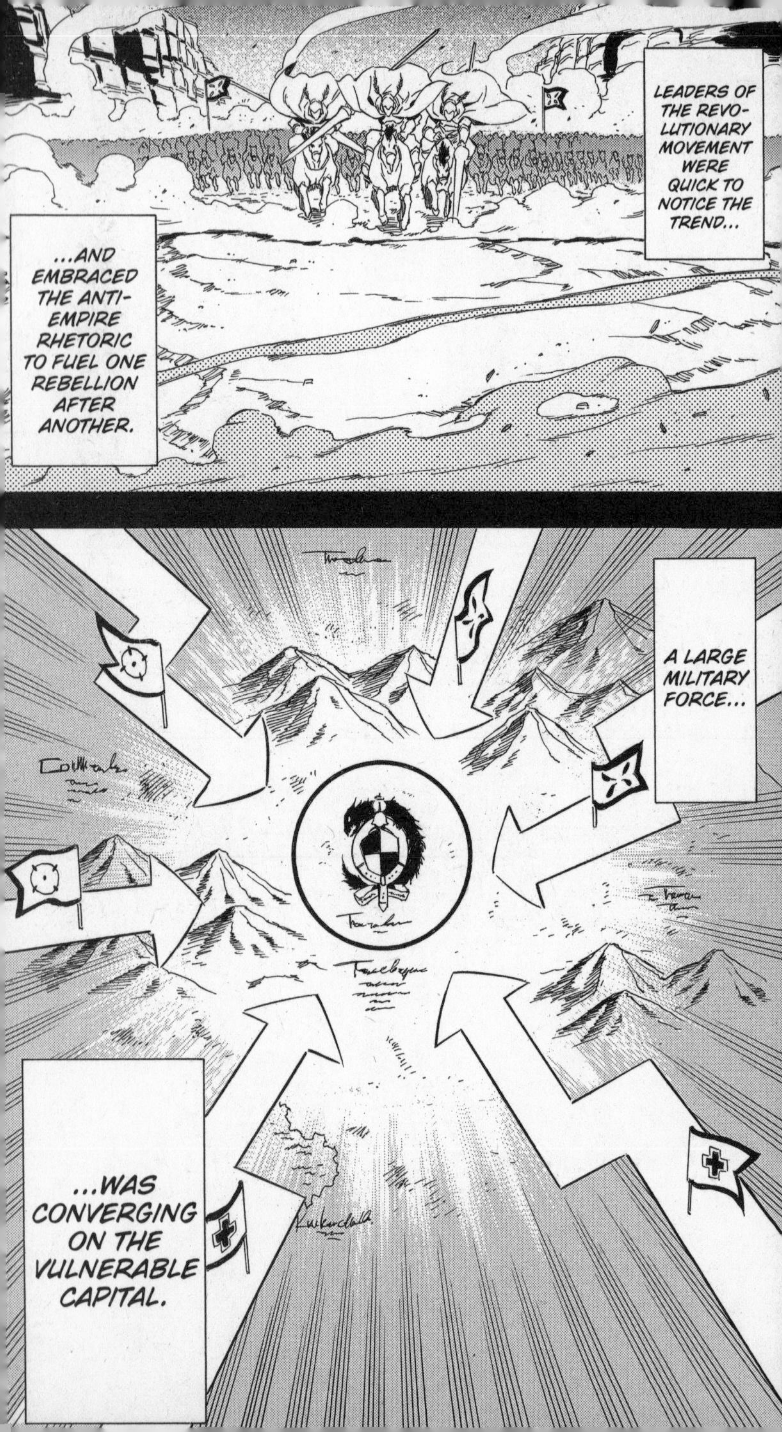
LEADERS OF THE REVOLUTIONARY MOVEMENT WERE QUICK TO NOTICE THE TREND...
...AND EMBRACED THE ANTI-EMPIRE RHETORIC TO FUEL ONE REBELLION AFTER ANOTHER.
A LARGE MILITARY FORCE...
...WAS CONVERGING ON THE VULNERABLE CAPITAL.

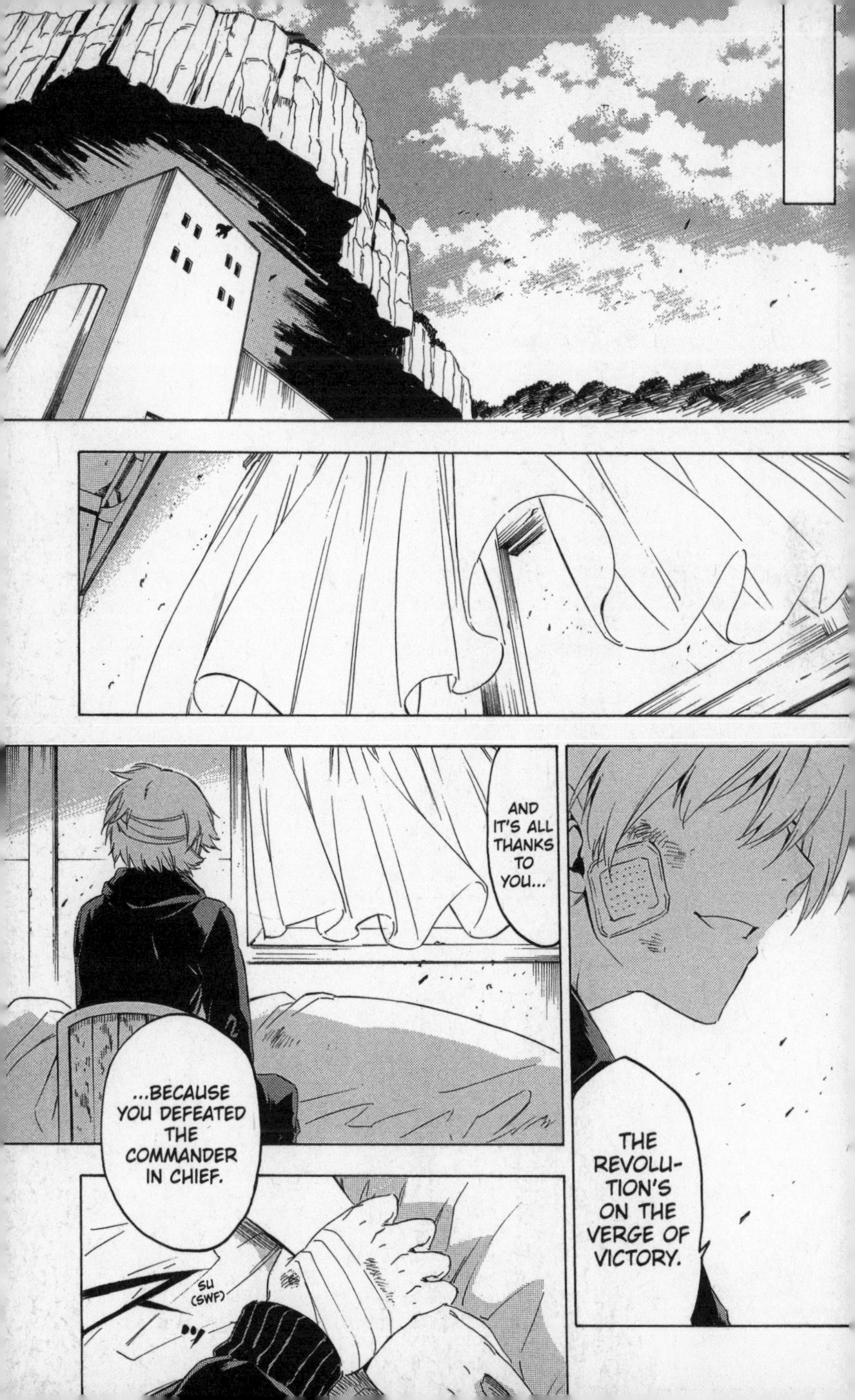
AND IT'S ALL THANKS TO YOU...
THE REVOLUTION'S ON THE VERGE OF VICTORY.
...BECAUSE YOU DEFEATED THE COMMANDER IN CHIEF.
SU (SWF)

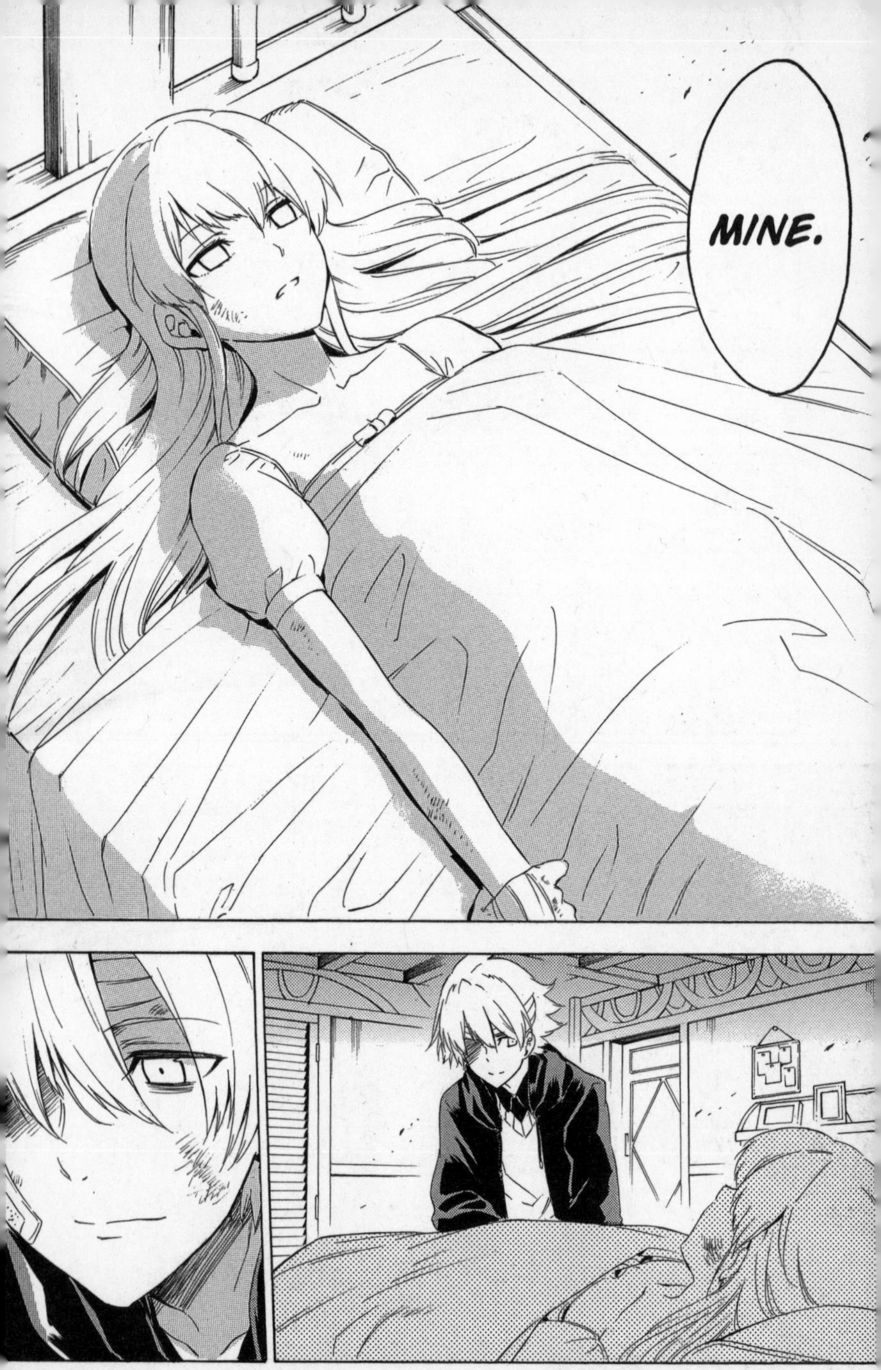
MINE.

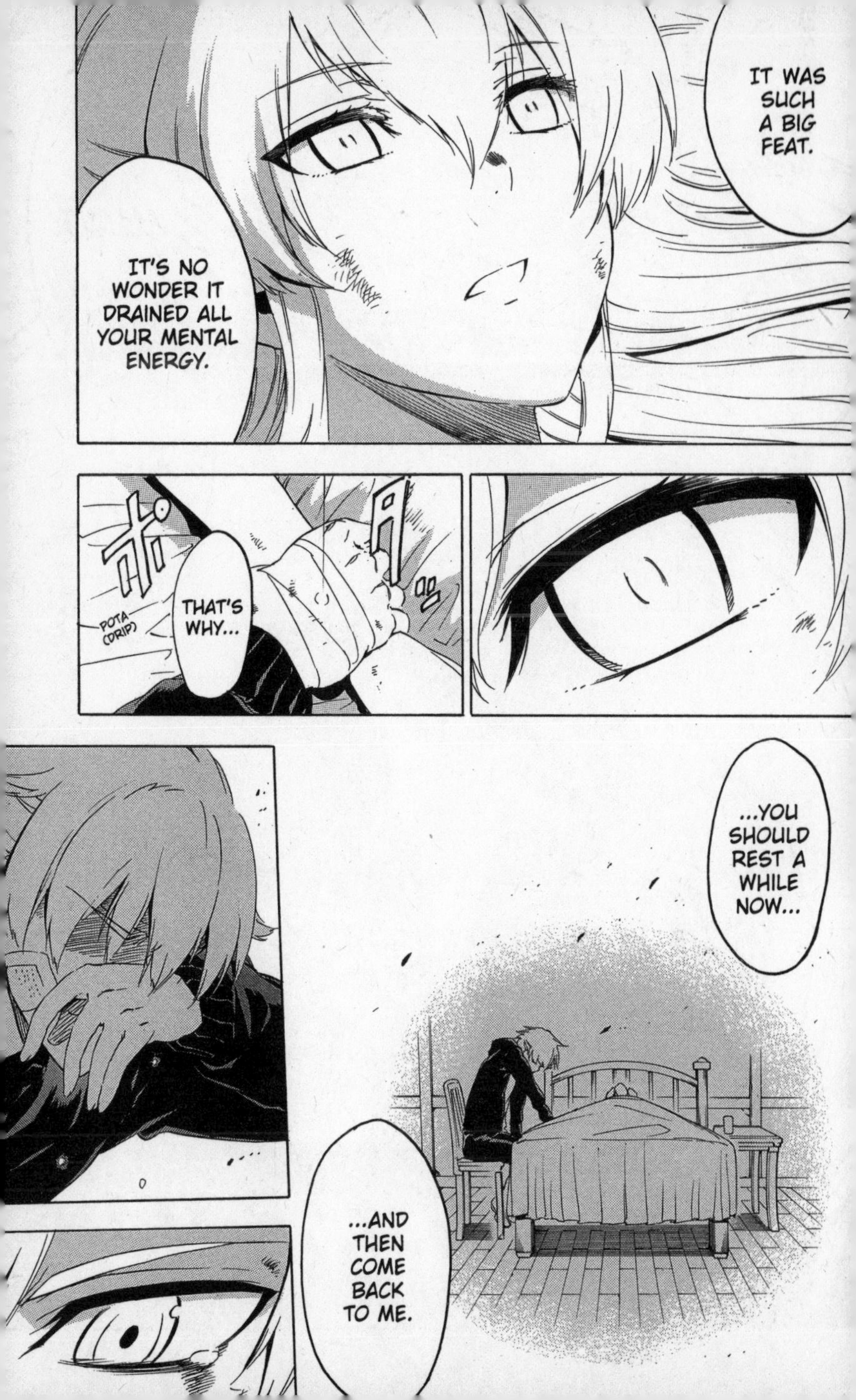
IT WAS SUCH A BIG FEAT.
IT'S NO WONDER IT DRAINED ALL YOUR MENTAL ENERGY.
THAT'S WHY...
POTA (DRIP)
...YOU SHOULD REST A WHILE NOW...
...AND THEN COME BACK TO ME.

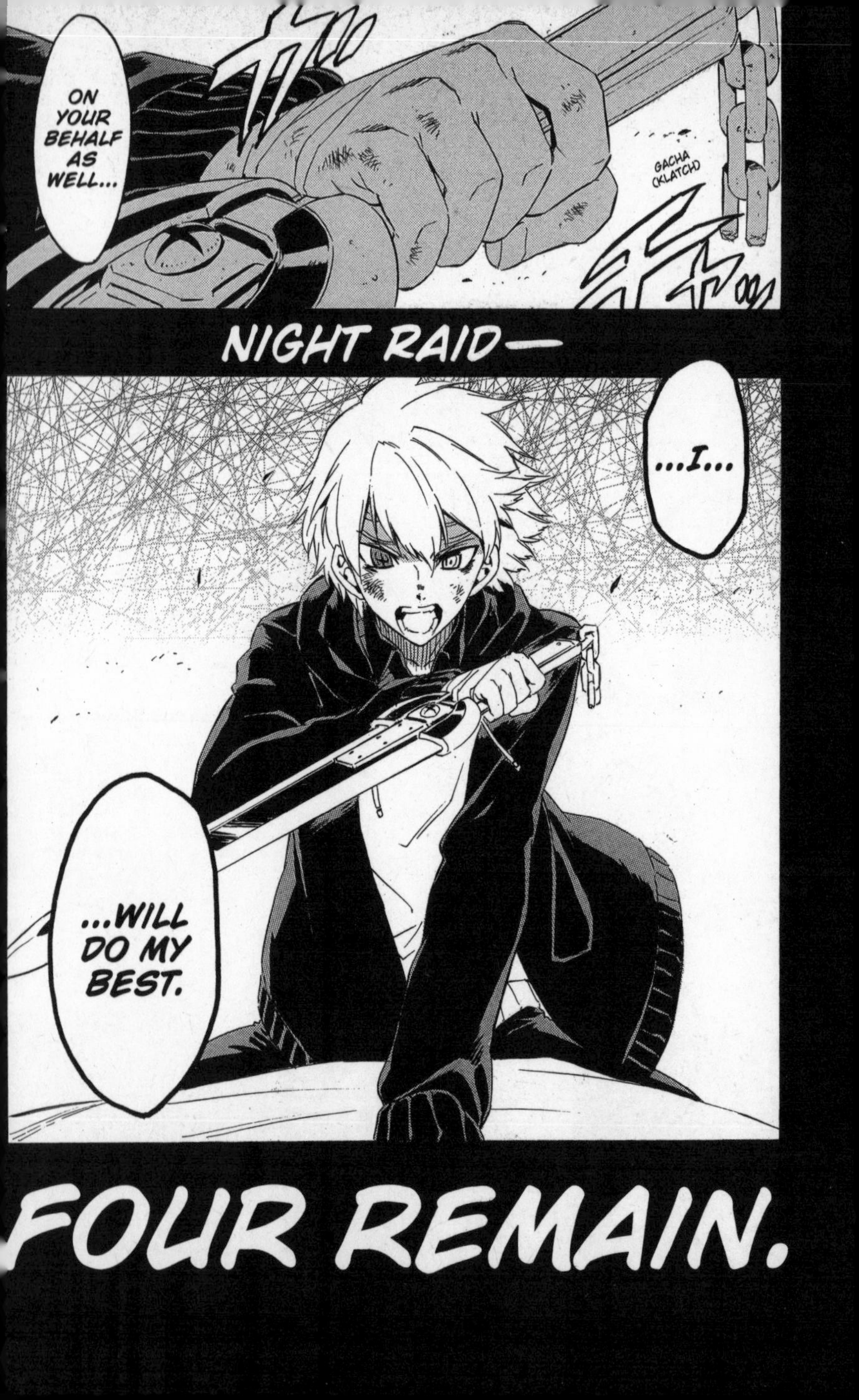
ON YOUR BEHALF AS WELL...
GACHA (KLATCH)
NIGHT RAID—
...I...
...WILL DO MY BEST.
FOUR REMAIN.

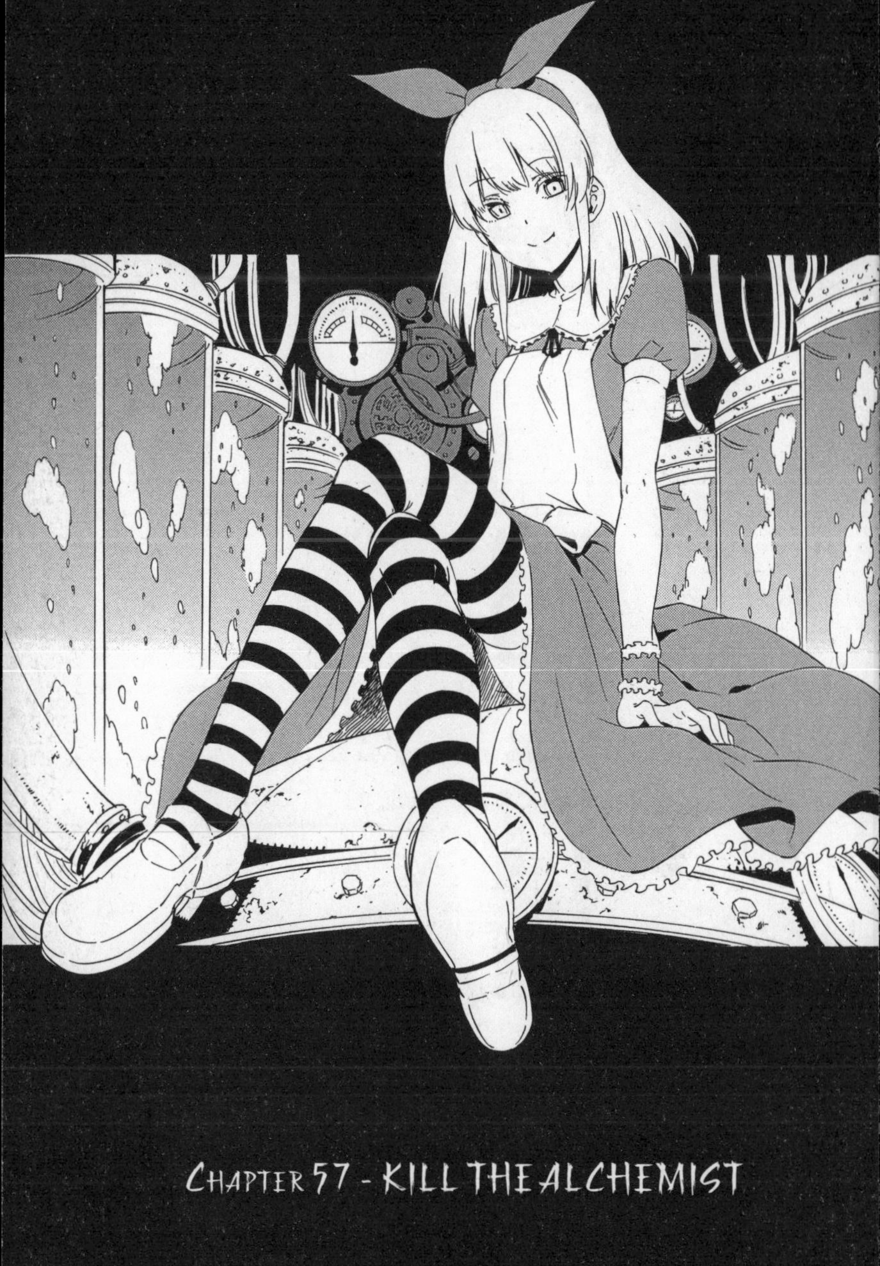

Chapter 57 - Kill the Alchemist

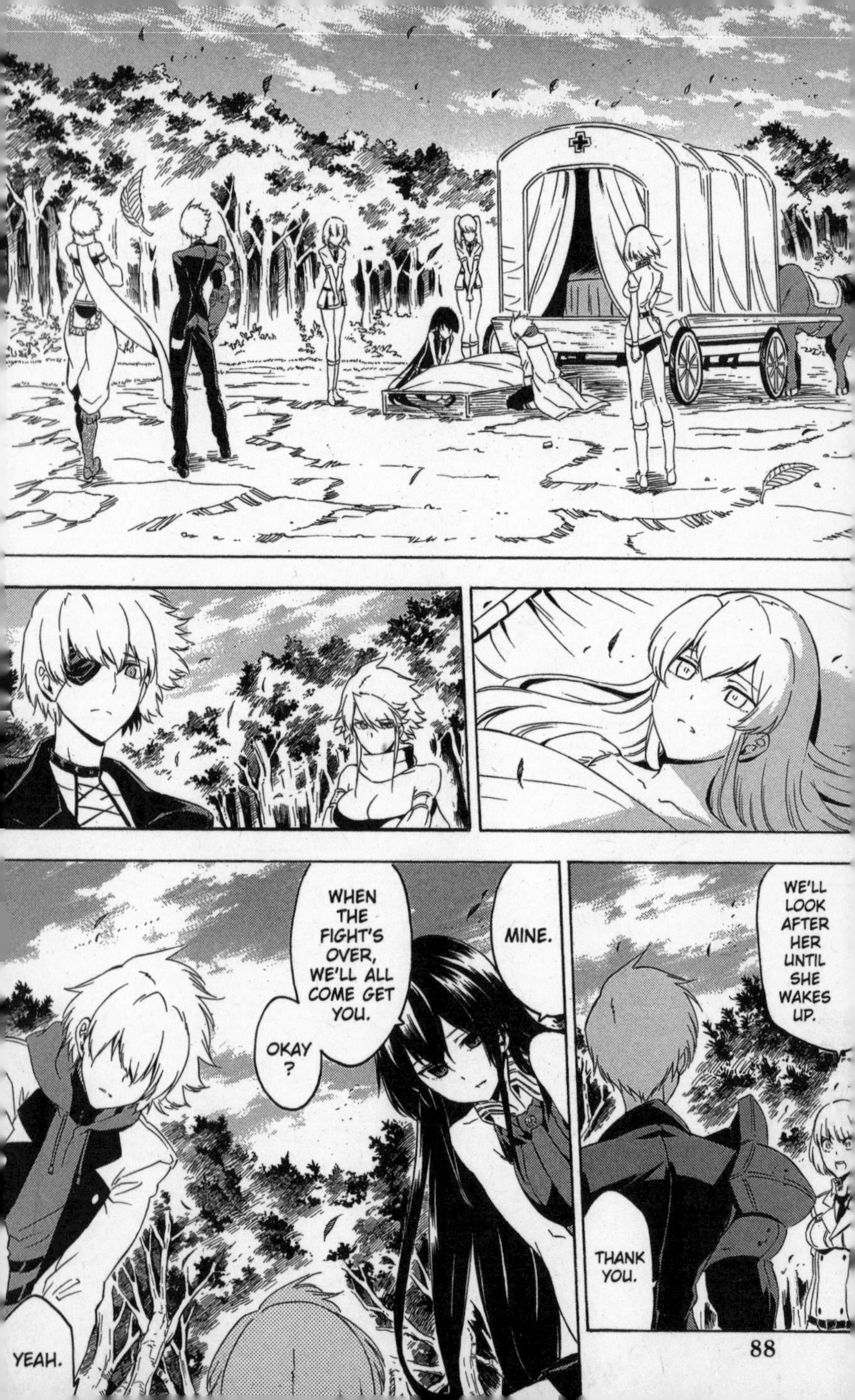
WE'LL LOOK AFTER HER UNTIL SHE WAKES UP.
THANK YOU.
MINE.
WHEN THE FIGHT'S OVER, WE'LL ALL COME GET YOU.
OKAY?
YEAH.

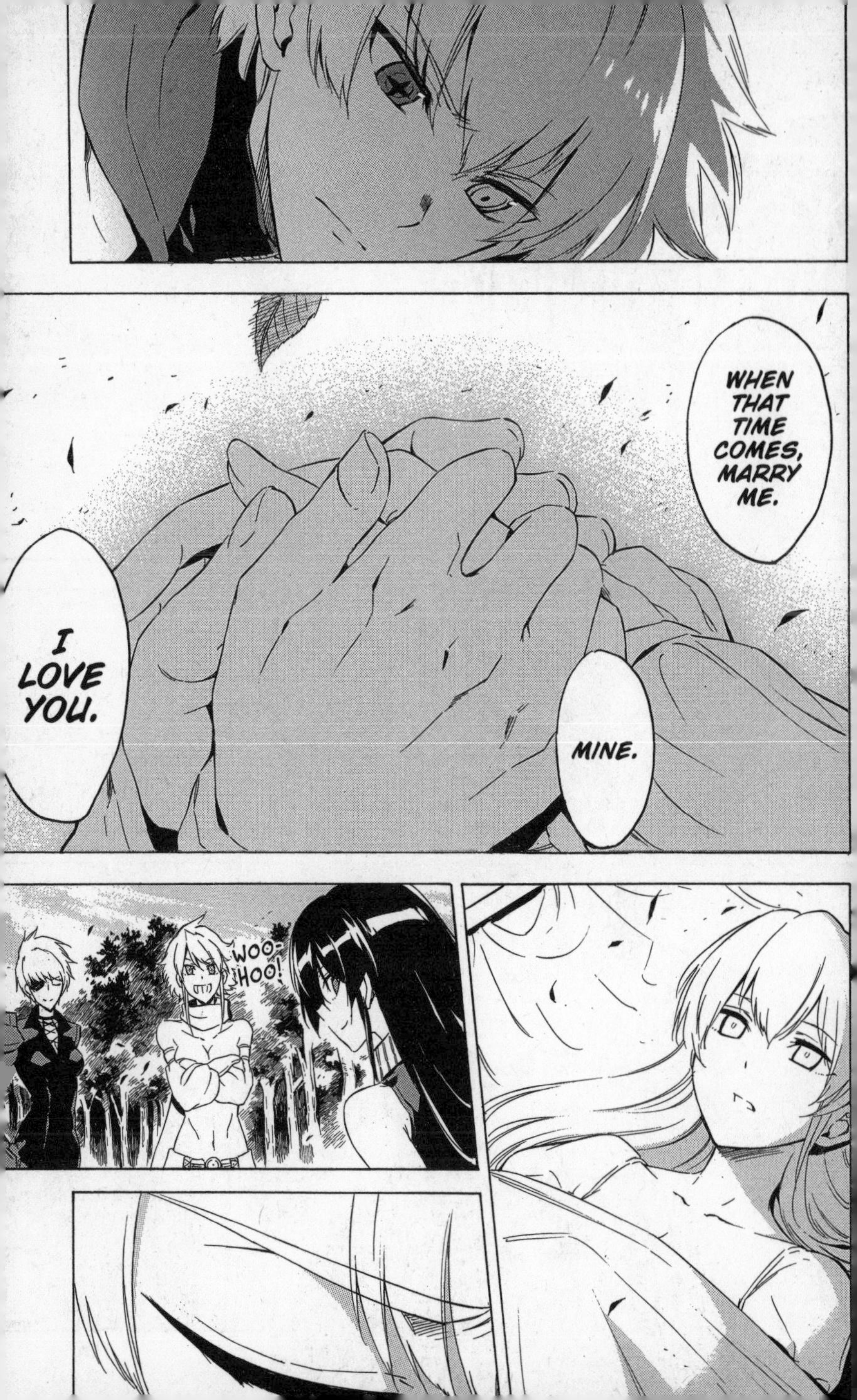
WHEN THAT TIME COMES, MARRY ME.
MINE.
I LOVE YOU.
WOO-HOO!

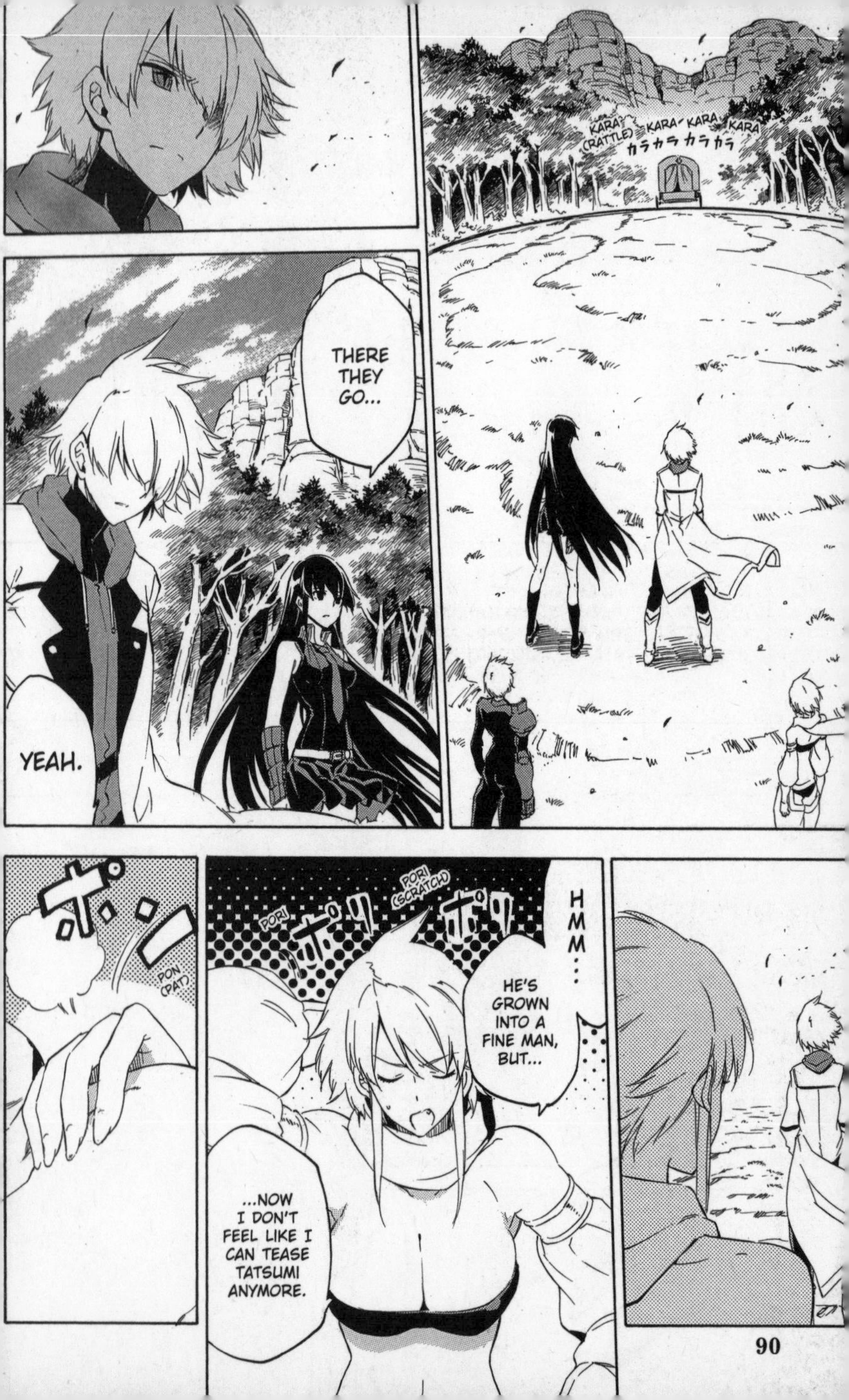
KARA (RATTLE) KARA KARA KARA
カラカラ カラカラ
THERE THEY GO...
YEAH.
PORI (SCRATCH) PORI
ポリ ポリ
HMM...
HE'S GROWN INTO A FINE MAN, BUT...
...NOW I DON'T FEEL LIKE I CAN TEASE TATSUMI ANYMORE.
PON (PAT)
ポン

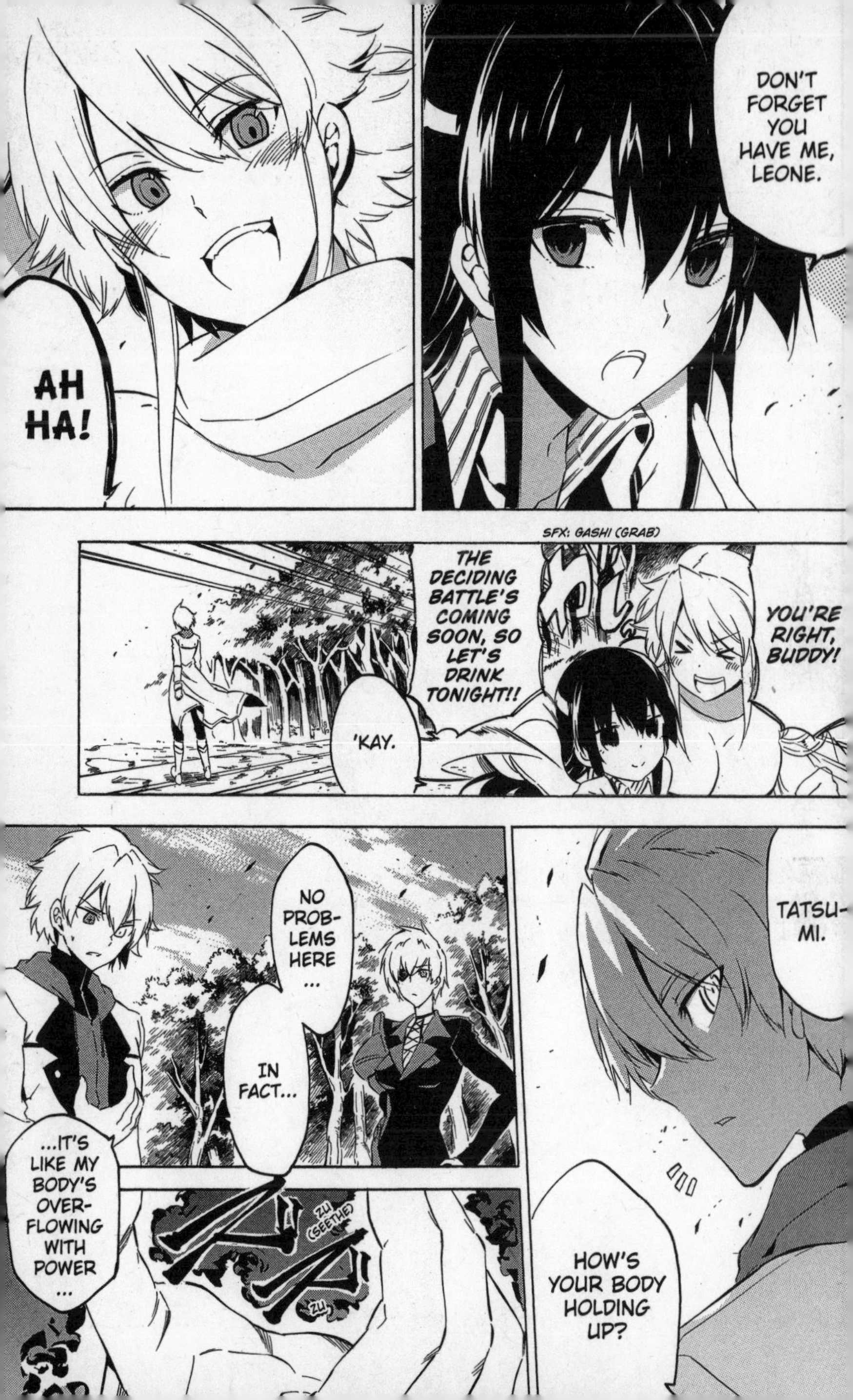
DON'T FORGET YOU HAVE ME, LEONE.
AH HA!
SFX: GASHI (GRAB)
YOU'RE RIGHT, BUDDY!
THE DECIDING BATTLE'S COMING SOON, SO LET'S DRINK TONIGHT!!
'KAY.
TATSUMI.
HOW'S YOUR BODY HOLDING UP?
NO PROBLEMS HERE ...
IN FACT...
...IT'S LIKE MY BODY'S OVERFLOWING WITH POWER ...
ZU (SEETHE)
ZU

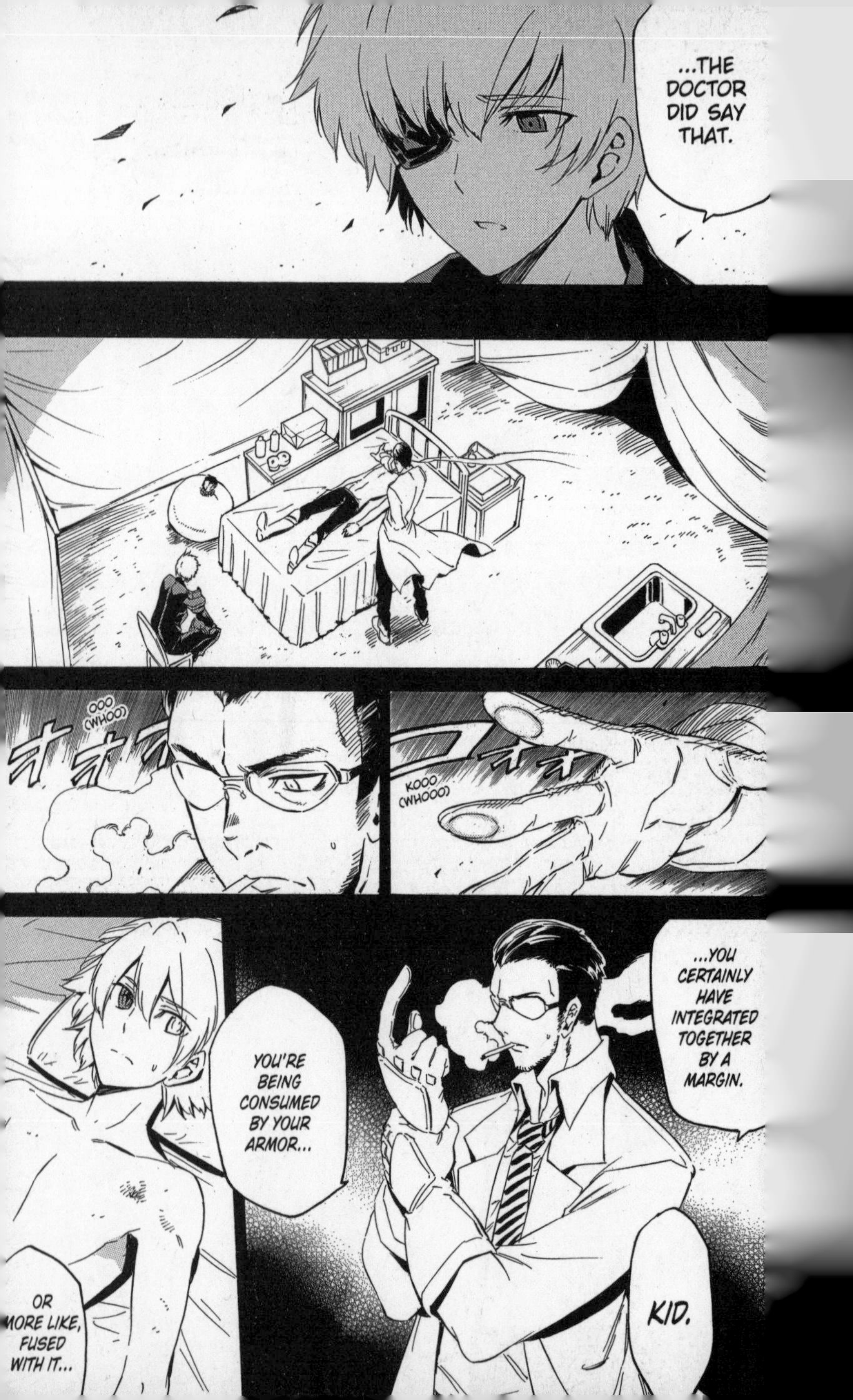

...THE DOCTOR DID SAY THAT.
OOO (WHOO)
KOOO (WHOOO)
...YOU CERTAINLY HAVE INTEGRATED TOGETHER BY A MARGIN.
KID.
YOU'RE BEING CONSUMED BY YOUR ARMOR...
OR MORE LIKE, FUSED WITH IT...

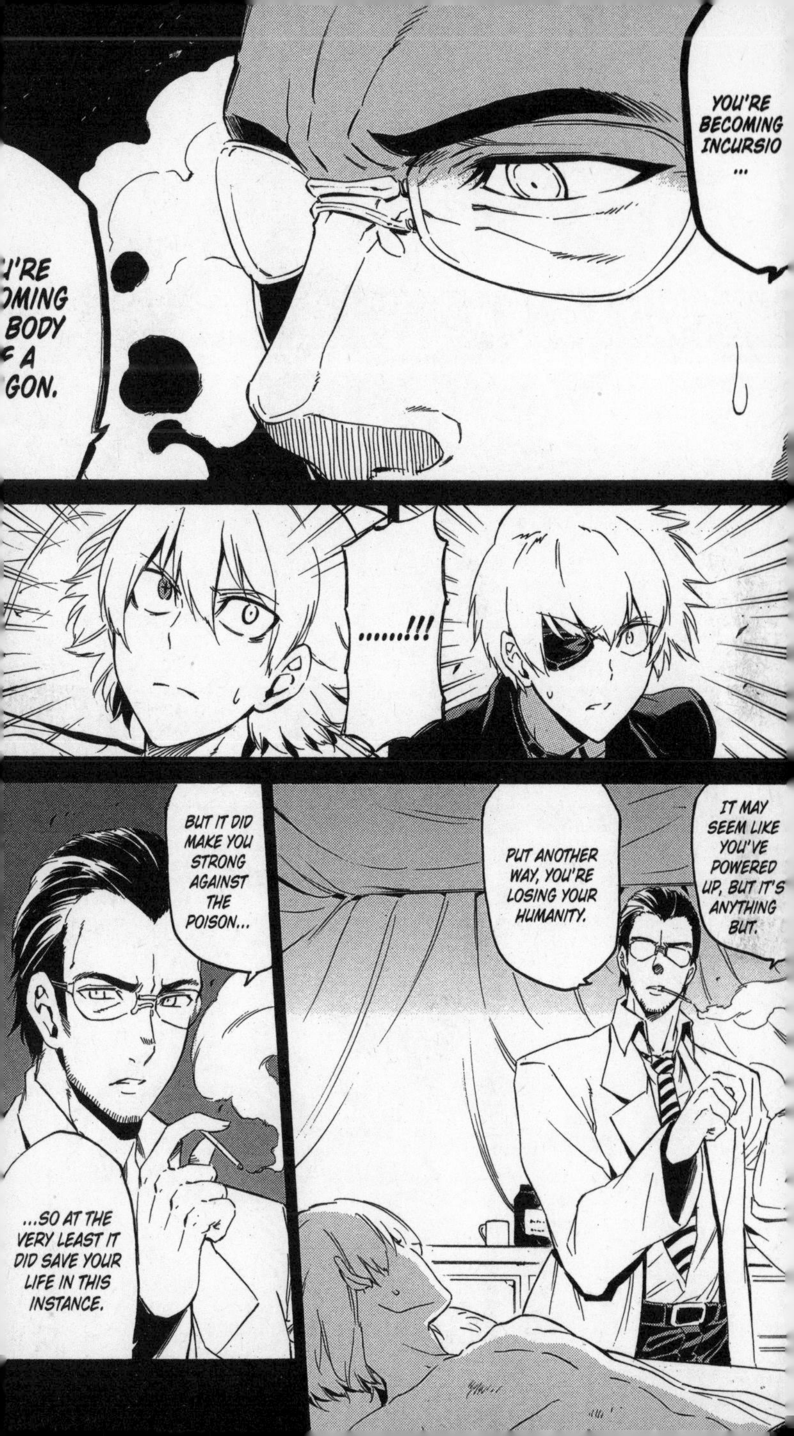
YOU'RE BECOMING INCURSIO ...
'RE OMING BODY A GON.
......!!!
IT MAY SEEM LIKE YOU'VE POWERED UP, BUT IT'S ANYTHING BUT.
PUT ANOTHER WAY, YOU'RE LOSING YOUR HUMANITY.
BUT IT DID MAKE YOU STRONG AGAINST THE POISON...
...SO AT THE VERY LEAST IT DID SAVE YOUR LIFE IN THIS INSTANCE.

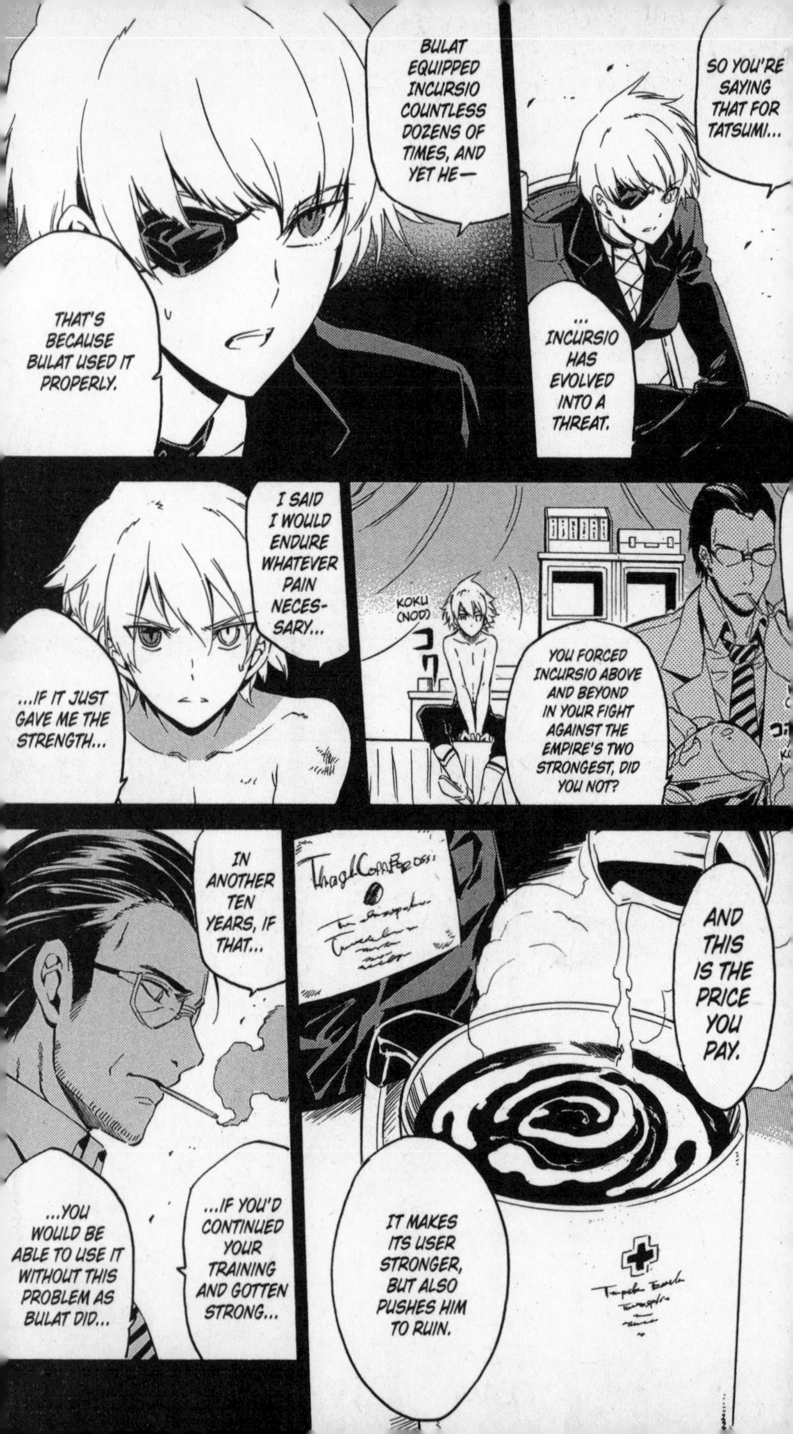

SO YOU'RE SAYING THAT FOR TATSUMI...
... INCURSIO HAS EVOLVED INTO A THREAT.
BULAT EQUIPPED INCURSIO COUNTLESS DOZENS OF TIMES, AND YET HE—
THAT'S BECAUSE BULAT USED IT PROPERLY.
KOKU (NOD)
YOU FORCED INCURSIO ABOVE AND BEYOND IN YOUR FIGHT AGAINST THE EMPIRE'S TWO STRONGEST, DID YOU NOT?
I SAID I WOULD ENDURE WHATEVER PAIN NECES-SARY...
...IF IT JUST GAVE ME THE STRENGTH...
AND THIS IS THE PRICE YOU PAY.
IT MAKES ITS USER STRONGER, BUT ALSO PUSHES HIM TO RUIN.
IN ANOTHER TEN YEARS, IF THAT...
...IF YOU'D CONTINUED YOUR TRAINING AND GOTTEN STRONG...
...YOU WOULD BE ABLE TO USE IT WITHOUT THIS PROBLEM AS BULAT DID...

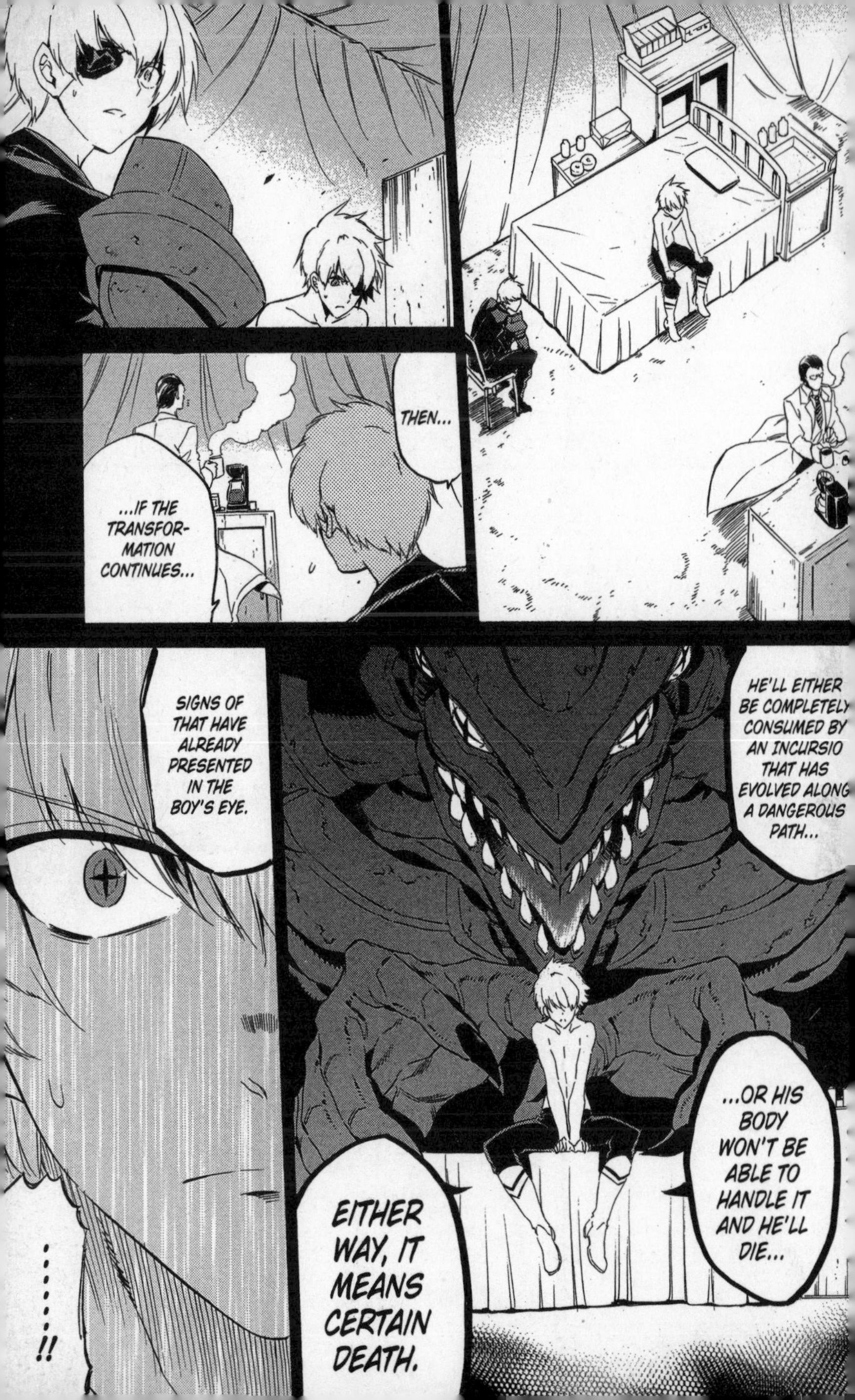

THEN...
...IF THE TRANSFOR-MATION CONTINUES...
HE'LL EITHER BE COMPLETELY CONSUMED BY AN INCURSIO THAT HAS EVOLVED ALONG A DANGEROUS PATH...
...OR HIS BODY WON'T BE ABLE TO HANDLE IT AND HE'LL DIE...
EITHER WAY, IT MEANS CERTAIN DEATH.
SIGNS OF THAT HAVE ALREADY PRESENTED IN THE BOY'S EYE.
......!!

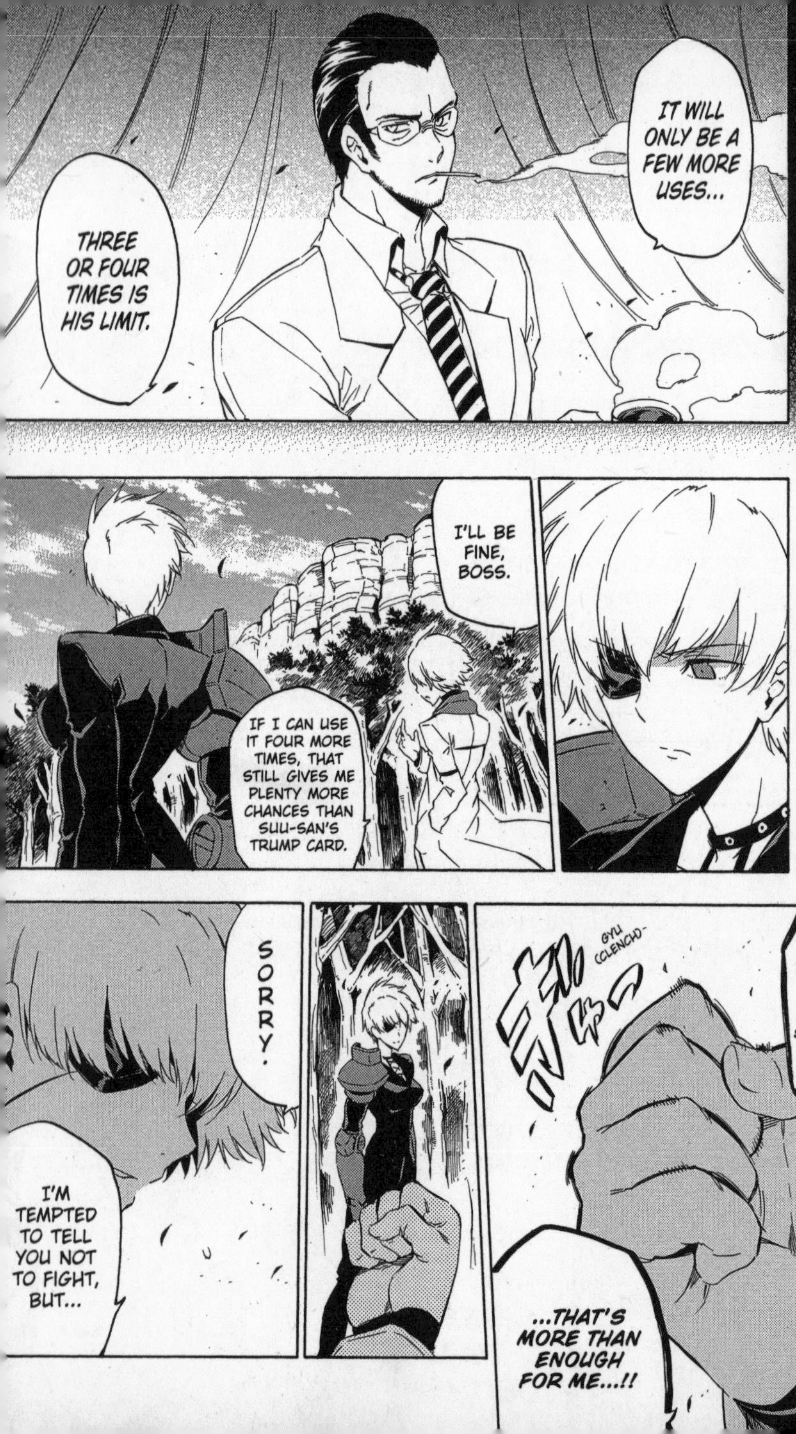
IT WILL ONLY BE A FEW MORE USES...
THREE OR FOUR TIMES IS HIS LIMIT.
I'LL BE FINE, BOSS.
IF I CAN USE IT FOUR MORE TIMES, THAT STILL GIVES ME PLENTY MORE CHANCES THAN SUU-SAN'S TRUMP CARD.
IN THE FINAL STANDOFF...
GYU (CLENCH)
...THAT'S MORE THAN ENOUGH FOR ME...!!
SORRY.
I'M TEMPTED TO TELL YOU NOT TO FIGHT, BUT...

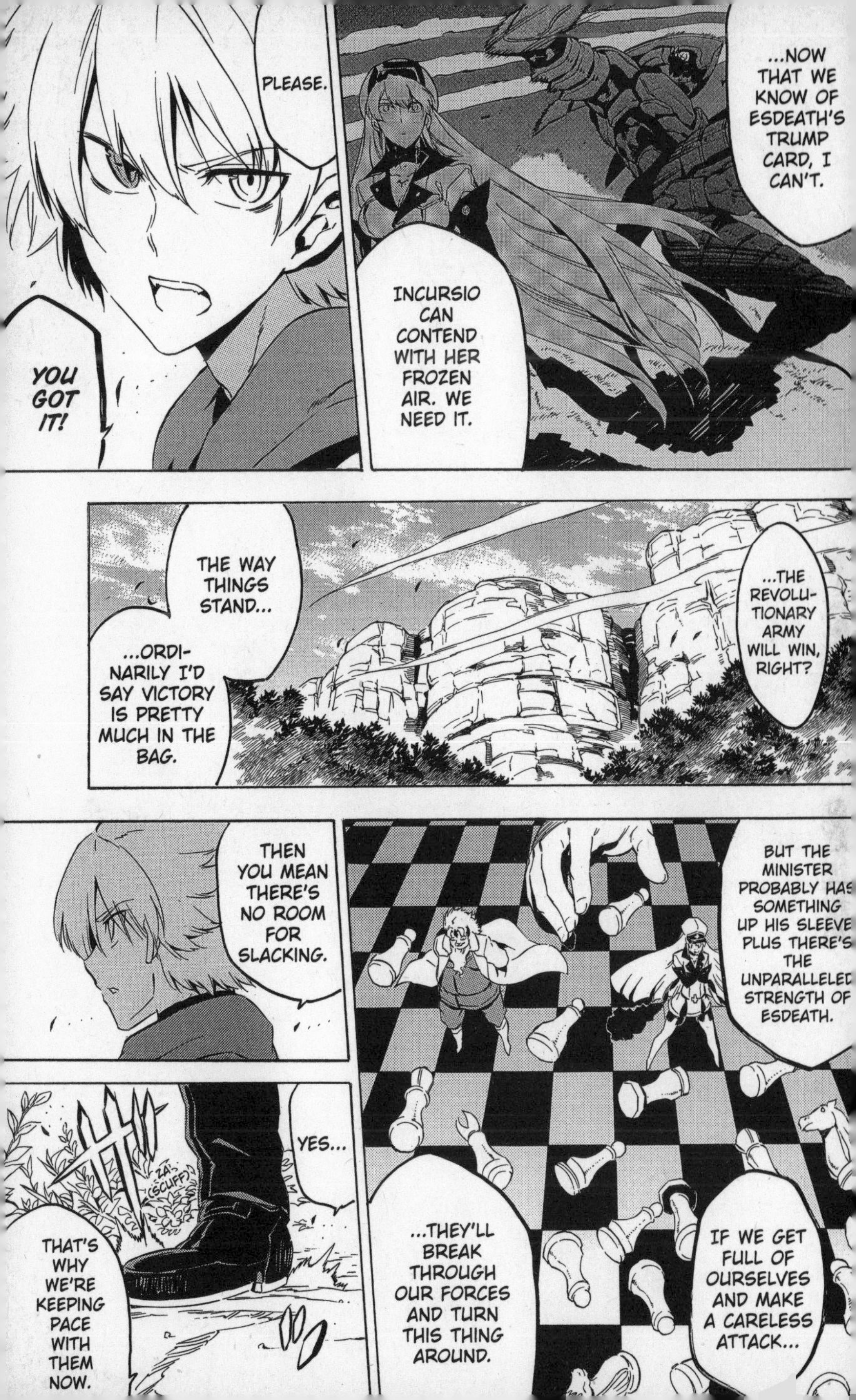
...NOW THAT WE KNOW OF ESDEATH'S TRUMP CARD, I CAN'T.
INCURSIO CAN CONTEND WITH HER FROZEN AIR. WE NEED IT.
PLEASE.
YOU GOT IT!
...THE REVOLUTIONARY ARMY WILL WIN, RIGHT?
THE WAY THINGS STAND...
...ORDINARILY I'D SAY VICTORY IS PRETTY MUCH IN THE BAG.
BUT THE MINISTER PROBABLY HAS SOMETHING UP HIS SLEEVE PLUS THERE'S THE UNPARALLELED STRENGTH OF ESDEATH.
IF WE GET FULL OF OURSELVES AND MAKE A CARELESS ATTACK...
...THEY'LL BREAK THROUGH OUR FORCES AND TURN THIS THING AROUND.
THEN YOU MEAN THERE'S NO ROOM FOR SLACKING.
...
YES...
ZA! (SCUFF)
THAT'S WHY WE'RE KEEPING PACE WITH THEM NOW.

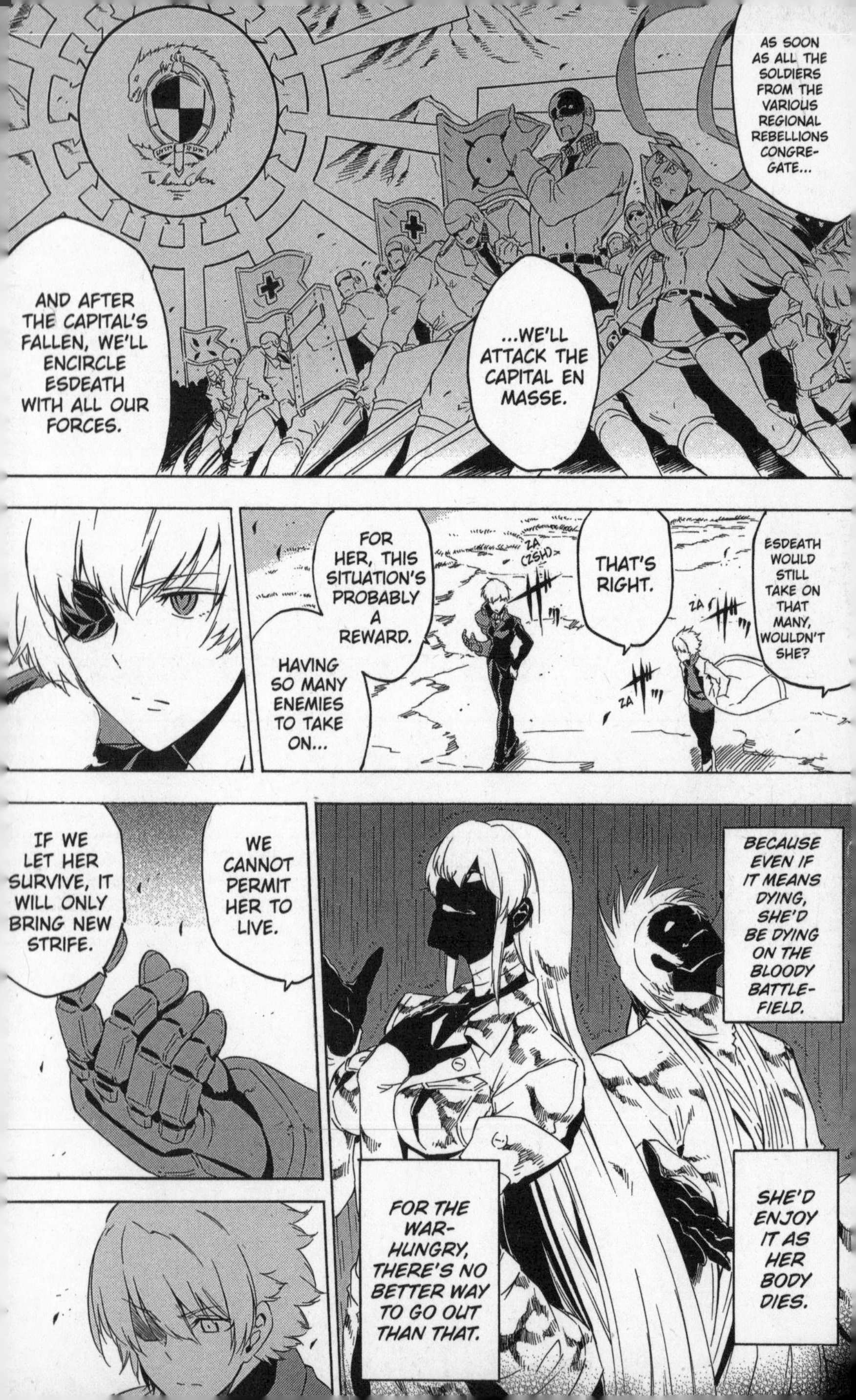
AS SOON AS ALL THE SOLDIERS FROM THE VARIOUS REGIONAL REBELLIONS CONGREGATE...
...WE'LL ATTACK THE CAPITAL EN MASSE.
AND AFTER THE CAPITAL'S FALLEN, WE'LL ENCIRCLE ESDEATH WITH ALL OUR FORCES.
ESDEATH WOULD STILL TAKE ON THAT MANY, WOULDN'T SHE?
ZA
ZA
THAT'S RIGHT.
ZA (ZSH)
FOR HER, THIS SITUATION'S PROBABLY A REWARD.
HAVING SO MANY ENEMIES TO TAKE ON...
BECAUSE EVEN IF IT MEANS DYING, SHE'D BE DYING ON THE BLOODY BATTLEFIELD.
SHE'D ENJOY IT AS HER BODY DIES.
FOR THE WAR-HUNGRY, THERE'S NO BETTER WAY TO GO OUT THAN THAT.
WE CANNOT PERMIT HER TO LIVE.
IF WE LET HER SURVIVE, IT WILL ONLY BRING NEW STRIFE.

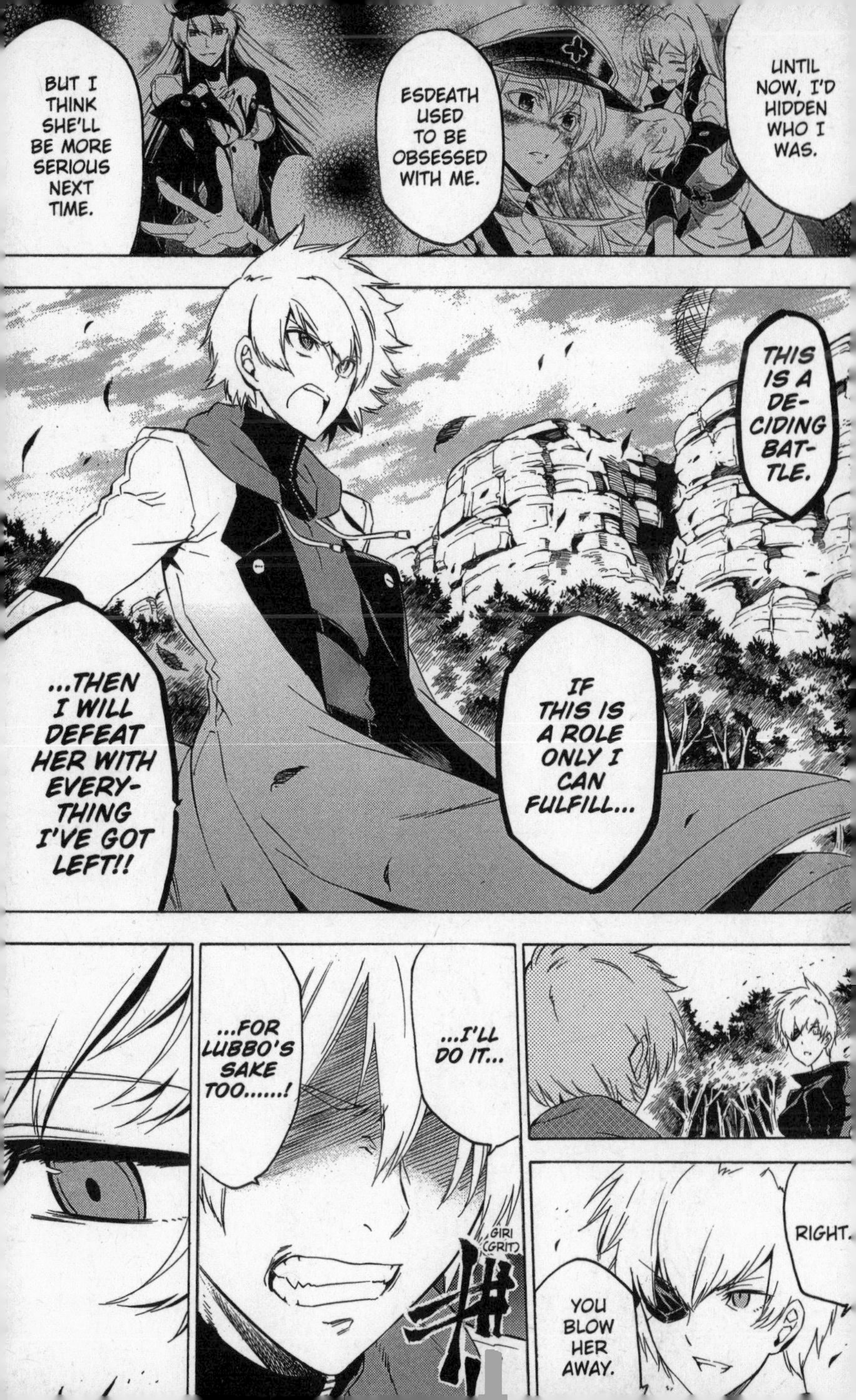
UNTIL NOW, I'D HIDDEN WHO I WAS.
ESDEATH USED TO BE OBSESSED WITH ME.
BUT I THINK SHE'LL BE MORE SERIOUS NEXT TIME.
THIS IS A DECIDING BATTLE.
IF THIS IS A ROLE ONLY I CAN FULFILL...
...THEN I WILL DEFEAT HER WITH EVERYTHING I'VE GOT LEFT!!
RIGHT.
YOU BLOW HER AWAY.
...I'LL DO IT...
...FOR LUBBO'S SAKE TOO......!
GIRI (GRIT)

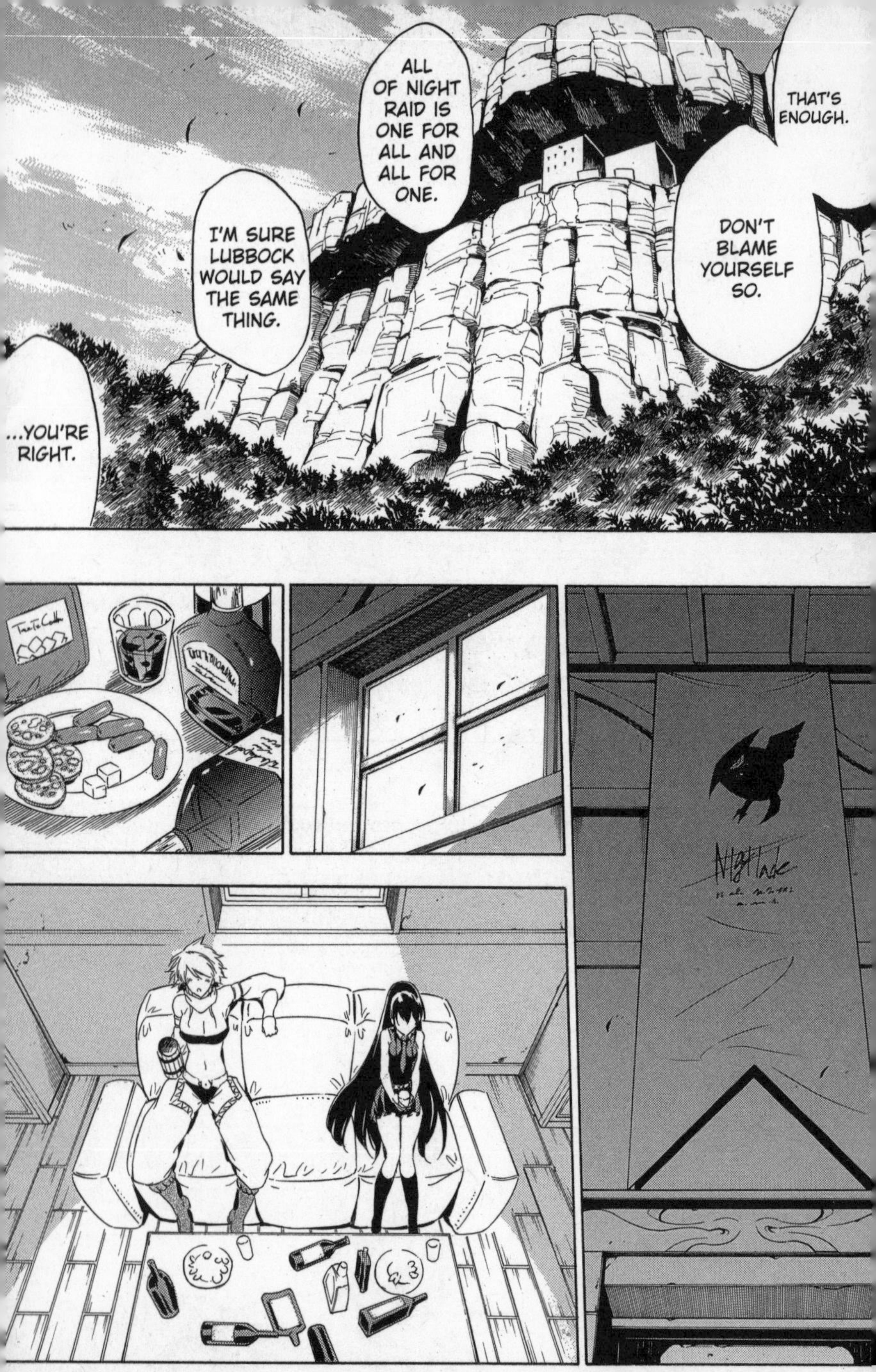
THAT'S ENOUGH.
DON'T BLAME YOURSELF SO.
ALL OF NIGHT RAID IS ONE FOR ALL AND ALL FOR ONE.
I'M SURE LUBBOCK WOULD SAY THE SAME THING.
...YOU'RE RIGHT.

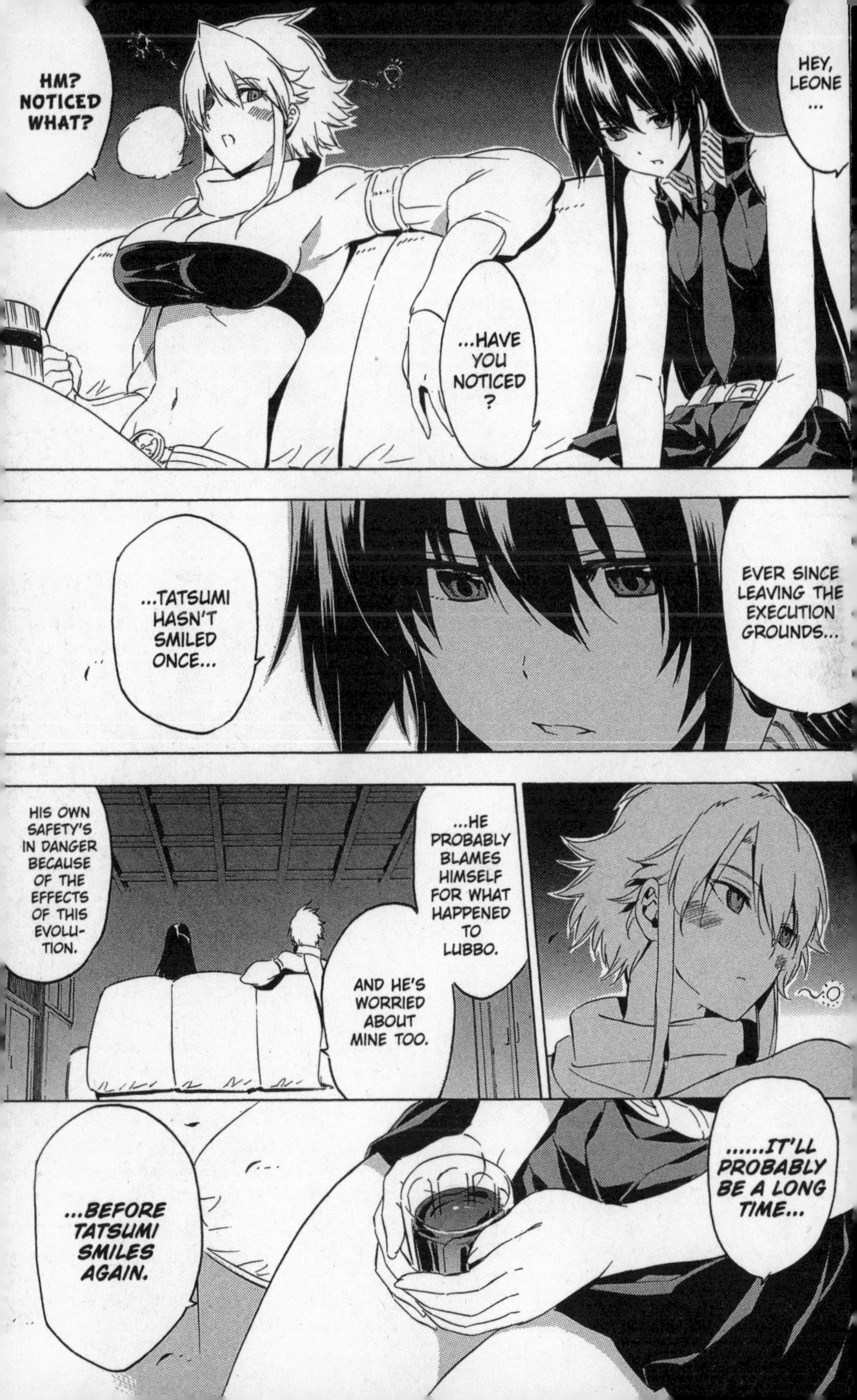
HEY, LEONE ...
...HAVE YOU NOTICED ?
HM? NOTICED WHAT?
EVER SINCE LEAVING THE EXECUTION GROUNDS...
...TATSUMI HASN'T SMILED ONCE...
...HE PROBABLY BLAMES HIMSELF FOR WHAT HAPPENED TO LUBBO.
AND HE'S WORRIED ABOUT MINE TOO.
HIS OWN SAFETY'S IN DANGER BECAUSE OF THE EFFECTS OF THIS EVOLUTION.
......IT'LL PROBABLY BE A LONG TIME...
...BEFORE TATSUMI SMILES AGAIN.

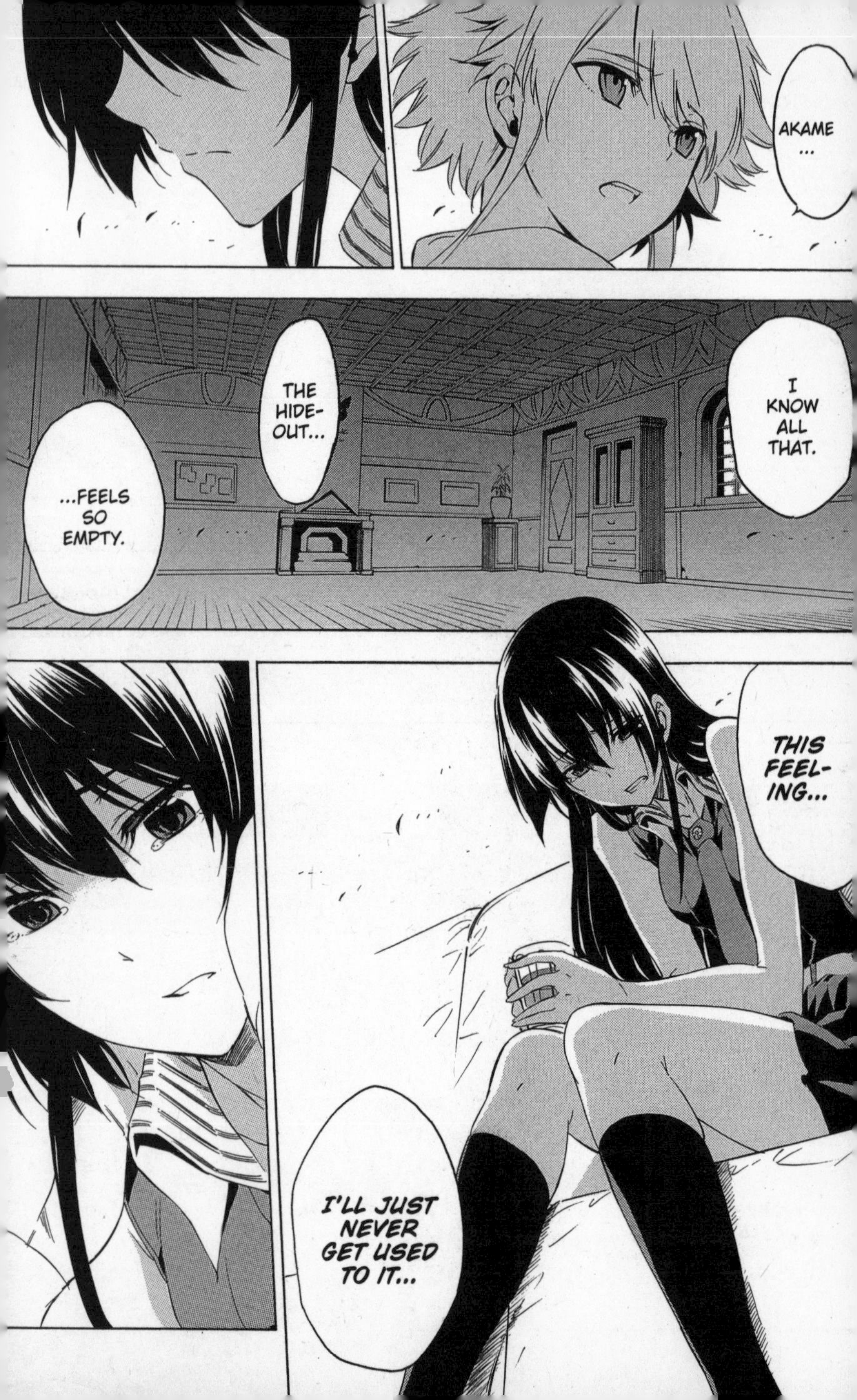

AKAME ...
I KNOW ALL THAT.
THE HIDE-OUT...
...FEELS SO EMPTY.
THIS FEEL-ING...
I'LL JUST NEVER GET USED TO IT...

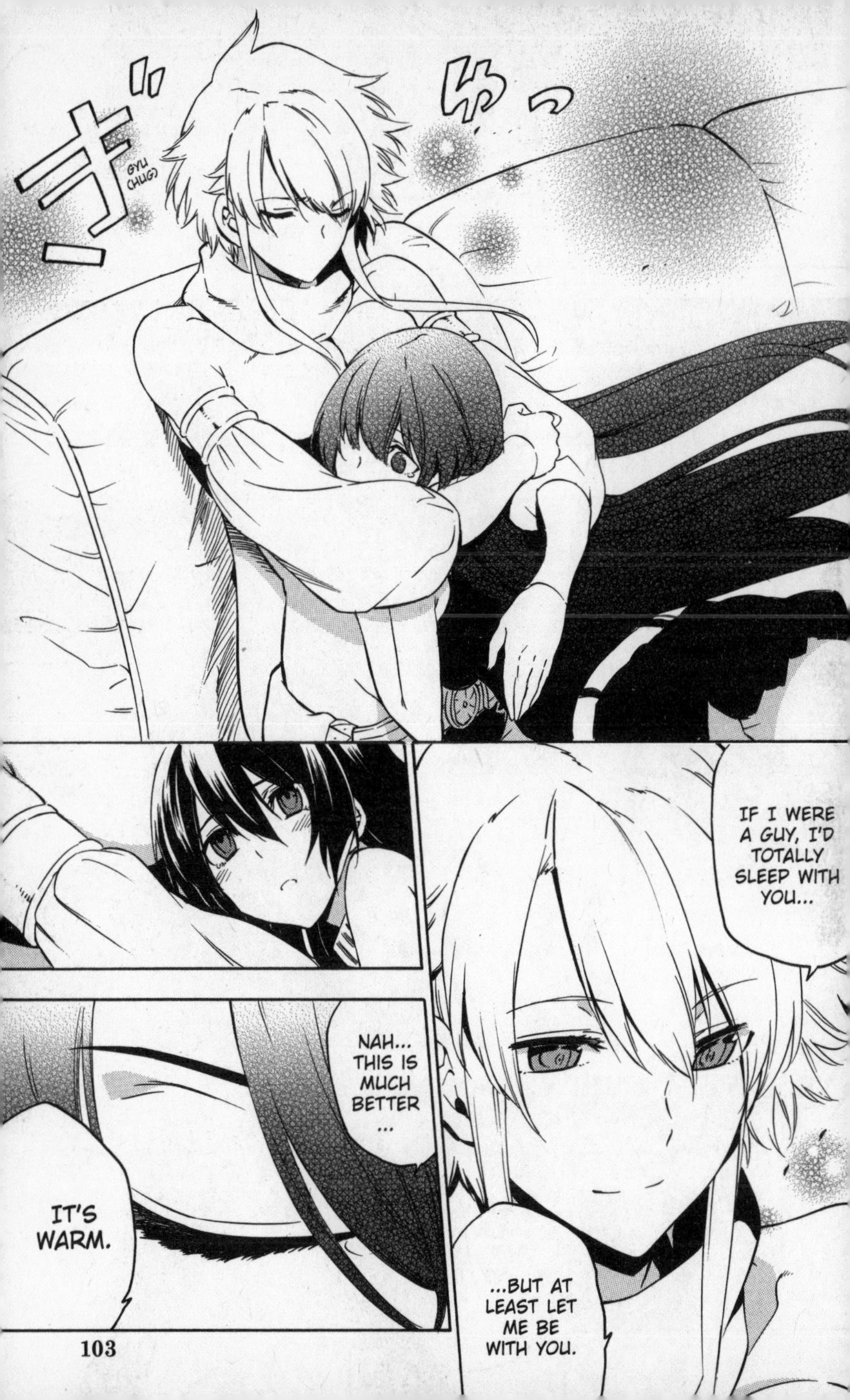
ぎゅっ
GYU (HUG)
IF I WERE A GUY, I'D TOTALLY SLEEP WITH YOU...
NAH... THIS IS MUCH BETTER ...
...BUT AT LEAST LET ME BE WITH YOU.
IT'S WARM.

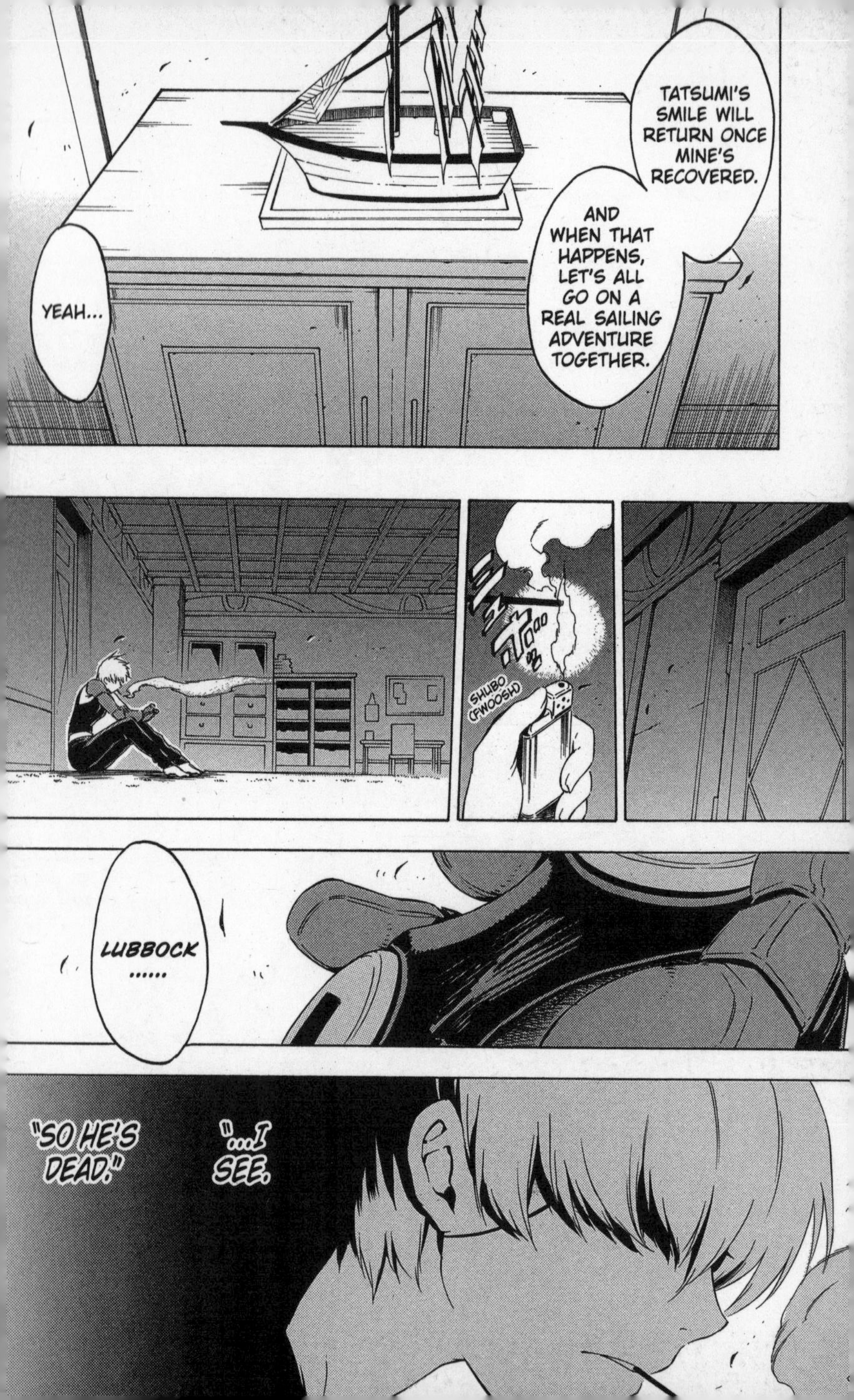
TATSUMI'S SMILE WILL RETURN ONCE MINE'S RECOVERED.
AND WHEN THAT HAPPENS, LET'S ALL GO ON A REAL SAILING ADVENTURE TOGETHER.
YEAH...
SHUBO (FWOOSH)
LUBBOCK ......
"...I SEE.
"SO HE'S DEAD."

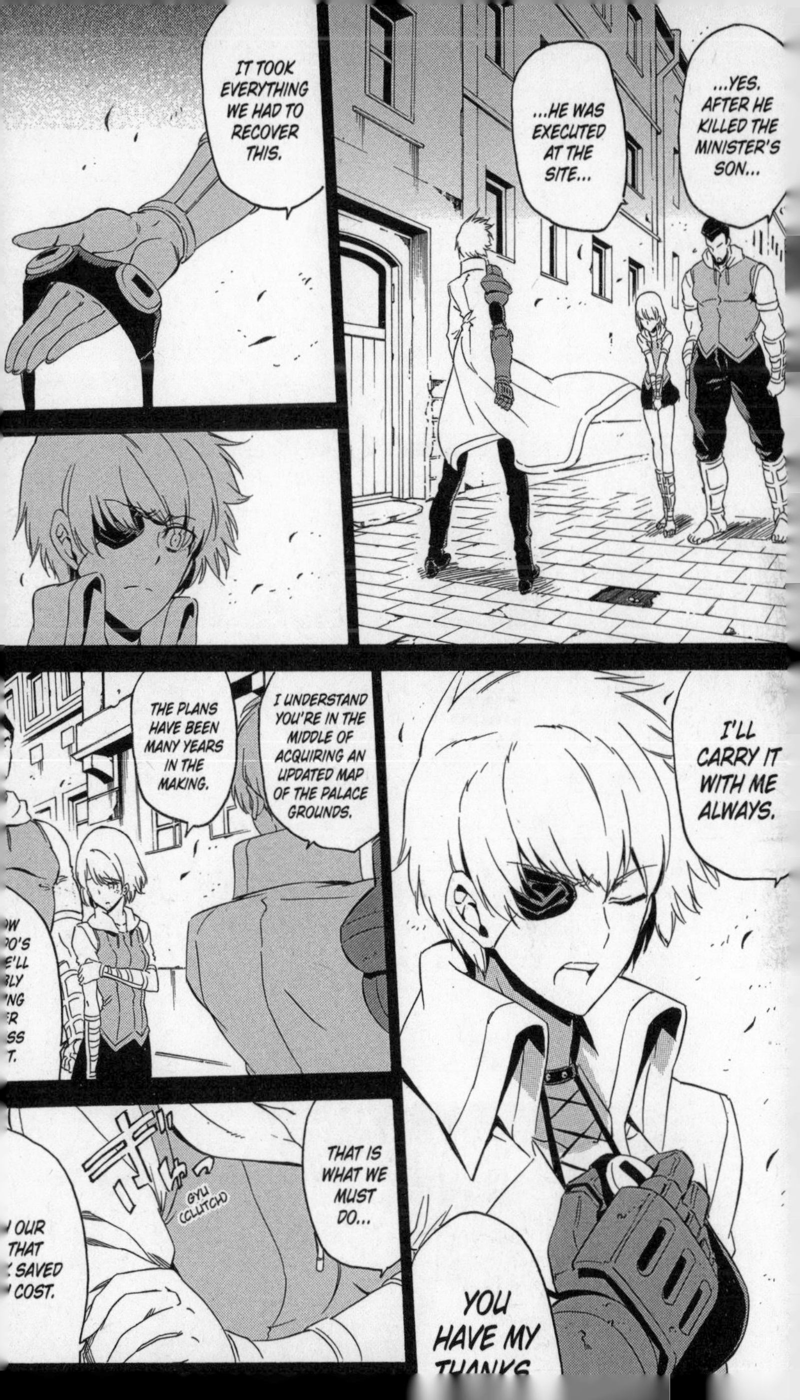
...YES. AFTER HE KILLED THE MINISTER'S SON...
...HE WAS EXECUTED AT THE SITE...
IT TOOK EVERYTHING WE HAD TO RECOVER THIS.
I'LL CARRY IT WITH ME ALWAYS.
YOU HAVE MY
I UNDERSTAND YOU'RE IN THE MIDDLE OF ACQUIRING AN UPDATED MAP OF THE PALACE GROUNDS.
THE PLANS HAVE BEEN MANY YEARS IN THE MAKING.
THAT IS WHAT WE MUST DO...
GYU (CLUTCH)

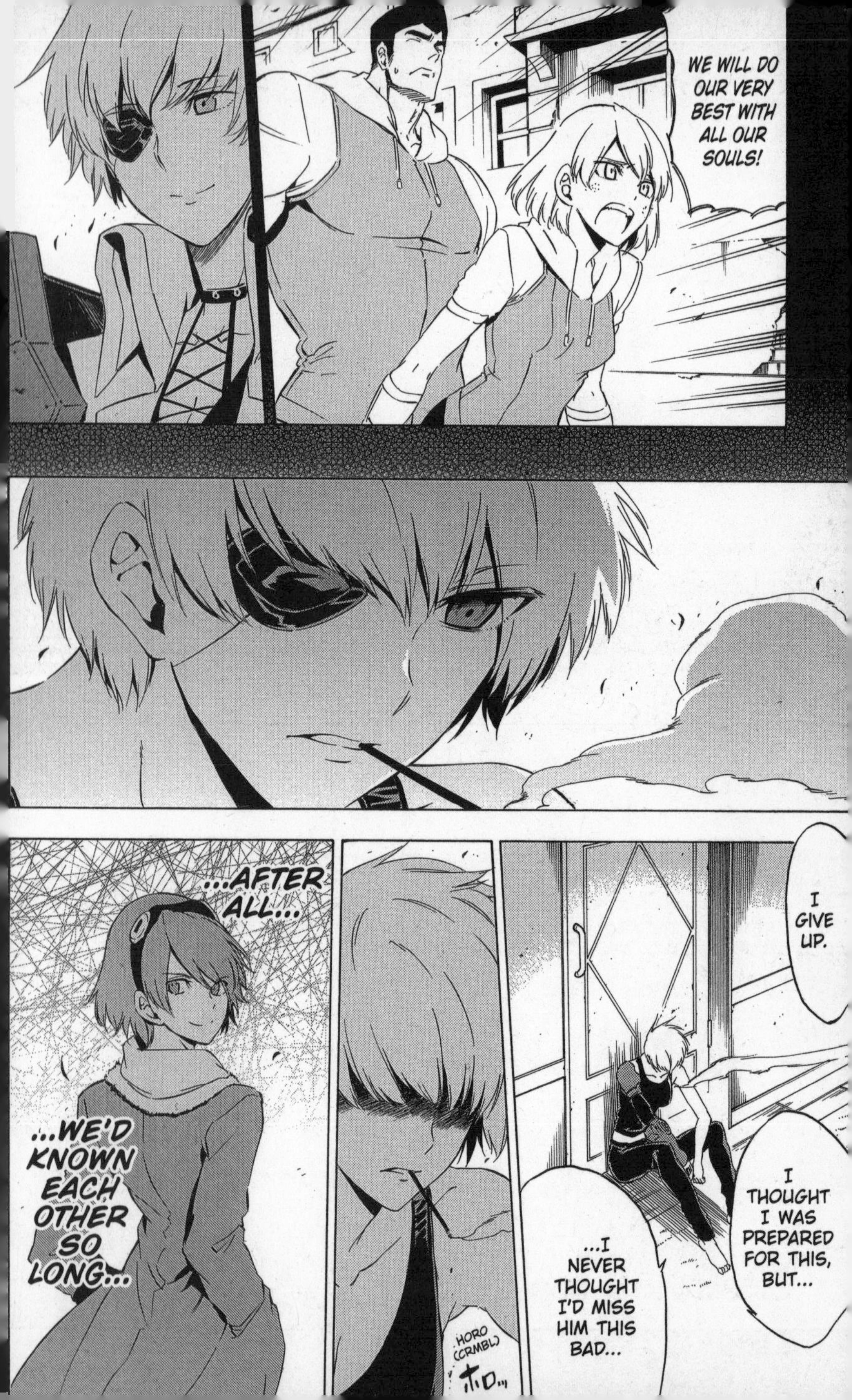
WE WILL DO OUR VERY BEST WITH ALL OUR SOULS!
I GIVE UP.
I THOUGHT I WAS PREPARED FOR THIS, BUT...
...I NEVER THOUGHT I'D MISS HIM THIS BAD...
HORO (CRMBL)
...AFTER ALL...
...WE'D KNOWN EACH OTHER SO LONG...

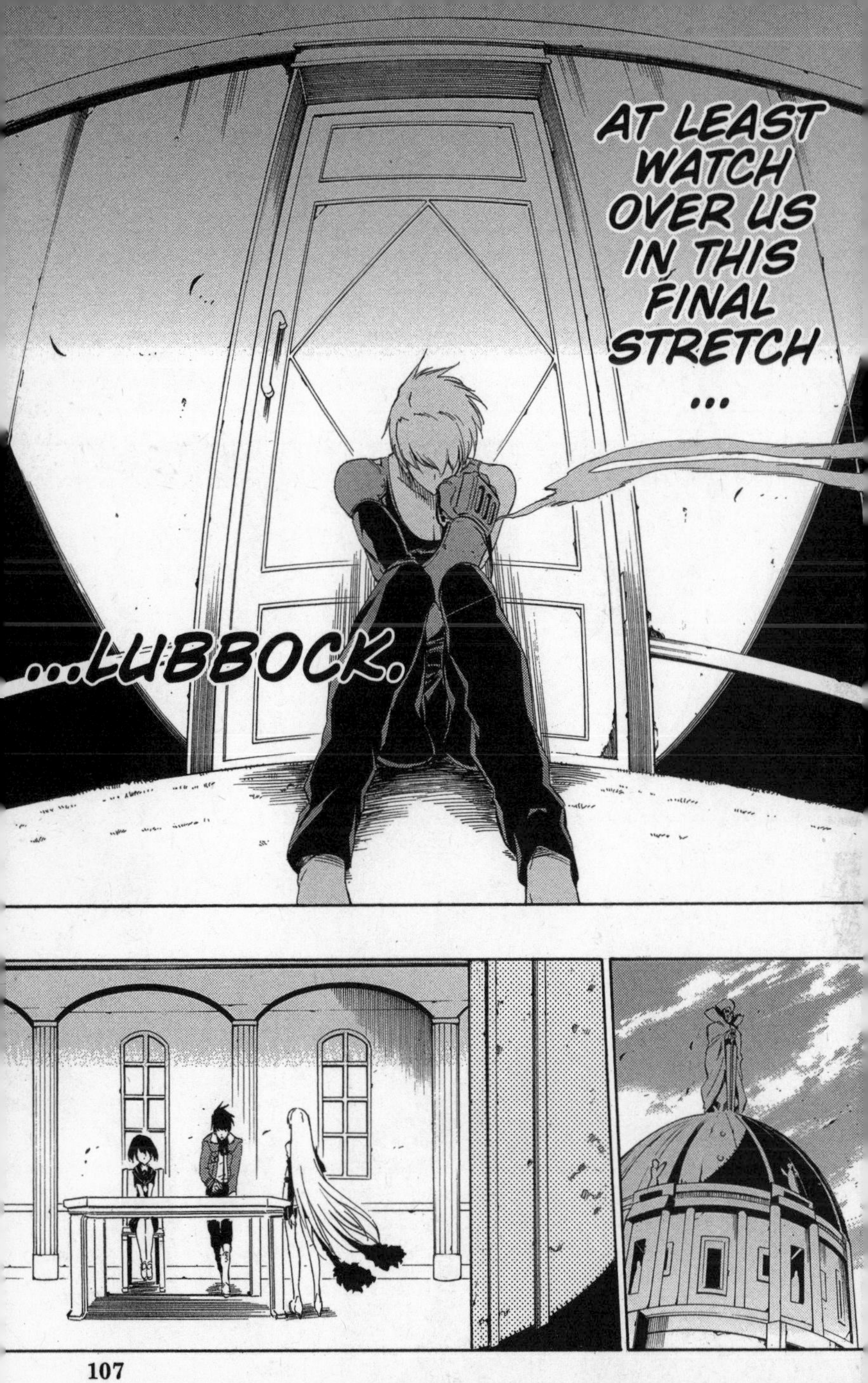
AT LEAST WATCH OVER US IN THIS FINAL STRETCH...
...LUBBOCK.

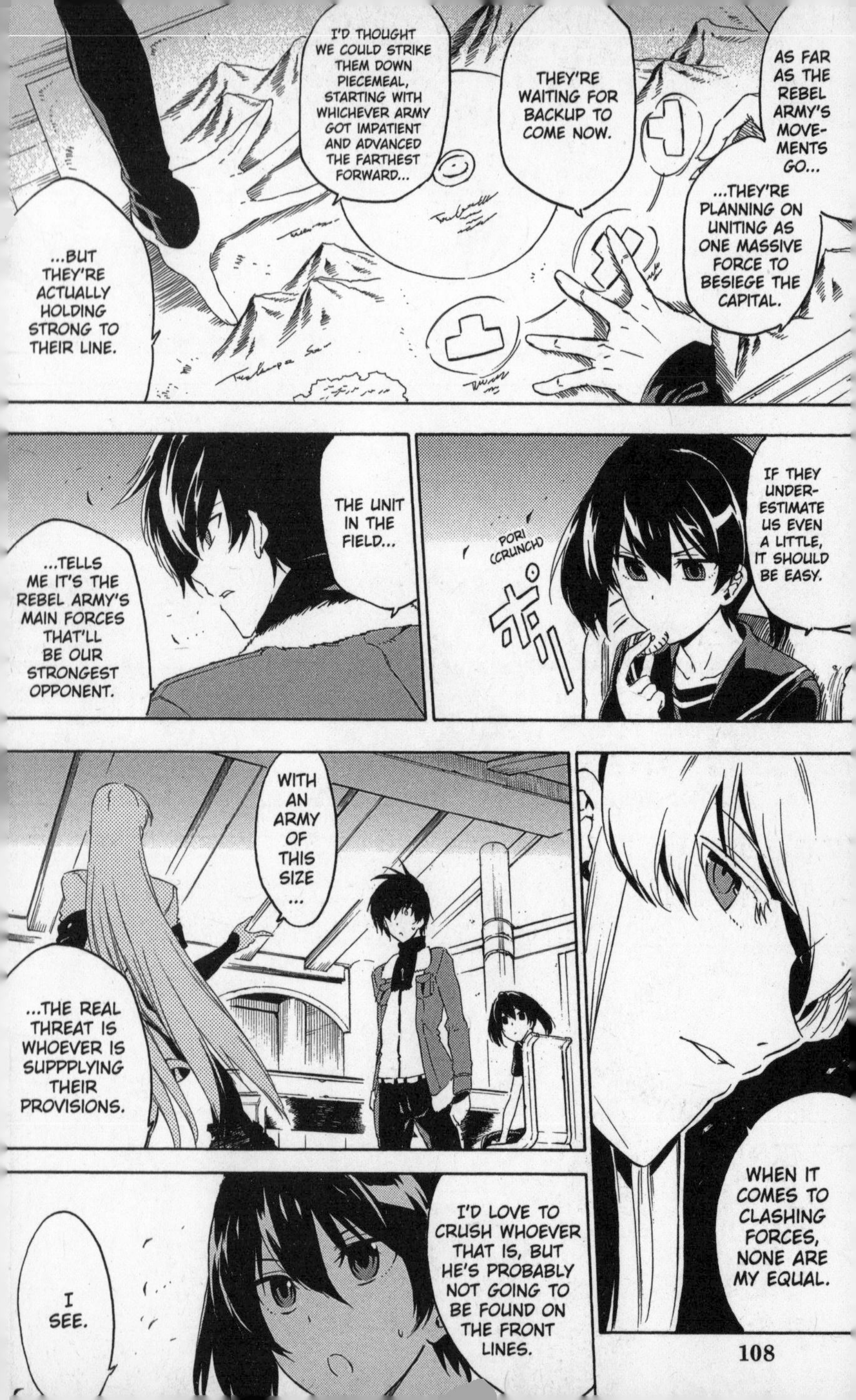
AS FAR AS THE REBEL ARMY'S MOVEMENTS GO...
...THEY'RE PLANNING ON UNITING AS ONE MASSIVE FORCE TO BESIEGE THE CAPITAL.
THEY'RE WAITING FOR BACKUP TO COME NOW.
I'D THOUGHT WE COULD STRIKE THEM DOWN PIECEMEAL, STARTING WITH WHICHEVER ARMY GOT IMPATIENT AND ADVANCED THE FARTHEST FORWARD...
...BUT THEY'RE ACTUALLY HOLDING STRONG TO THEIR LINE.
IF THEY UNDERESTIMATE US EVEN A LITTLE, IT SHOULD BE EASY.
PORI (CRUNCH)
THE UNIT IN THE FIELD...
...TELLS ME IT'S THE REBEL ARMY'S MAIN FORCES THAT'LL BE OUR STRONGEST OPPONENT.
WITH AN ARMY OF THIS SIZE...
...THE REAL THREAT IS WHOEVER IS SUPPPLYING THEIR PROVISIONS.
WHEN IT COMES TO CLASHING FORCES, NONE ARE MY EQUAL.
I'D LOVE TO CRUSH WHOEVER THAT IS, BUT HE'S PROBABLY NOT GOING TO BE FOUND ON THE FRONT LINES.
I SEE.

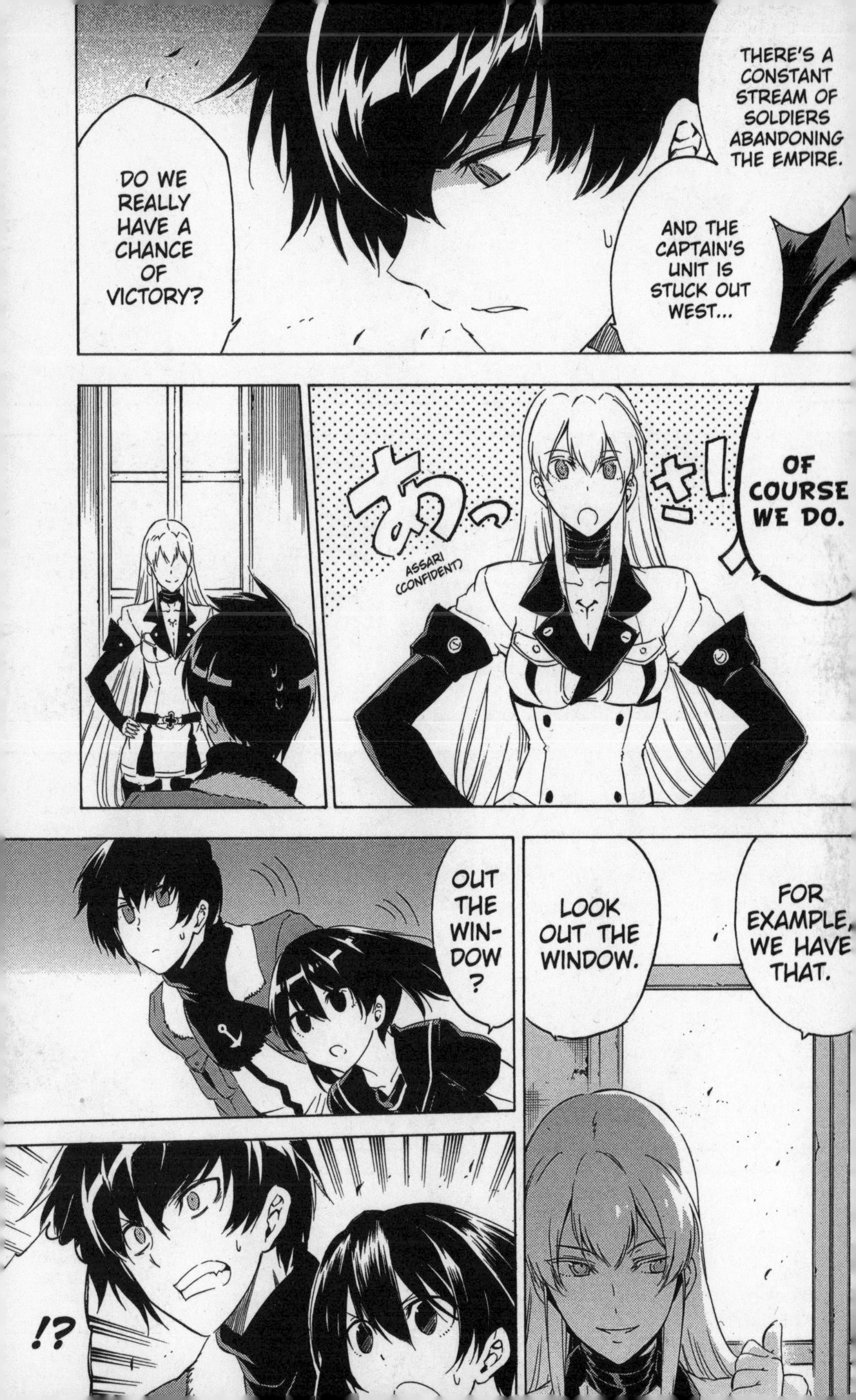
THERE'S A CONSTANT STREAM OF SOLDIERS ABANDONING THE EMPIRE.
AND THE CAPTAIN'S UNIT IS STUCK OUT WEST...
DO WE REALLY HAVE A CHANCE OF VICTORY?
OF COURSE WE DO.
あっさり
ASSARI (CONFIDENT)
FOR EXAMPLE, WE HAVE THAT.
LOOK OUT THE WINDOW.
OUT THE WIN-DOW?
!?

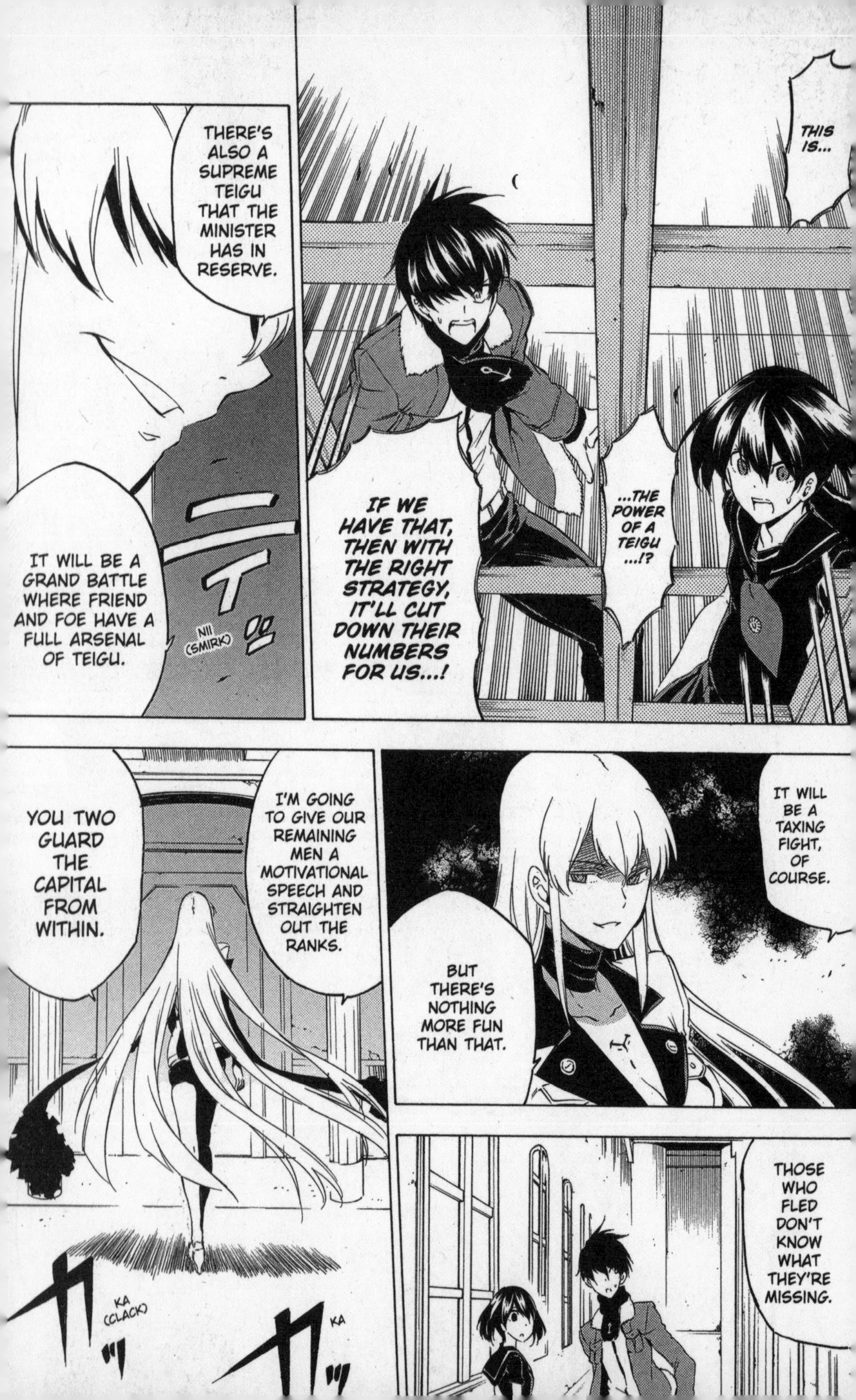
THIS IS...
...THE POWER OF A TEIGU ...!?
IF WE HAVE THAT, THEN WITH THE RIGHT STRATEGY, IT'LL CUT DOWN THEIR NUMBERS FOR US...!
THERE'S ALSO A SUPREME TEIGU THAT THE MINISTER HAS IN RESERVE.
NII (SMIRK)
IT WILL BE A GRAND BATTLE WHERE FRIEND AND FOE HAVE A FULL ARSENAL OF TEIGU.
IT WILL BE A TAXING FIGHT, OF COURSE.
BUT THERE'S NOTHING MORE FUN THAN THAT.
I'M GOING TO GIVE OUR REMAINING MEN A MOTIVATIONAL SPEECH AND STRAIGHTEN OUT THE RANKS.
YOU TWO GUARD THE CAPITAL FROM WITHIN.
KA (CLACK)
KA
THOSE WHO FLED DON'T KNOW WHAT THEY'RE MISSING.

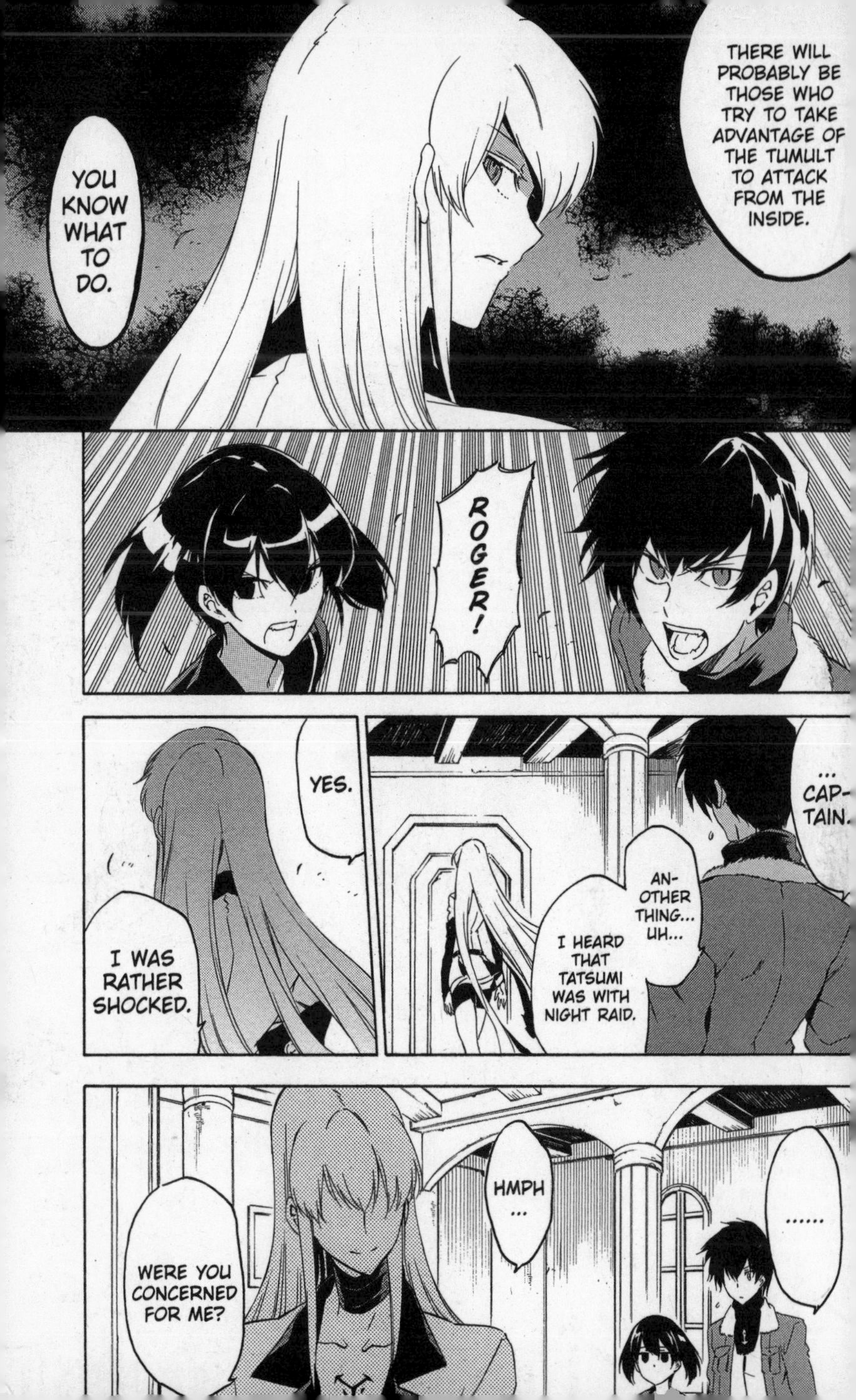
THERE WILL PROBABLY BE THOSE WHO TRY TO TAKE ADVANTAGE OF THE TUMULT TO ATTACK FROM THE INSIDE.
YOU KNOW WHAT TO DO.
ROGER!
... CAP-TAIN.
AN-OTHER THING... UH...
I HEARD THAT TATSUMI WAS WITH NIGHT RAID.
YES.
I WAS RATHER SHOCKED.
......
HMPH ...
WERE YOU CONCERNED FOR ME?

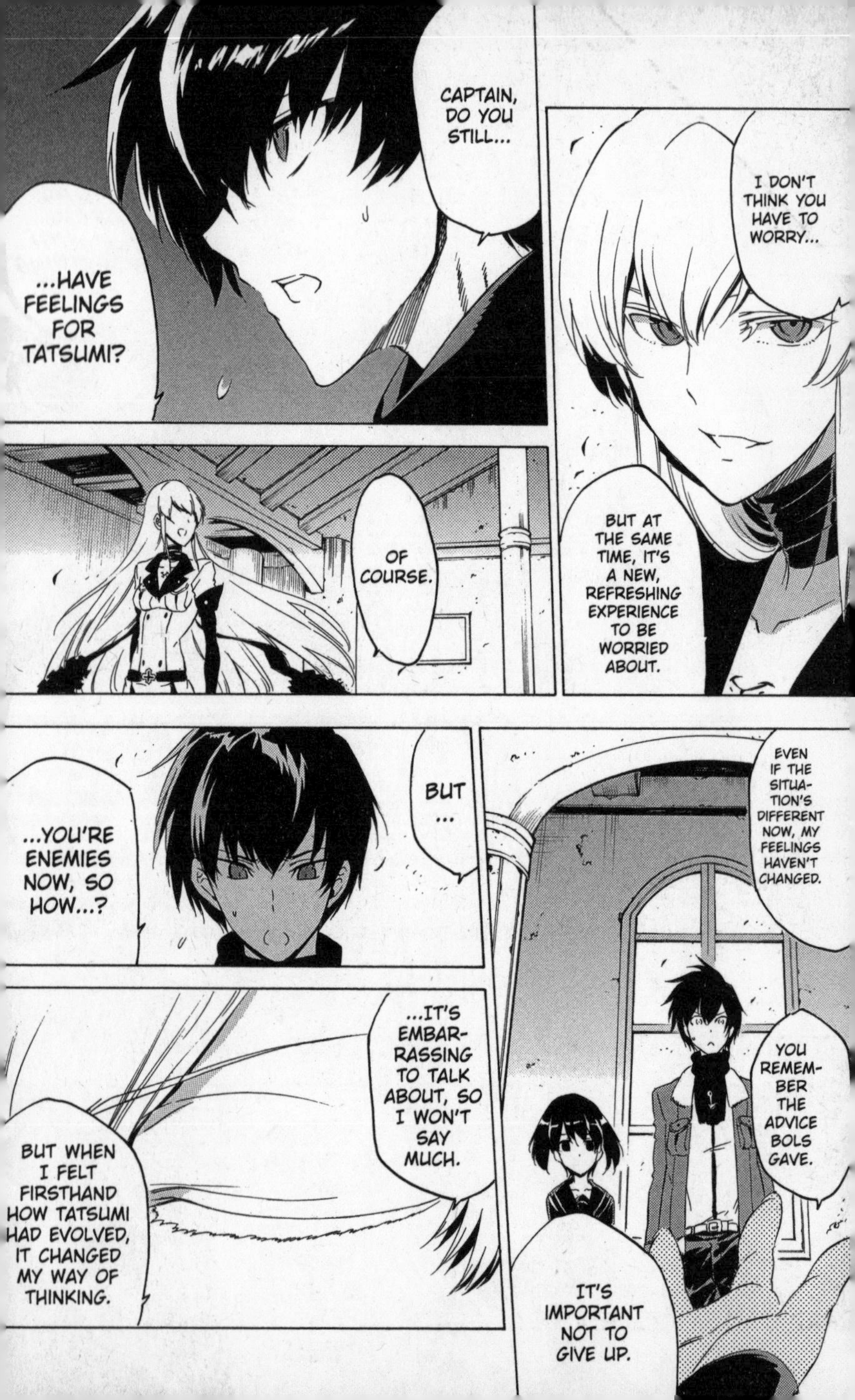
CAPTAIN, DO YOU STILL...
...HAVE FEELINGS FOR TATSUMI?
OF COURSE.
I DON'T THINK YOU HAVE TO WORRY...
BUT AT THE SAME TIME, IT'S A NEW, REFRESHING EXPERIENCE TO BE WORRIED ABOUT.
EVEN IF THE SITUATION'S DIFFERENT NOW, MY FEELINGS HAVEN'T CHANGED.
BUT ...
...YOU'RE ENEMIES NOW, SO HOW...?
...IT'S EMBARRASSING TO TALK ABOUT, SO I WON'T SAY MUCH.
BUT WHEN I FELT FIRSTHAND HOW TATSUMI HAD EVOLVED, IT CHANGED MY WAY OF THINKING.
YOU REMEMBER THE ADVICE BOLS GAVE.
IT'S IMPORTANT NOT TO GIVE UP.

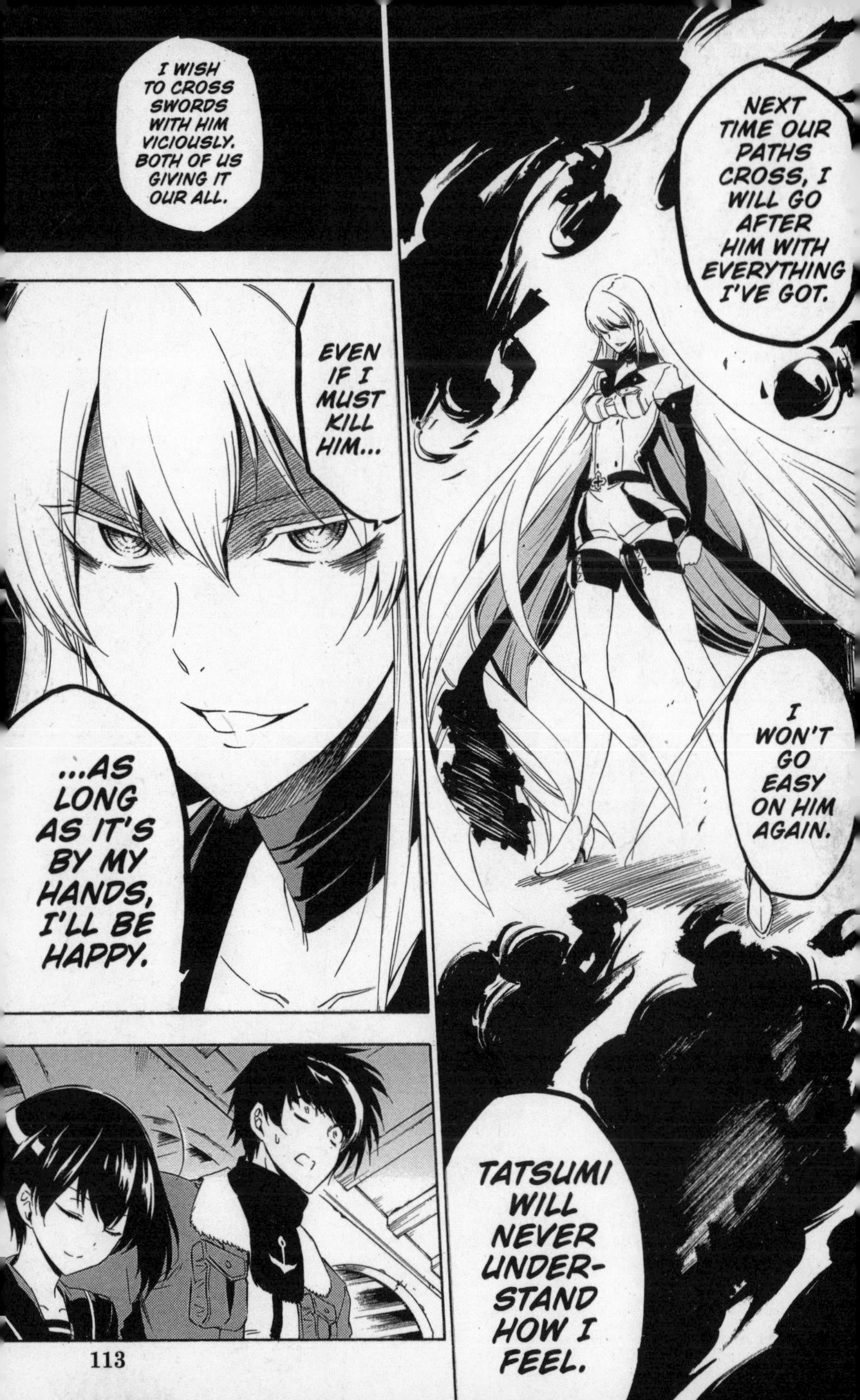
NEXT TIME OUR PATHS CROSS, I WILL GO AFTER HIM WITH EVERYTHING I'VE GOT.
I WON'T GO EASY ON HIM AGAIN.
I WISH TO CROSS SWORDS WITH HIM VICIOUSLY. BOTH OF US GIVING IT OUR ALL.
EVEN IF I MUST KILL HIM...
...AS LONG AS IT'S BY MY HANDS, I'LL BE HAPPY.
TATSUMI WILL NEVER UNDER-STAND HOW I FEEL.

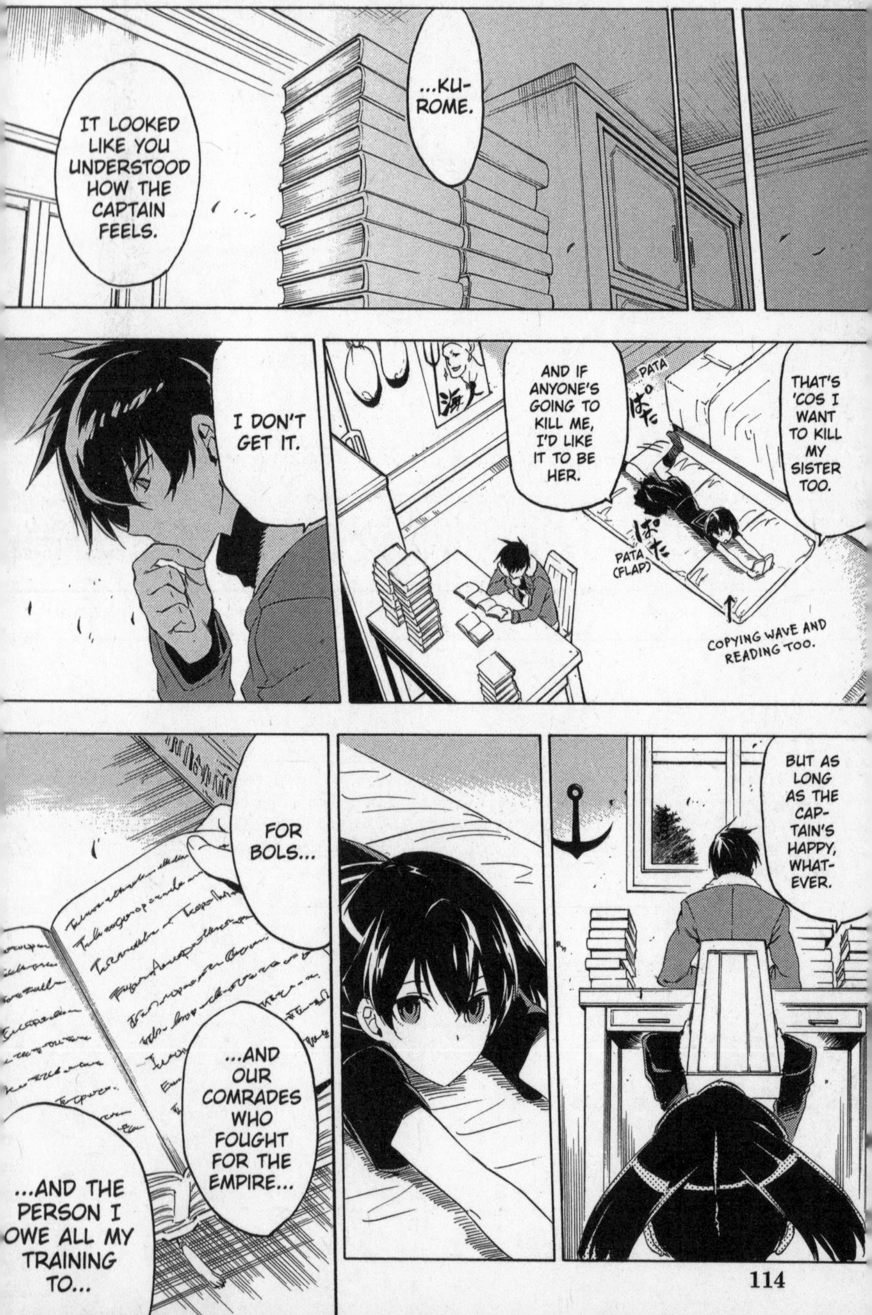
...KUROME.
IT LOOKED LIKE YOU UNDERSTOOD HOW THE CAPTAIN FEELS.
THAT'S 'COS I WANT TO KILL MY SISTER TOO.
PATA
ぱた
AND IF ANYONE'S GOING TO KILL ME, I'D LIKE IT TO BE HER.
ぱた
PATA (FLAP)
COPYING WAVE AND READING TOO.
I DON'T GET IT.
BUT AS LONG AS THE CAPTAIN'S HAPPY, WHATEVER.
FOR BOLS...
...AND OUR COMRADES WHO FOUGHT FOR THE EMPIRE...
...AND THE PERSON I OWE ALL MY TRAINING TO...

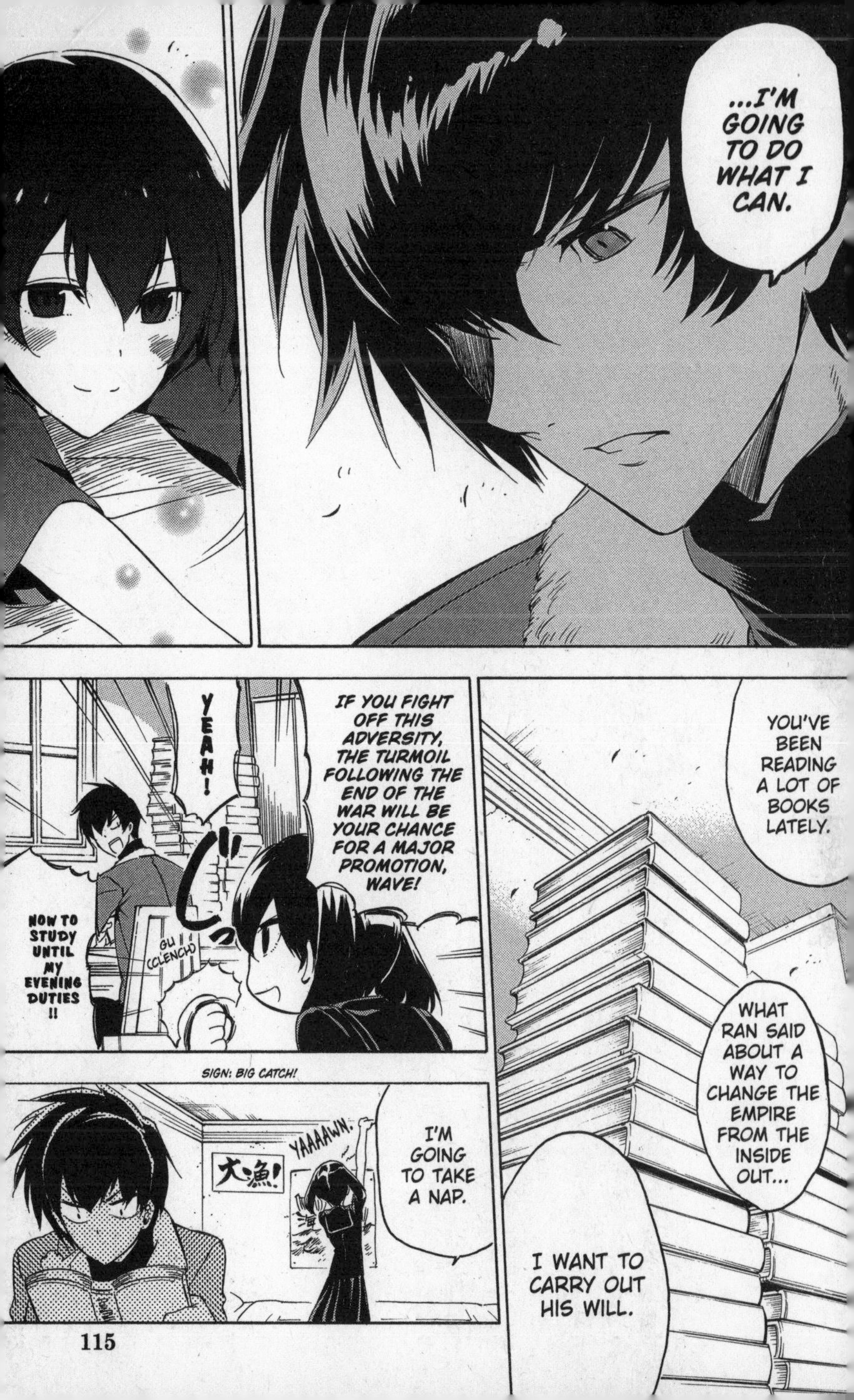
...I'M GOING TO DO WHAT I CAN.
YOU'VE BEEN READING A LOT OF BOOKS LATELY.
WHAT RAN SAID ABOUT A WAY TO CHANGE THE EMPIRE FROM THE INSIDE OUT...
I WANT TO CARRY OUT HIS WILL.
IF YOU FIGHT OFF THIS ADVERSITY, THE TURMOIL FOLLOWING THE END OF THE WAR WILL BE YOUR CHANCE FOR A MAJOR PROMOTION, WAVE!
YEAH!
GU (CLENCH)
NOW TO STUDY UNTIL MY EVENING DUTIES !!
SIGN: BIG CATCH!
I'M GOING TO TAKE A NAP.
YAAAAWN.
大漁!

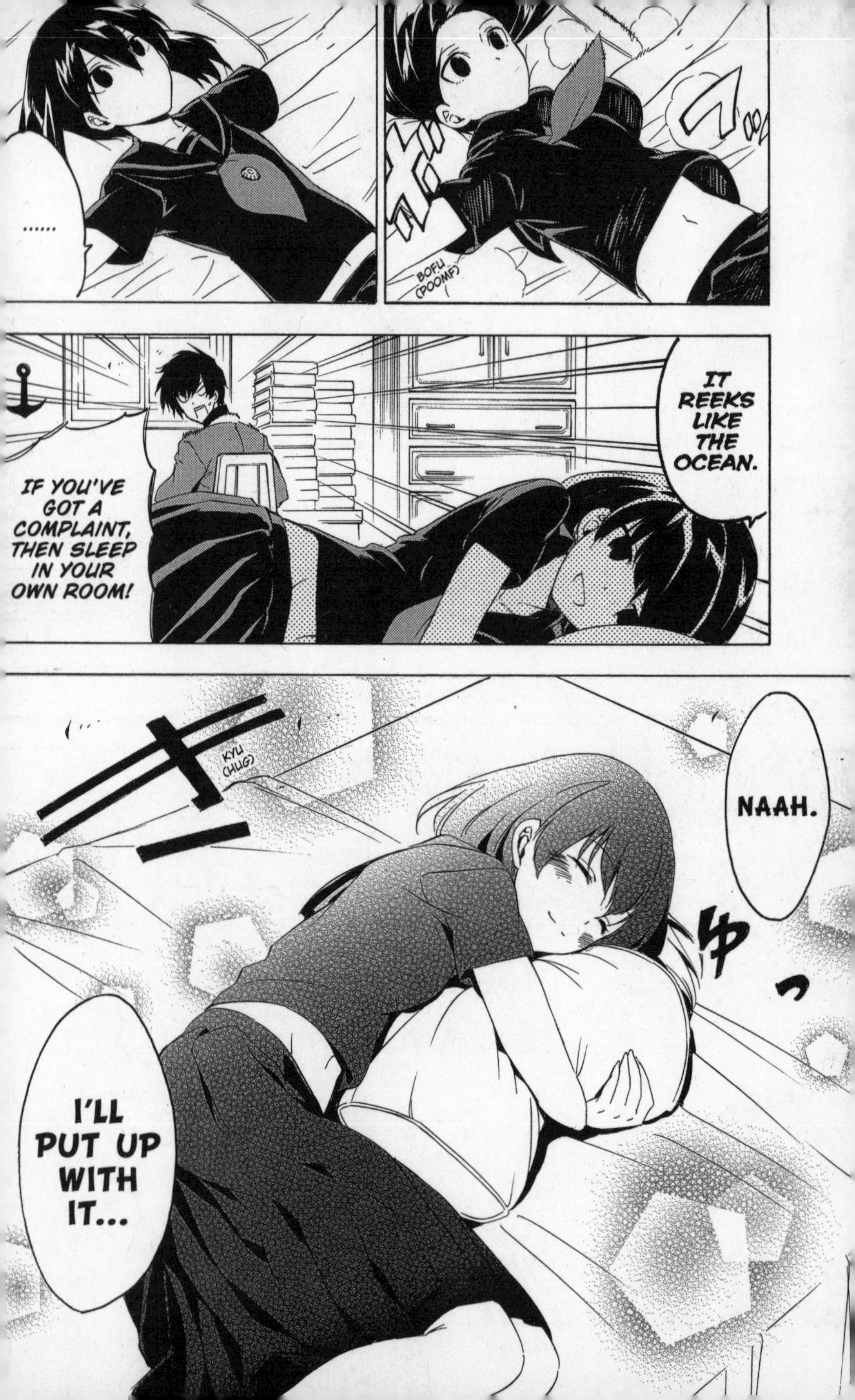

BOFU (POOMF)
......
IT REEKS LIKE THE OCEAN.
IF YOU'VE GOT A COMPLAINT, THEN SLEEP IN YOUR OWN ROOM!
NAAH.
KYU (HUG)
I'LL PUT UP WITH IT...

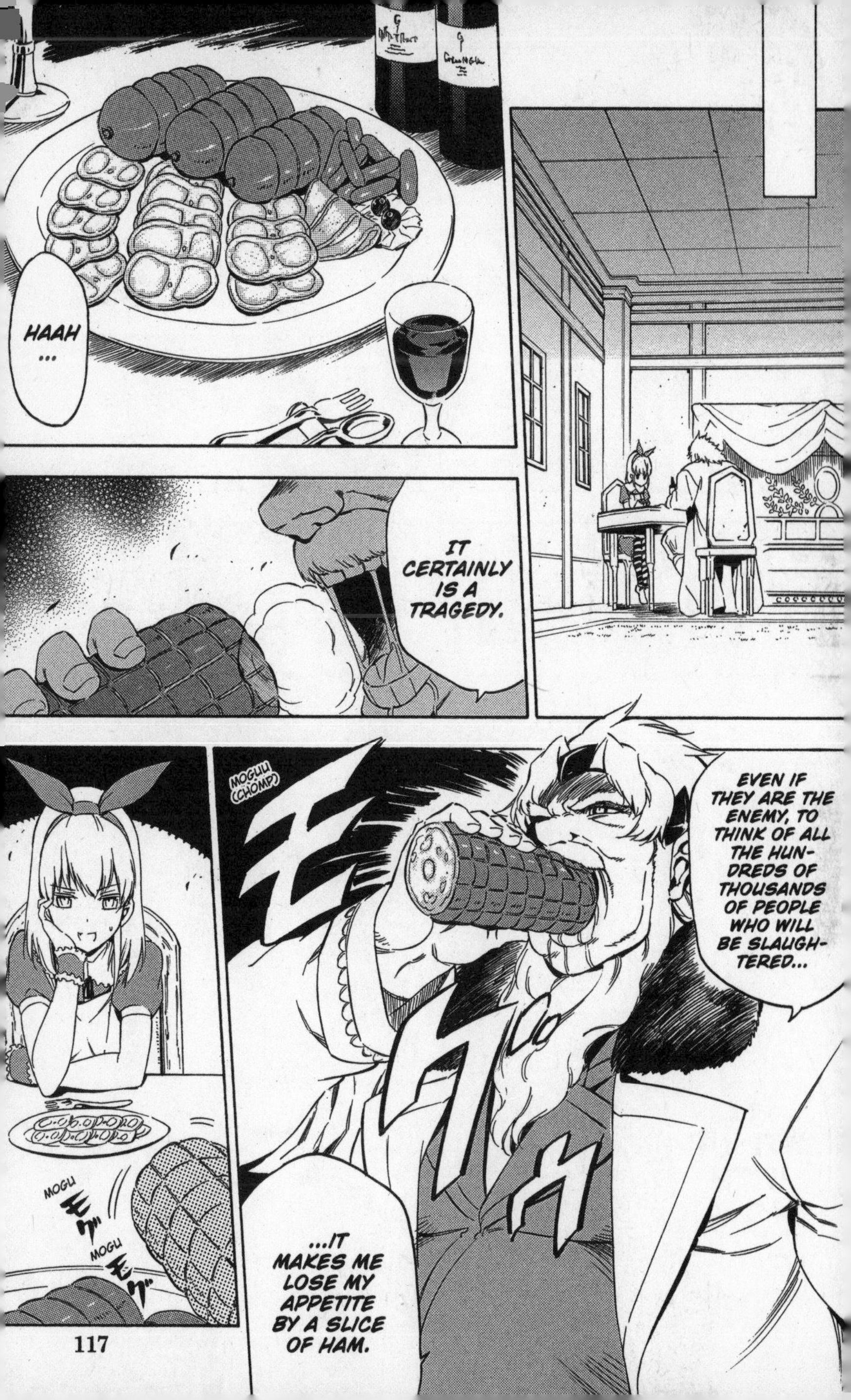
HAAH ...
IT CERTAINLY IS A TRAGEDY.
MOGU (CHOMP)
EVEN IF THEY ARE THE ENEMY, TO THINK OF ALL THE HUNDREDS OF THOUSANDS OF PEOPLE WHO WILL BE SLAUGHTERED...
...IT MAKES ME LOSE MY APPETITE BY A SLICE OF HAM.
MOGU
MOGU

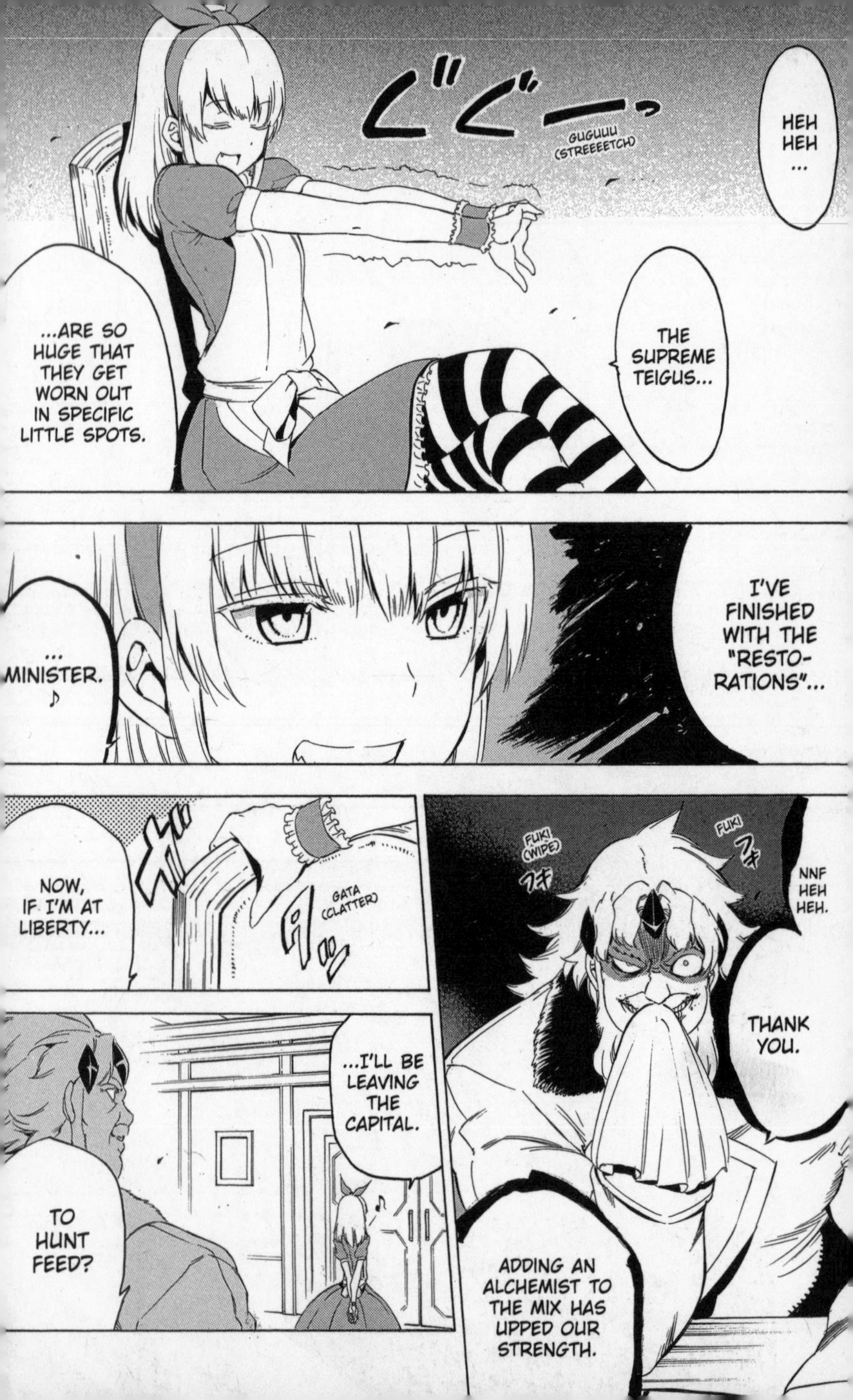
HEH HEH ...
ぐぐーっ
GUGUUU (STREEEETCH)
THE SUPREME TEIGUS...
...ARE SO HUGE THAT THEY GET WORN OUT IN SPECIFIC LITTLE SPOTS.
I'VE FINISHED WITH THE "RESTO-RATIONS"...
... MINISTER. ♪
FUKI
FUKI (WIPE)
NNF HEH HEH.
THANK YOU.
ADDING AN ALCHEMIST TO THE MIX HAS UPPED OUR STRENGTH.
GATA (CLATTER)
NOW, IF I'M AT LIBERTY...
...I'LL BE LEAVING THE CAPITAL.
TO HUNT FEED?

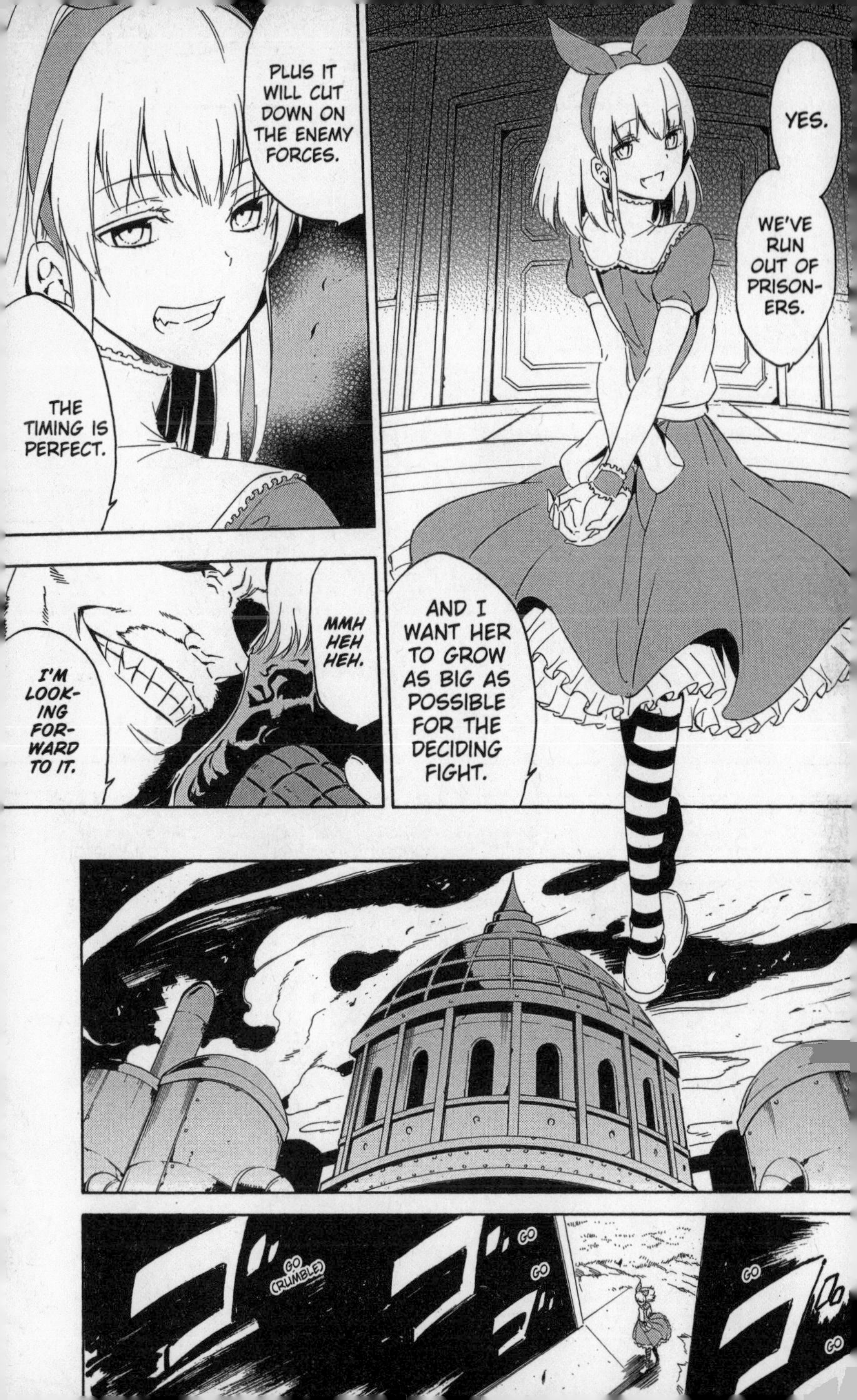
YES.
WE'VE RUN OUT OF PRISON-ERS.
PLUS IT WILL CUT DOWN ON THE ENEMY FORCES.
THE TIMING IS PERFECT.
AND I WANT HER TO GROW AS BIG AS POSSIBLE FOR THE DECIDING FIGHT.
MMH HEH HEH.
I'M LOOK-ING FOR-WARD TO IT.
GO
GO
GO
GO
GO (RUMBLE)

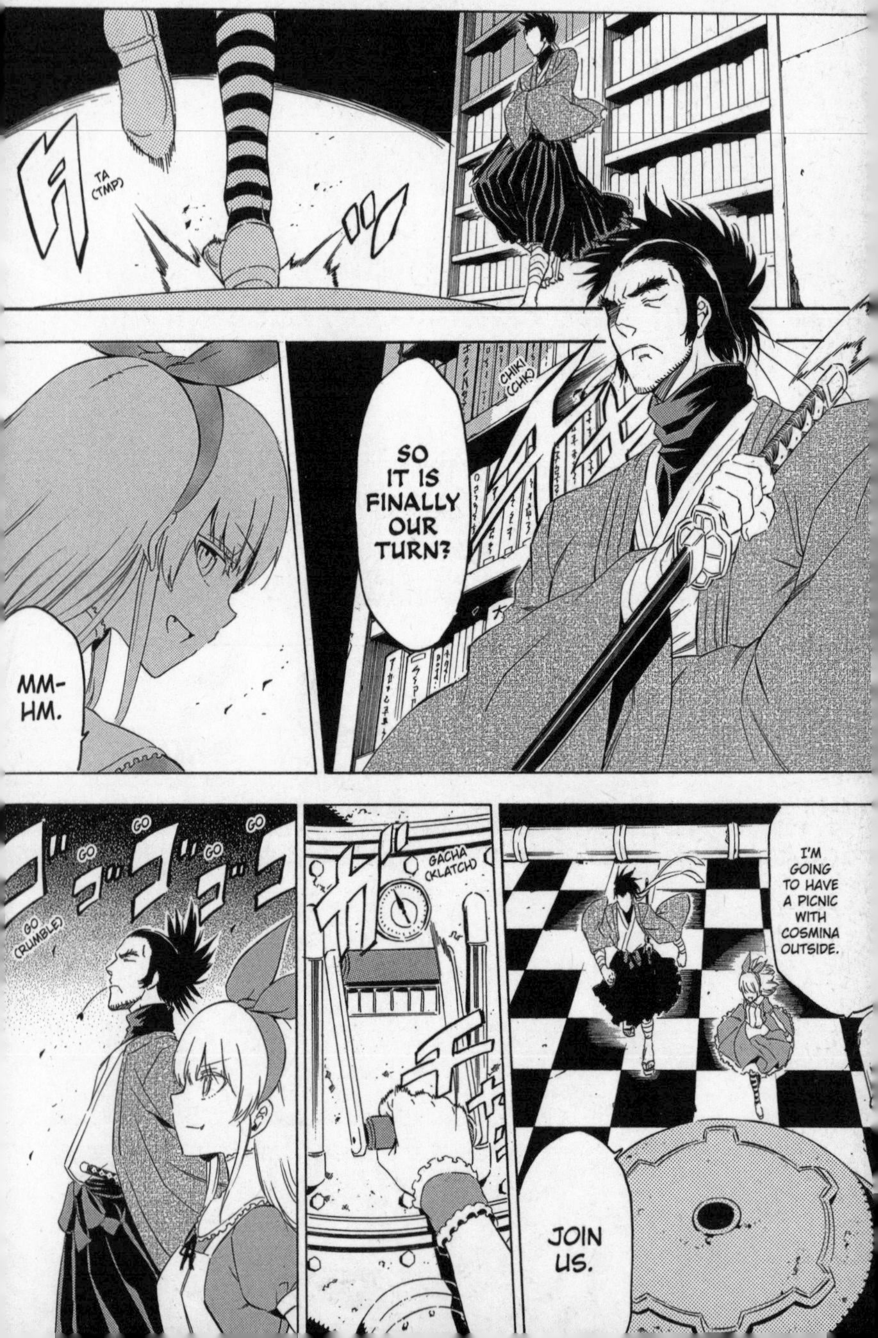
TA (TMP)
CHIKI (CHK)
SO IT IS FINALLY OUR TURN?
MM-HM.
I'M GOING TO HAVE A PICNIC WITH COSMINA OUTSIDE.
JOIN US.
GACHA (KLATCH)
GO GO GO GO (RUMBLE)

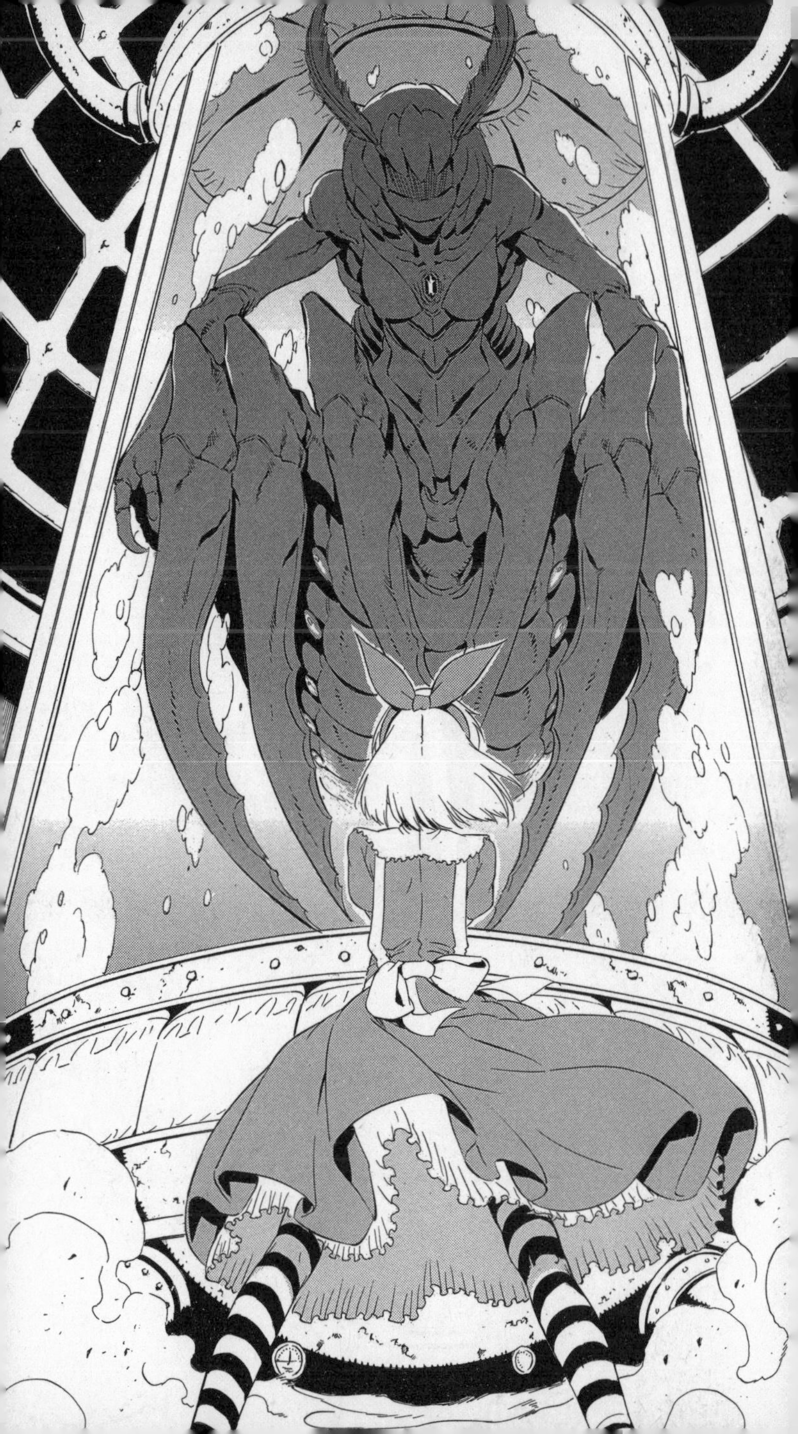

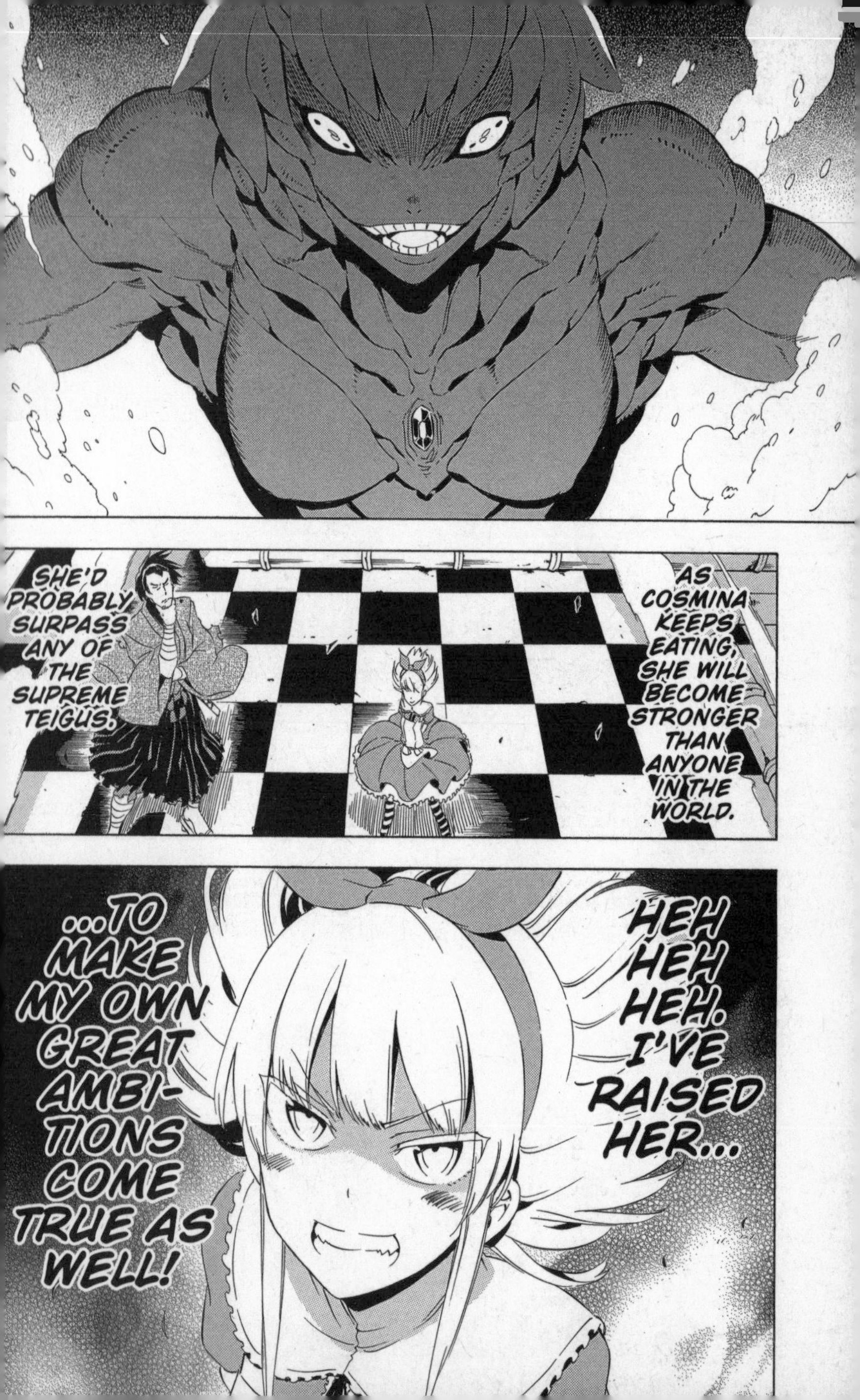
AS COSMINA KEEPS EATING, SHE WILL BECOME STRONGER THAN ANYONE IN THE WORLD.
SHE'D PROBABLY SURPASS ANY OF THE SUPREME TEIGUS.
HEH HEH HEH. I'VE RAISED HER...
...TO MAKE MY OWN GREAT AMBITIONS COME TRUE AS WELL!

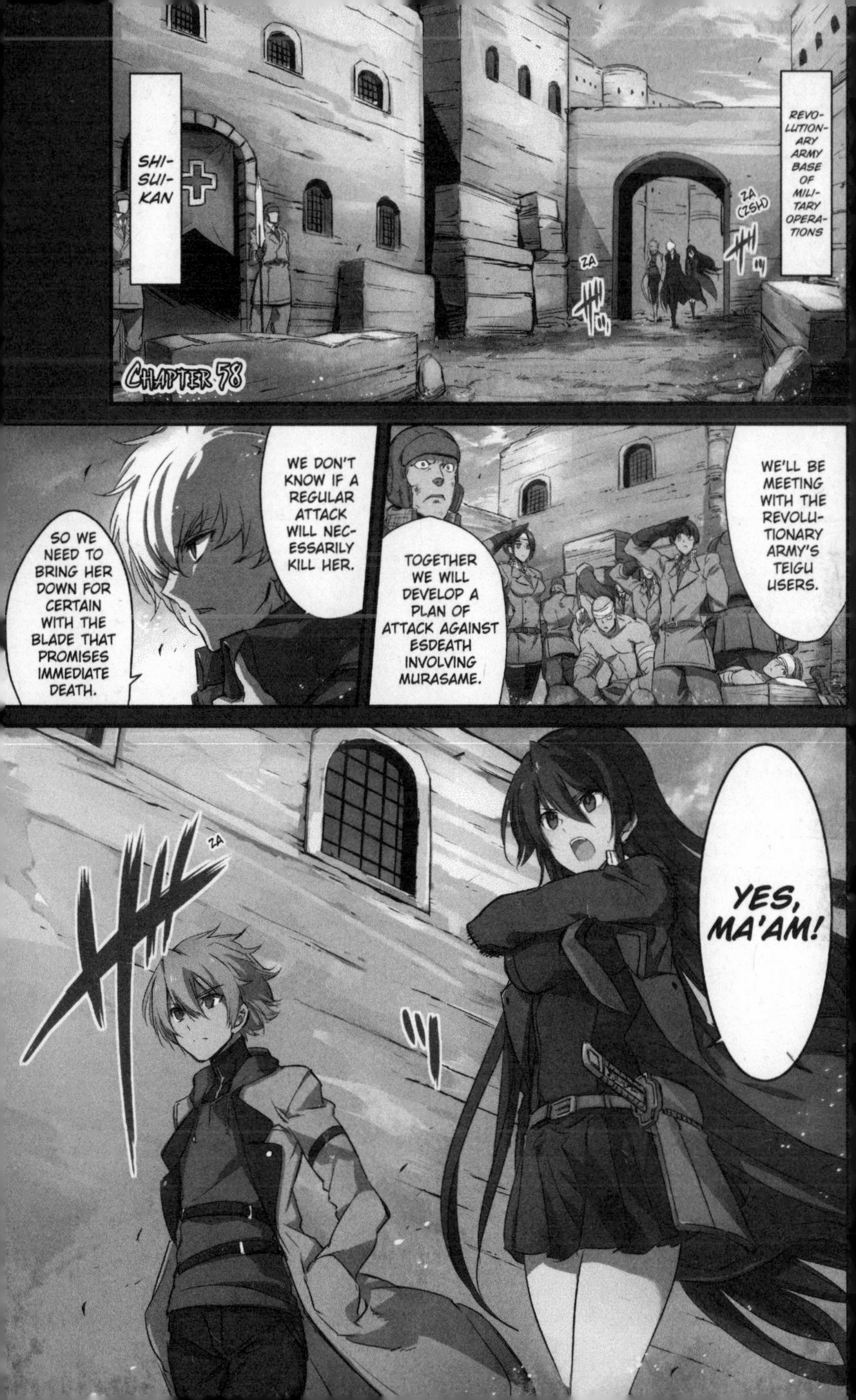
REVOLUTIONARY ARMY BASE OF MILITARY OPERATIONS
ZA (ZSH)
ZA
SHISUIKAN
CHAPTER 58
WE'LL BE MEETING WITH THE REVOLUTIONARY ARMY'S TEIGU USERS.
TOGETHER WE WILL DEVELOP A PLAN OF ATTACK AGAINST ESDEATH INVOLVING MURASAME.
WE DON'T KNOW IF A REGULAR ATTACK WILL NECESSARILY KILL HER.
SO WE NEED TO BRING HER DOWN FOR CERTAIN WITH THE BLADE THAT PROMISES IMMEDIATE DEATH.
YES, MA'AM!
ZA

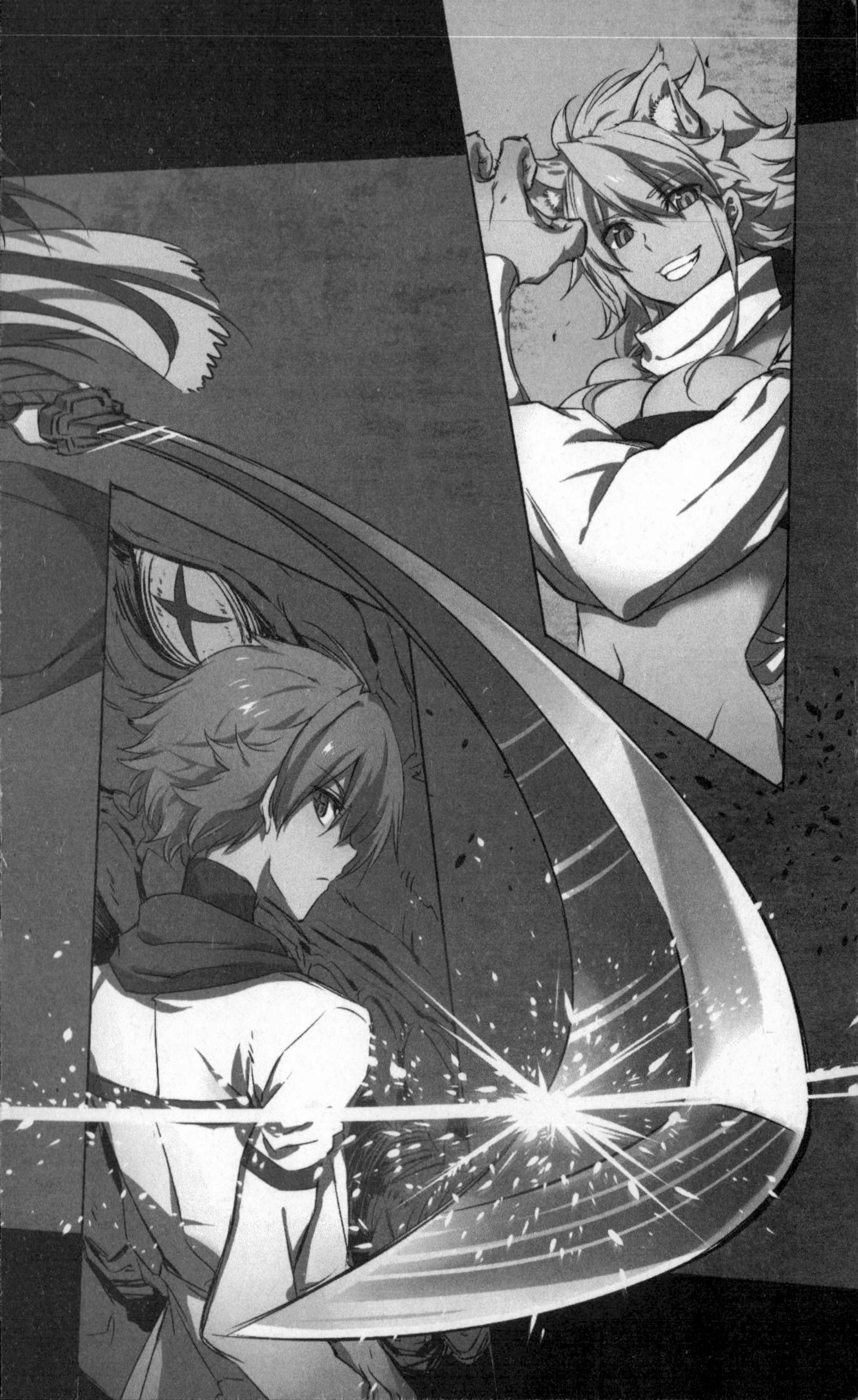

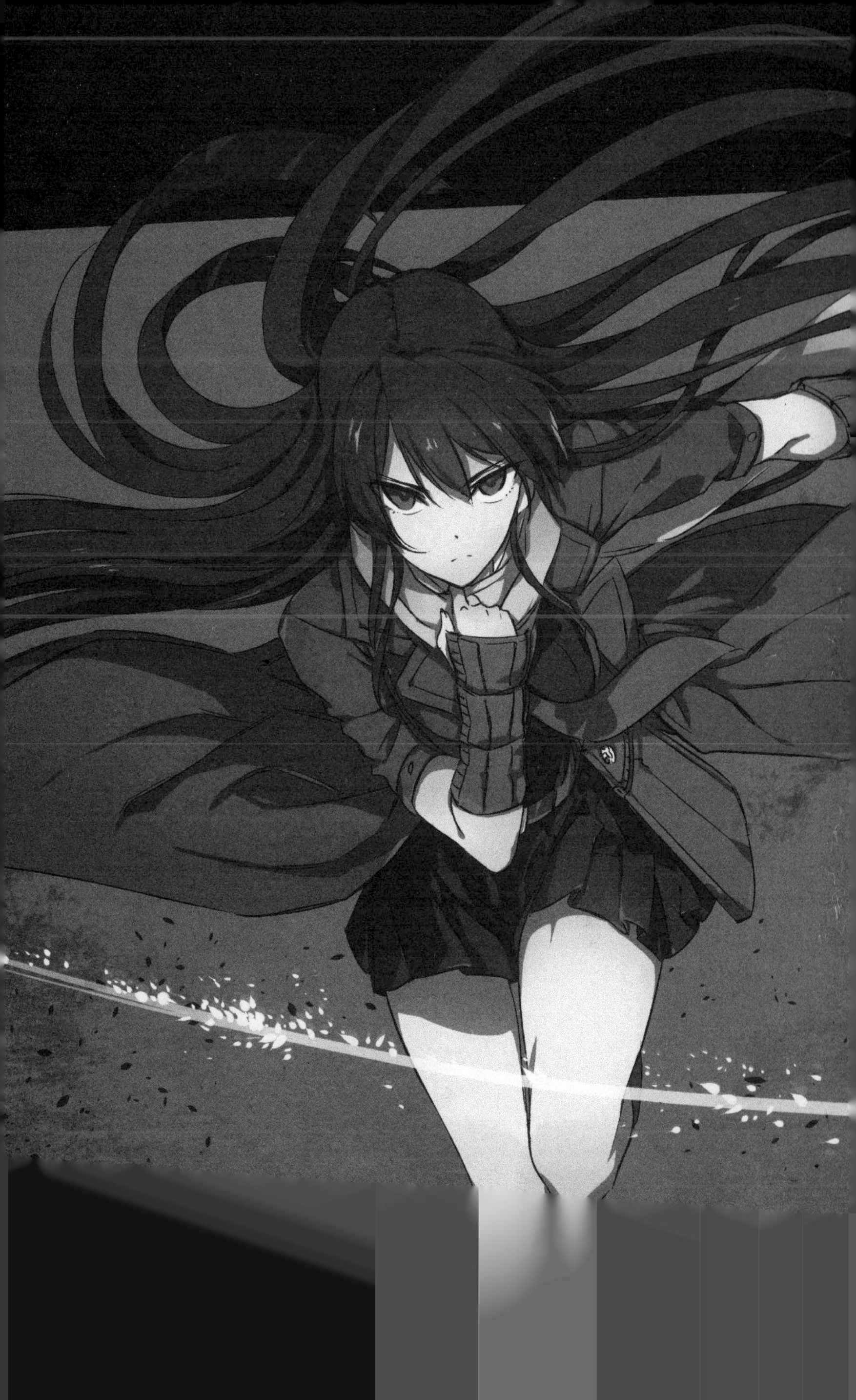

REV-
OLU-
TION-
ARY
ARMY
CAMP

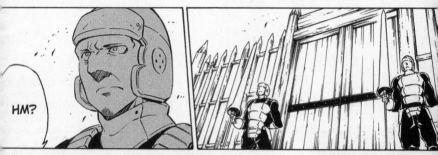

HM?

SFX: ZA (ZSH) ZA ZA ZA ZA ZA

HEY.

IS THERE
SOMETHING
HEADING
THIS WAY?

WHAT
!?

126

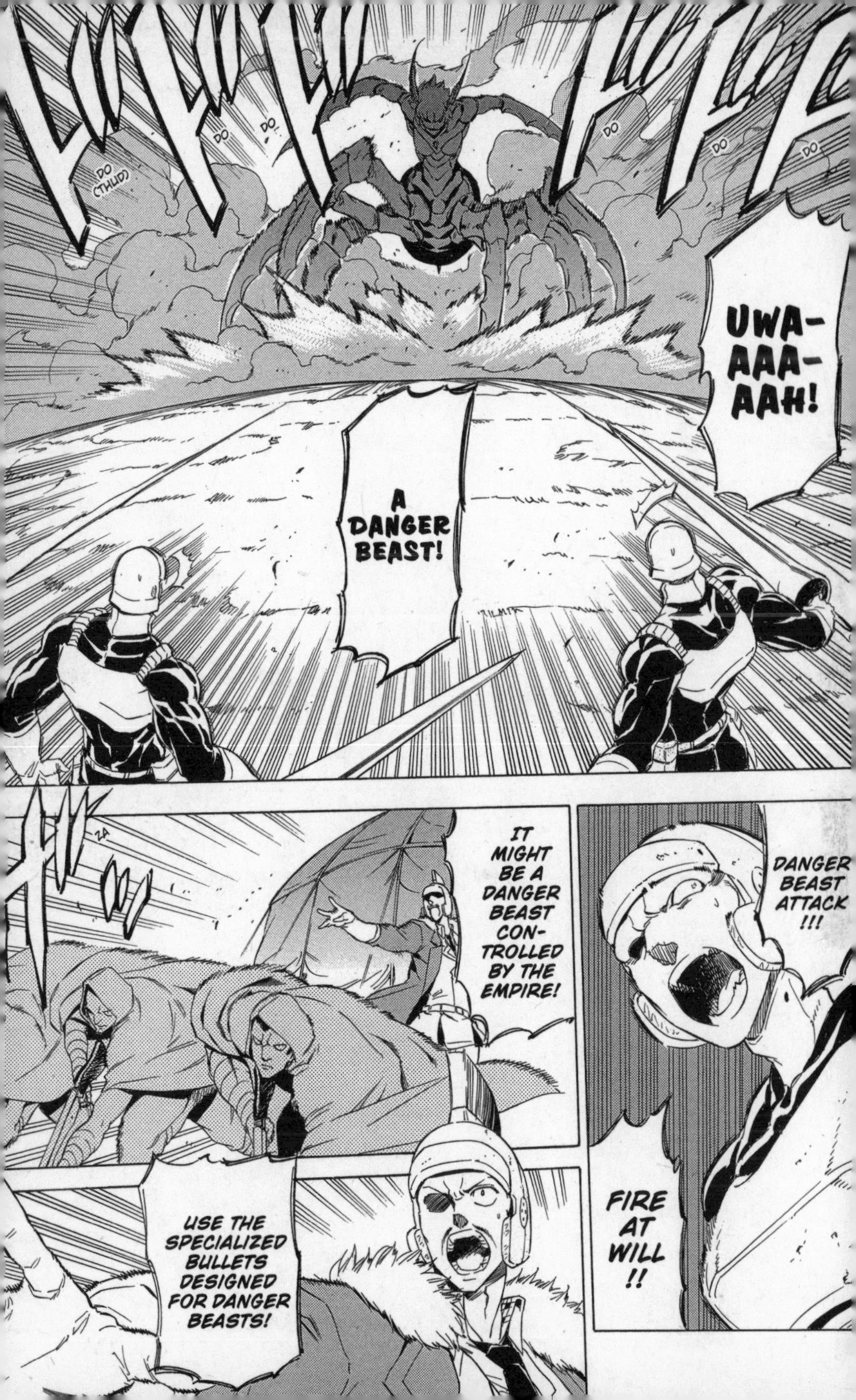
DO
DO
DO
UWA-AAA-AAH!
A DANGER BEAST!
DO
DO
DO (THUD)
DANGER BEAST ATTACK!!!
IT MIGHT BE A DANGER BEAST CONTROLLED BY THE EMPIRE!
ZA
FIRE AT WILL!!
USE THE SPECIALIZED BULLETS DESIGNED FOR DANGER BEASTS!

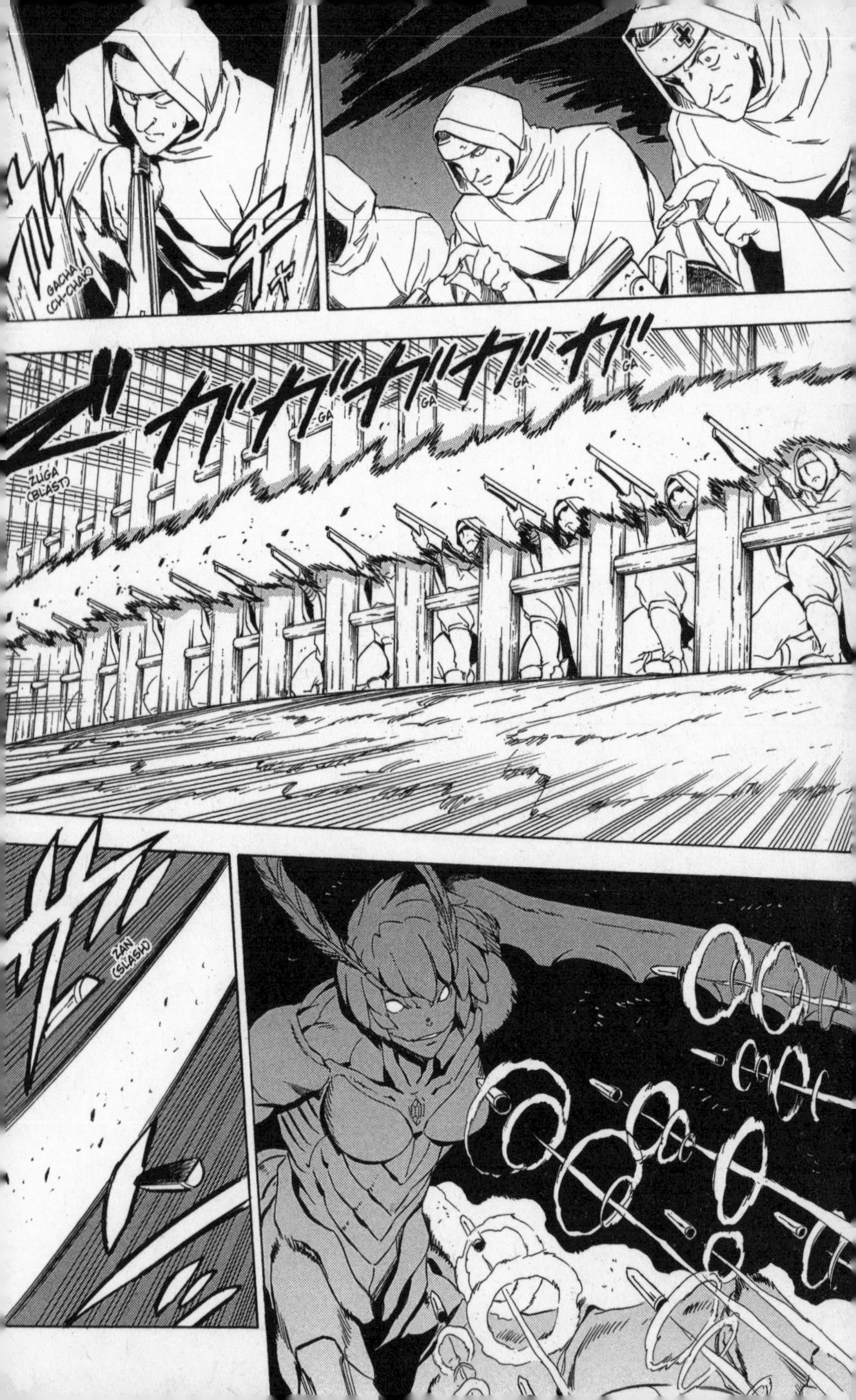
GACHA (CH-CHAK)
ZUGA (BLAST)
GA
GA
GA
GA
ZAN (SLASH)

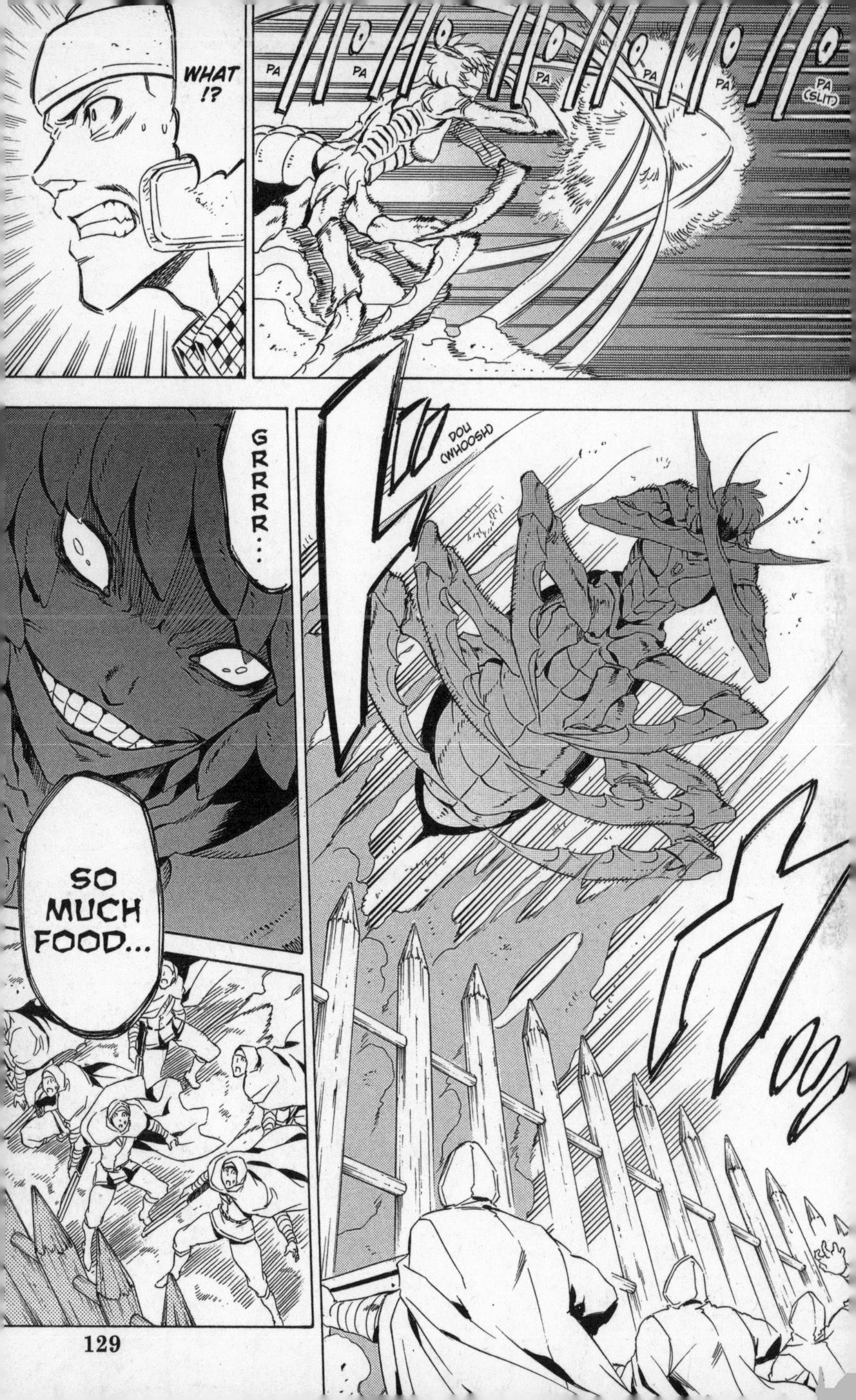
PA
PA
PA
PA
PA
PA (SLIT)
WHAT!?
DOU (WHOOSH)
GRRRR...
SO MUCH FOOD...

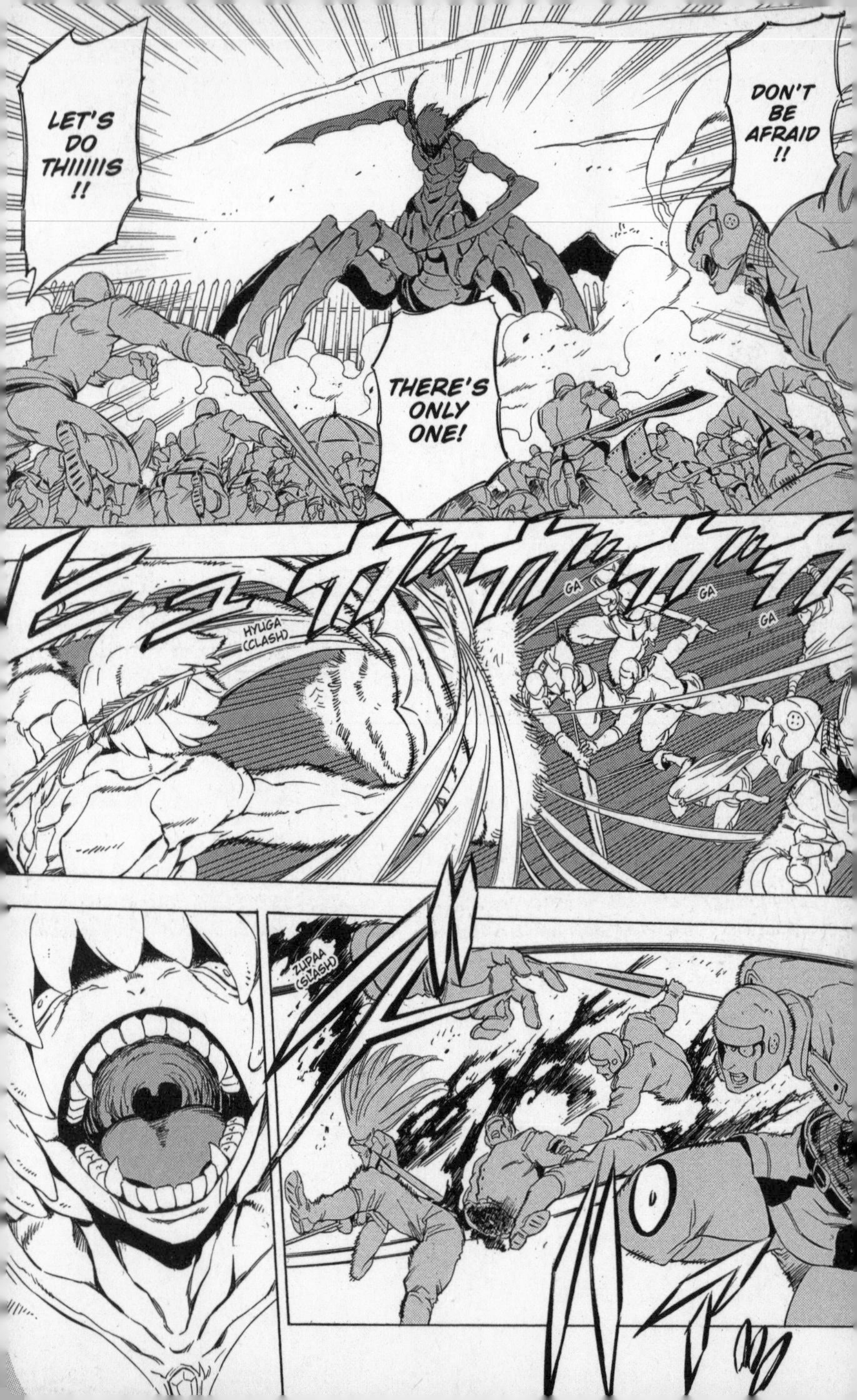
DON'T BE AFRAID !!
LET'S DO THIIIIIS !!
THERE'S ONLY ONE!
GA
GA
GA
HYUGA (CLASH)
ZUPAA (SLASH)

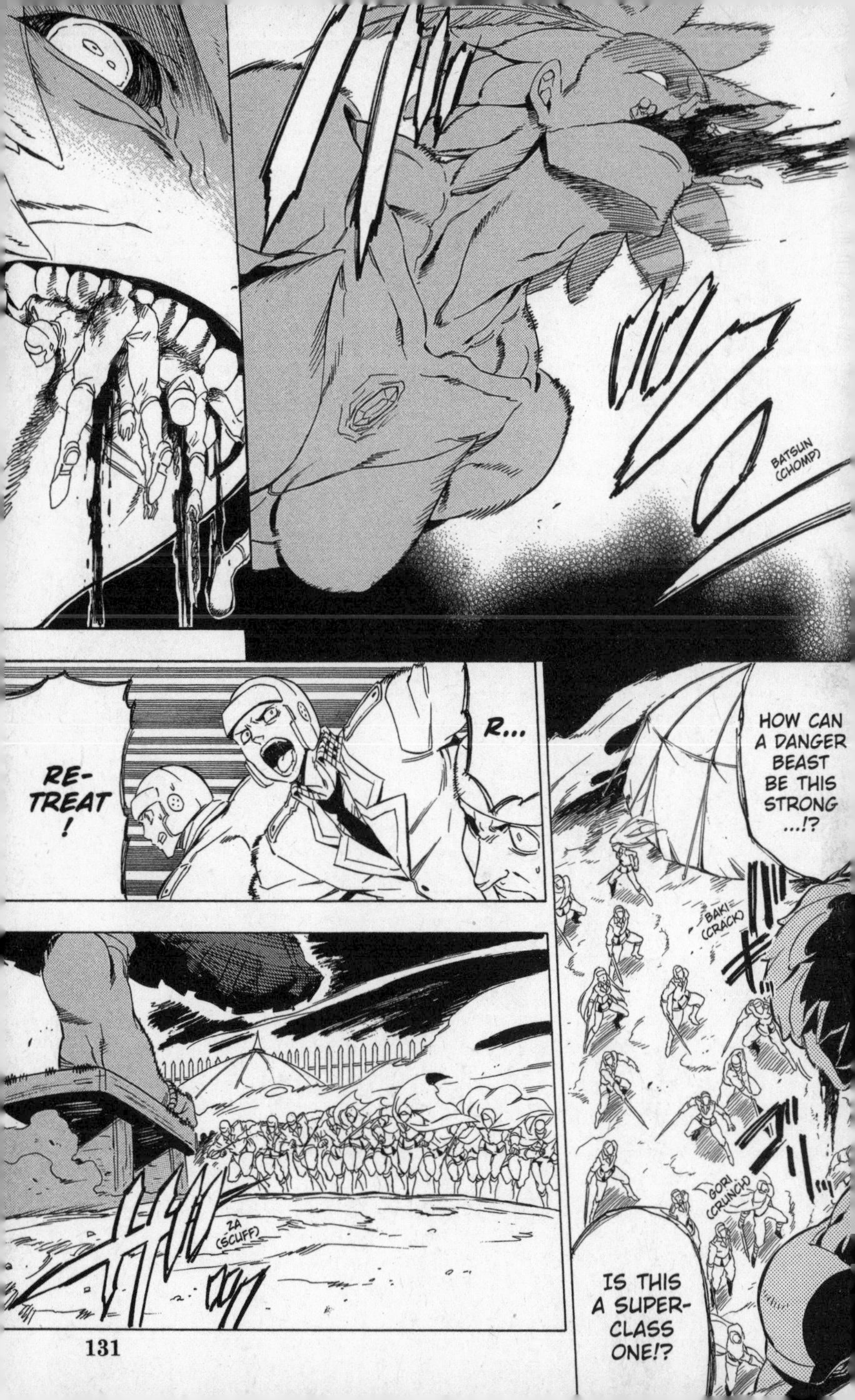
BATSUN (CHOMP)
HOW CAN A DANGER BEAST BE THIS STRONG ...!?
R...
RE-TREAT!
BAKI (CRACK)
GORI (CRUNCH)
IS THIS A SUPER-CLASS ONE!?
ZA (SCUFF)

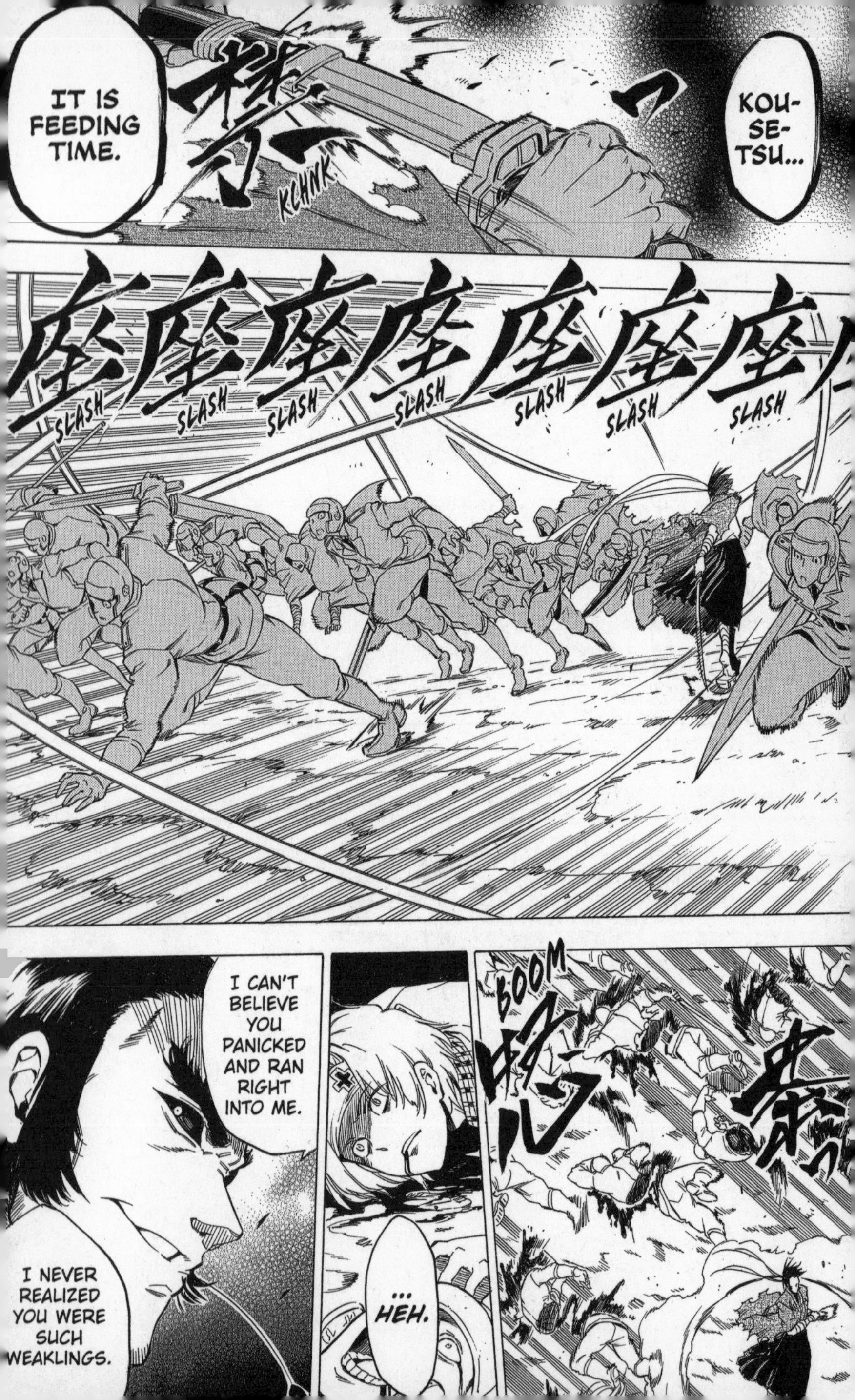
KOU-SE-TSU...
IT IS FEEDING TIME.
KCHNK
SLASH
SLASH
SLASH
SLASH
SLASH
SLASH
SLASH
BOOM
I CAN'T BELIEVE YOU PANICKED AND RAN RIGHT INTO ME.
...HEH.
I NEVER REALIZED YOU WERE SUCH WEAKLINGS.

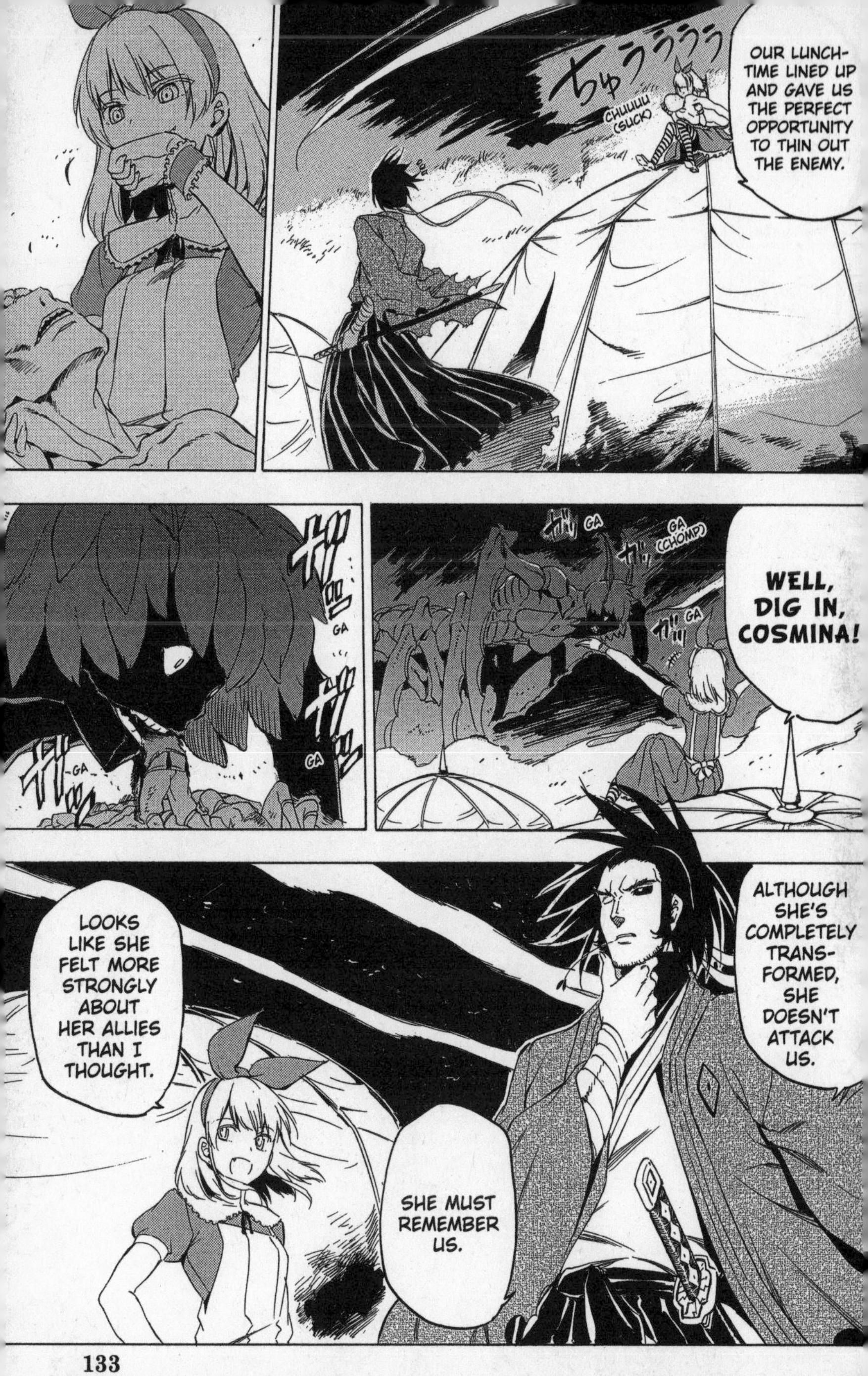

OUR LUNCH-TIME LINED UP AND GAVE US THE PERFECT OPPORTUNITY TO THIN OUT THE ENEMY.
CHUUUUU (SUCK)
GA
GA (CHOMP)
GA
WELL, DIG IN, COSMINA!
GA
GA
GA
ALTHOUGH SHE'S COMPLETELY TRANS-FORMED, SHE DOESN'T ATTACK US.
SHE MUST REMEMBER US.
LOOKS LIKE SHE FELT MORE STRONGLY ABOUT HER ALLIES THAN I THOUGHT.

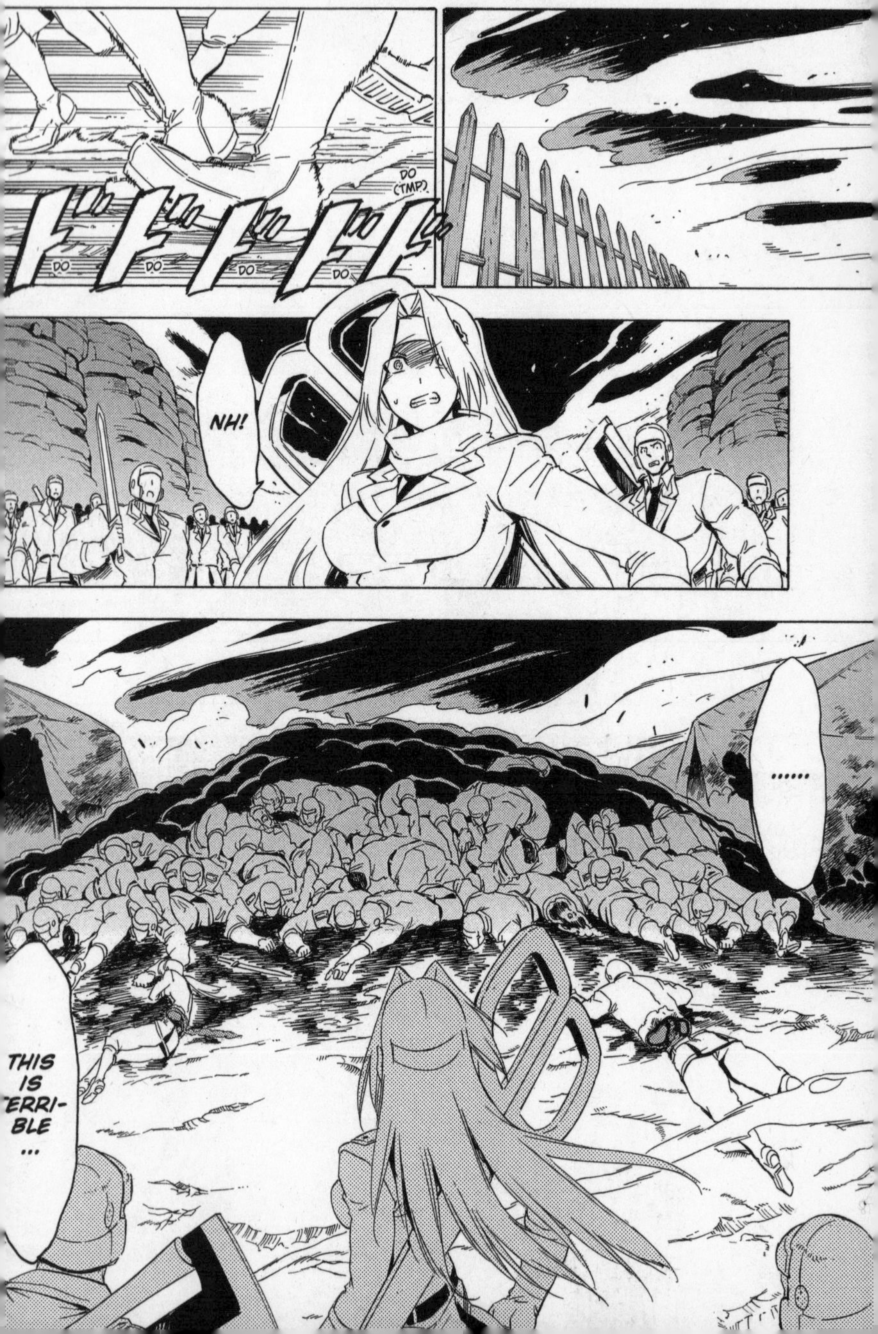
DO (TMP)
DO
DO
DO
DO
NH!
......
THIS IS TERRIBLE...

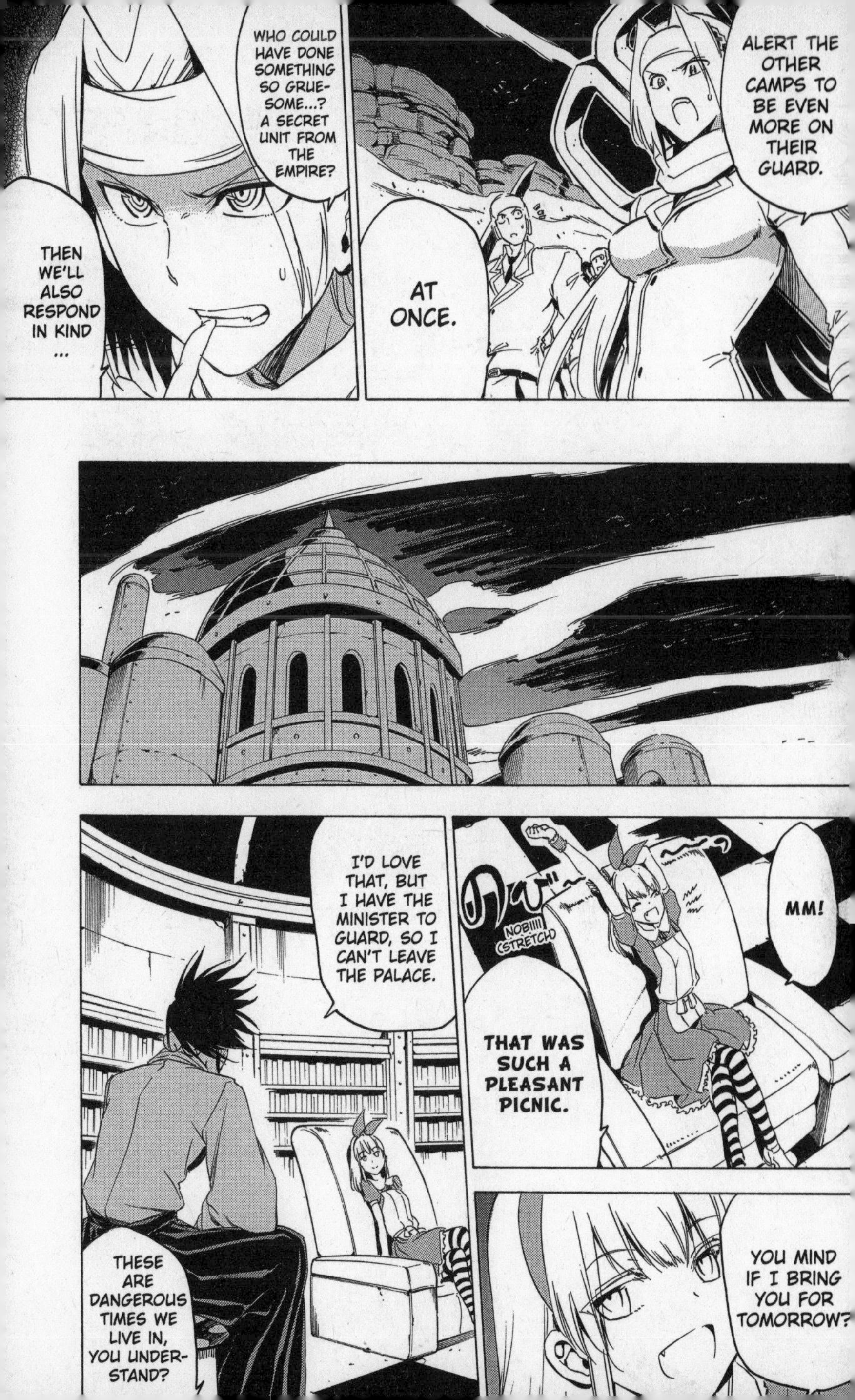
ALERT THE OTHER CAMPS TO BE EVEN MORE ON THEIR GUARD.
AT ONCE.
WHO COULD HAVE DONE SOMETHING SO GRUE-SOME...? A SECRET UNIT FROM THE EMPIRE?
THEN WE'LL ALSO RESPOND IN KIND...
MM!
NOBIIII (STRETCH)
THAT WAS SUCH A PLEASANT PICNIC.
YOU MIND IF I BRING YOU FOR TOMORROW?
I'D LOVE THAT, BUT I HAVE THE MINISTER TO GUARD, SO I CAN'T LEAVE THE PALACE.
THESE ARE DANGEROUS TIMES WE LIVE IN, YOU UNDER-STAND?

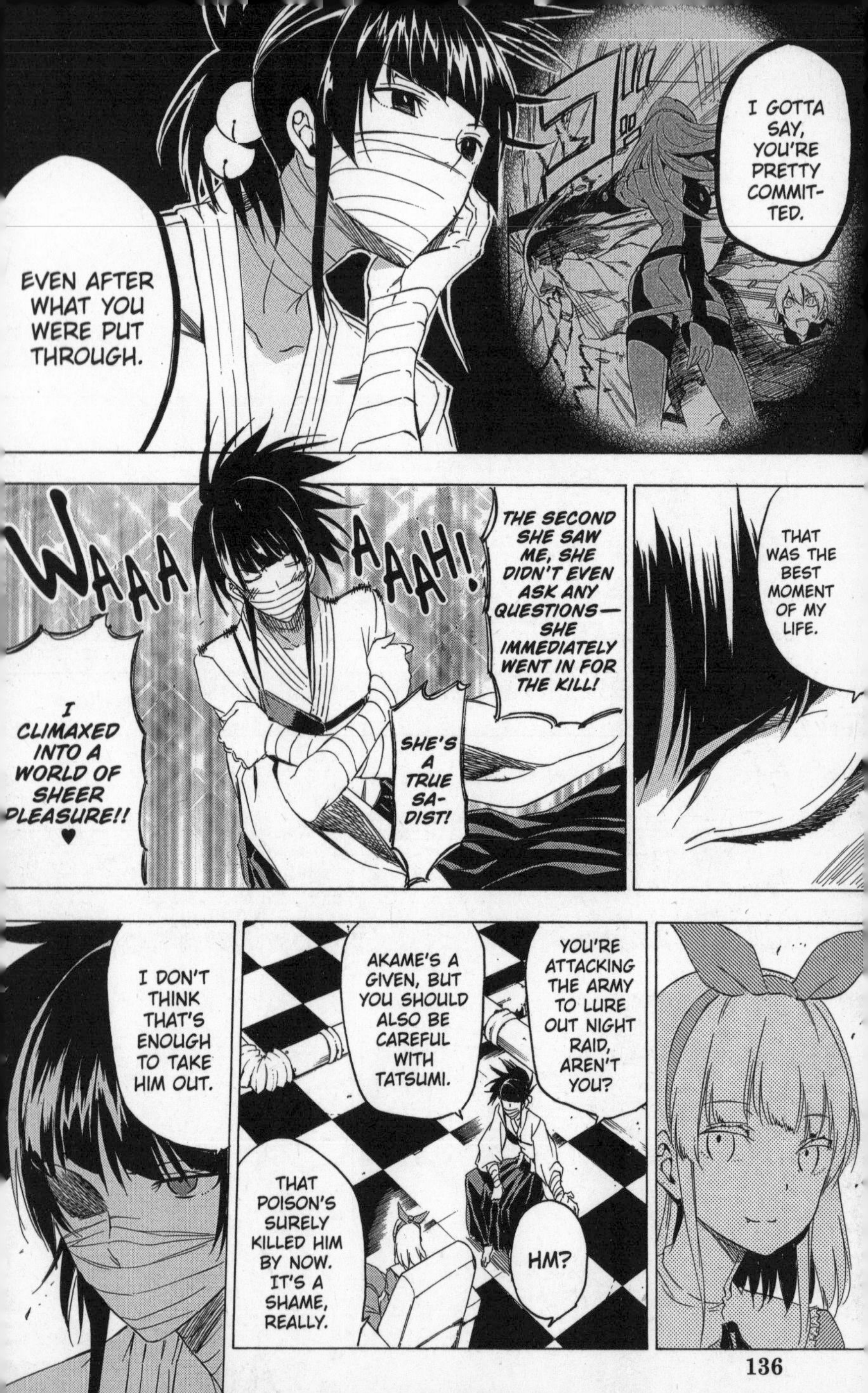
I GOTTA SAY, YOU'RE PRETTY COMMIT- TED.
EVEN AFTER WHAT YOU WERE PUT THROUGH.
THAT WAS THE BEST MOMENT OF MY LIFE.
THE SECOND SHE SAW ME, SHE DIDN'T EVEN ASK ANY QUESTIONS— SHE IMMEDIATELY WENT IN FOR THE KILL!
SHE'S A TRUE SA- DIST!
WAAAAAAH!
I CLIMAXED INTO A WORLD OF SHEER PLEASURE!! ♥
YOU'RE ATTACKING THE ARMY TO LURE OUT NIGHT RAID, AREN'T YOU?
HM?
AKAME'S A GIVEN, BUT YOU SHOULD ALSO BE CAREFUL WITH TATSUMI.
THAT POISON'S SURELY KILLED HIM BY NOW. IT'S A SHAME, REALLY.
I DON'T THINK THAT'S ENOUGH TO TAKE HIM OUT.

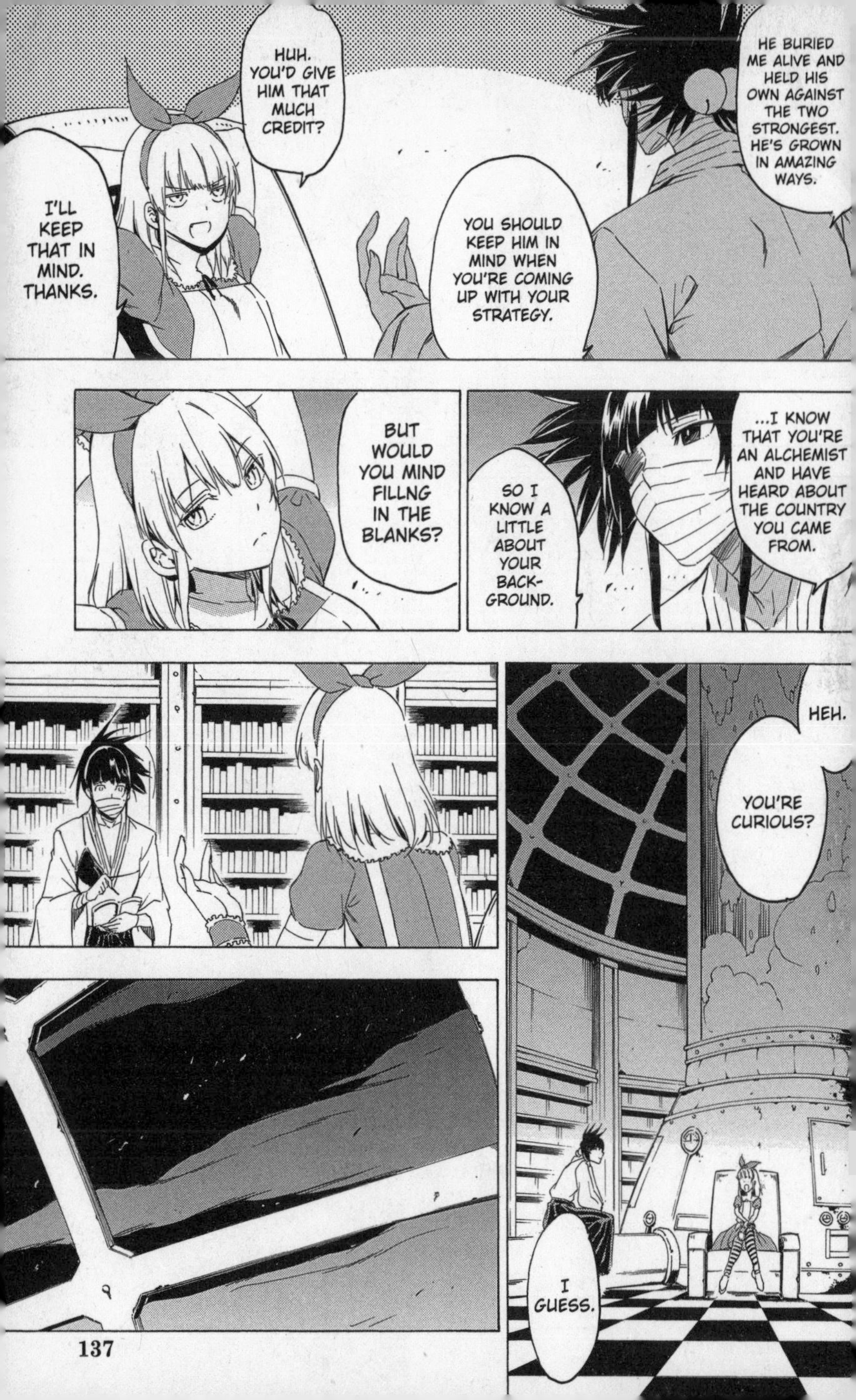
HE BURIED ME ALIVE AND HELD HIS OWN AGAINST THE TWO STRONGEST. HE'S GROWN IN AMAZING WAYS.
YOU SHOULD KEEP HIM IN MIND WHEN YOU'RE COMING UP WITH YOUR STRATEGY.
HUH. YOU'D GIVE HIM THAT MUCH CREDIT?
I'LL KEEP THAT IN MIND. THANKS.
...I KNOW THAT YOU'RE AN ALCHEMIST AND HAVE HEARD ABOUT THE COUNTRY YOU CAME FROM.
SO I KNOW A LITTLE ABOUT YOUR BACK-GROUND.
BUT WOULD YOU MIND FILLNG IN THE BLANKS?
HEH.
YOU'RE CURIOUS?
I GUESS.

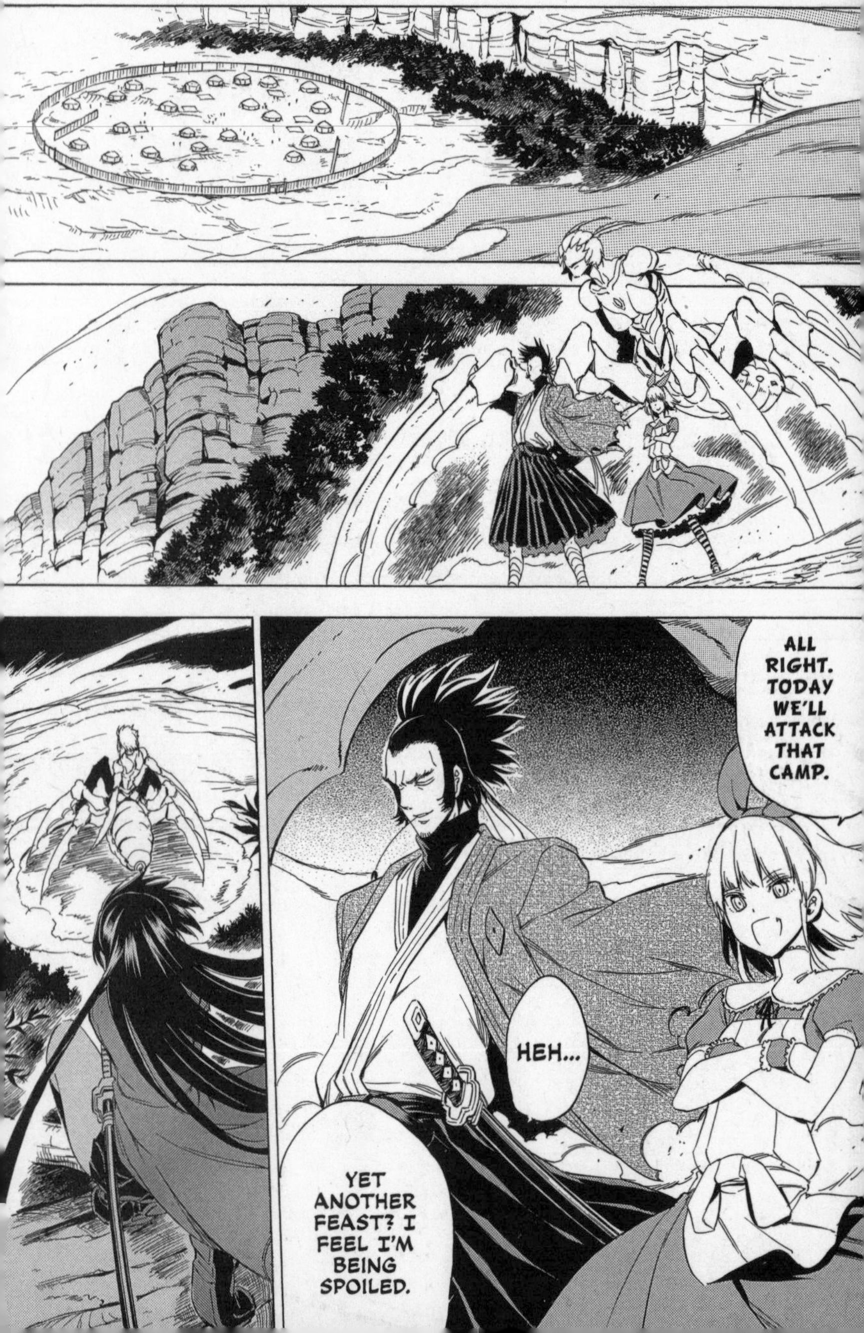
ALL RIGHT. TODAY WE'LL ATTACK THAT CAMP.
HEH...
YET ANOTHER FEAST? I FEEL I'M BEING SPOILED.

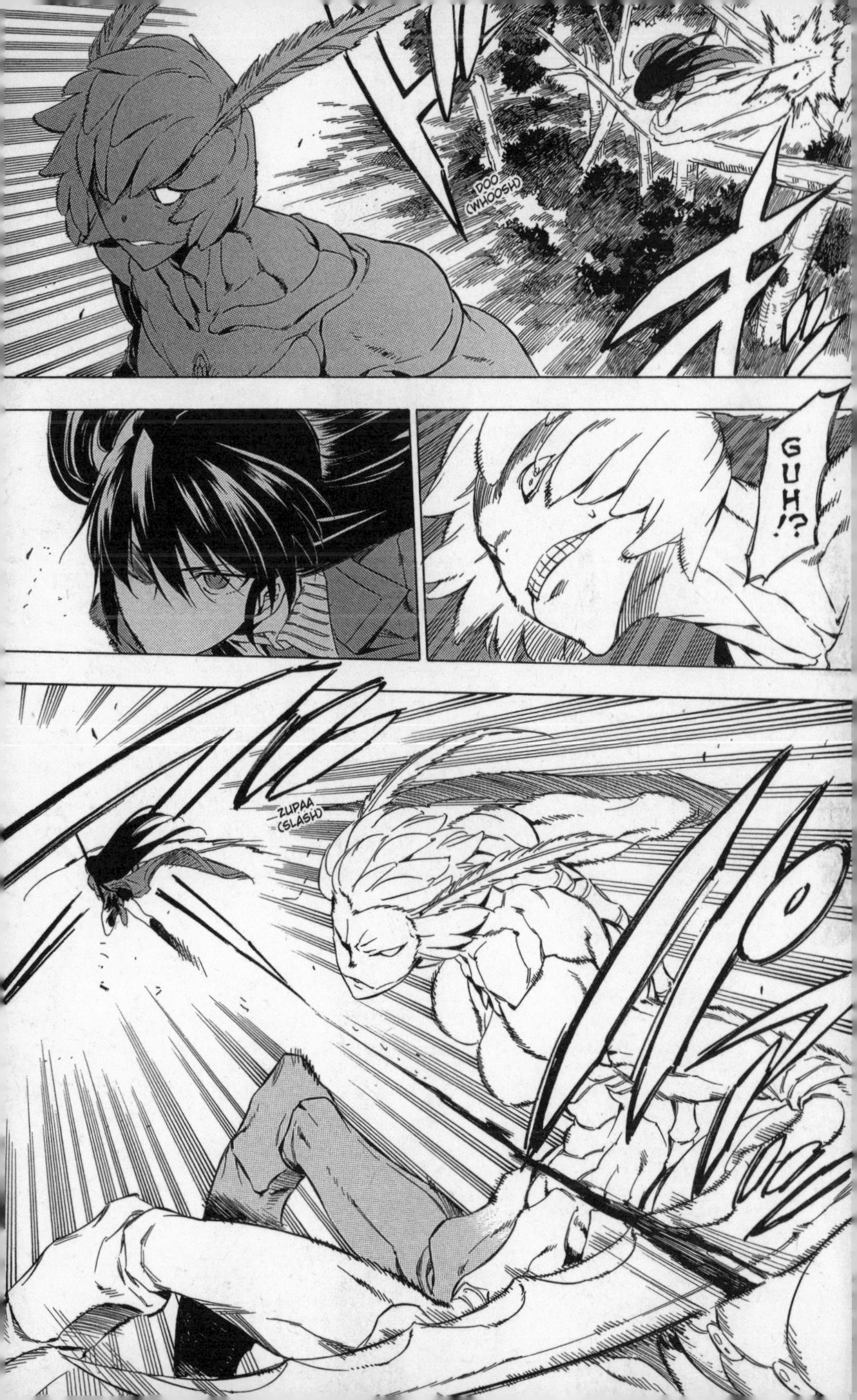
DOO
(WHOOSH)
GUH!?
ZUPAA
(SLASH)

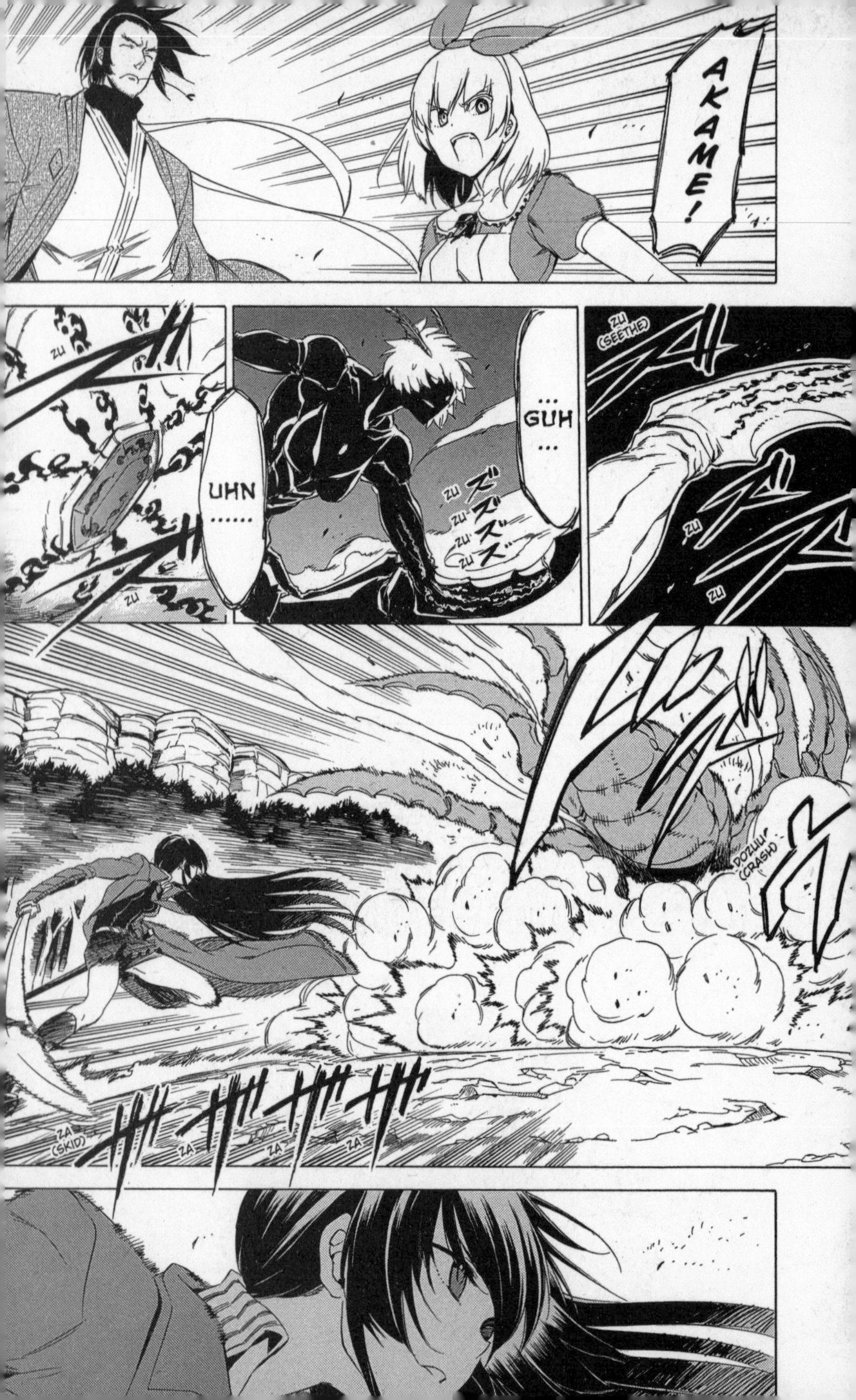
AKAME!
ZU (SEETHE)
ZU
ZU
... GUH ...
UHN ......
ズズズズ
ZU ZU ZU ZU
ZU
ZU
DOZUU (CRASH)
ZA (SKID)
ZA
ZA
ZA

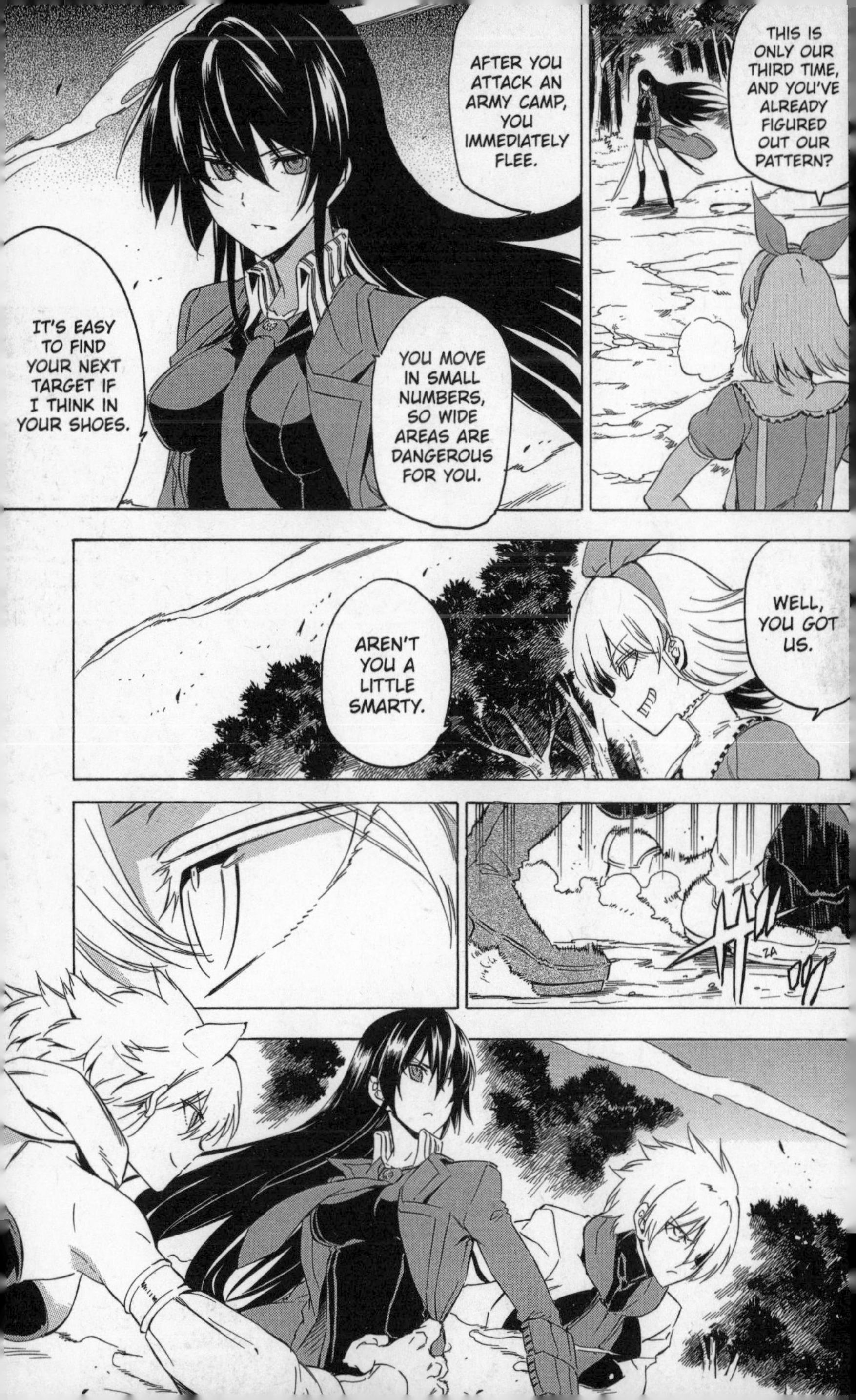
THIS IS ONLY OUR THIRD TIME, AND YOU'VE ALREADY FIGURED OUT OUR PATTERN?
AFTER YOU ATTACK AN ARMY CAMP, YOU IMMEDIATELY FLEE.
YOU MOVE IN SMALL NUMBERS, SO WIDE AREAS ARE DANGEROUS FOR YOU.
IT'S EASY TO FIND YOUR NEXT TARGET IF I THINK IN YOUR SHOES.
WELL, YOU GOT US.
AREN'T YOU A LITTLE SMARTY.
ZA

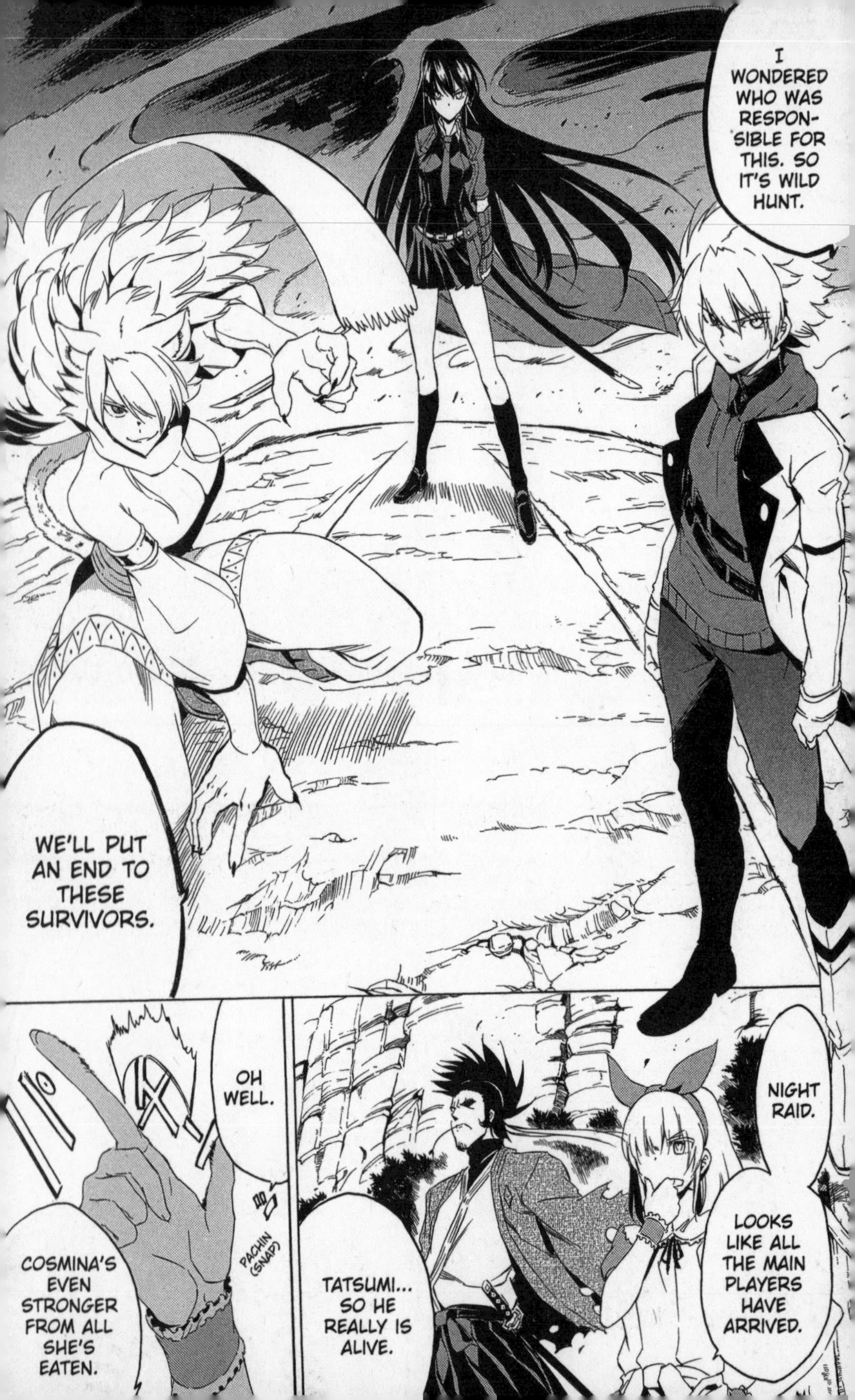
I WONDERED WHO WAS RESPONSIBLE FOR THIS. SO IT'S WILD HUNT.
WE'LL PUT AN END TO THESE SURVIVORS.
NIGHT RAID.
LOOKS LIKE ALL THE MAIN PLAYERS HAVE ARRIVED.
TATSUMI... SO HE REALLY IS ALIVE.
OH WELL.
PACHIN (SNAP)
COSMINA'S EVEN STRONGER FROM ALL SHE'S EATEN.

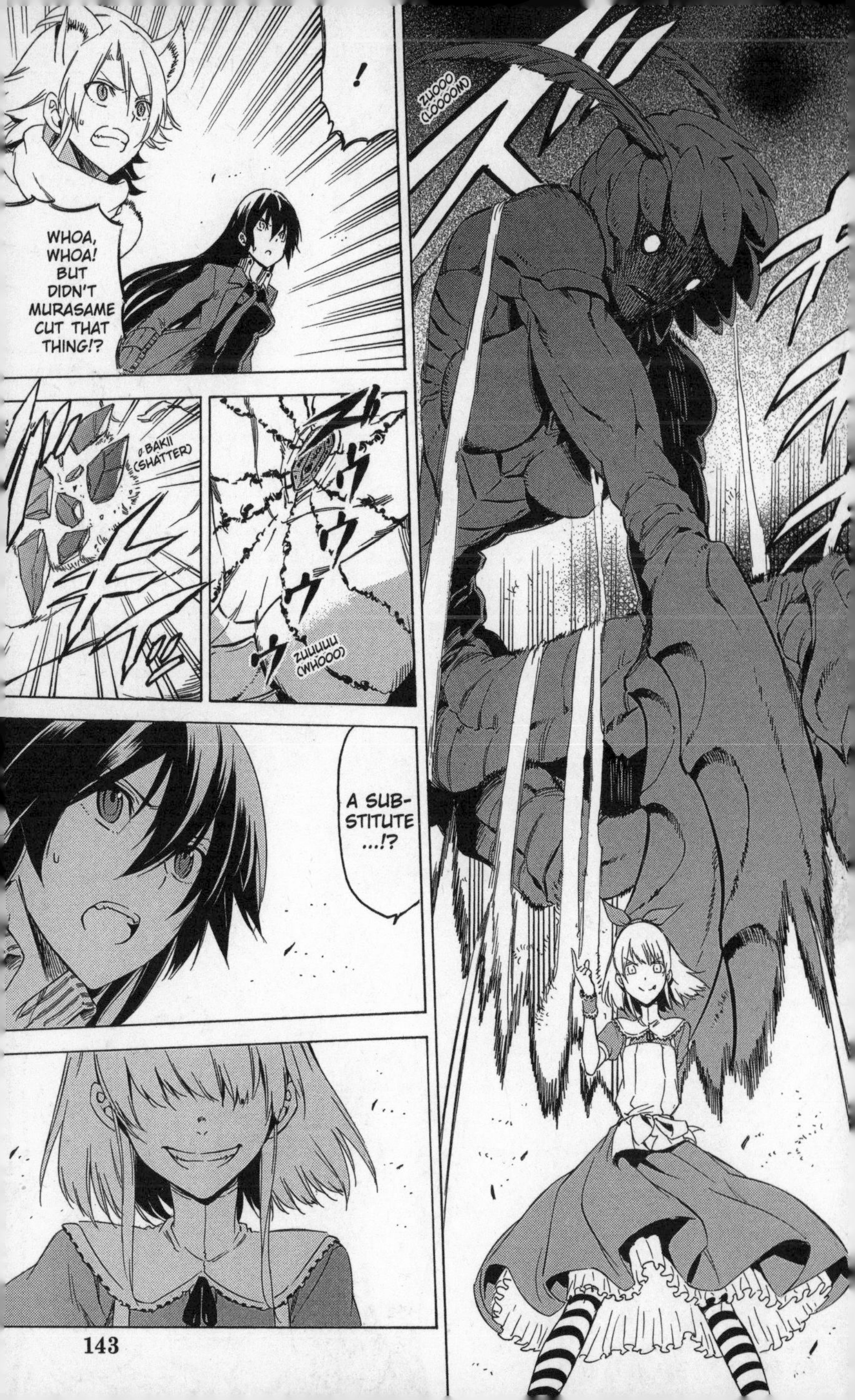

ZUOOO
(WOOOOM)
!
WHOA, WHOA! BUT DIDN'T MURASAME CUT THAT THING!?
ZUNNNN
(WHOOO)
O-BAKII
(SHATTER)
A SUB-STITUTE ...!?

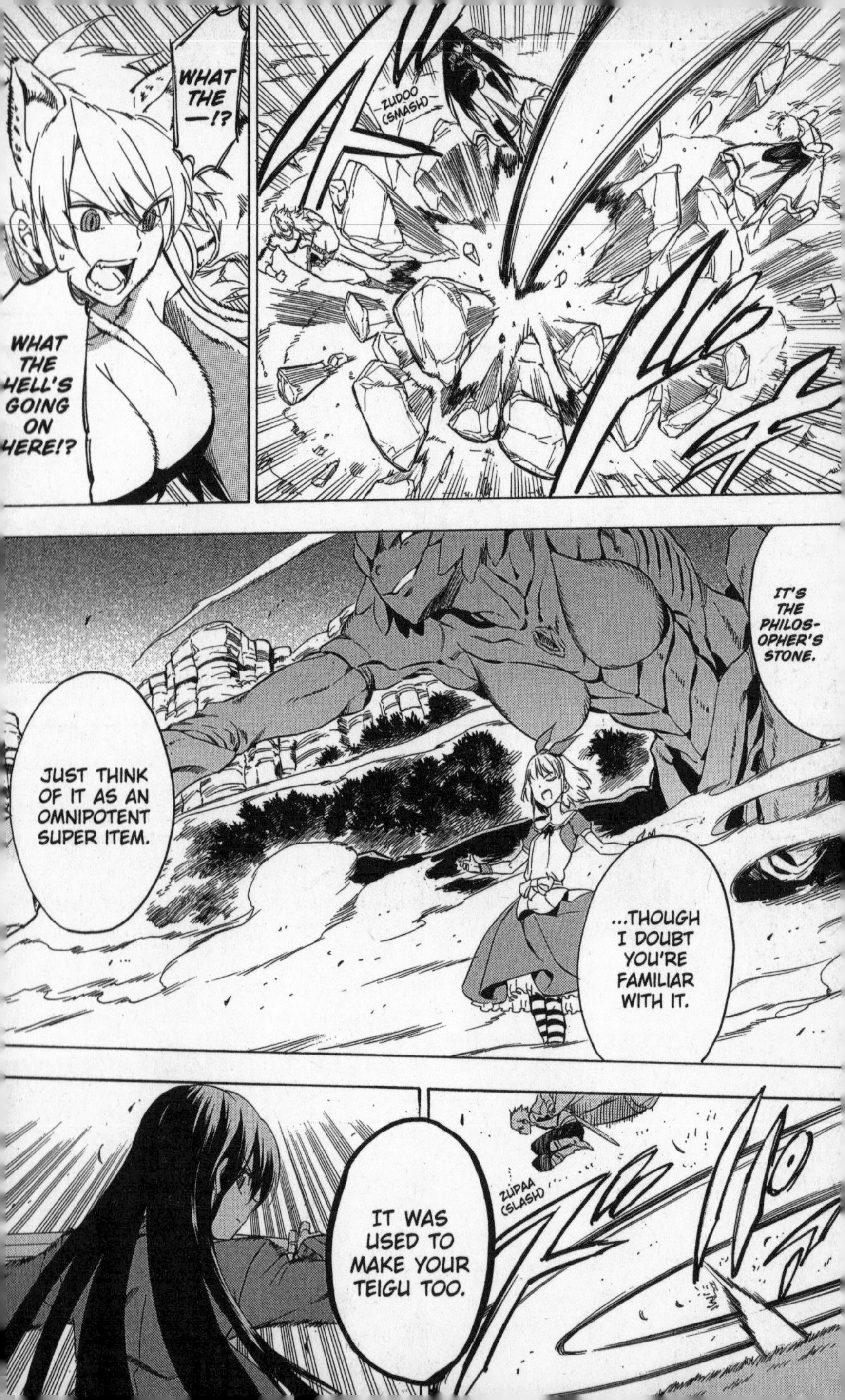
WHAT THE —!?
WHAT THE HELL'S GOING ON HERE!?
ZUDOO (SMASH)
IT'S THE PHILOS-OPHER'S STONE.
JUST THINK OF IT AS AN OMNIPOTENT SUPER ITEM.
...THOUGH I DOUBT YOU'RE FAMILIAR WITH IT.
ZUPAA (SLASH)
IT WAS USED TO MAKE YOUR TEIGU TOO.

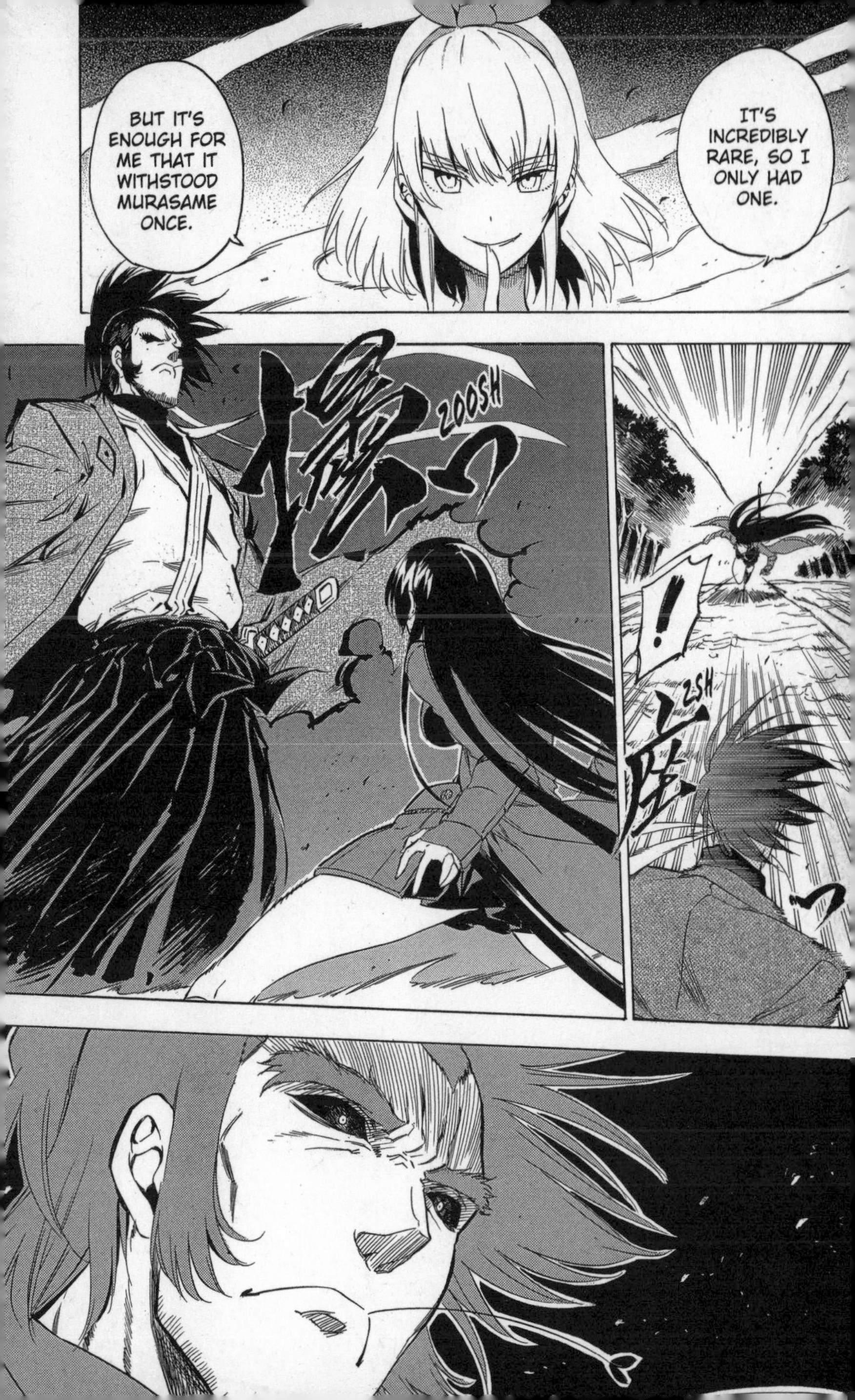
IT'S INCREDIBLY RARE, SO I ONLY HAD ONE.
BUT IT'S ENOUGH FOR ME THAT IT WITHSTOOD MURASAME ONCE.
!
ZSH
ZOOSH

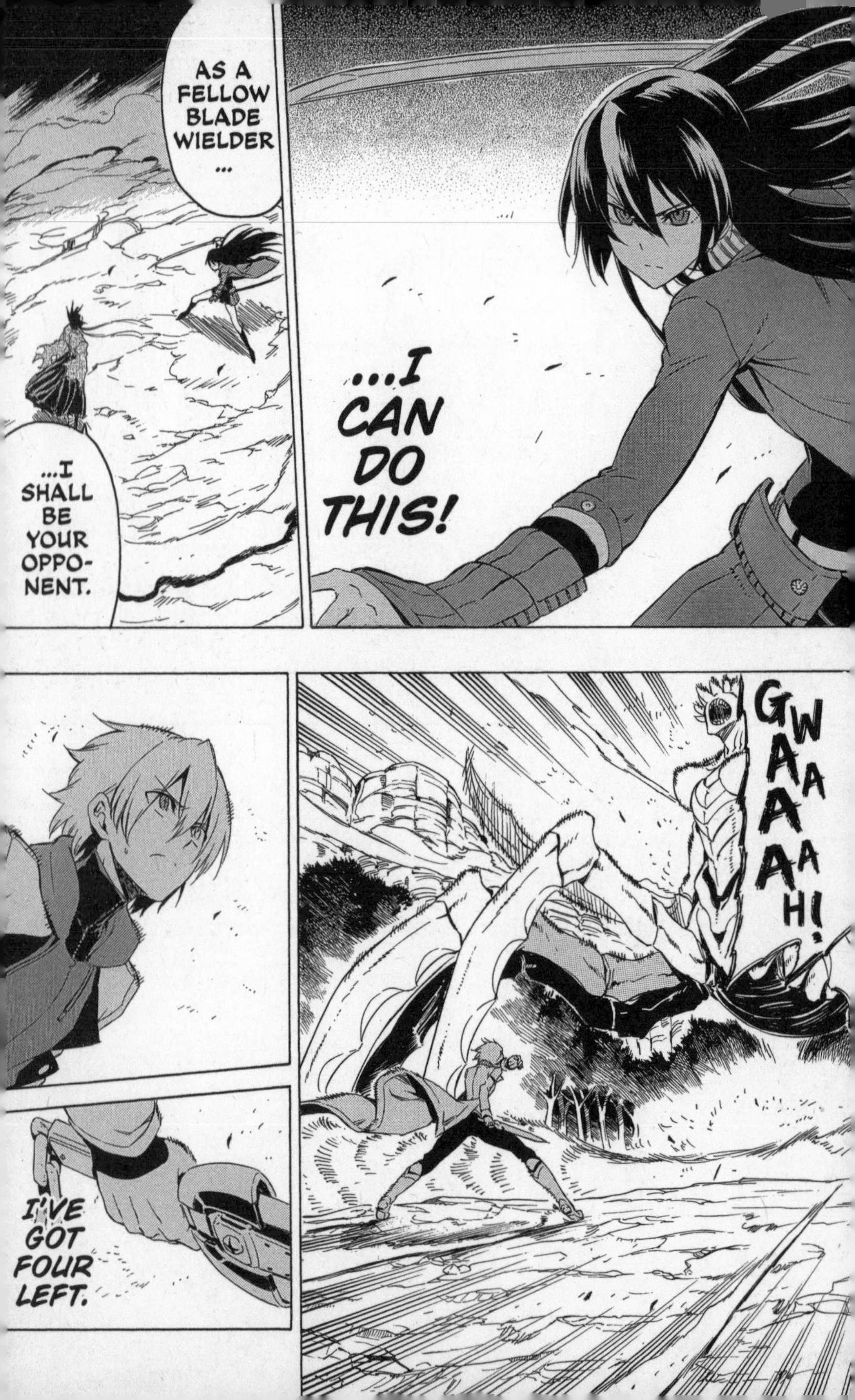
...I CAN DO THIS!
AS A FELLOW BLADE WIELDER ...
...I SHALL BE YOUR OPPONENT.
GWAAAAAAH!
I'VE GOT FOUR LEFT.

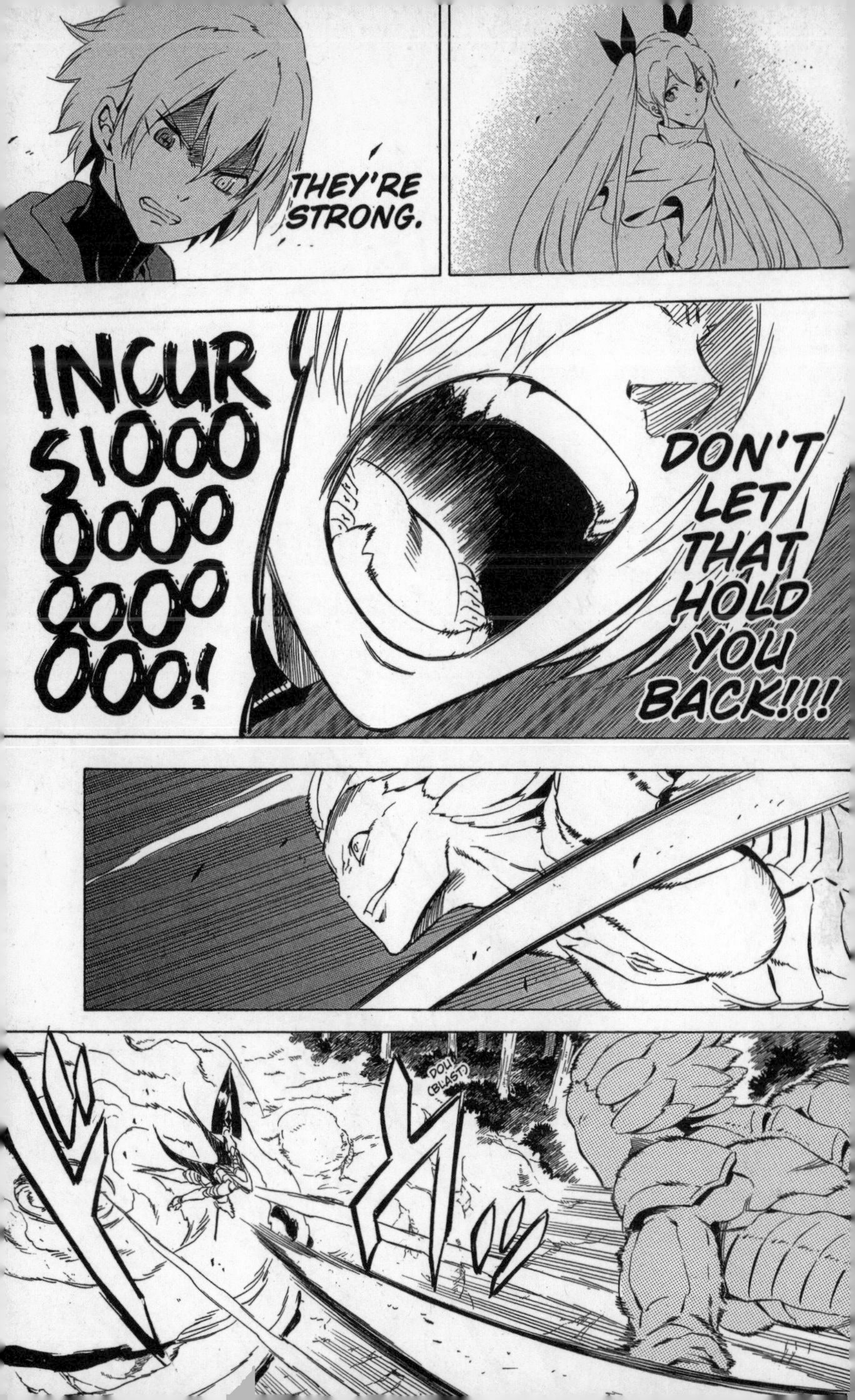
THEY'RE STRONG.
INCUR $1000000000000000!
DON'T LET THAT HOLD YOU BACK!!!
DOU (BLAST)

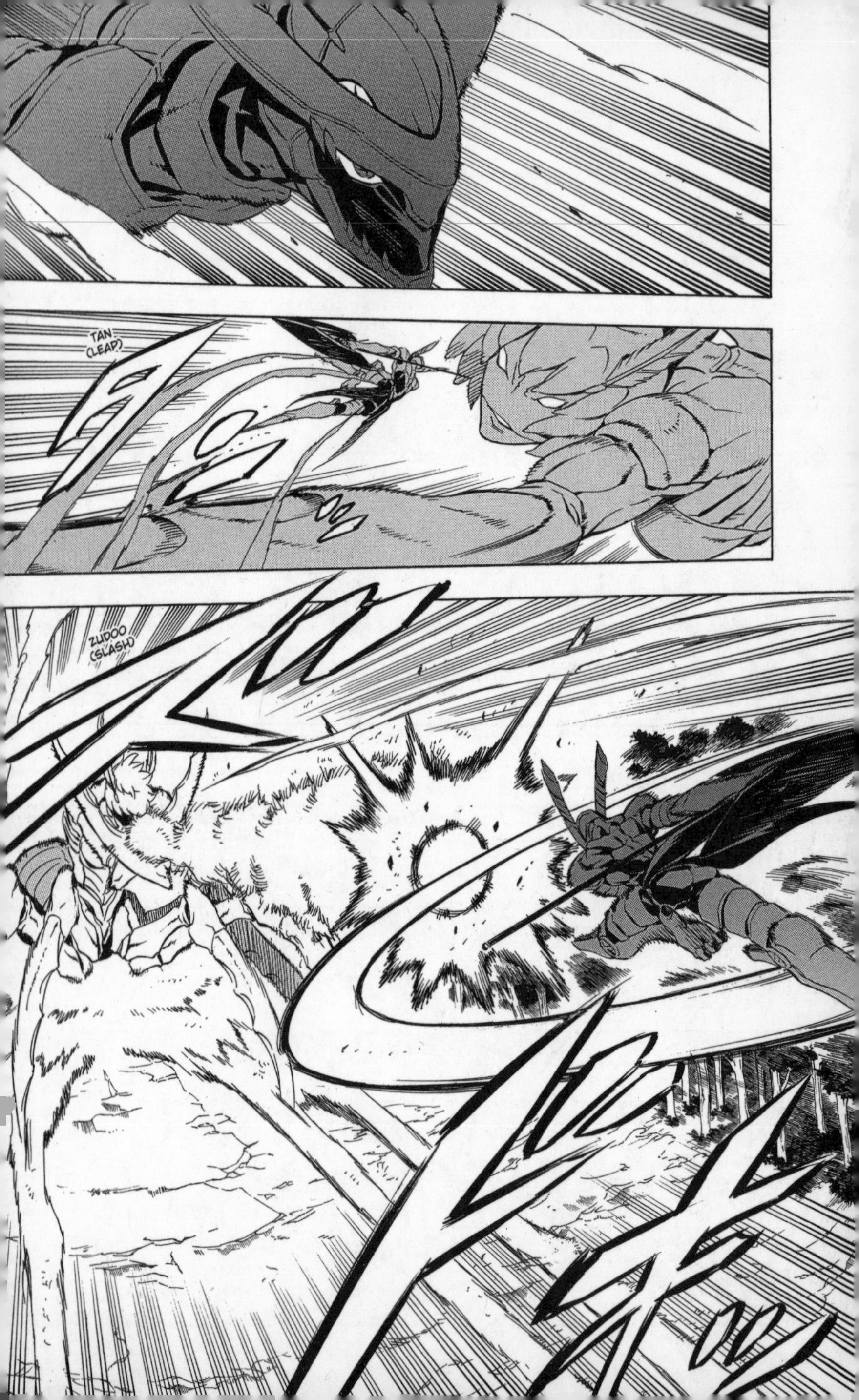
TAN
(LEAP)
ZUDOO
(SLASH)

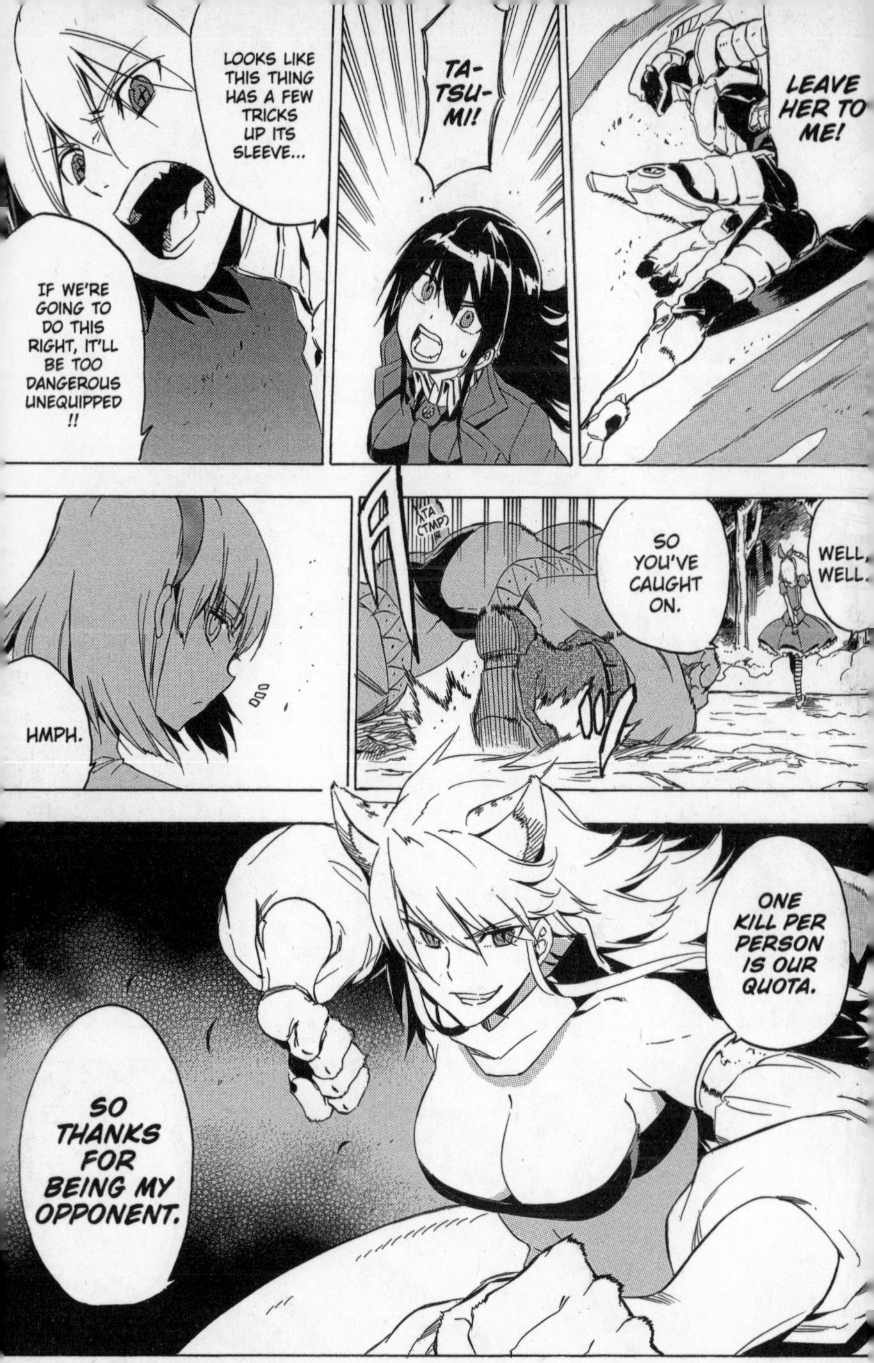
LEAVE HER TO ME!
TA-TSU-MI!
LOOKS LIKE THIS THING HAS A FEW TRICKS UP ITS SLEEVE...
IF WE'RE GOING TO DO THIS RIGHT, IT'LL BE TOO DANGEROUS UNEQUIPPED !!
WELL, WELL.
SO YOU'VE CAUGHT ON.
TA (TMP)
HMPH.
ONE KILL PER PERSON IS OUR QUOTA.
SO THANKS FOR BEING MY OPPONENT.

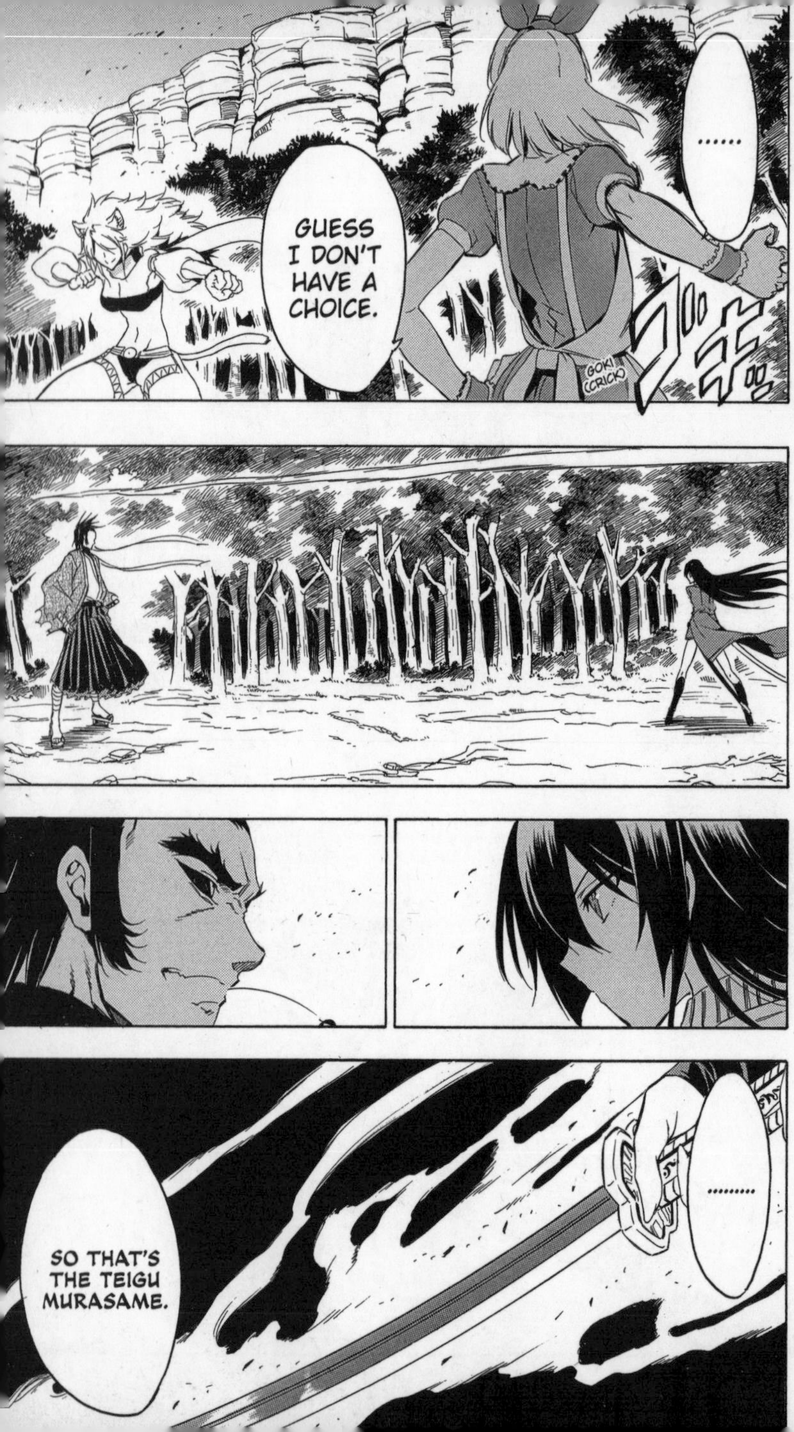

......
GUESS I DON'T HAVE A CHOICE.
GOKI (CRICK)
SO THAT'S THE TEIGU MURASAME.
....

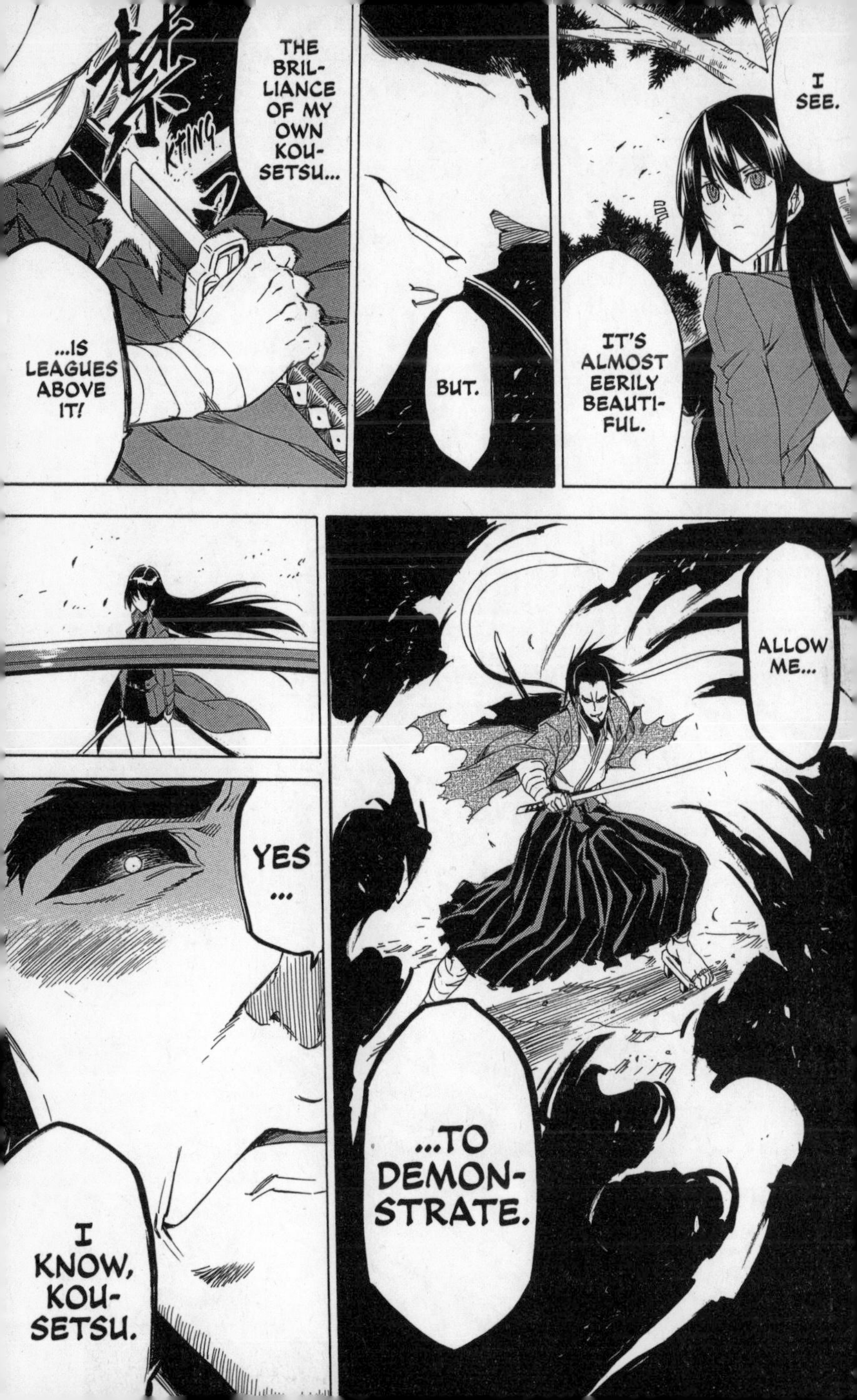
I SEE.
IT'S ALMOST EERILY BEAUTIFUL.
BUT.
THE BRILLIANCE OF MY OWN KOUSETSU...
K'TING
...IS LEAGUES ABOVE IT!
ALLOW ME...
...TO DEMONSTRATE.
YES...
I KNOW, KOUSETSU.

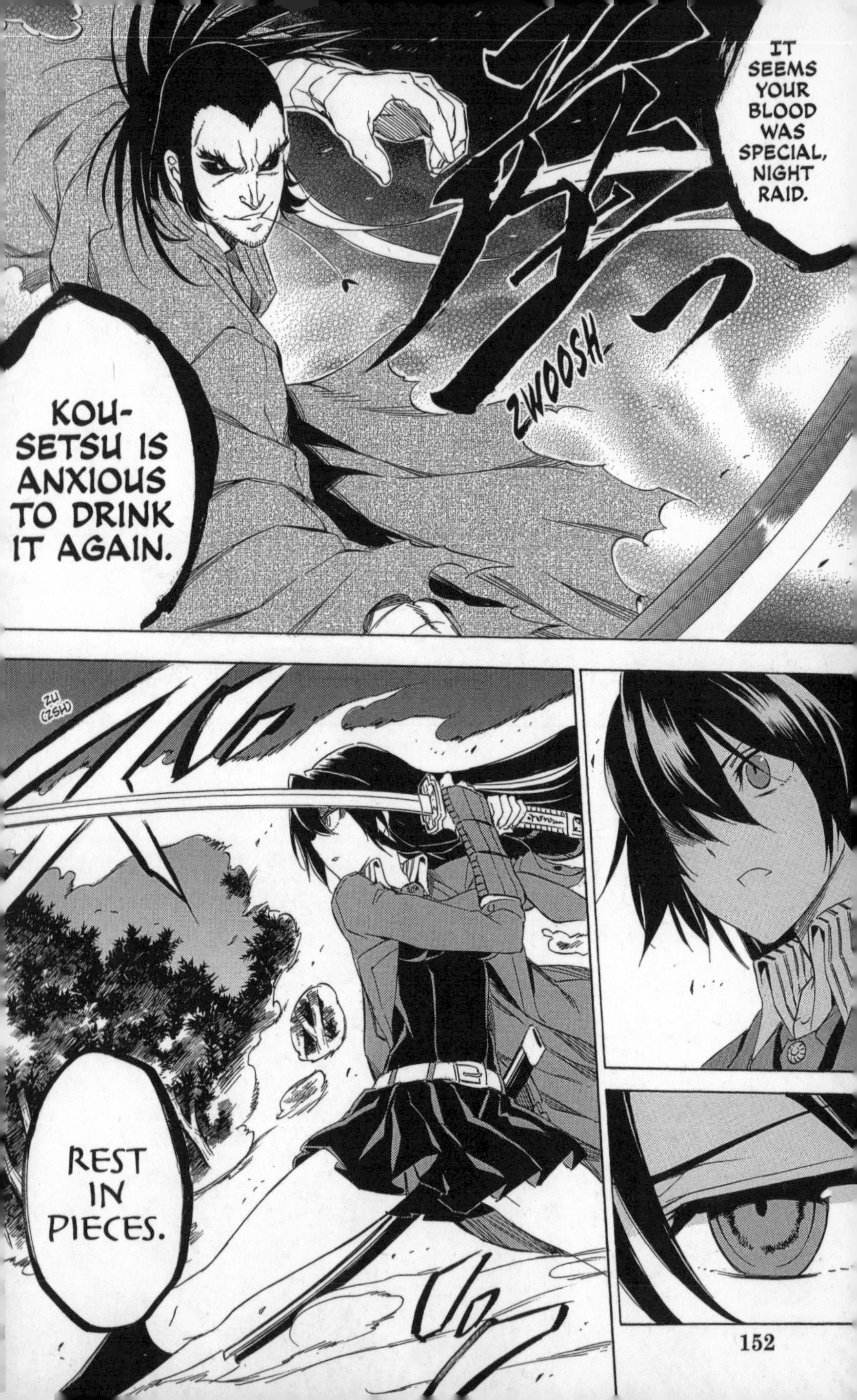
IT SEEMS YOUR BLOOD WAS SPECIAL, NIGHT RAID.
KOU-SETSU IS ANXIOUS TO DRINK IT AGAIN.
ZWOOSH
ZU (ZSH)
REST IN PIECES.

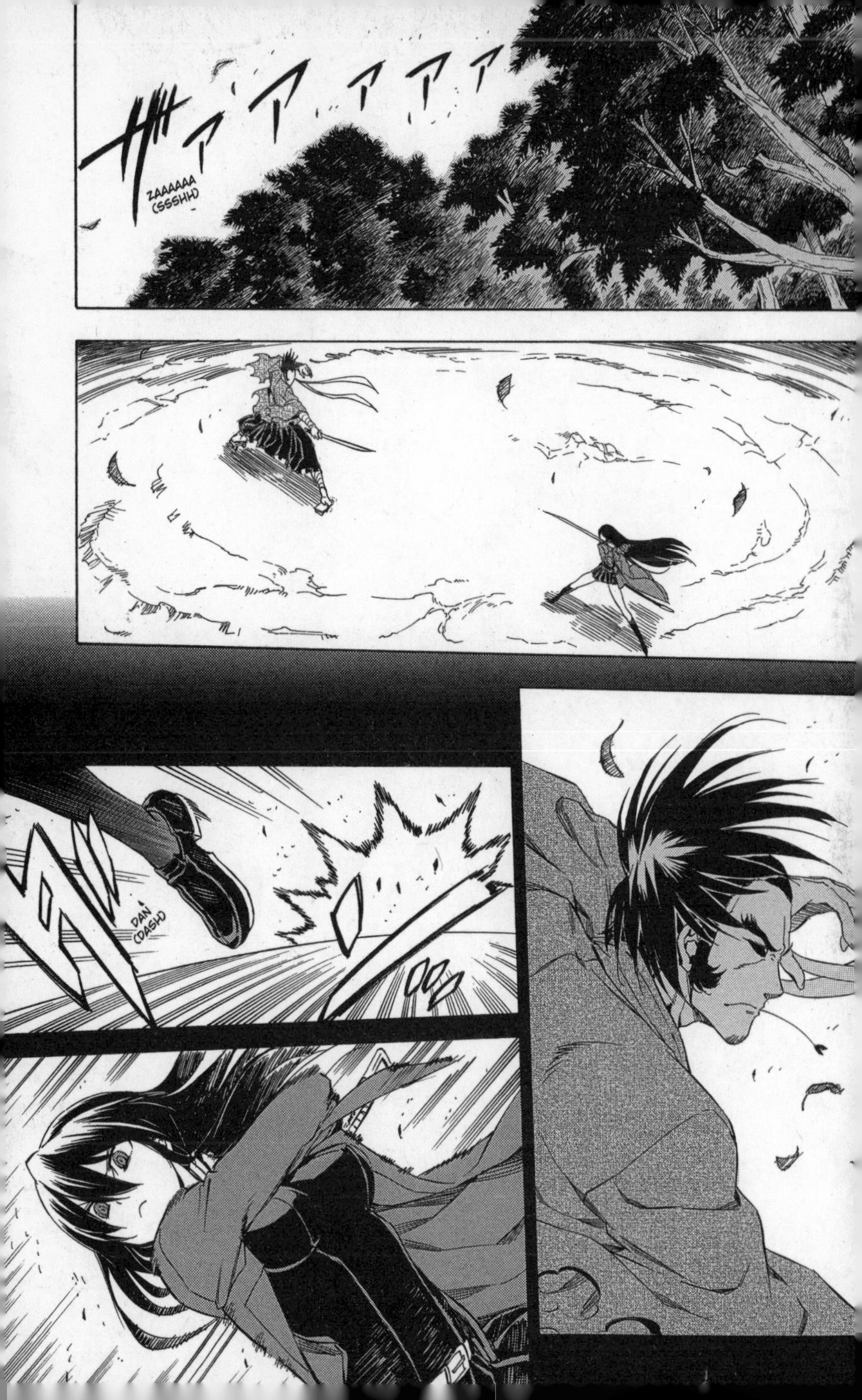
ザァァァァァ
ZAAAAAA (SSSHH)
ダン
DAN (DASH)

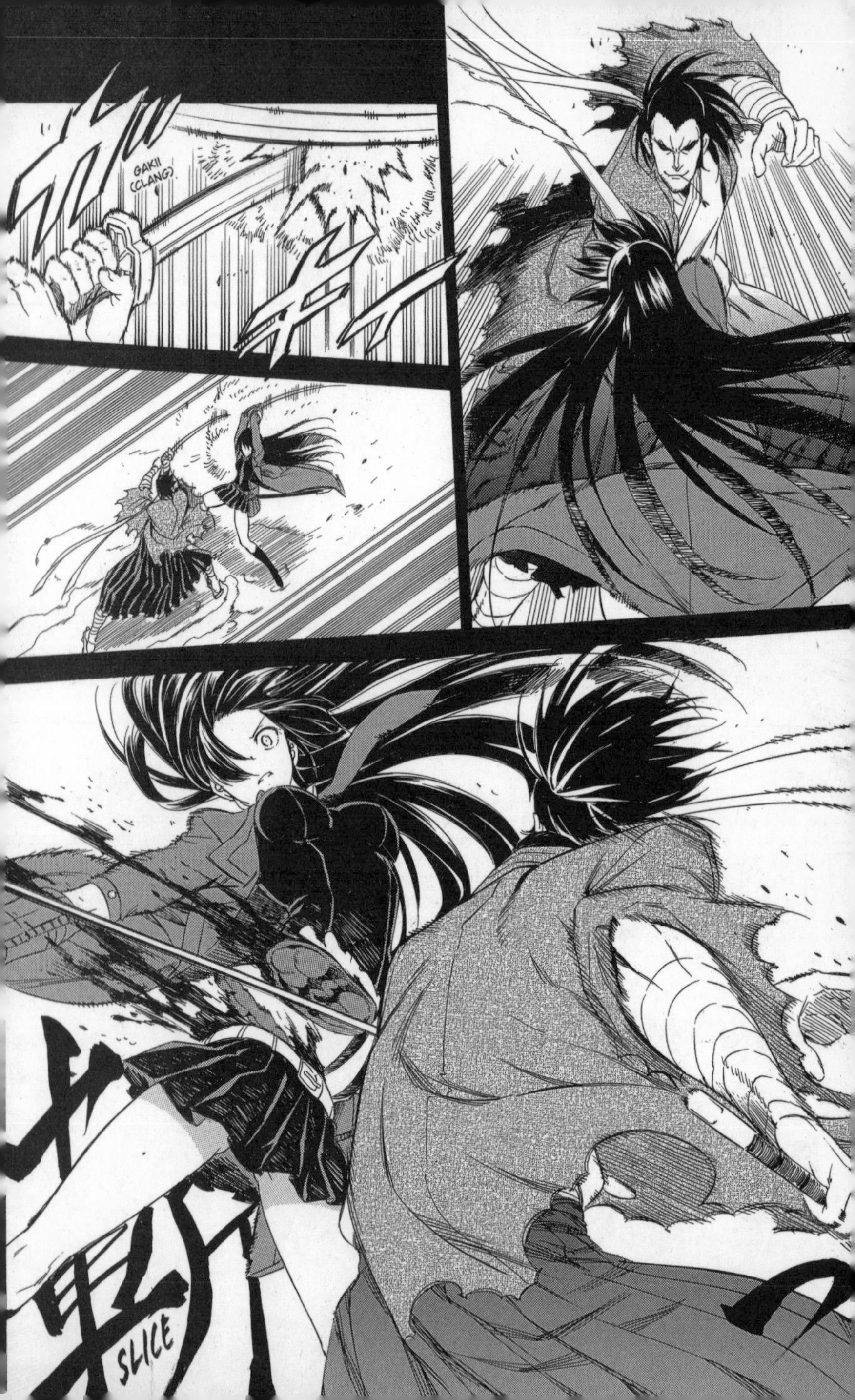
GAKII (CLANG)
SLICE

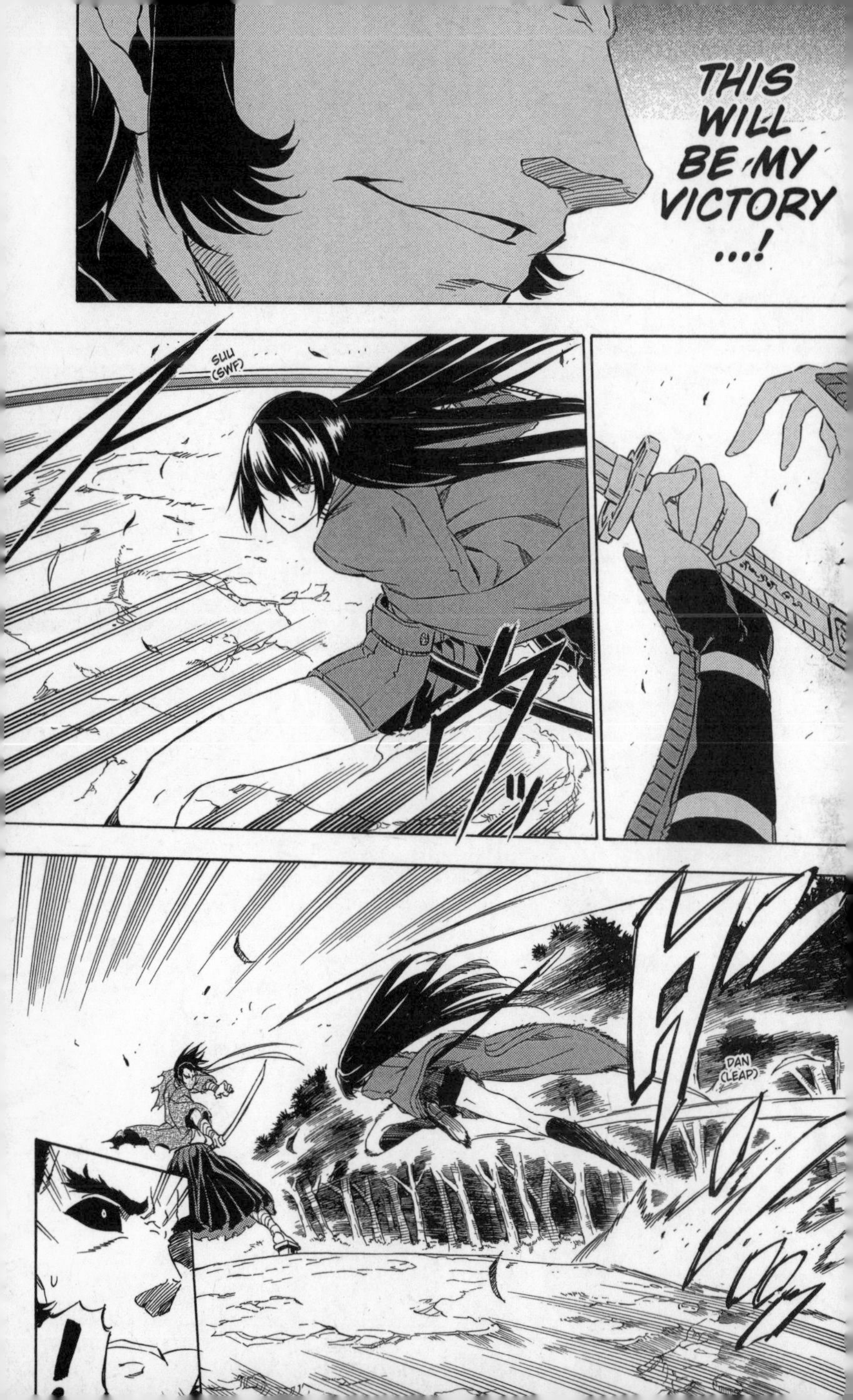
THIS WILL BE MY VICTORY ...!
SUU (SWF)
DAN (LEAP)

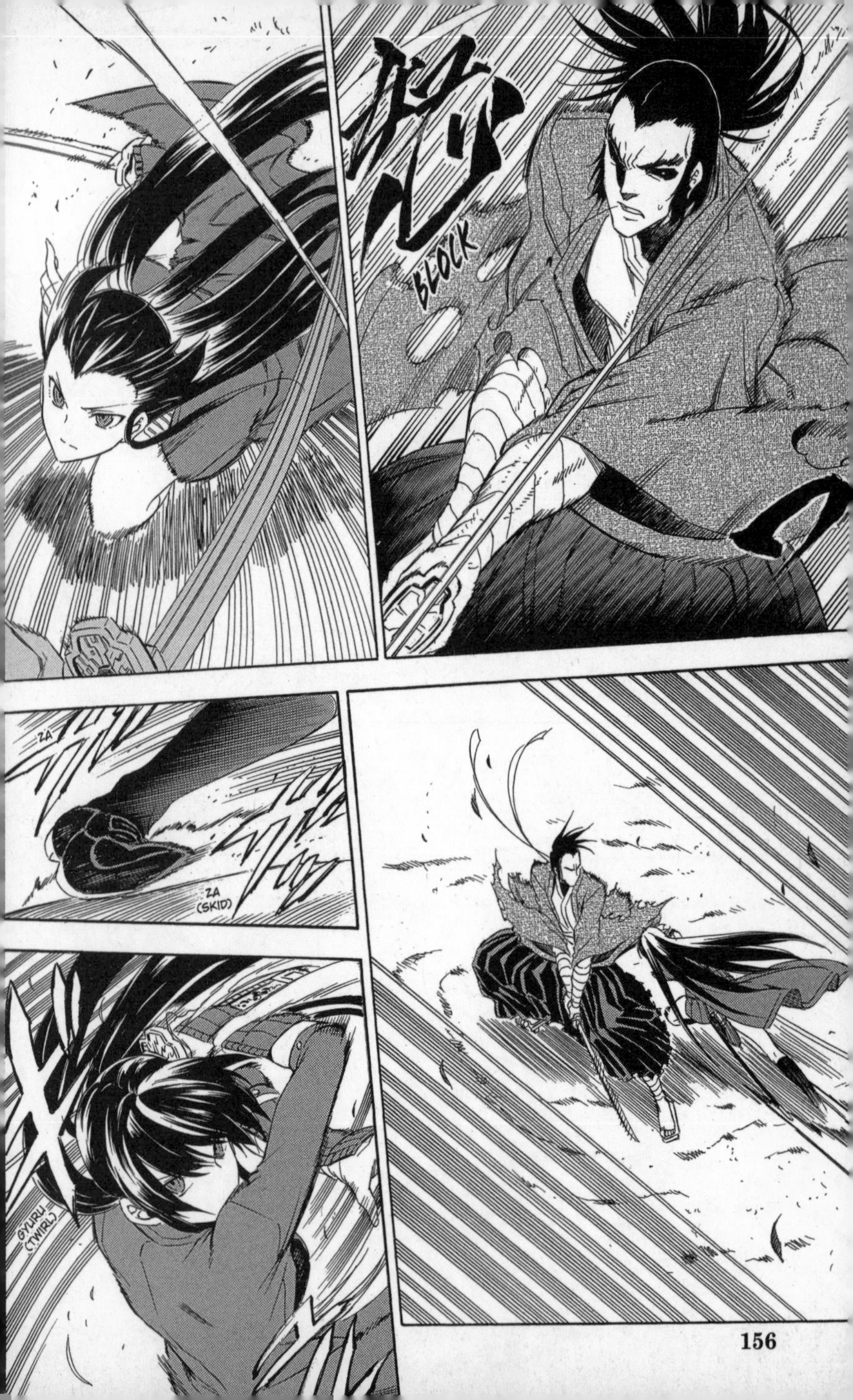

BLOCK
ZA
ZA
(SKID)
GYURU
(TWIRL)

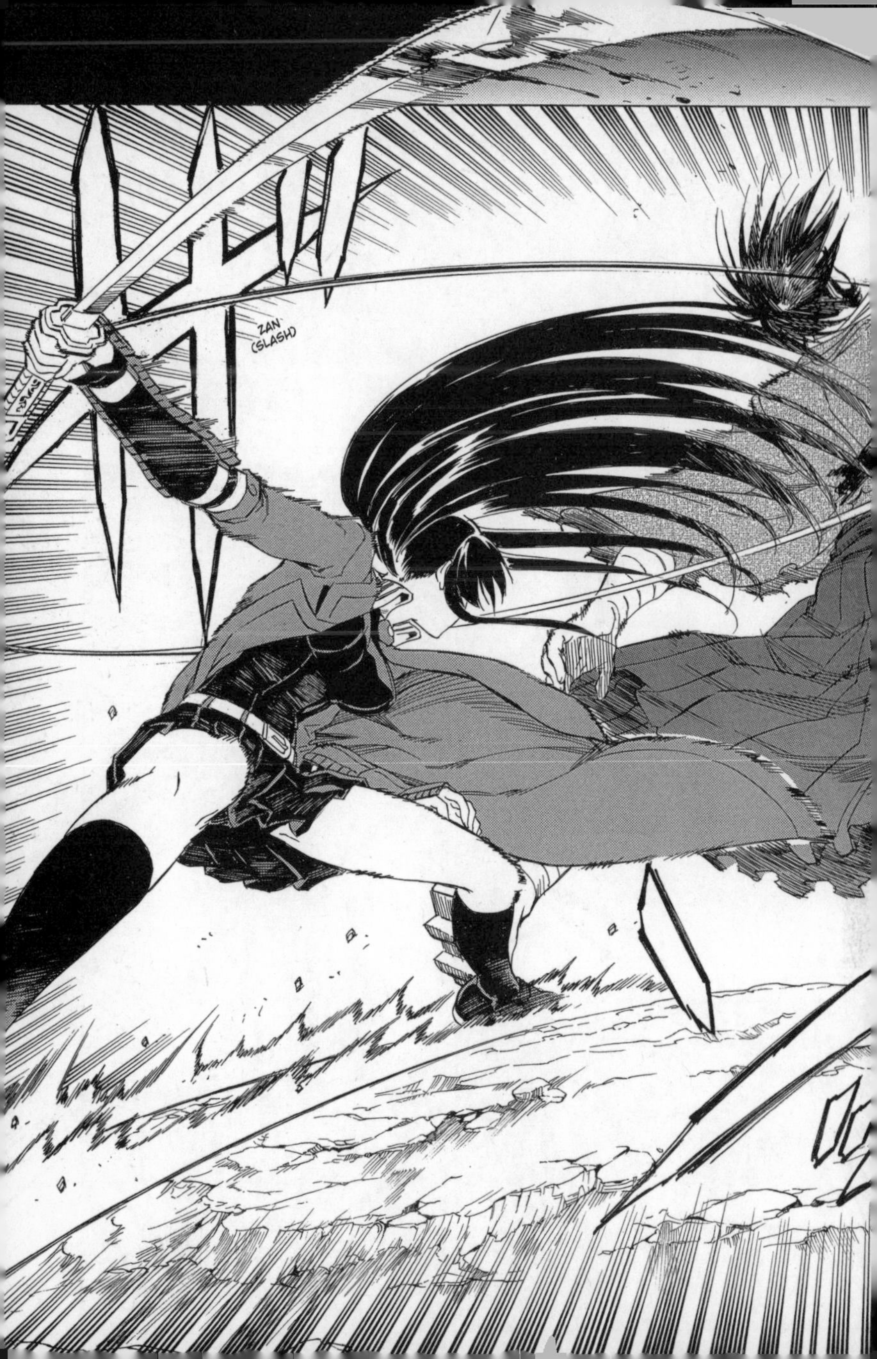
ZAN
(SLASH)

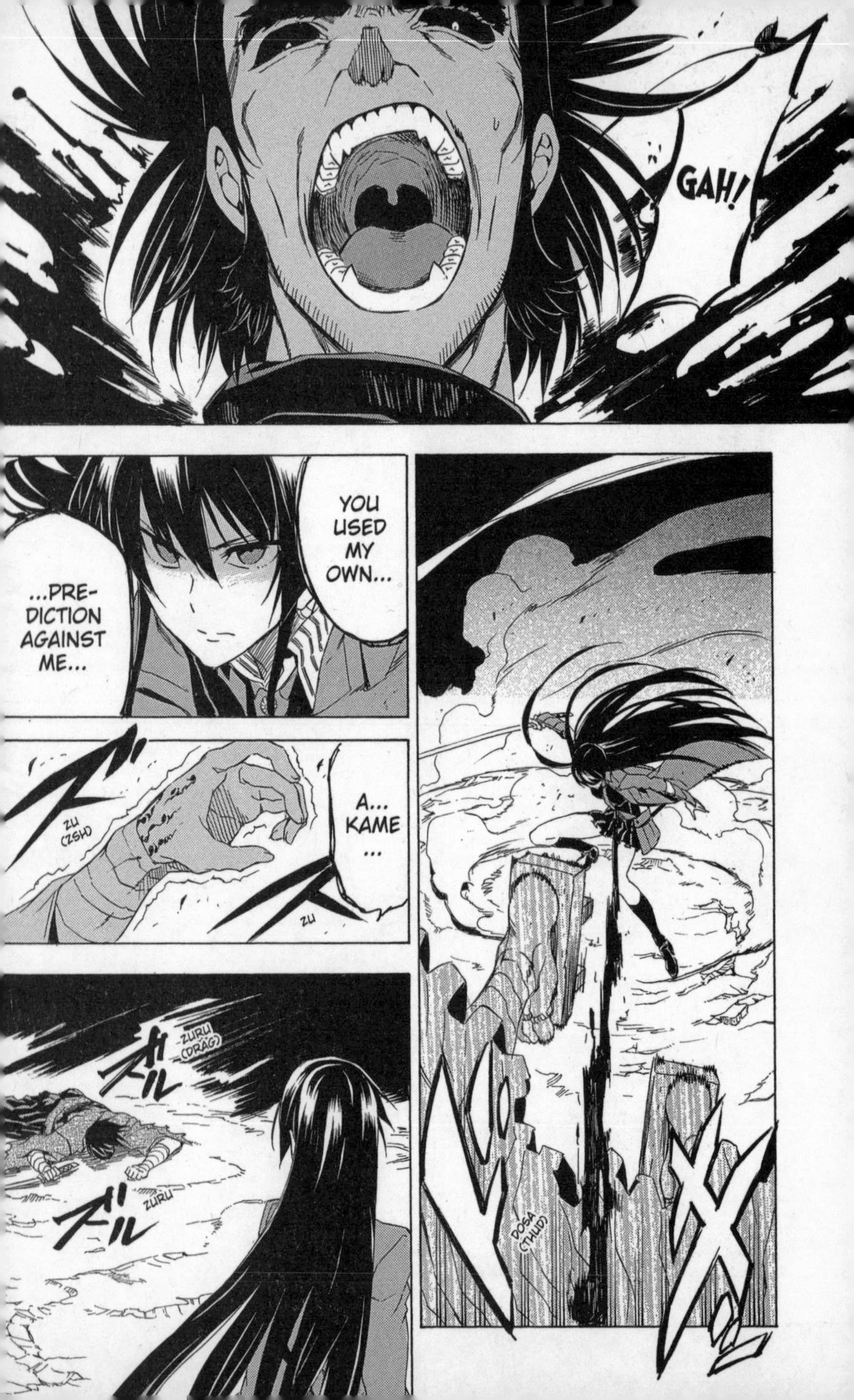
GAH!
DOSA (THUD)
YOU USED MY OWN...
...PREDICTION AGAINST ME...
ZU (ZSH)
A... KAME ...
ZU
ZURU (DRAG)
ZURU

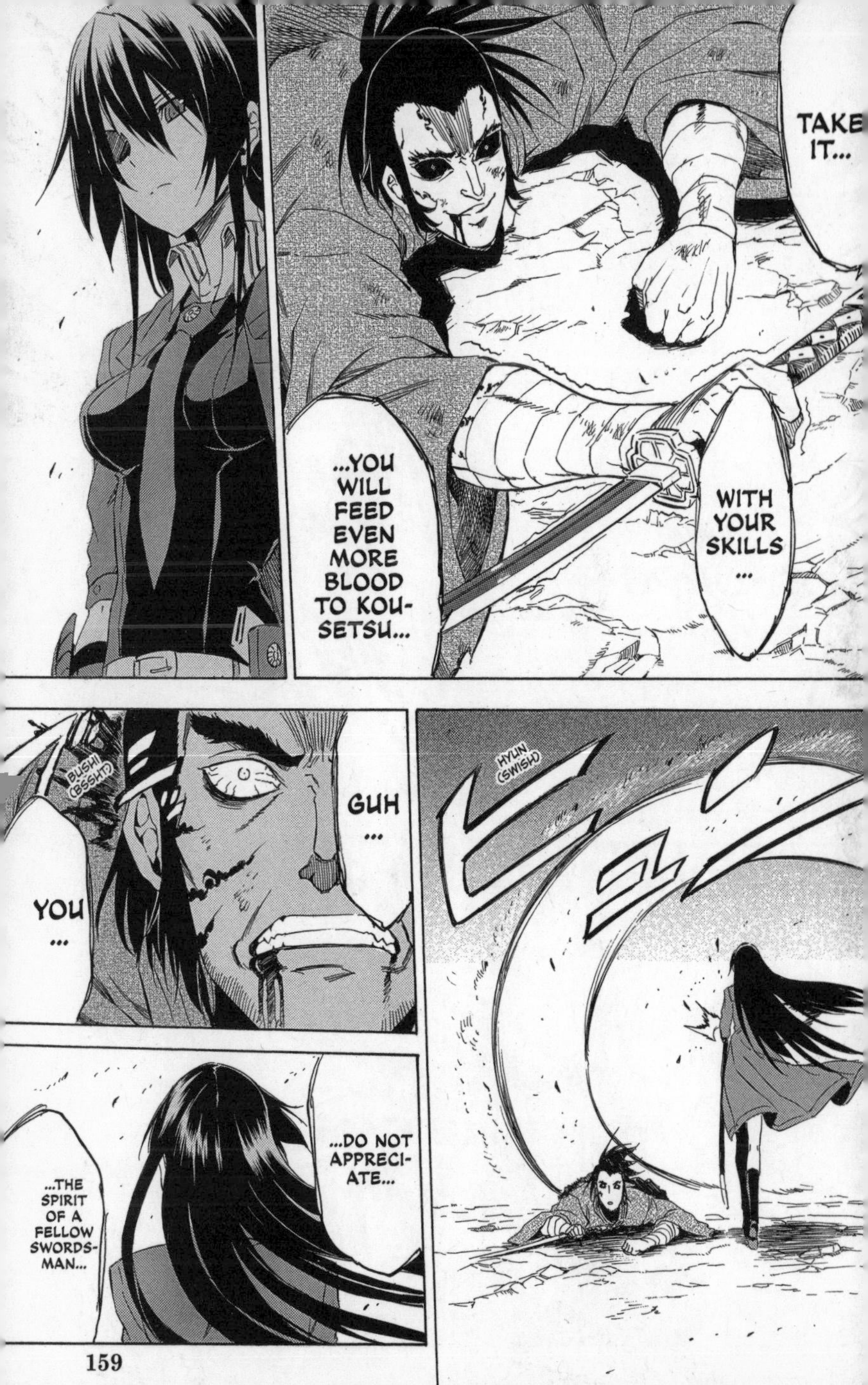
TAKE IT...
WITH YOUR SKILLS ...
...YOU WILL FEED EVEN MORE BLOOD TO KOU-SETSU...
HYUN (SWISH)
BUSHI (BSSHT!)
GUH ...
YOU ...
...DO NOT APPRECI-ATE...
...THE SPIRIT OF A FELLOW SWORDS-MAN...

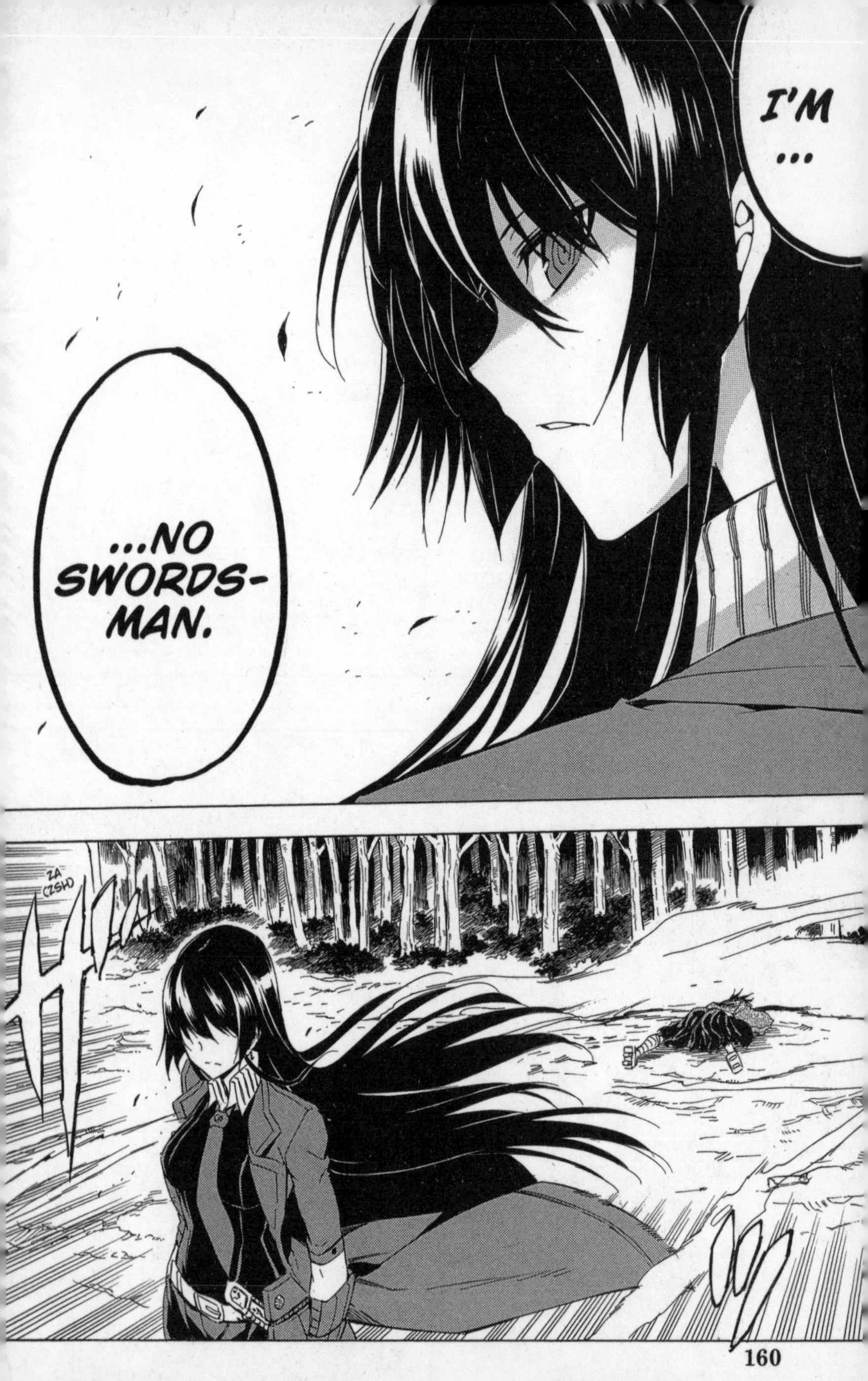
I'M ...
...NO SWORDS-MAN.
ZA (ZSH)

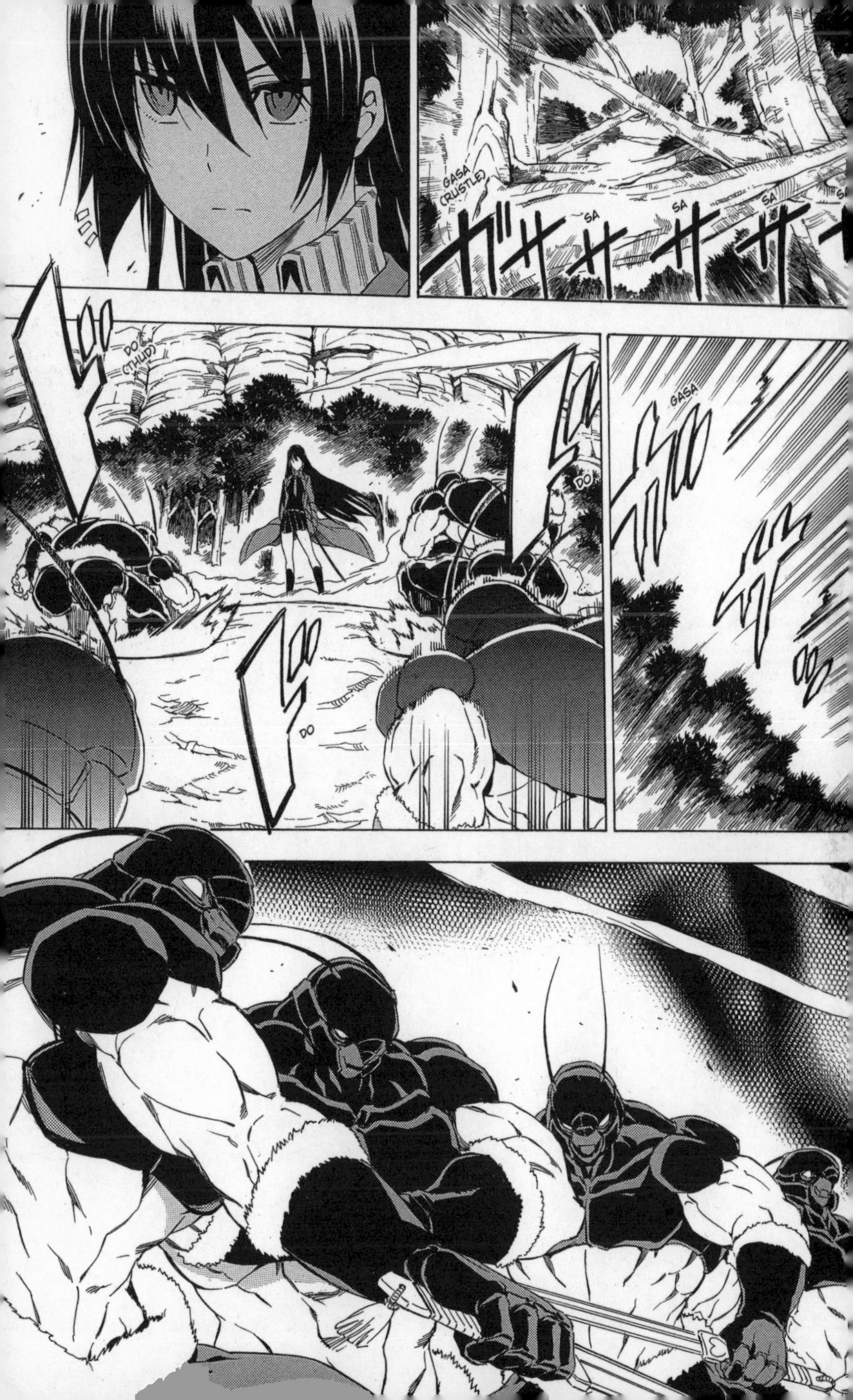
GASA (RUSTLE)
SA
SA
SA
DO (THUD)
DO
GASA
DO

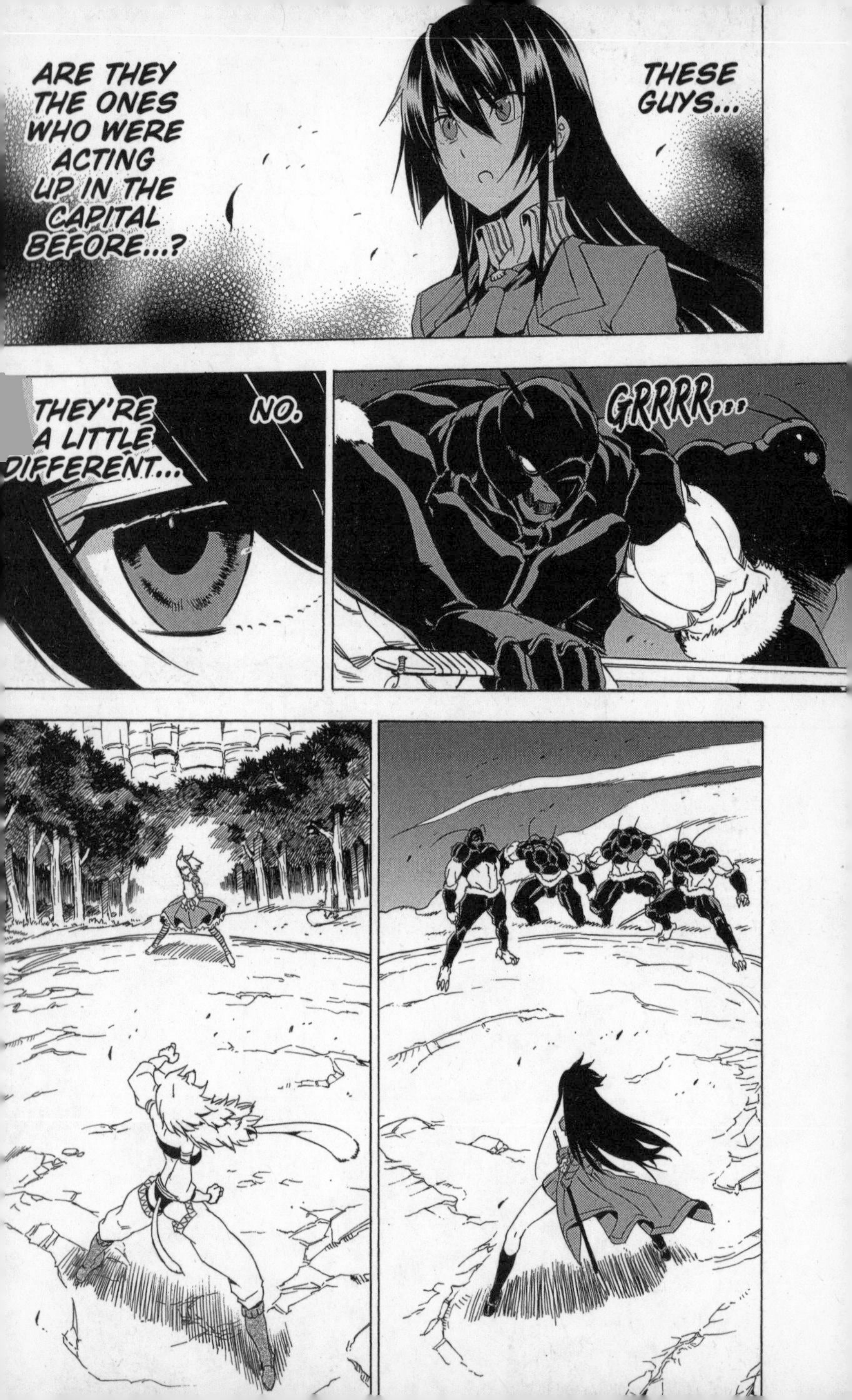
THESE GUYS...
ARE THEY THE ONES WHO WERE ACTING UP IN THE CAPITAL BEFORE...?
GRRRR...
NO.
THEY'RE A LITTLE DIFFERENT...

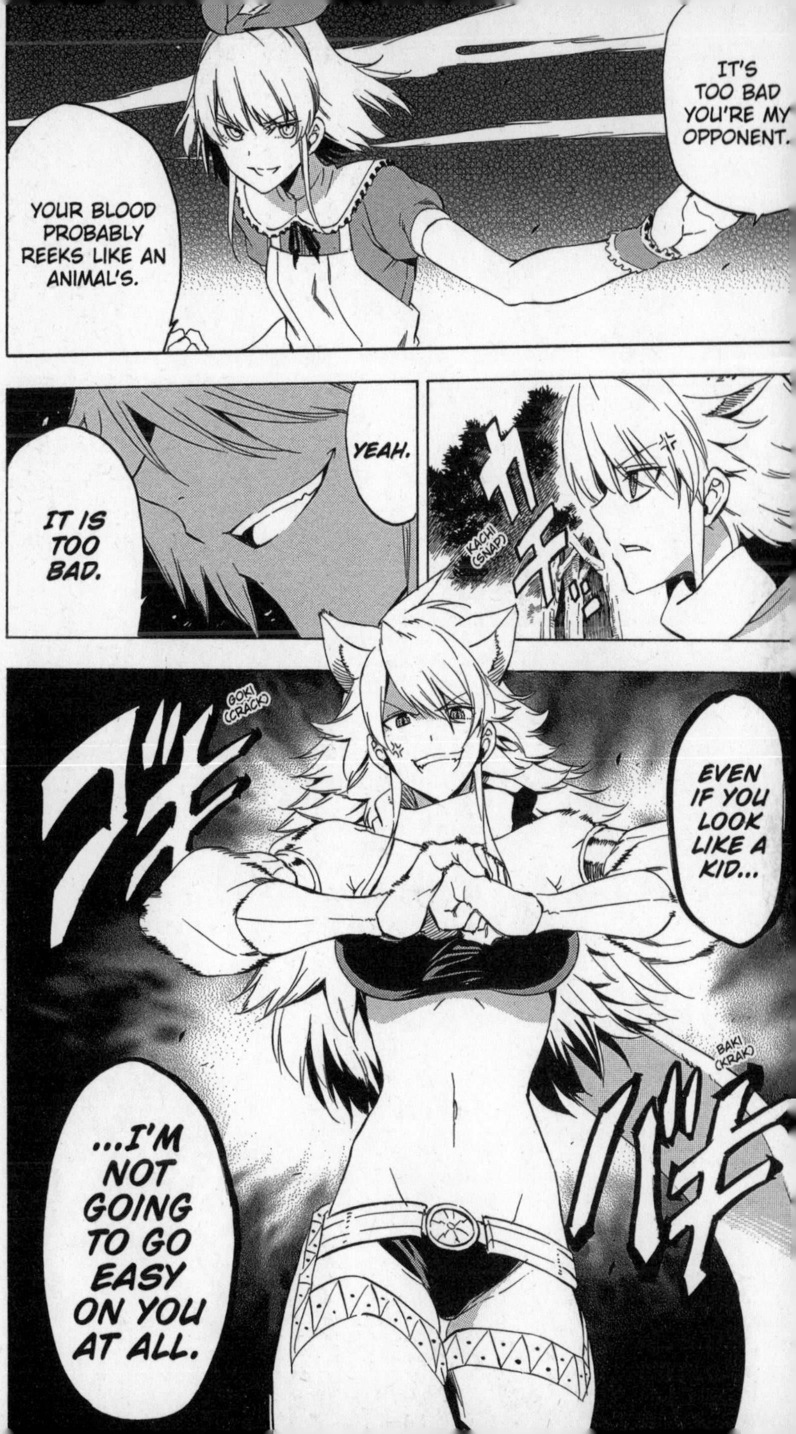
IT'S TOO BAD YOU'RE MY OPPONENT.
YOUR BLOOD PROBABLY REEKS LIKE AN ANIMAL'S.
KACHI (SNAP)
YEAH.
IT IS TOO BAD.
EVEN IF YOU LOOK LIKE A KID...
GOKI (CRACK)
BAKI (KRAK)
...I'M NOT GOING TO GO EASY ON YOU AT ALL.

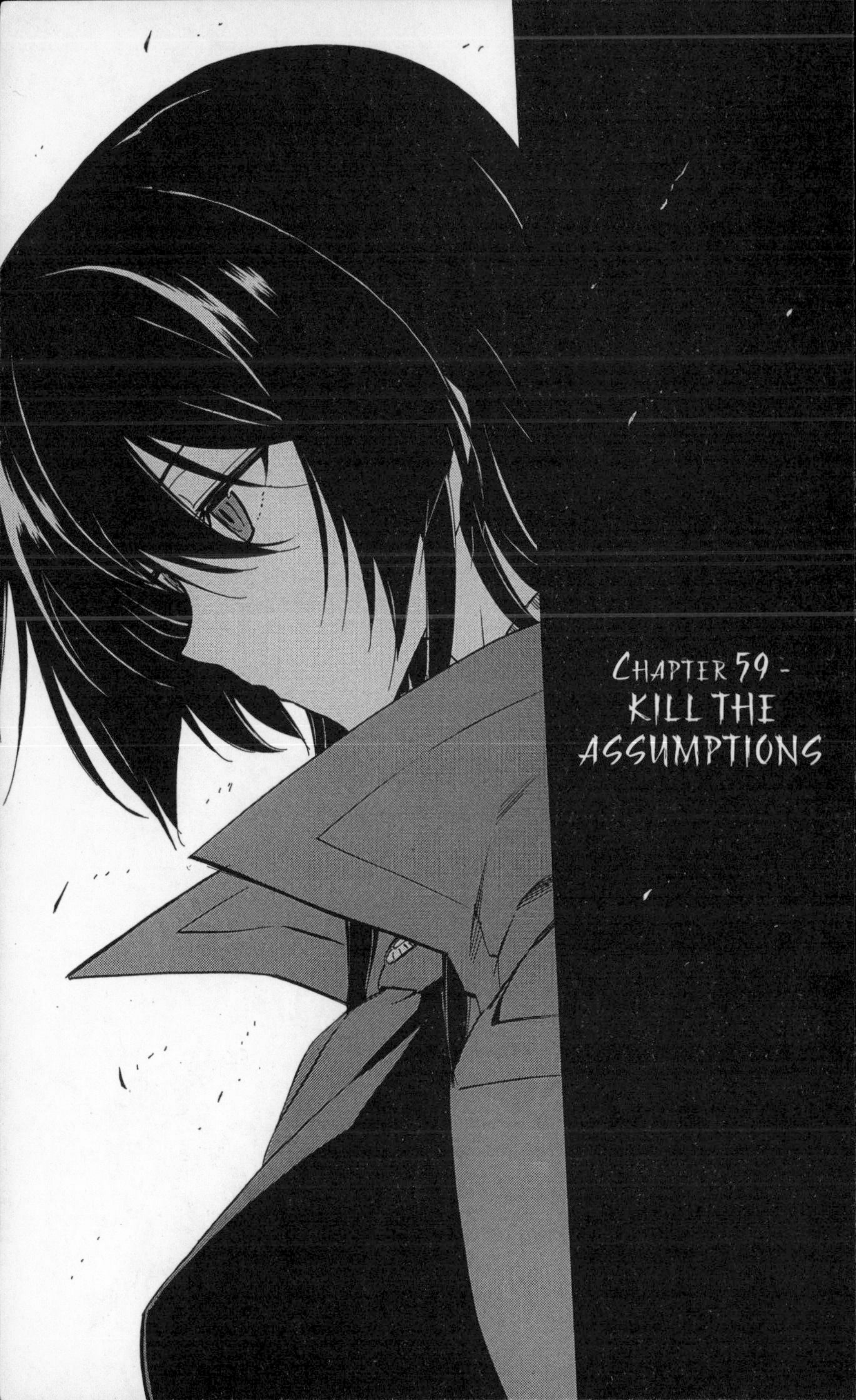
Chapter 59 -
Kill the
Assumptions

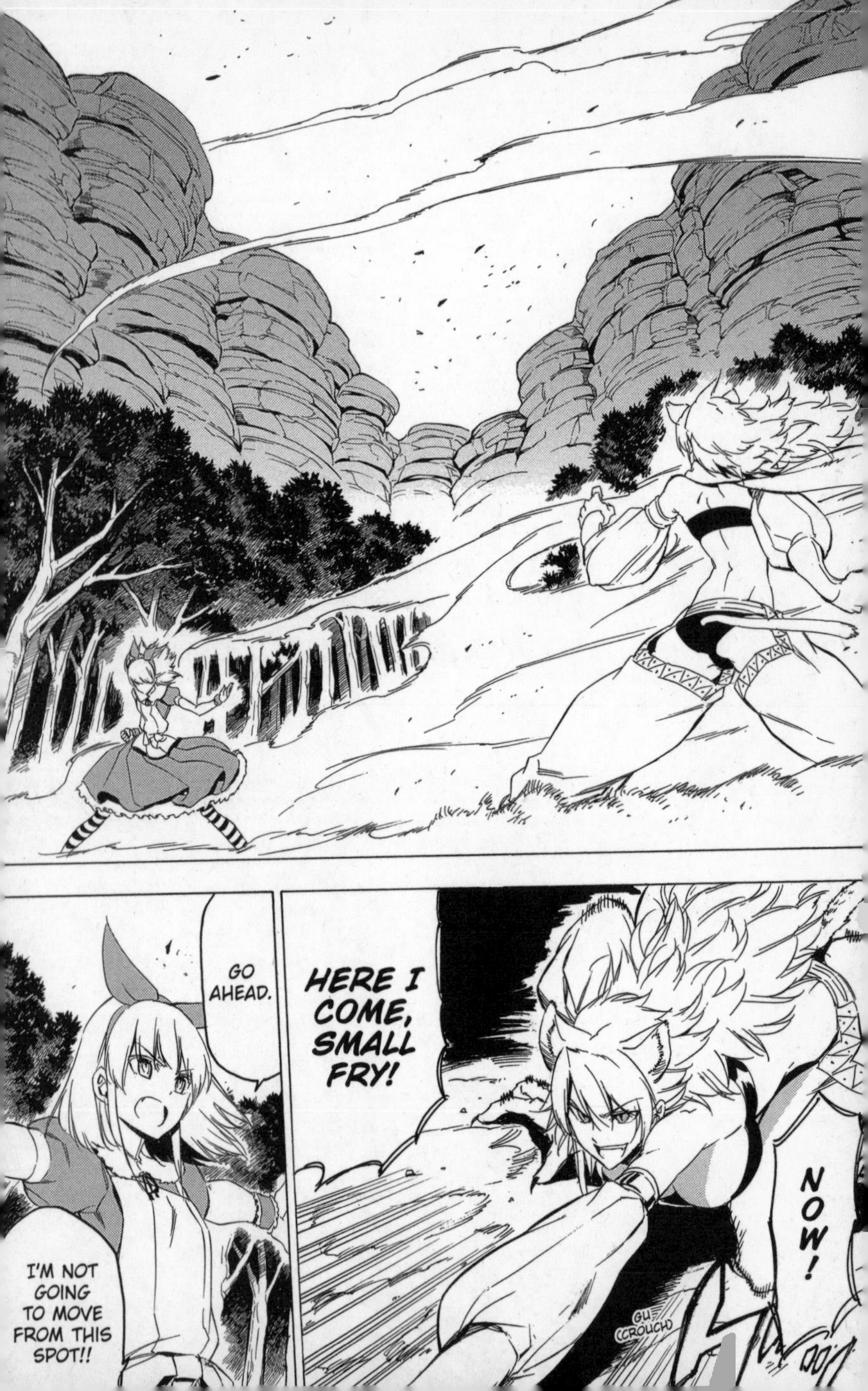
HERE I COME, SMALL FRY!
NOW!
GU (CROUCH)
GO AHEAD.
I'M NOT GOING TO MOVE FROM THIS SPOT!!

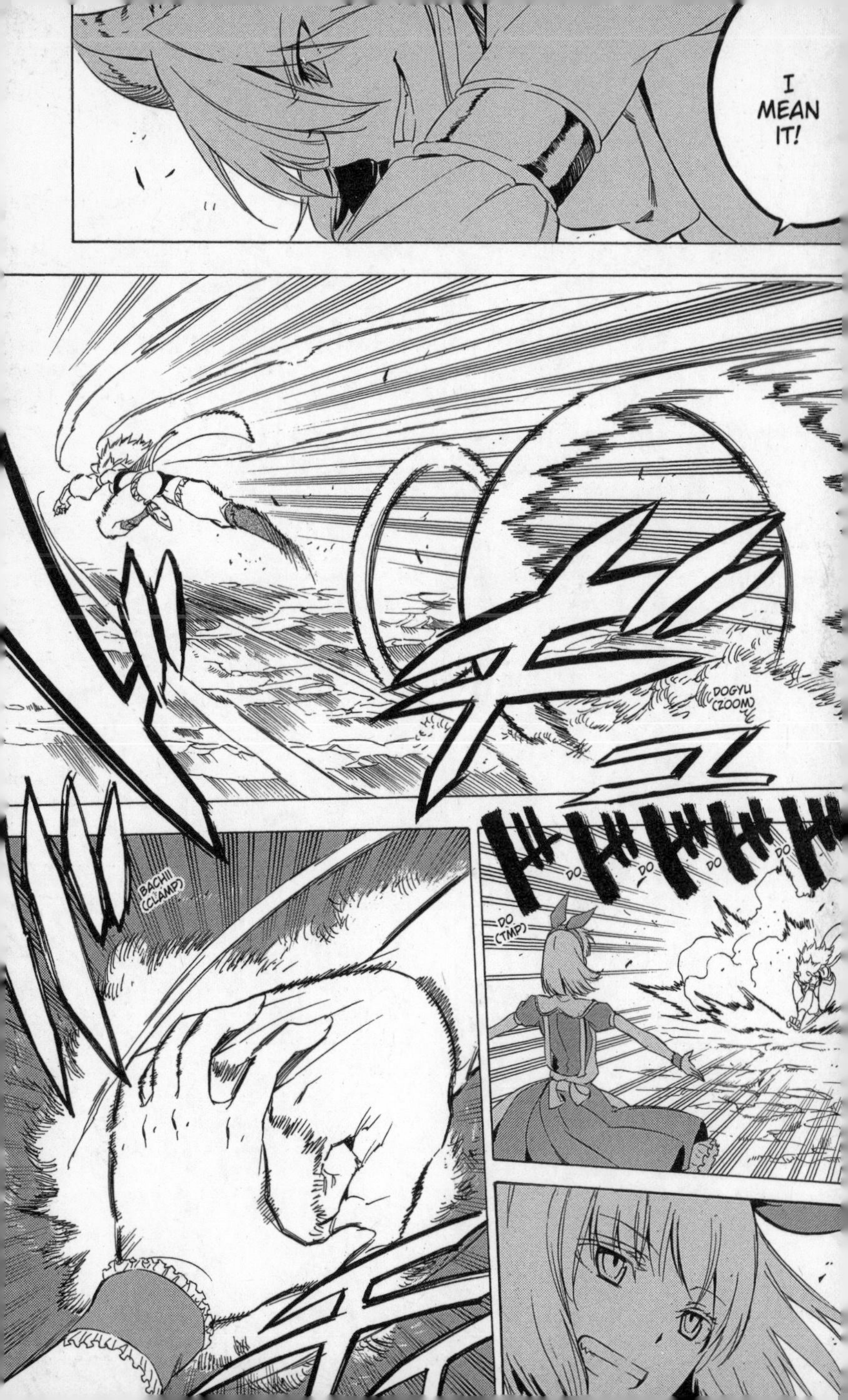
I MEAN IT!
DOGYU (ZOOM)
DO DO DO DO
DO (TMP)
BACHI! (CLAMP)

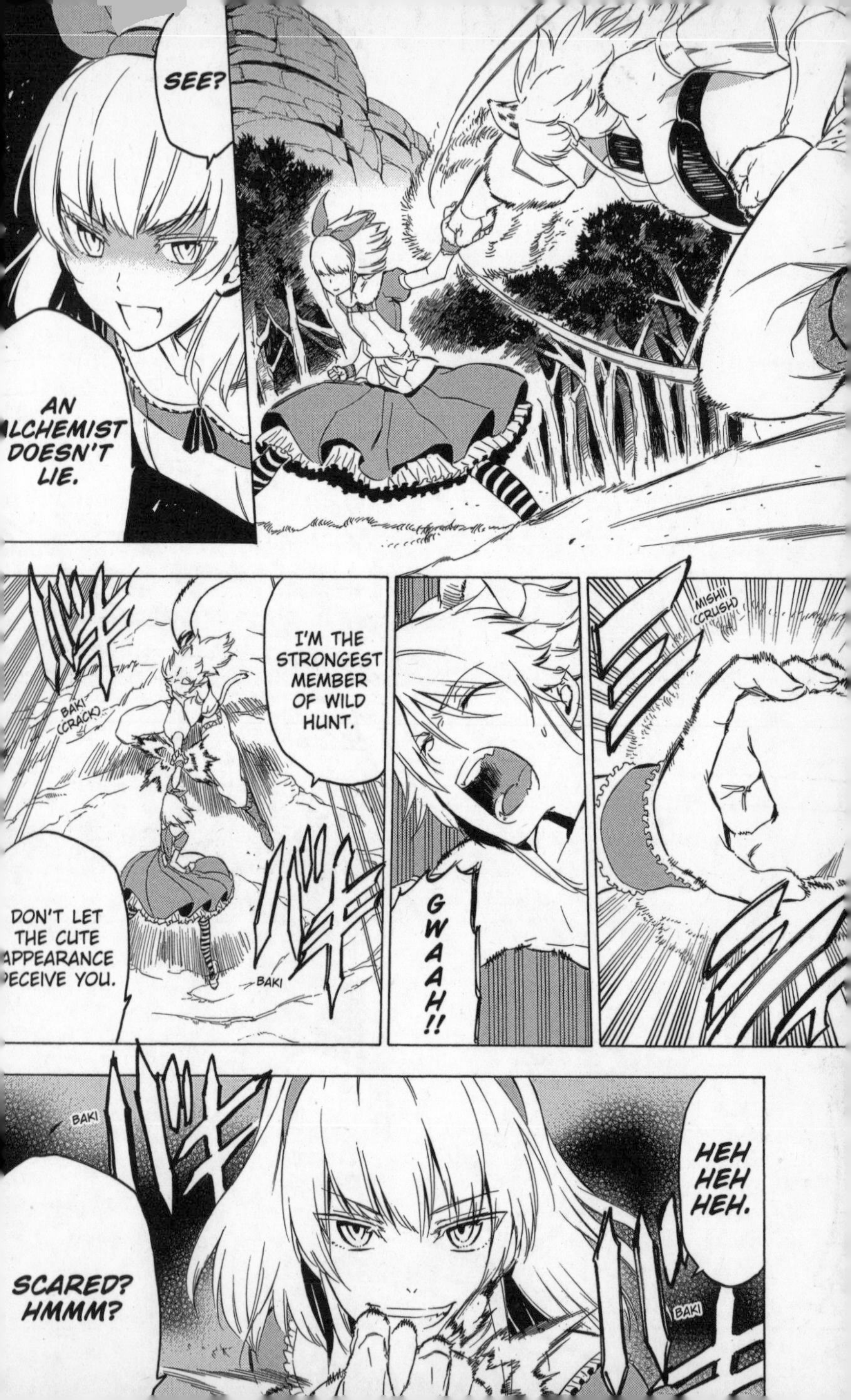
SEE?
AN LCHEMIST DOESN'T LIE.
MISHI (CRUSH)
GWAAAH!!
I'M THE STRONGEST MEMBER OF WILD HUNT.
BAKI (CRACK)
DON'T LET THE CUTE PPEARANCE ECEIVE YOU.
BAKI
HEH HEH HEH.
BAKI
SCARED? HMMM?
BAKI

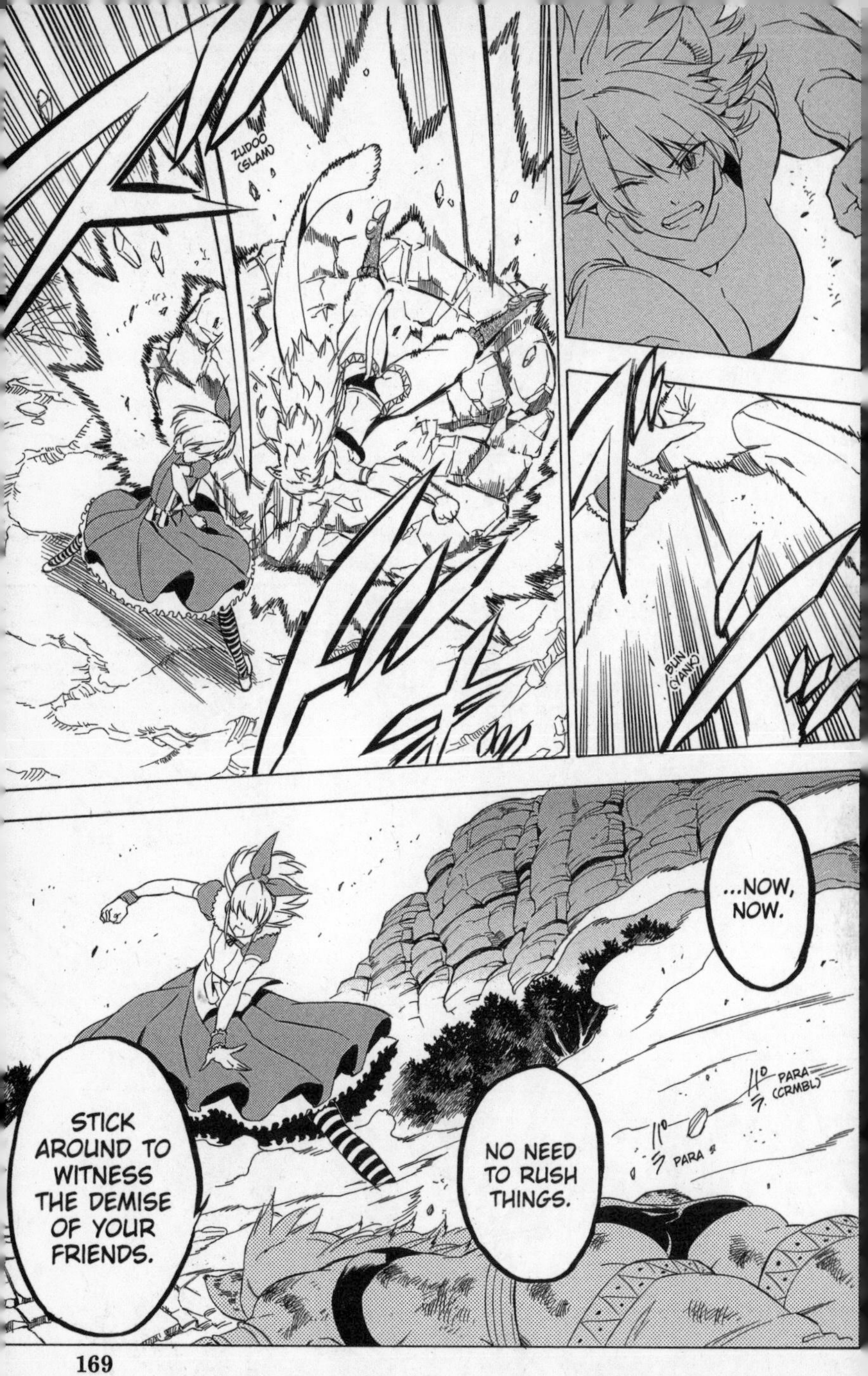
BUN (YANK)
ZUDOO (SLAM)
...NOW, NOW.
PARA (CRMBL)
PARA
NO NEED TO RUSH THINGS.
STICK AROUND TO WITNESS THE DEMISE OF YOUR FRIENDS.

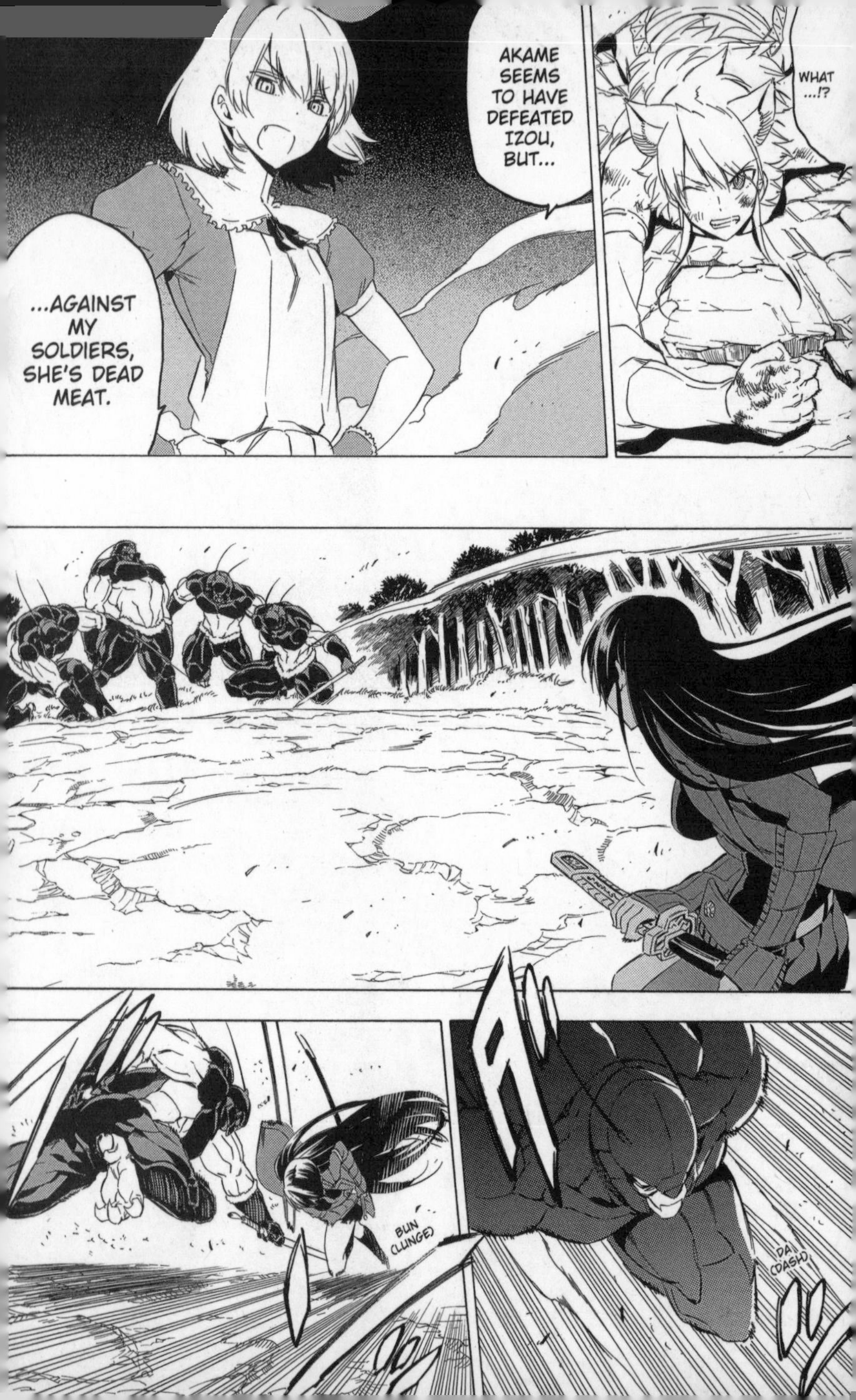
AKAME SEEMS TO HAVE DEFEATED IZOU, BUT...
...AGAINST MY SOLDIERS, SHE'S DEAD MEAT.
WHAT ...!?
DA (DASH)
BUN (LUNGE)

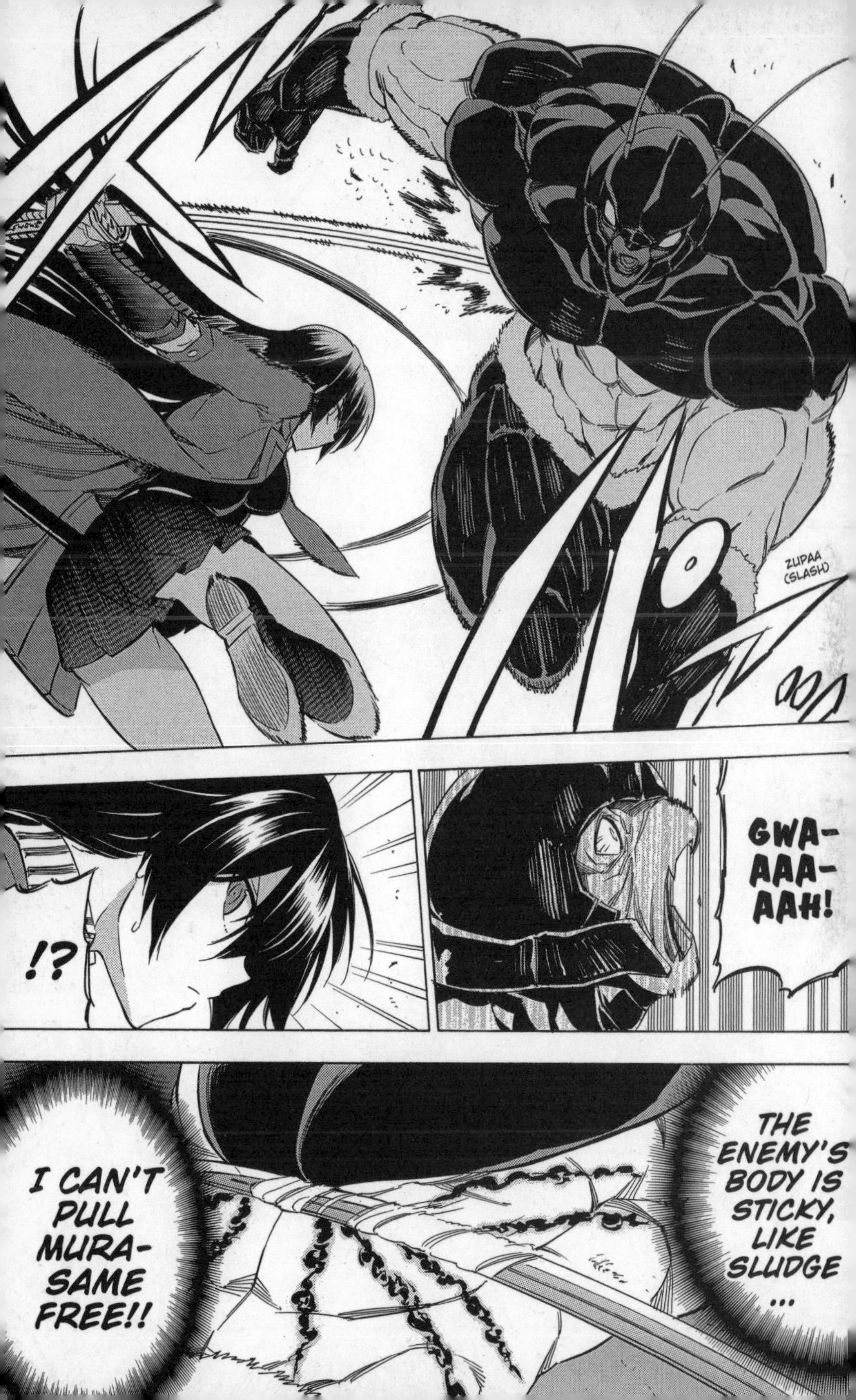
ZUPAA (SLASH)
GWA-AAA-AAH!
!?
THE ENEMY'S BODY IS STICKY, LIKE SLUDGE ...
I CAN'T PULL MURA-SAME FREE!!

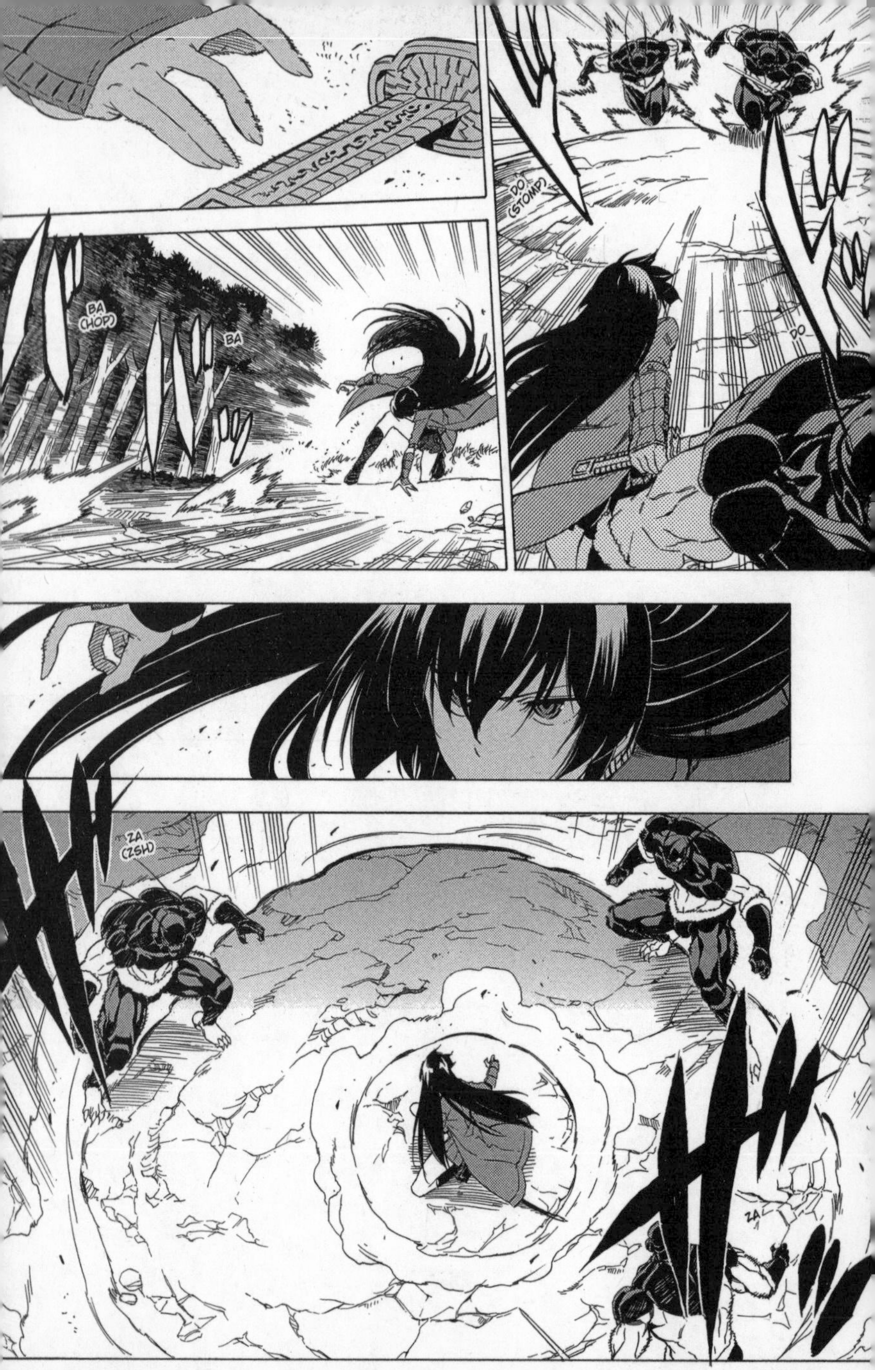
DO (STOMP)
DO
BA (HOP)
BA
ZA (ZSH)
ZA

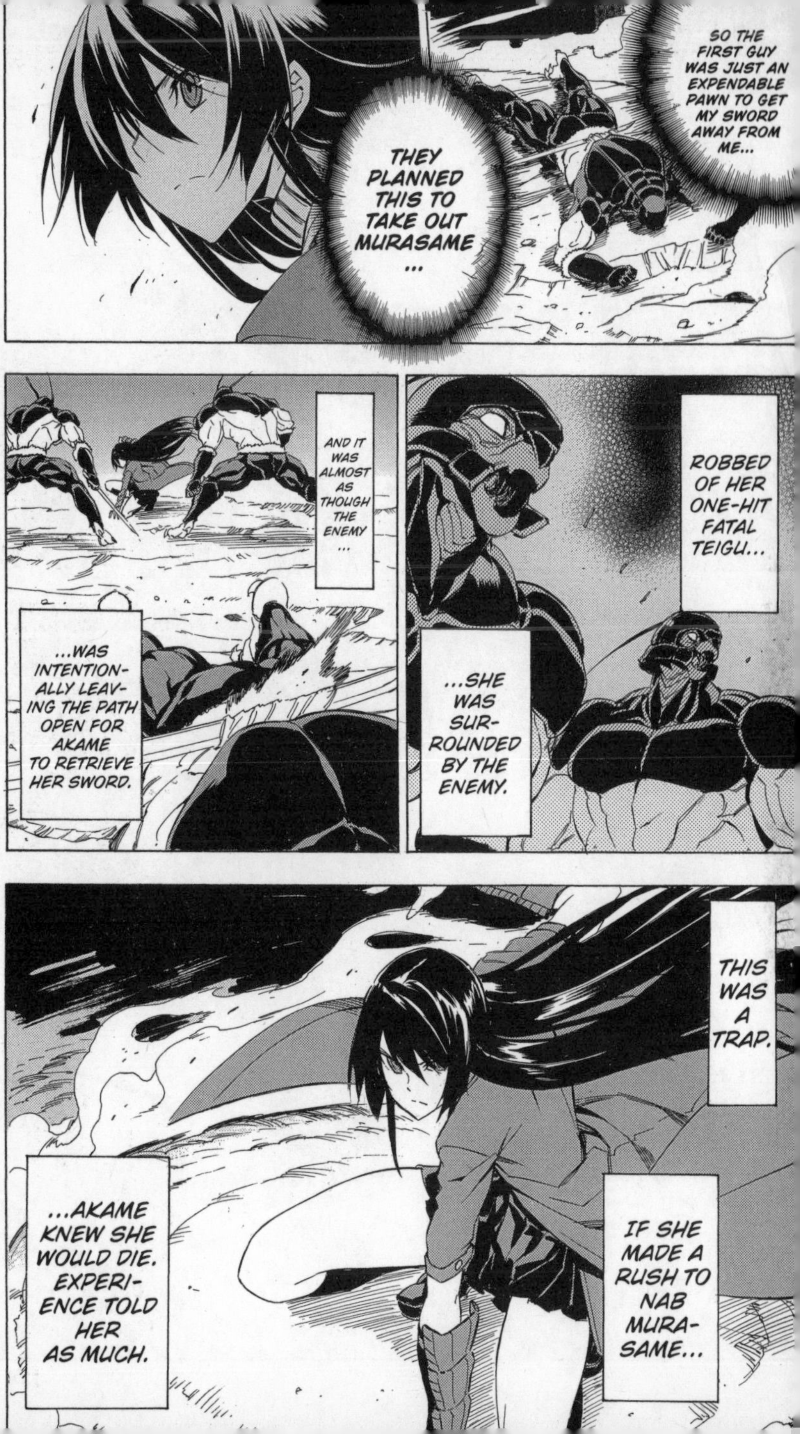
SO THE FIRST GUY WAS JUST AN EXPENDABLE PAWN TO GET MY SWORD AWAY FROM ME...
THEY PLANNED THIS TO TAKE OUT MURASAME ...
ROBBED OF HER ONE-HIT FATAL TEIGU...
...SHE WAS SURROUNDED BY THE ENEMY.
AND IT WAS ALMOST AS THOUGH THE ENEMY ...
...WAS INTENTIONALLY LEAVING THE PATH OPEN FOR AKAME TO RETRIEVE HER SWORD.
THIS WAS A TRAP.
IF SHE MADE A RUSH TO NAB MURASAME...
...AKAME KNEW SHE WOULD DIE. EXPERIENCE TOLD HER AS MUCH.

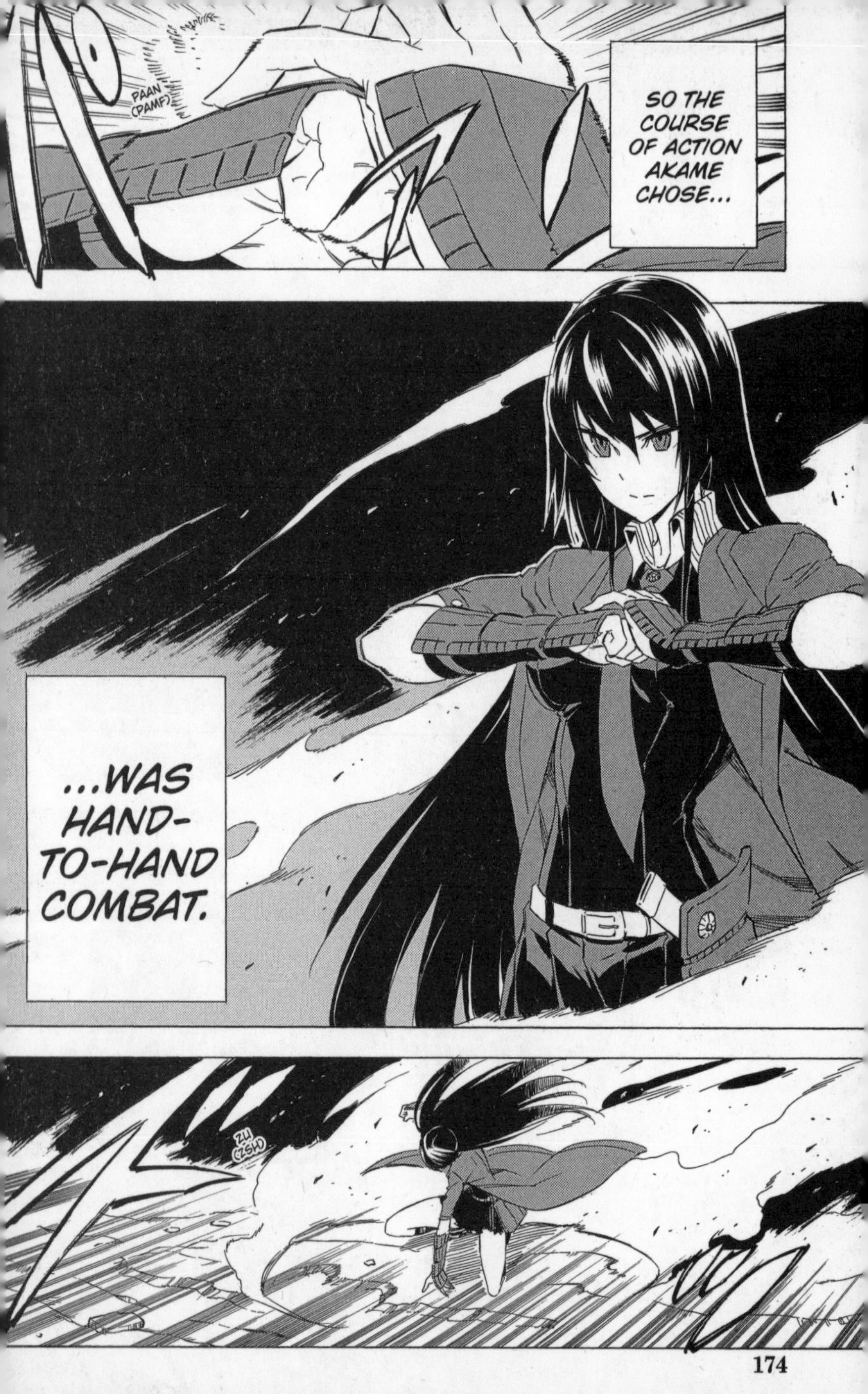
SO THE COURSE OF ACTION AKAME CHOSE...
PAAN (PAMF)
...WAS HAND-TO-HAND COMBAT.
ZU (ZSH)

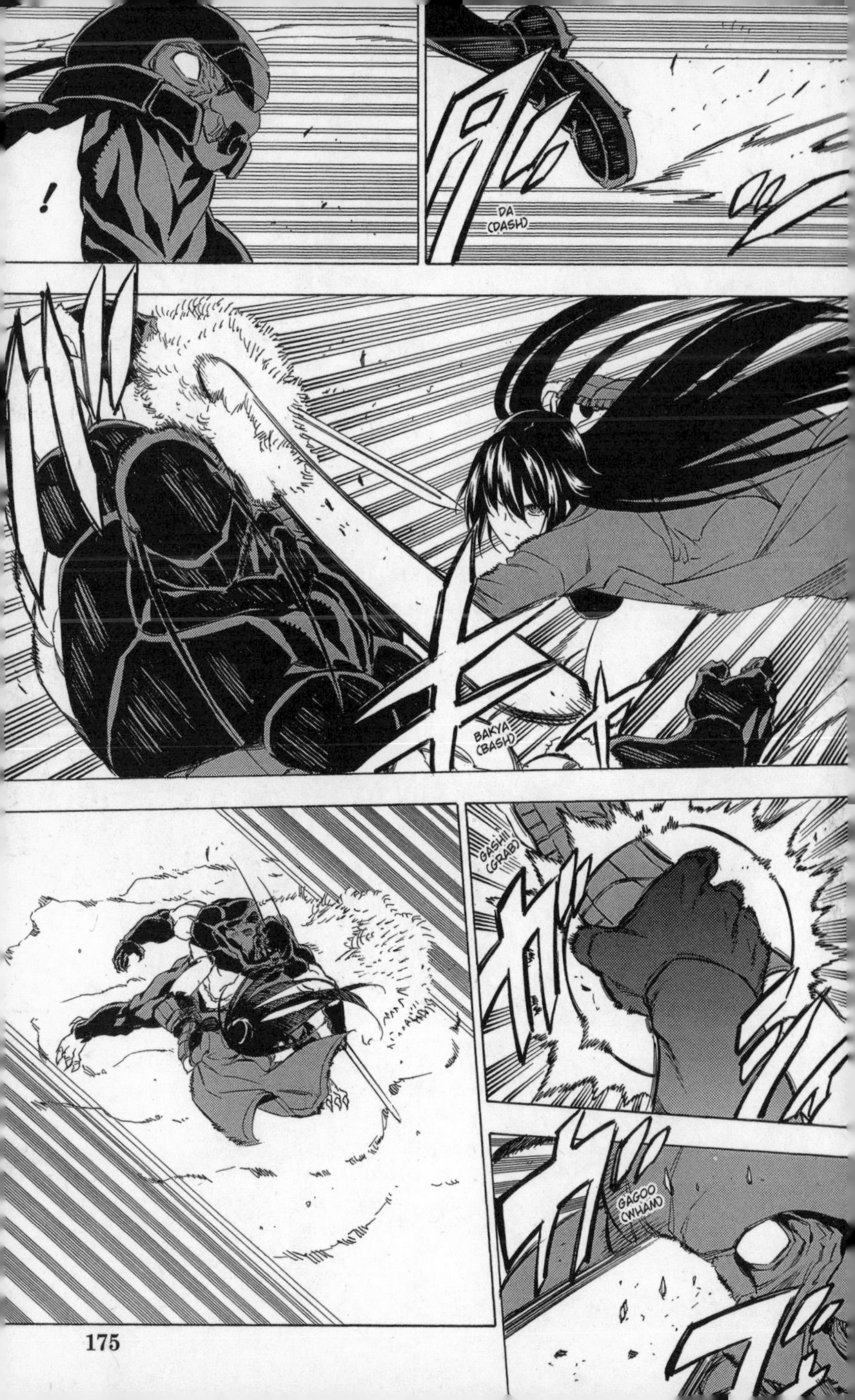
!
DA
(DASH)
BAKYA
(BASH)
GASHI
(GRAB)
GAGOO
(WHAM)

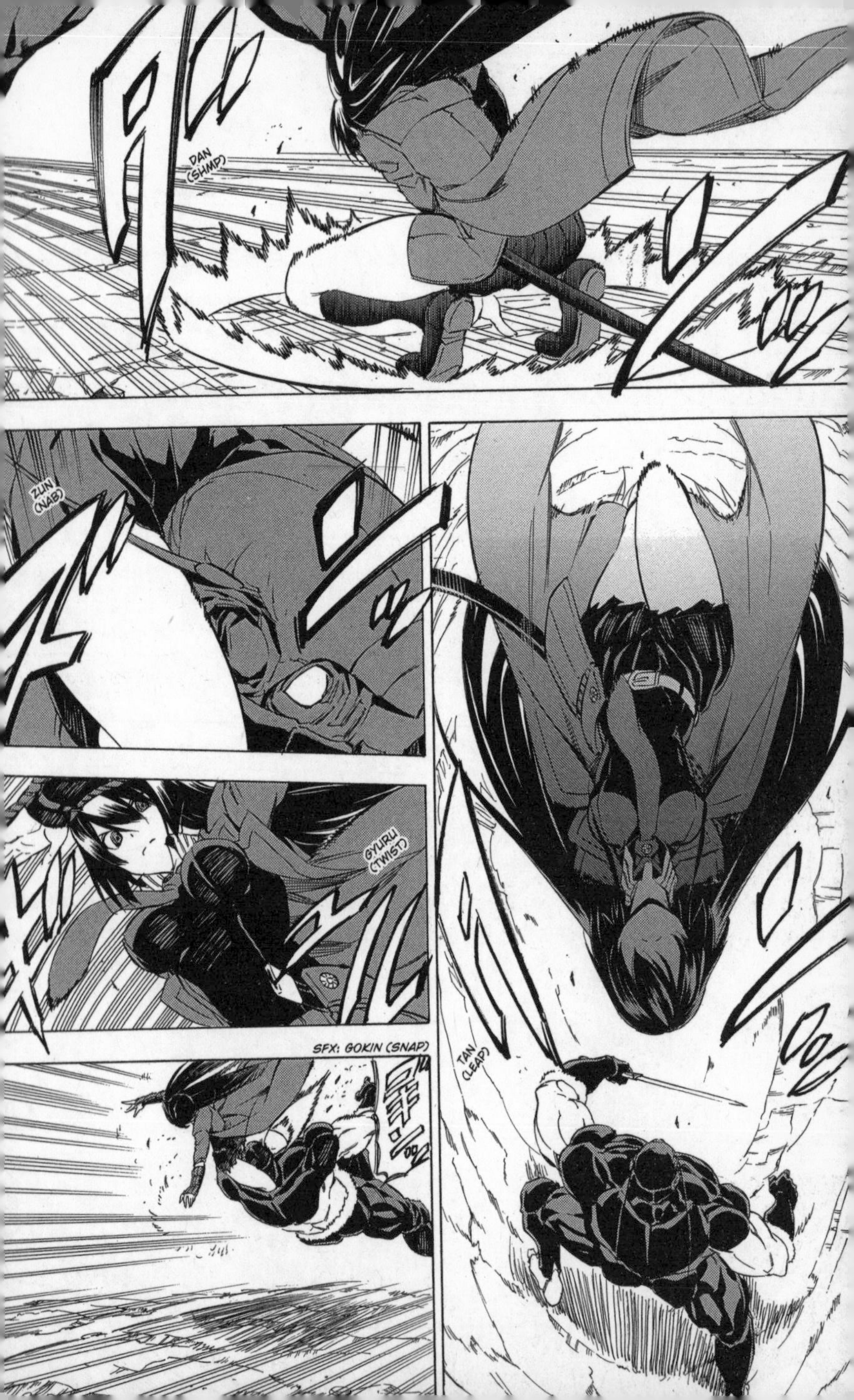
DAN (SHMP)
ZUN (NAB)
GYURU (TWIST)
TAN (LEAP)
SFX: GOKIN (SNAP)

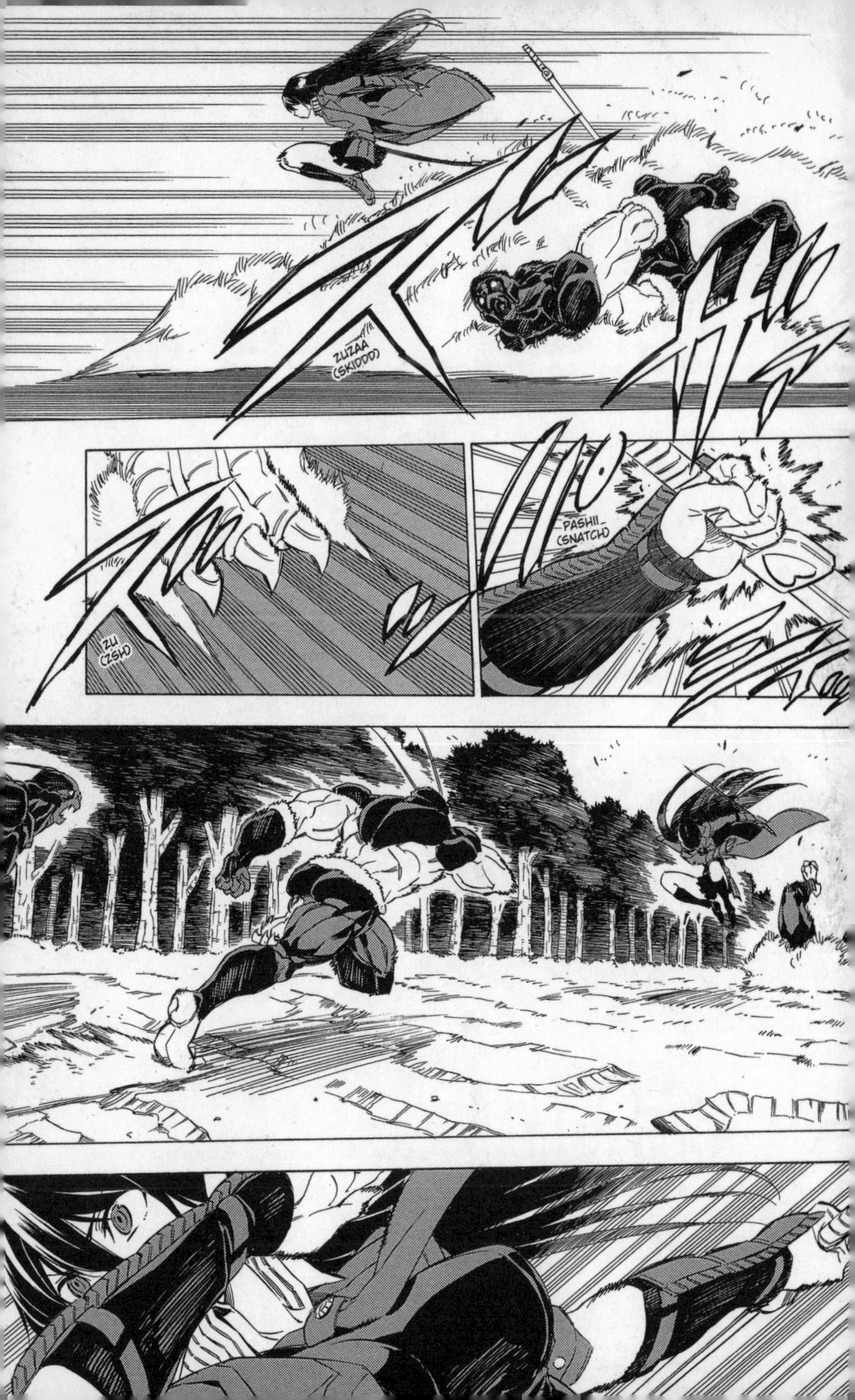
ZUZAA
(SKIDDD)
PASHII
(SNATCH)
ZU
(ZSH)

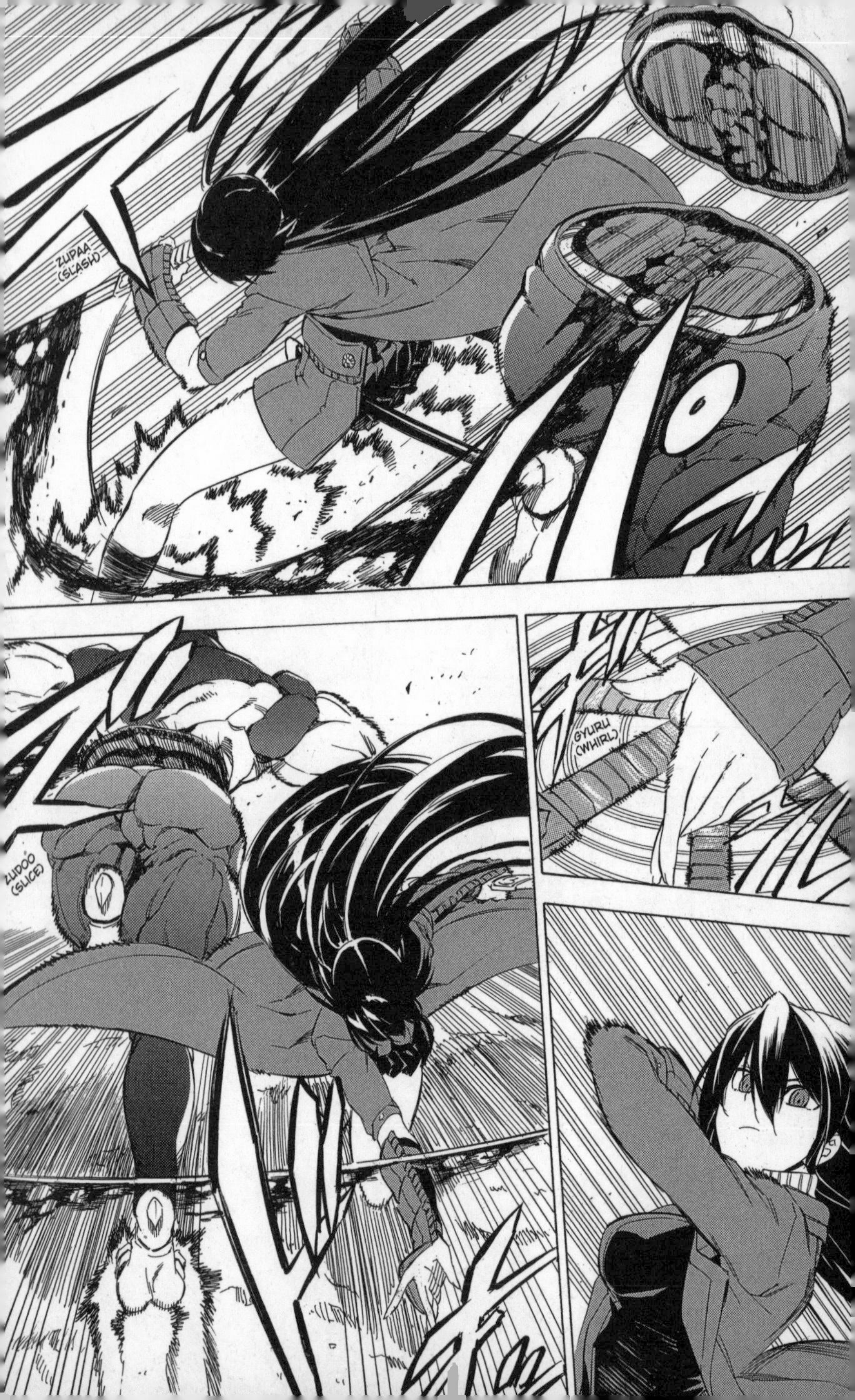
ZUPAA (SLASH)
GYURU (WHIRL)
ZUDOO (SLICE)

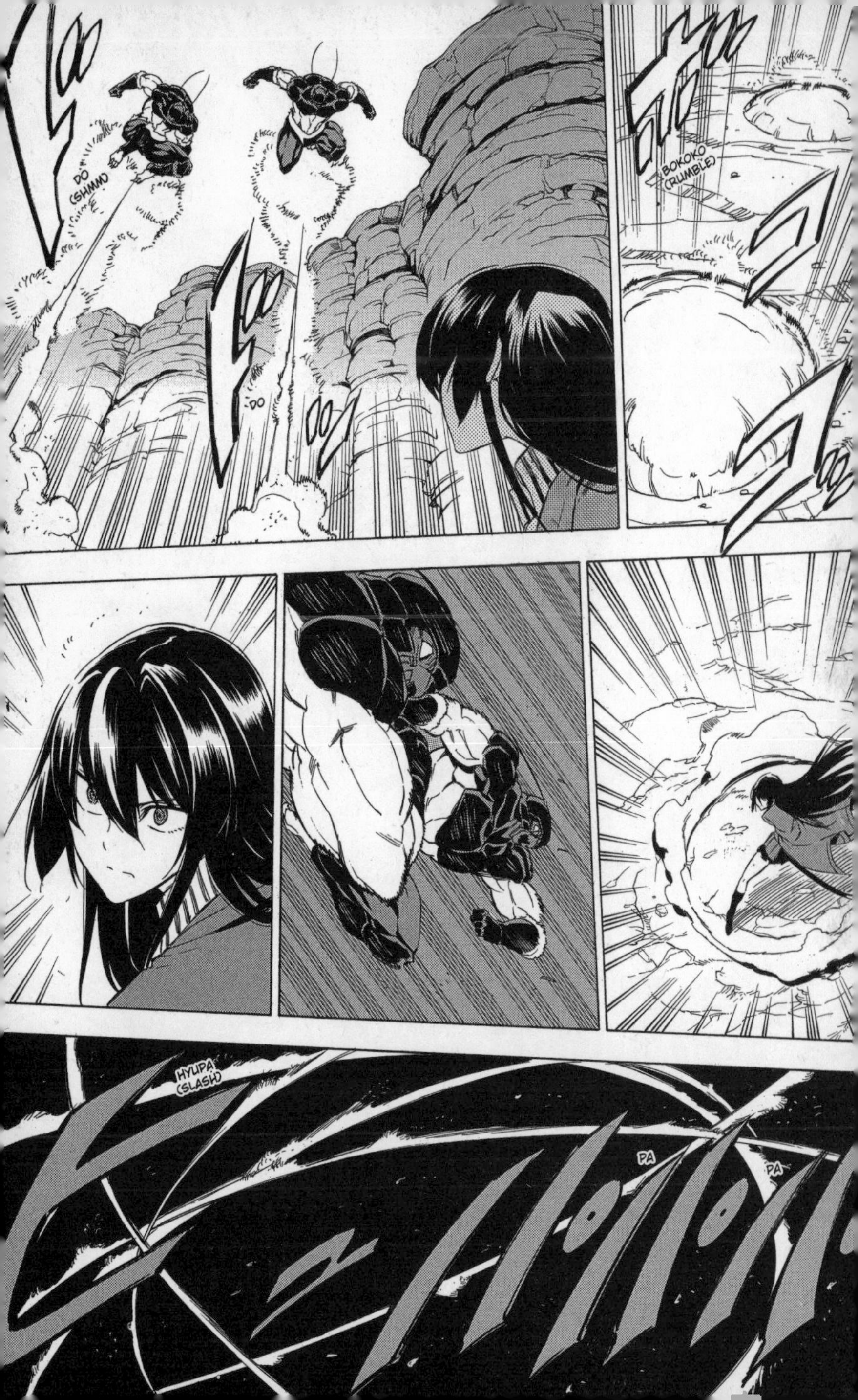
BOKOKO
(RUMBLE)
DO
(SHMM)
DO
HYUPA
(SLASH)
PA
PA

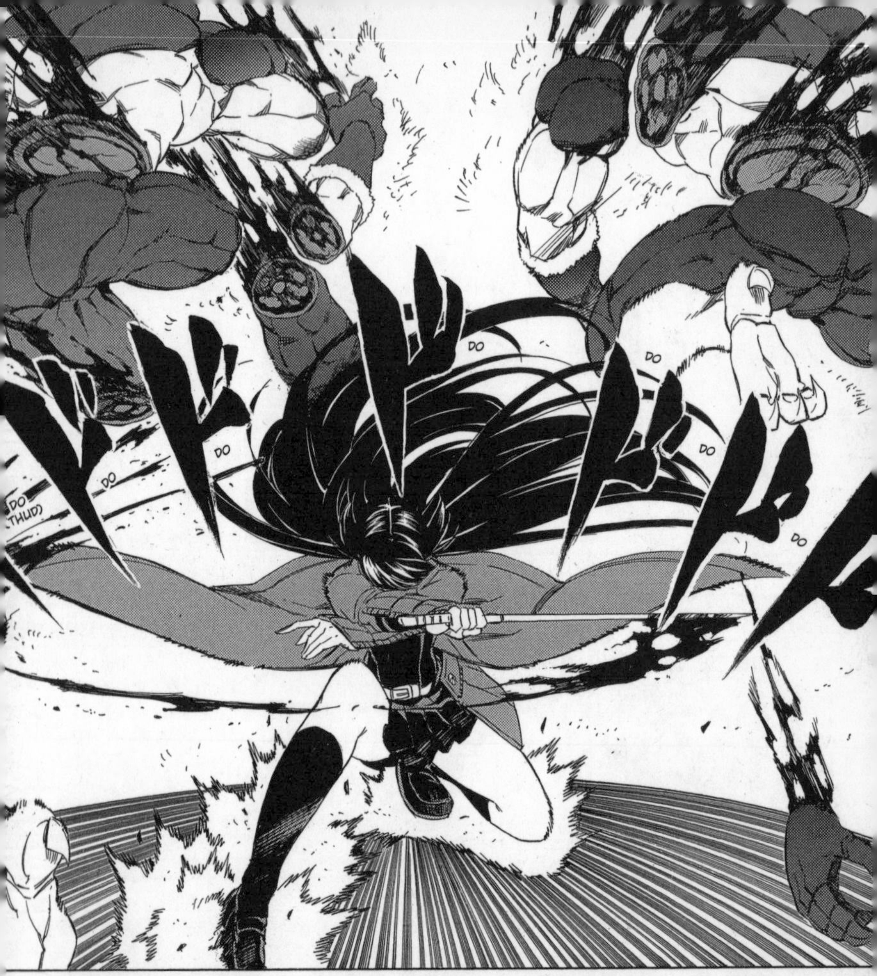

DO
DO
DO
DO
DO (THUD)
DO
DO
DO

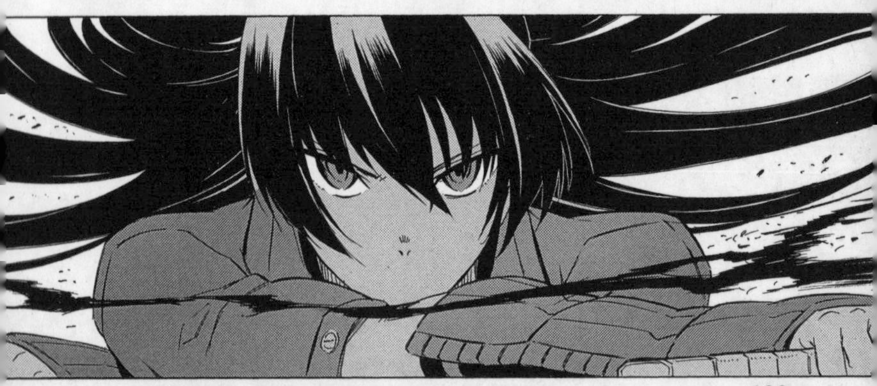

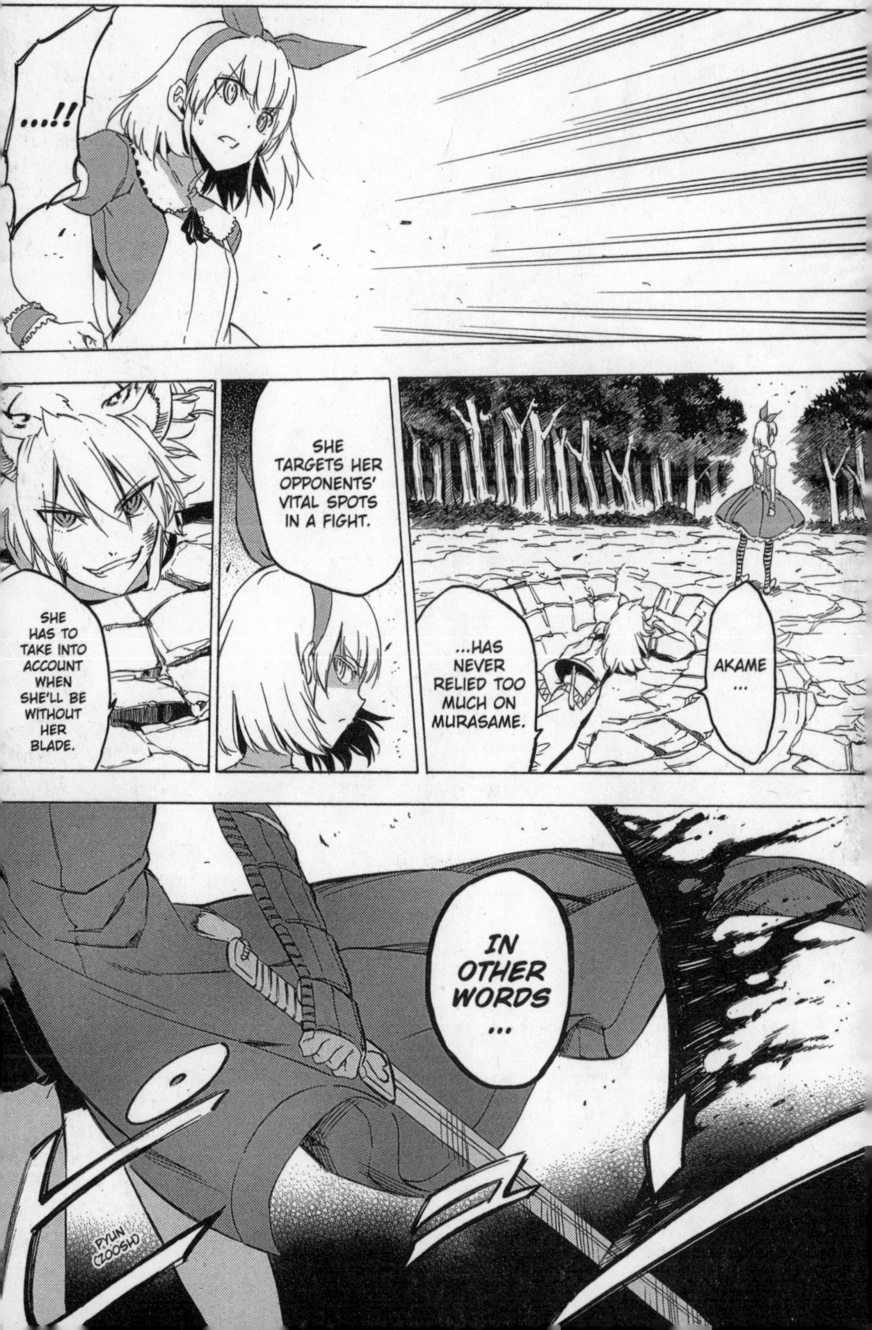
...!!
AKAME ...
...HAS NEVER RELIED TOO MUCH ON MURASAME.
SHE TARGETS HER OPPONENTS' VITAL SPOTS IN A FIGHT.
SHE HAS TO TAKE INTO ACCOUNT WHEN SHE'LL BE WITHOUT HER BLADE.
IN OTHER WORDS ...
PYUN (ZOOSH)

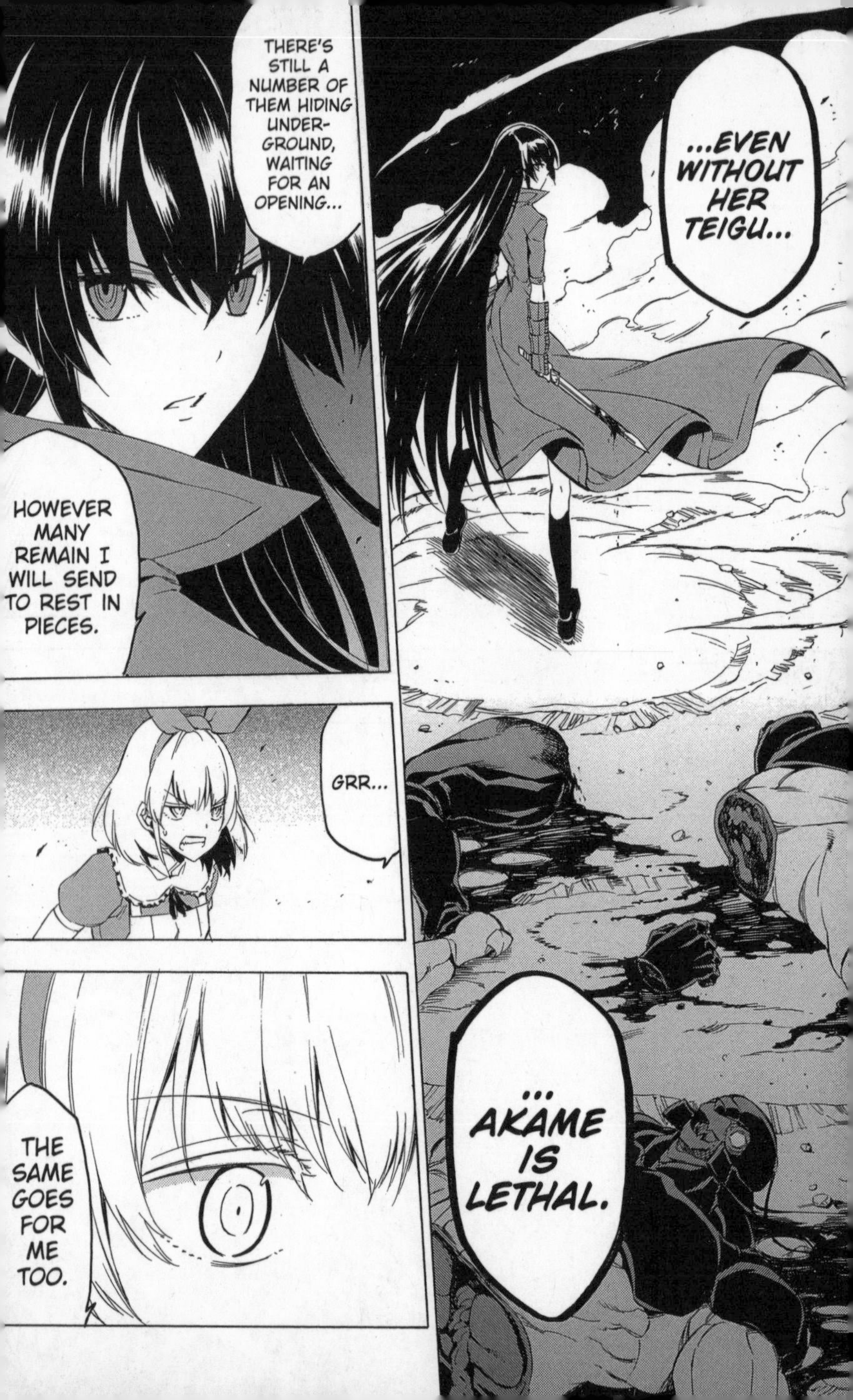
...EVEN WITHOUT HER TEIGU...
... AKÄME IS LETHAL.
THERE'S STILL A NUMBER OF THEM HIDING UNDER-GROUND, WAITING FOR AN OPENING...
HOWEVER MANY REMAIN I WILL SEND TO REST IN PIECES.
GRR...
THE SAME GOES FOR ME TOO.

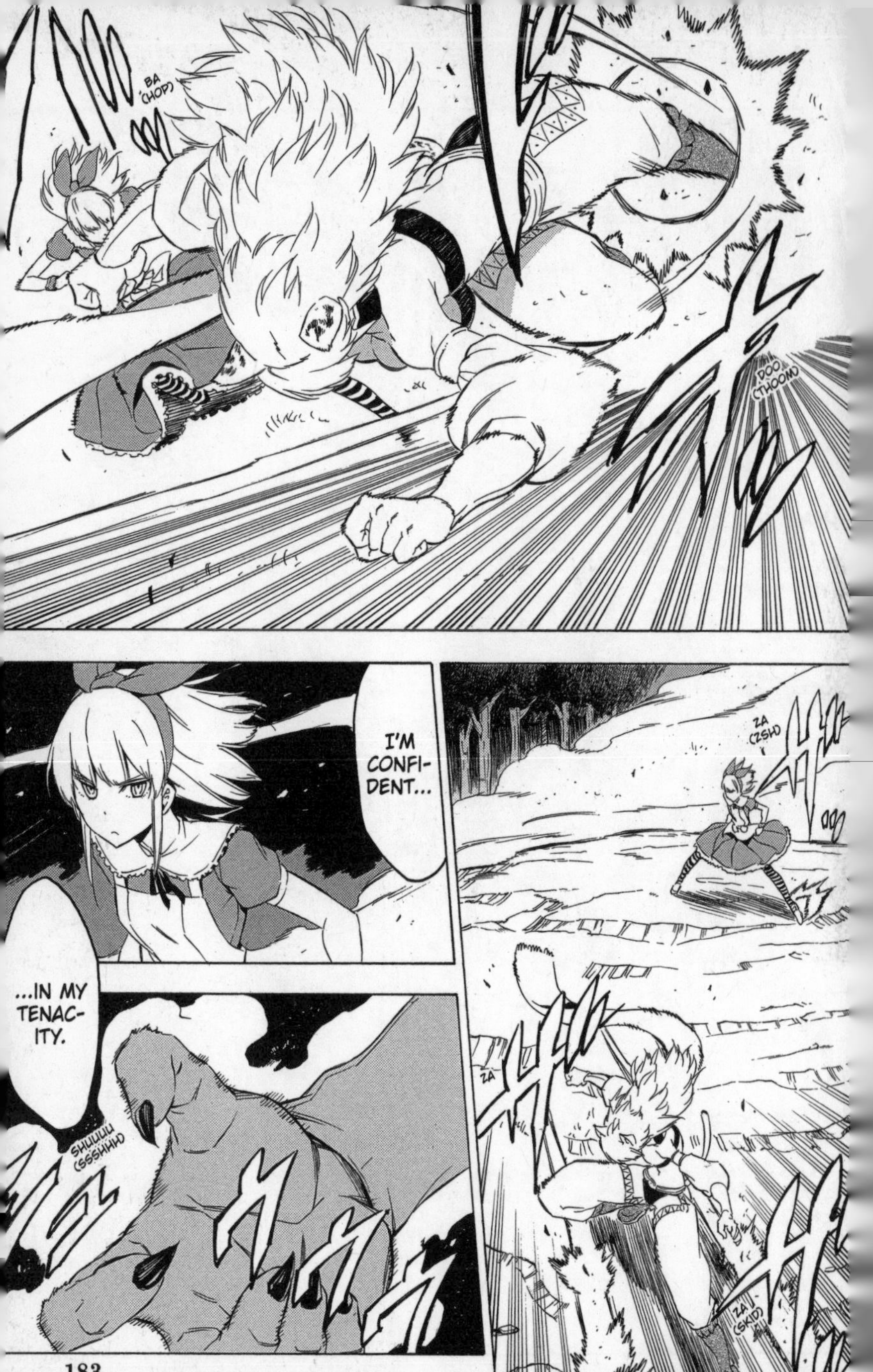

DOO (THOOM)
BA (HOP)
ZA (ZSH)
I'M CONFI-DENT...
...IN MY TENAC-ITY.
SHUUUU (SSSHHH)
ZA
ZA (SKID)

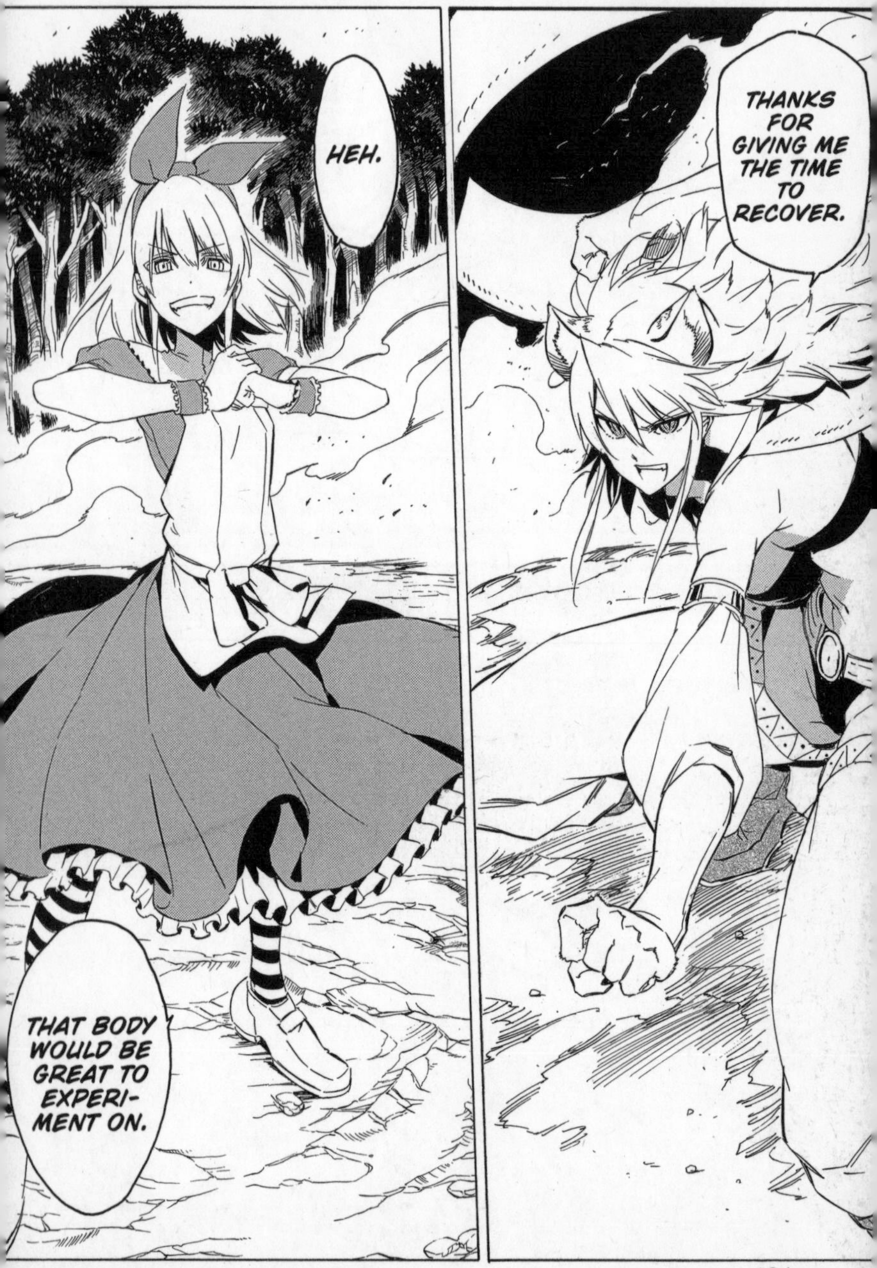
THANKS FOR GIVING ME THE TIME TO RECOVER.
HEH.
THAT BODY WOULD BE GREAT TO EXPERI-MENT ON.

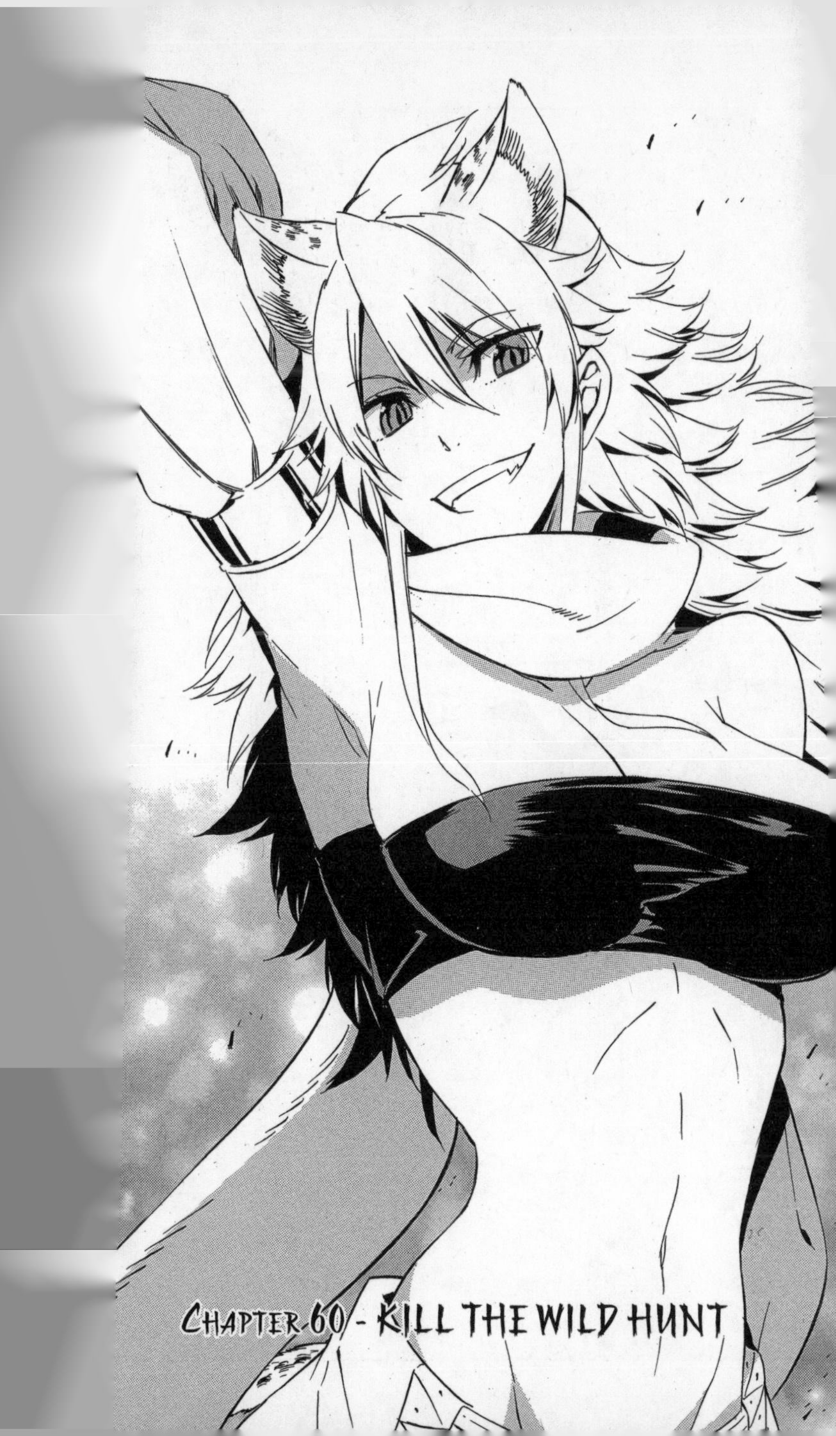
CHAPTER 60 - KILL THE WILD HUNT

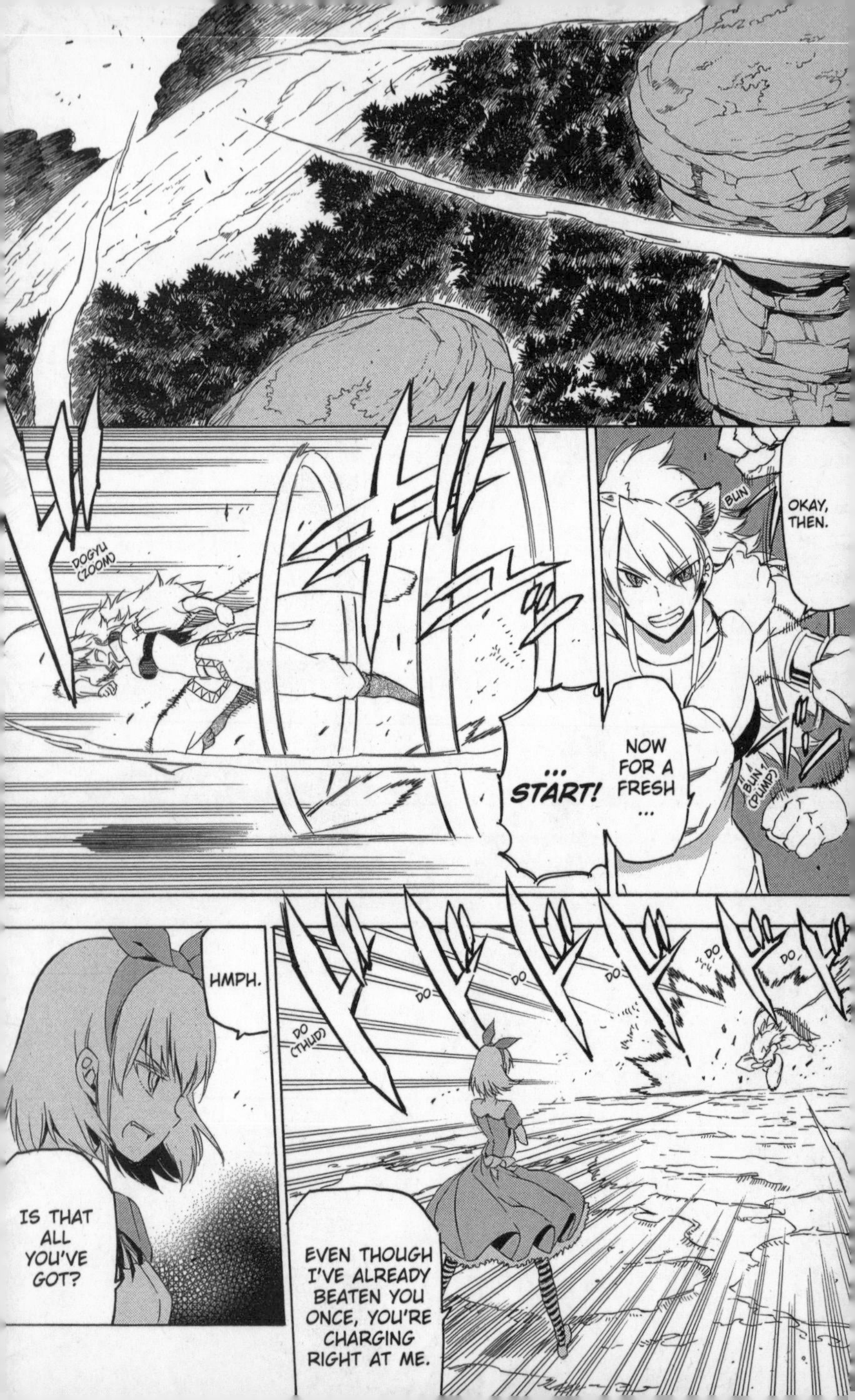
BUN
OKAY, THEN.
DOGYU (ZOOM)
NOW FOR A FRESH ...
... START!
BUN (PUMP)
DO
DO
DO
DO
DO
DO (THUD)
HMPH.
EVEN THOUGH I'VE ALREADY BEATEN YOU ONCE, YOU'RE CHARGING RIGHT AT ME.
IS THAT ALL YOU'VE GOT?

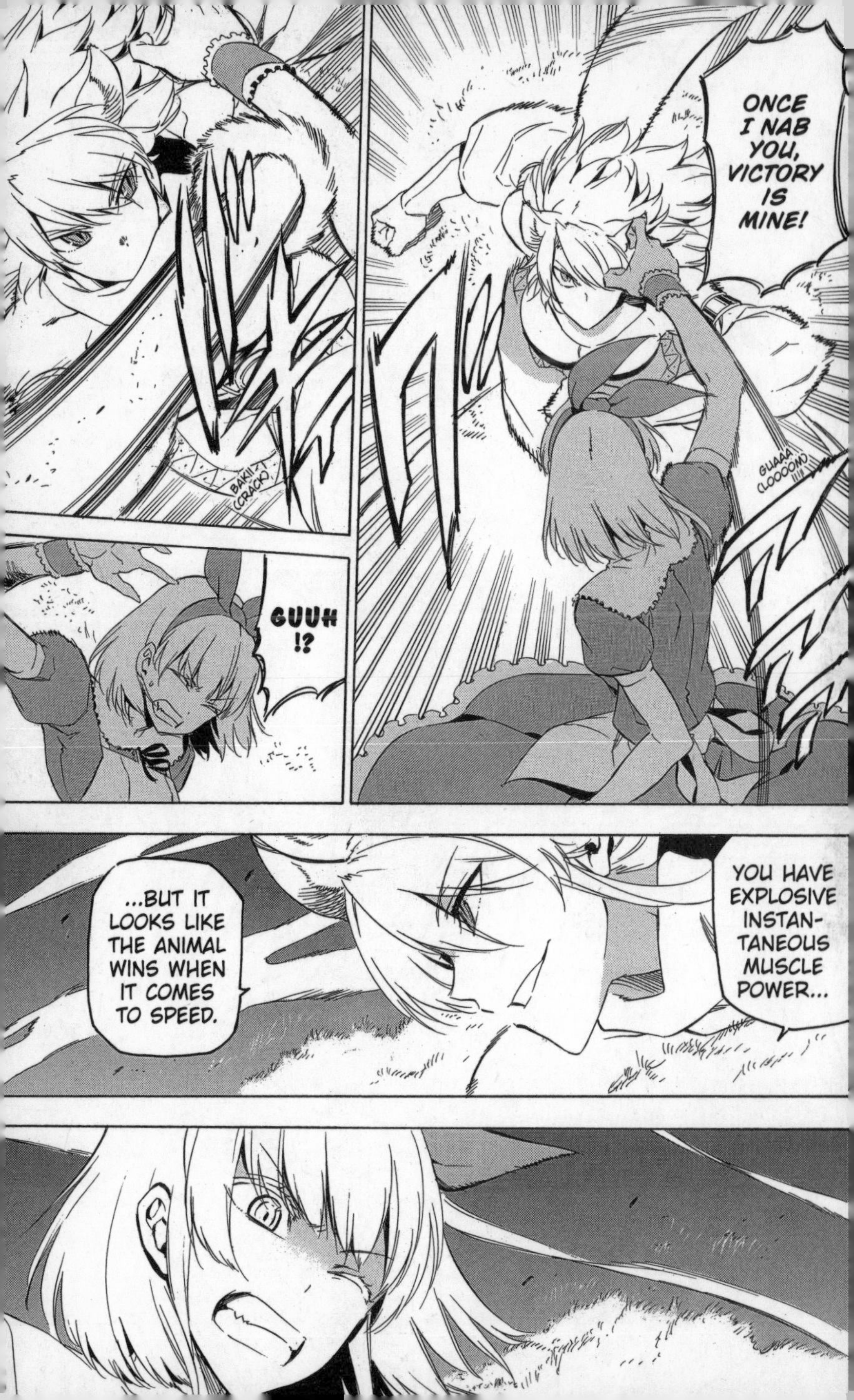
ONCE I NAB YOU, VICTORY IS MINE!
GUAAA (LOOOOOM)
BAKII (CRACK)
GUUH !?
YOU HAVE EXPLOSIVE INSTAN-TANEOUS MUSCLE POWER...
...BUT IT LOOKS LIKE THE ANIMAL WINS WHEN IT COMES TO SPEED.

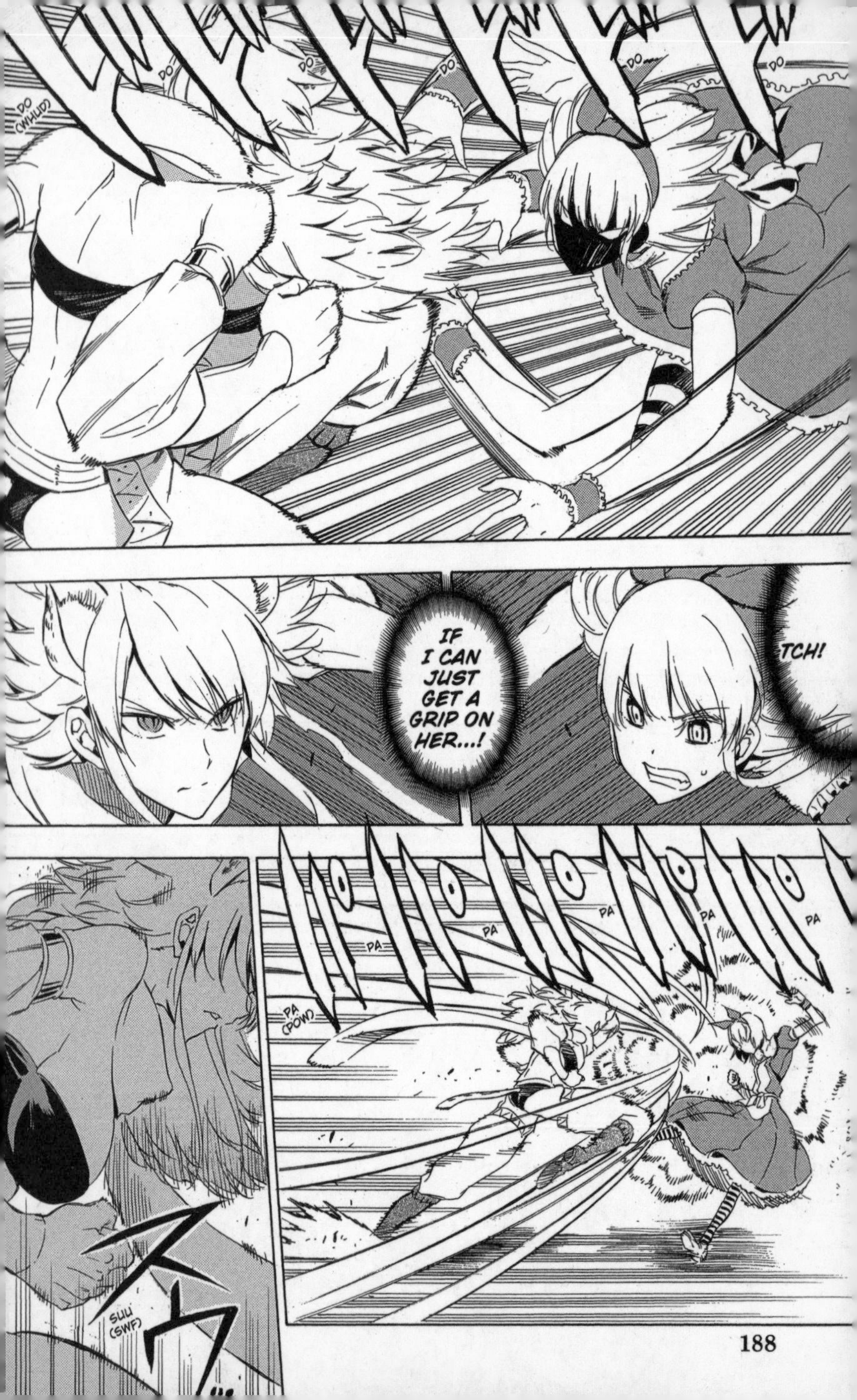
DO
DO
DO
DO
DO (WHUD)
TCH!
IF I CAN JUST GET A GRIP ON HER...!
PA
PA
PA
PA
PA (POW)
SUU (SWF)

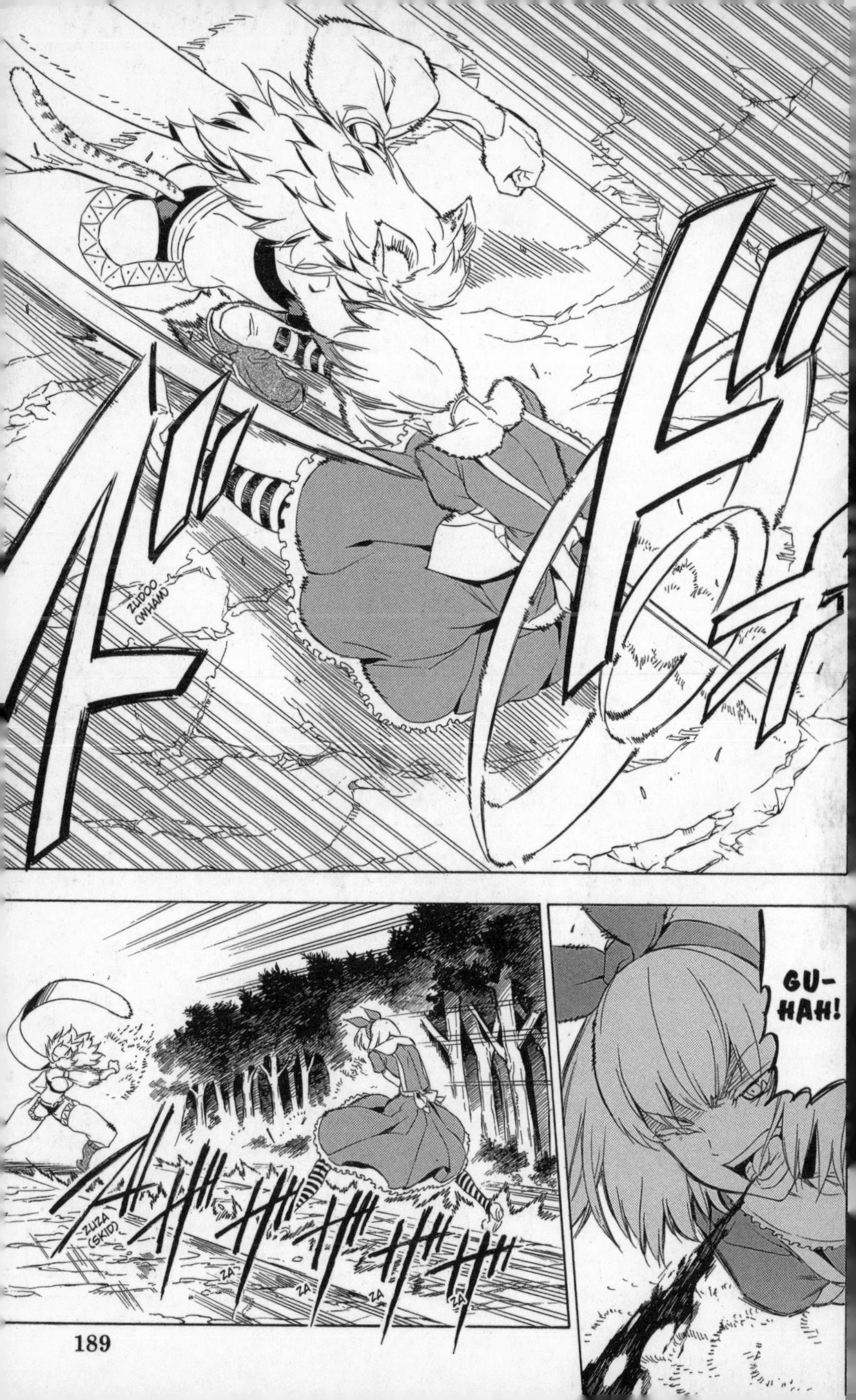
ZUDOO (WHAM)
GU-HAH!
ZUZA (SKID)
ZA
ZA
ZA

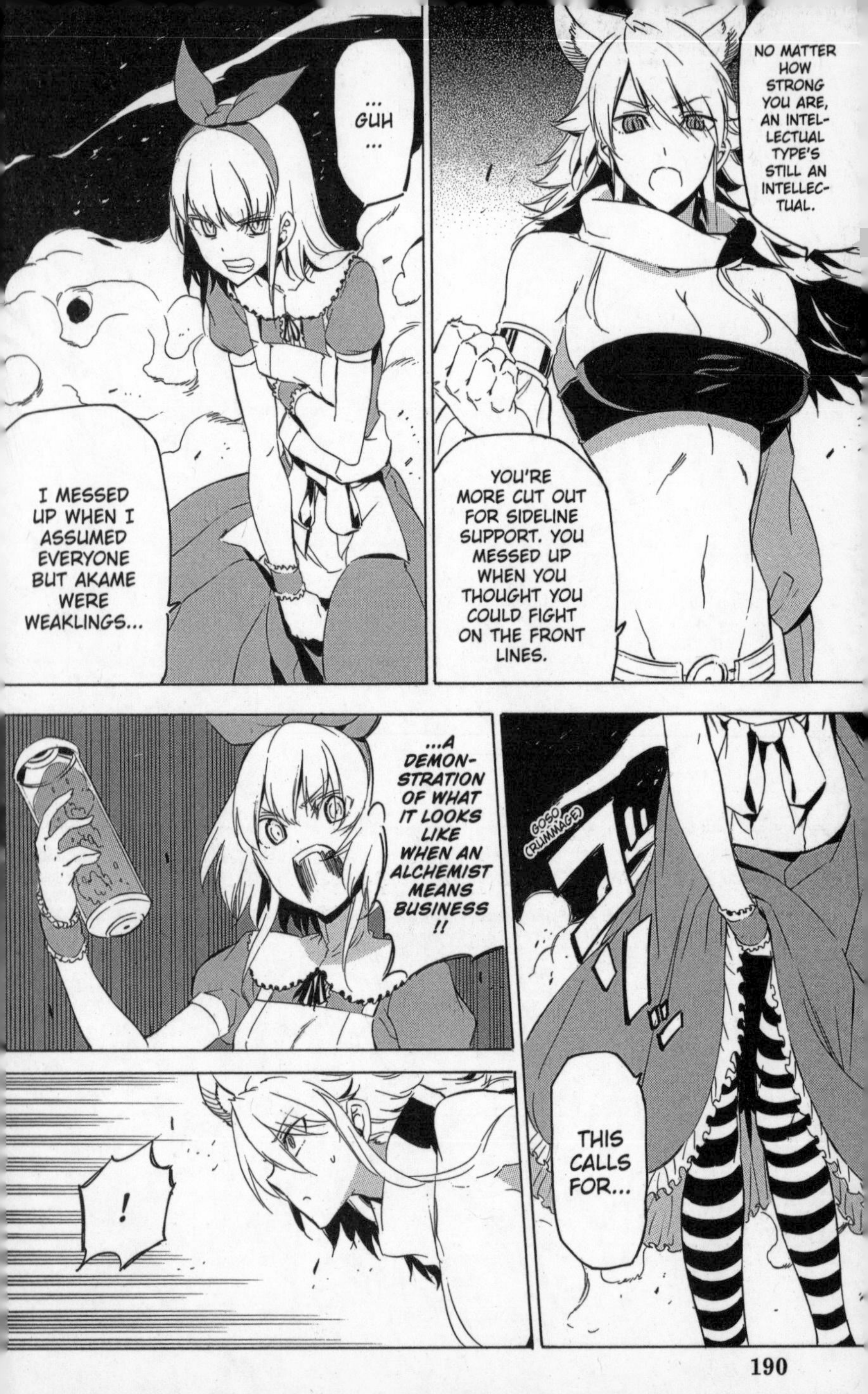
NO MATTER HOW STRONG YOU ARE, AN INTELLECTUAL TYPE'S STILL AN INTELLECTUAL.
YOU'RE MORE CUT OUT FOR SIDELINE SUPPORT. YOU MESSED UP WHEN YOU THOUGHT YOU COULD FIGHT ON THE FRONT LINES.
... GUH ...
I MESSED UP WHEN I ASSUMED EVERYONE BUT AKAME WERE WEAKLINGS...
GOSO (RUMMAGE)
THIS CALLS FOR...
...A DEMONSTRATION OF WHAT IT LOOKS LIKE WHEN AN ALCHEMIST MEANS BUSINESS!!
!

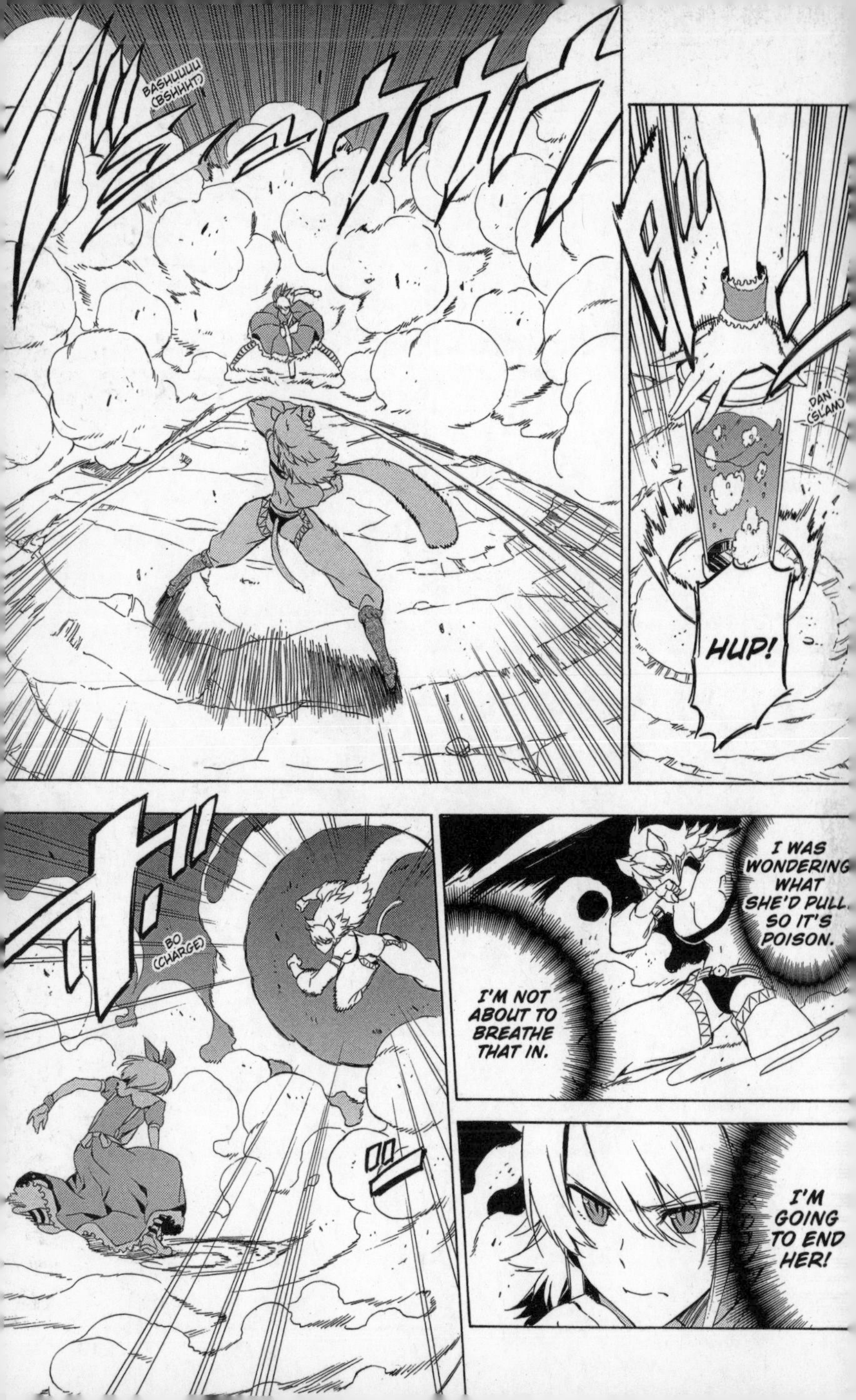
BASHUUUU
(BSHHHT)
DAN
(SLAM)
HUP!
I WAS WONDERING WHAT SHE'D PULL. SO IT'S POISON.
I'M NOT ABOUT TO BREATHE THAT IN.
BO
(CHARGE)
I'M GOING TO END HER!

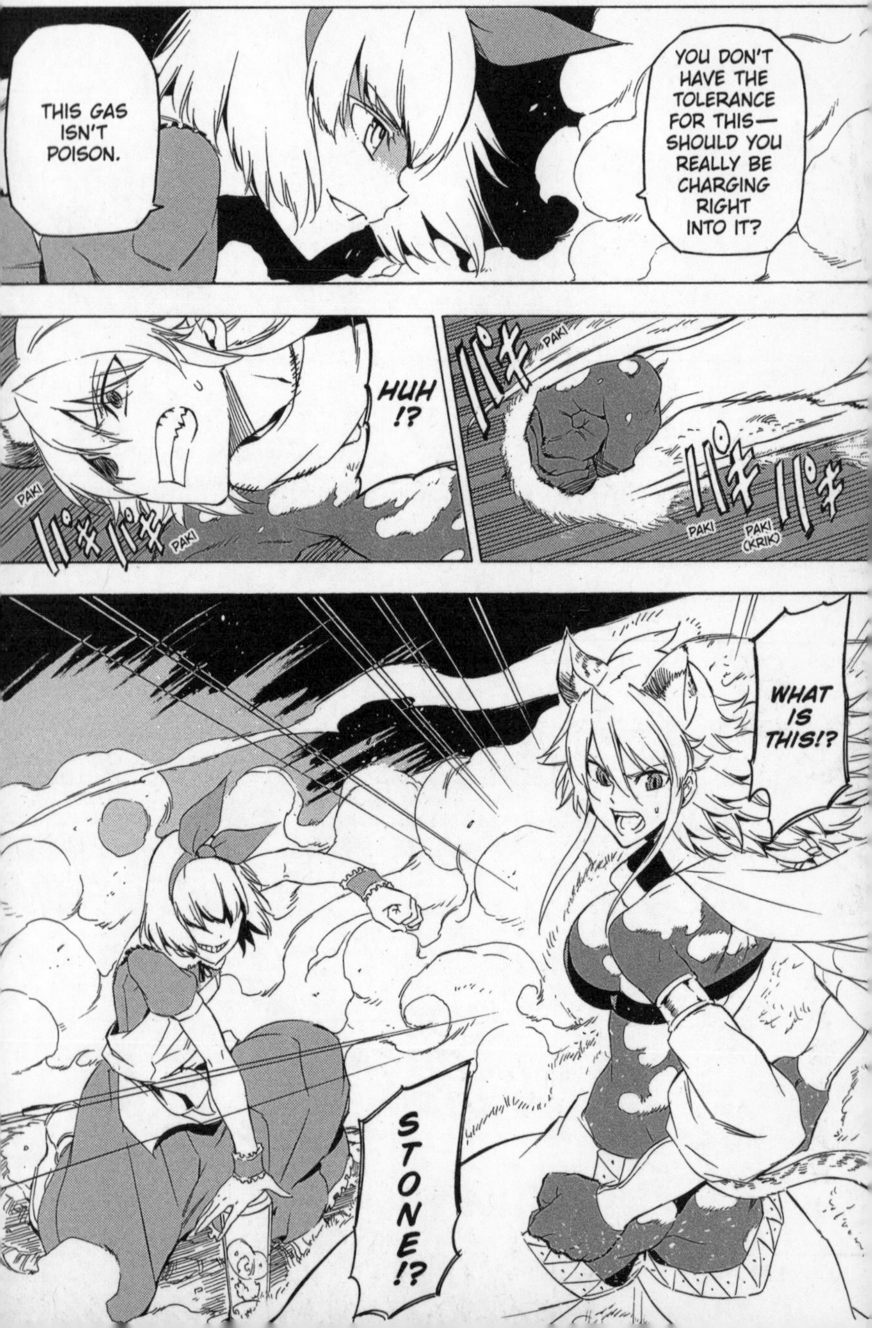

YOU DON'T HAVE THE TOLERANCE FOR THIS—SHOULD YOU REALLY BE CHARGING RIGHT INTO IT?
THIS GAS ISN'T POISON.
パキ
PAKI
パキパキ
PAKI
PAKI (KRIK)
HUH!?
パキパキ
PAKI
PAKI
WHAT IS THIS!?
STONE!?

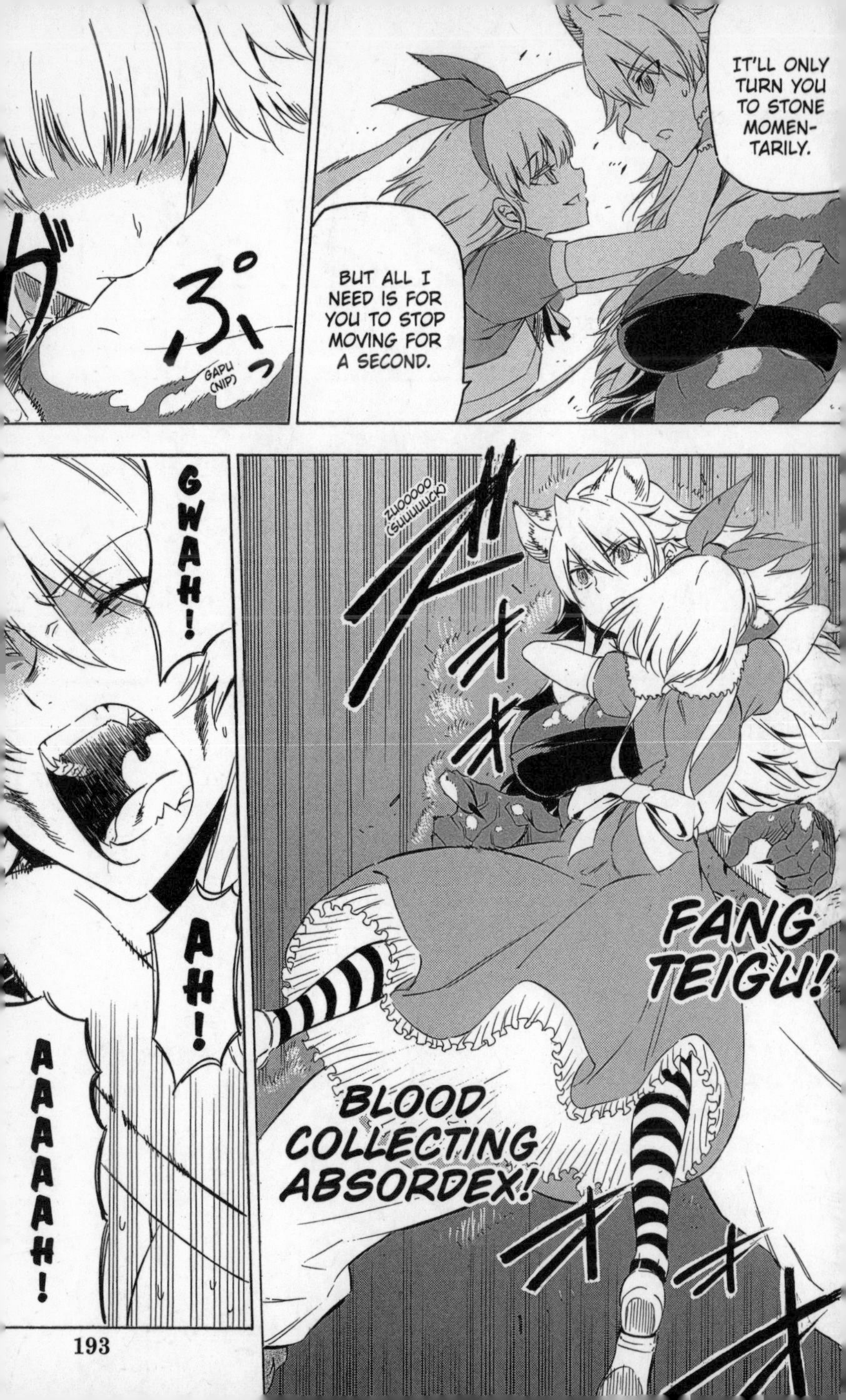
IT'LL ONLY TURN YOU TO STONE MOMENTARILY.
BUT ALL I NEED IS FOR YOU TO STOP MOVING FOR A SECOND.
GAPU (NIP)
FANG TEIGU!
BLOOD COLLECTING ABSORDEX!
GWAH!
AH!
AAAAAAH!

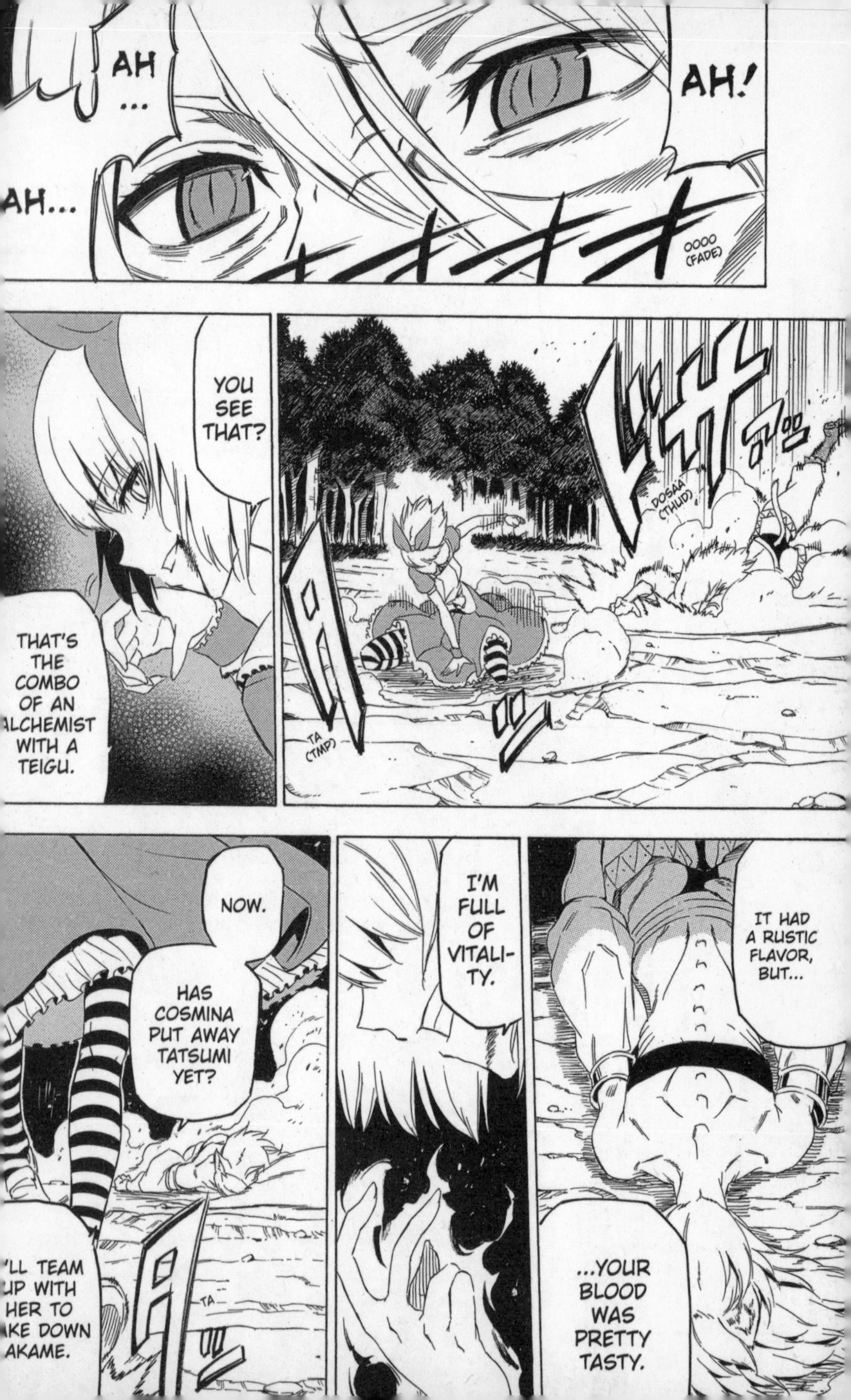
AH!
AH ...
AH...
OOOO (FADE)
DOSAA (THUD)
TA (TMP)
YOU SEE THAT?
THAT'S THE COMBO OF AN LCHEMIST WITH A TEIGU.
IT HAD A RUSTIC FLAVOR, BUT...
...YOUR BLOOD WAS PRETTY TASTY.
I'M FULL OF VITALITY.
NOW.
HAS COSMINA PUT AWAY TATSUMI YET?
'LL TEAM UP WITH HER TO AKE DOWN AKAME.
TA

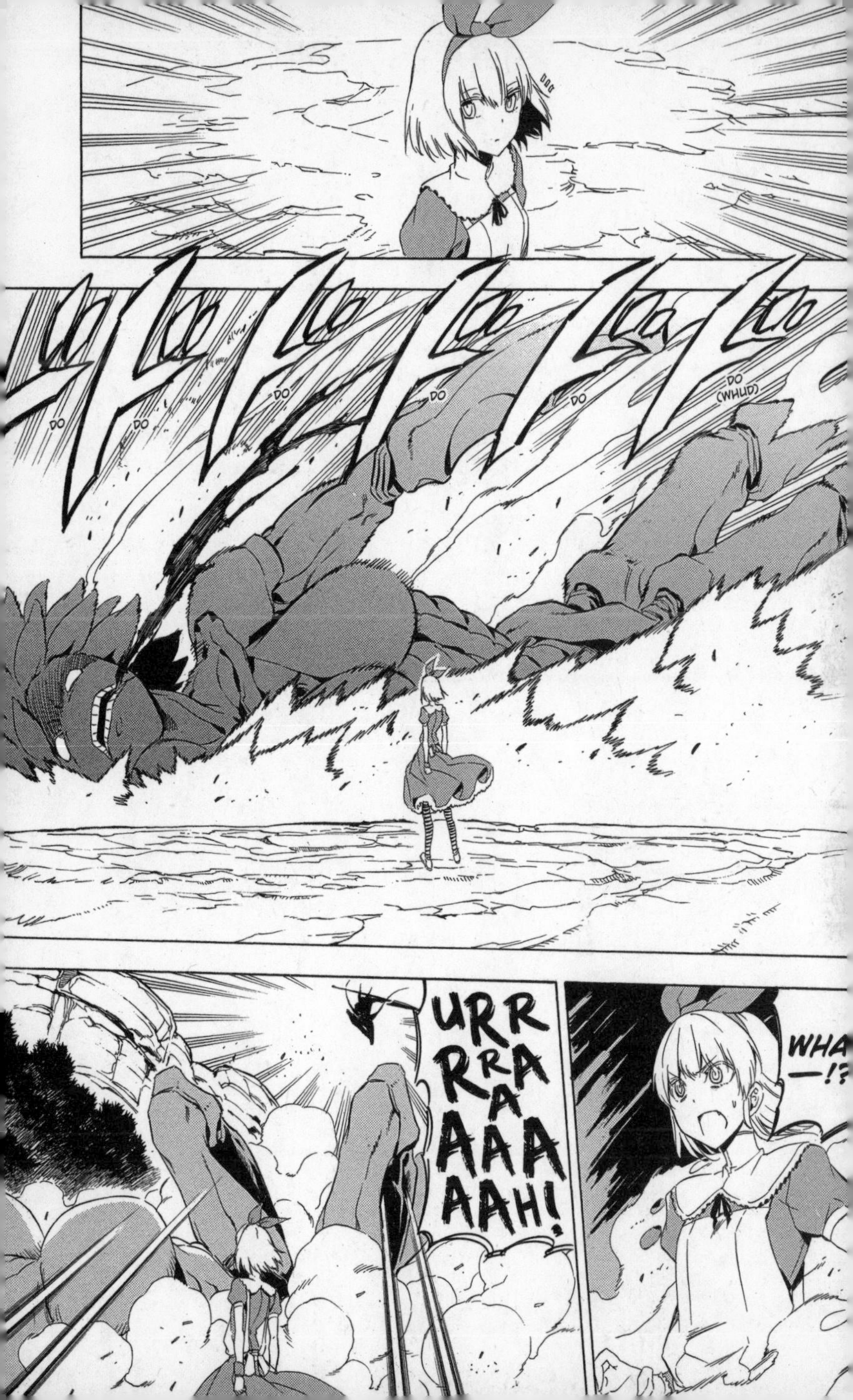
DO
(WHUD)
DO
DO
DO
DO
DO
WHA
—!?
URRRRAAAAAAAH!

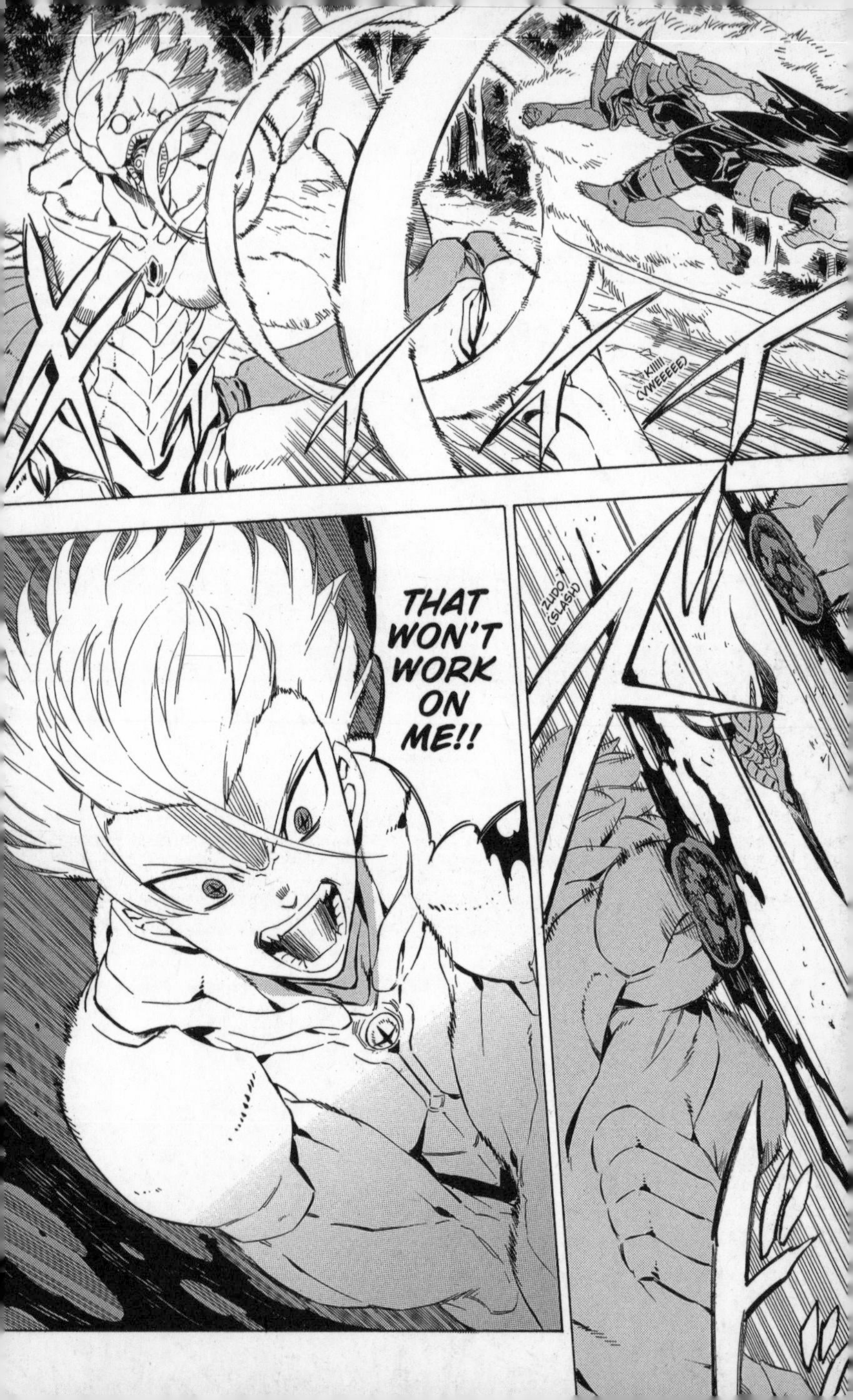
KIIIIII (VWEEEEE)
ZUDO (SLASH)
THAT WON'T WORK ON ME!!

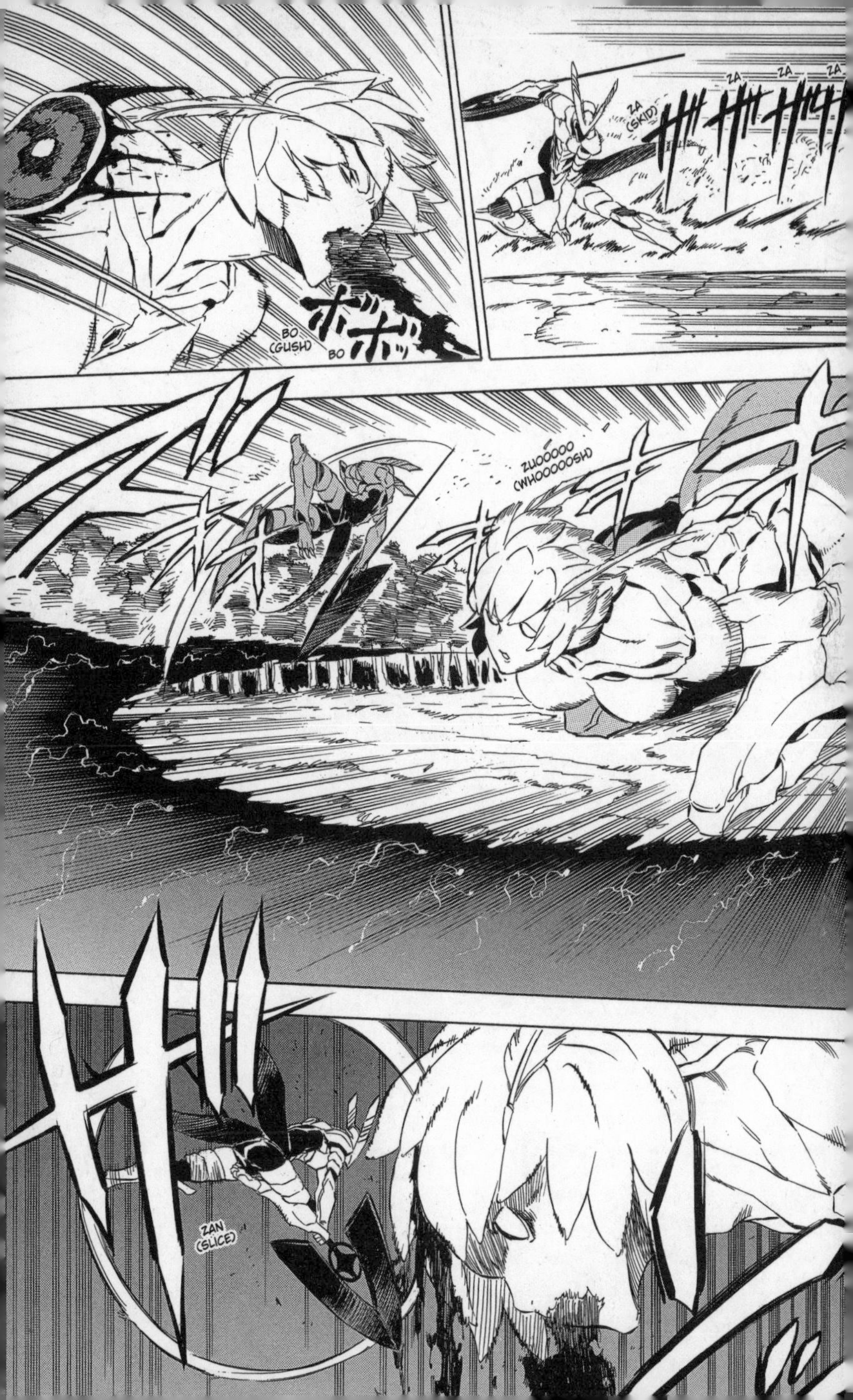
ZA ZA ZA
ZA (SKID)
ザザザザ
BO (GUSH) BO
ボボッ
ZUOOOOO (WHOOOOOSH)
ズオオオ
ザン
ZAN (SLICE)

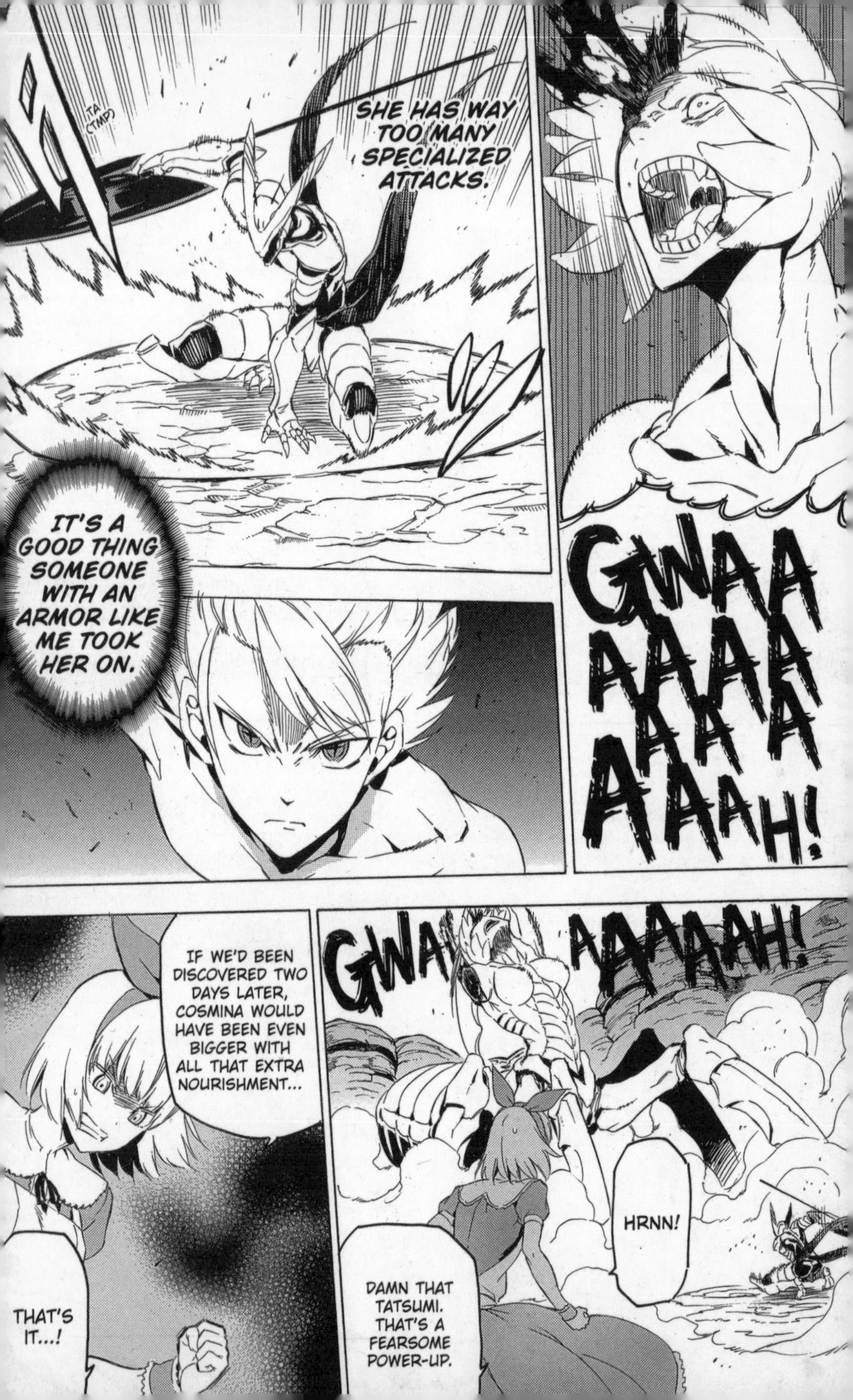
GWAAAAAAAAAAAAAH!
TA (TMP)
SHE HAS WAY TOO MANY SPECIALIZED ATTACKS.
IT'S A GOOD THING SOMEONE WITH AN ARMOR LIKE ME TOOK HER ON.
GWA
AAAAAH!
HRNN!
DAMN THAT TATSUMI. THAT'S A FEARSOME POWER-UP.
IF WE'D BEEN DISCOVERED TWO DAYS LATER, COSMINA WOULD HAVE BEEN EVEN BIGGER WITH ALL THAT EXTRA NOURISHMENT...
THAT'S IT...!

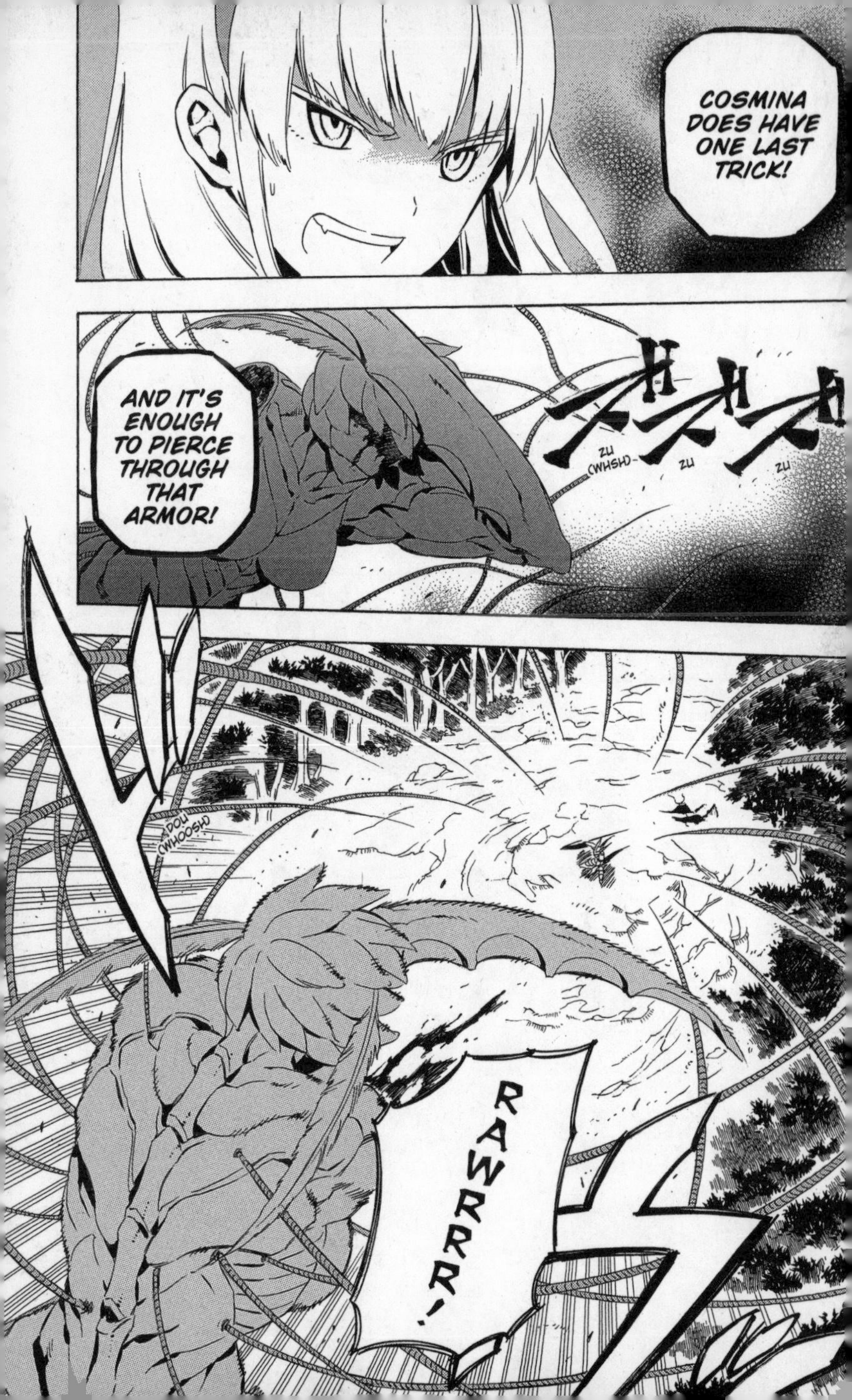
COSMINA DOES HAVE ONE LAST TRICK!
AND IT'S ENOUGH TO PIERCE THROUGH THAT ARMOR!
ZU (WHSH)-
ZU
ZU
DOU (WHOOSH)
RAWRRR!

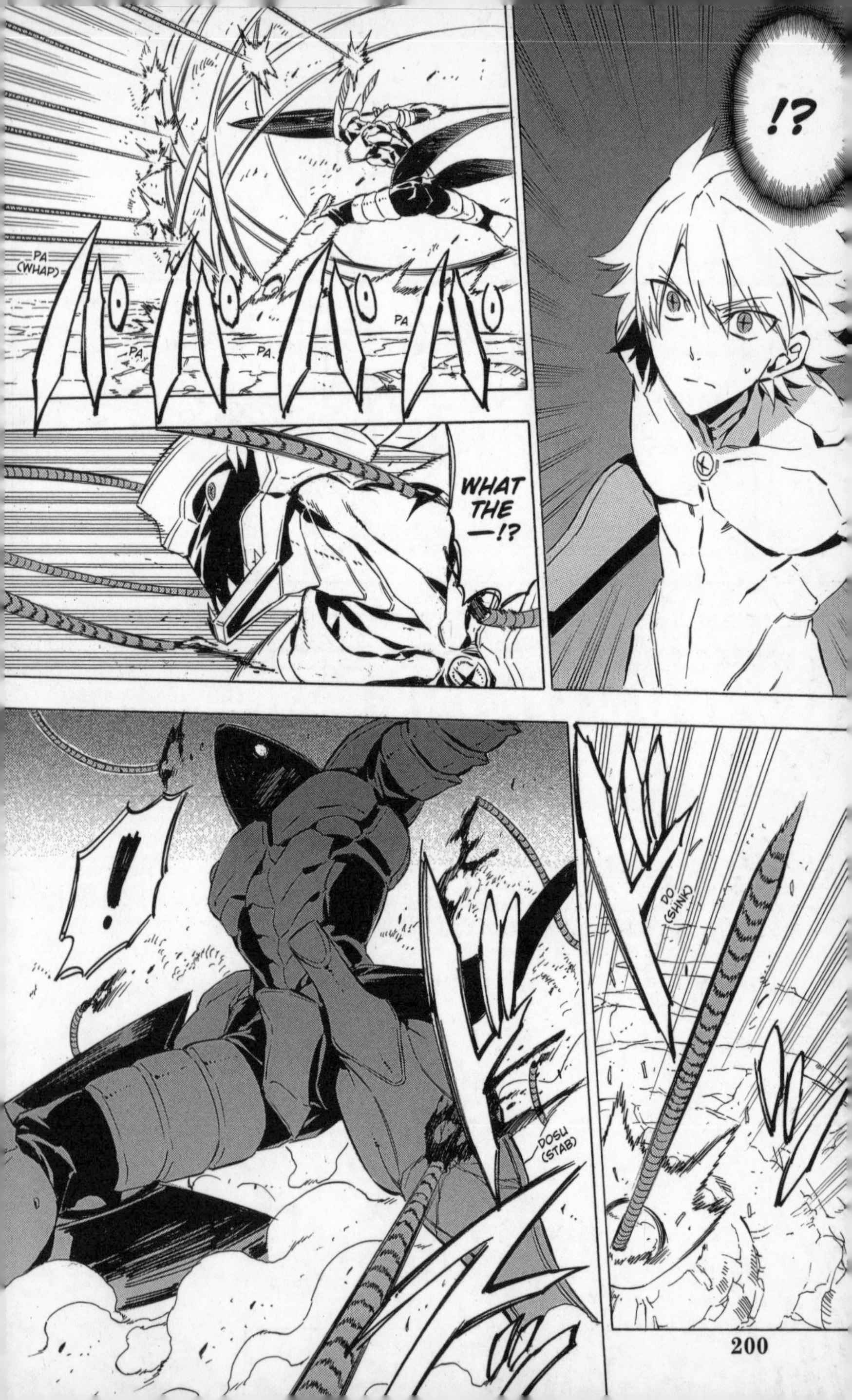
!?
PA (WHAP)
PA
PA
PA
WHAT THE—!?
DO (SHINK)
!
DOSU (STAB)

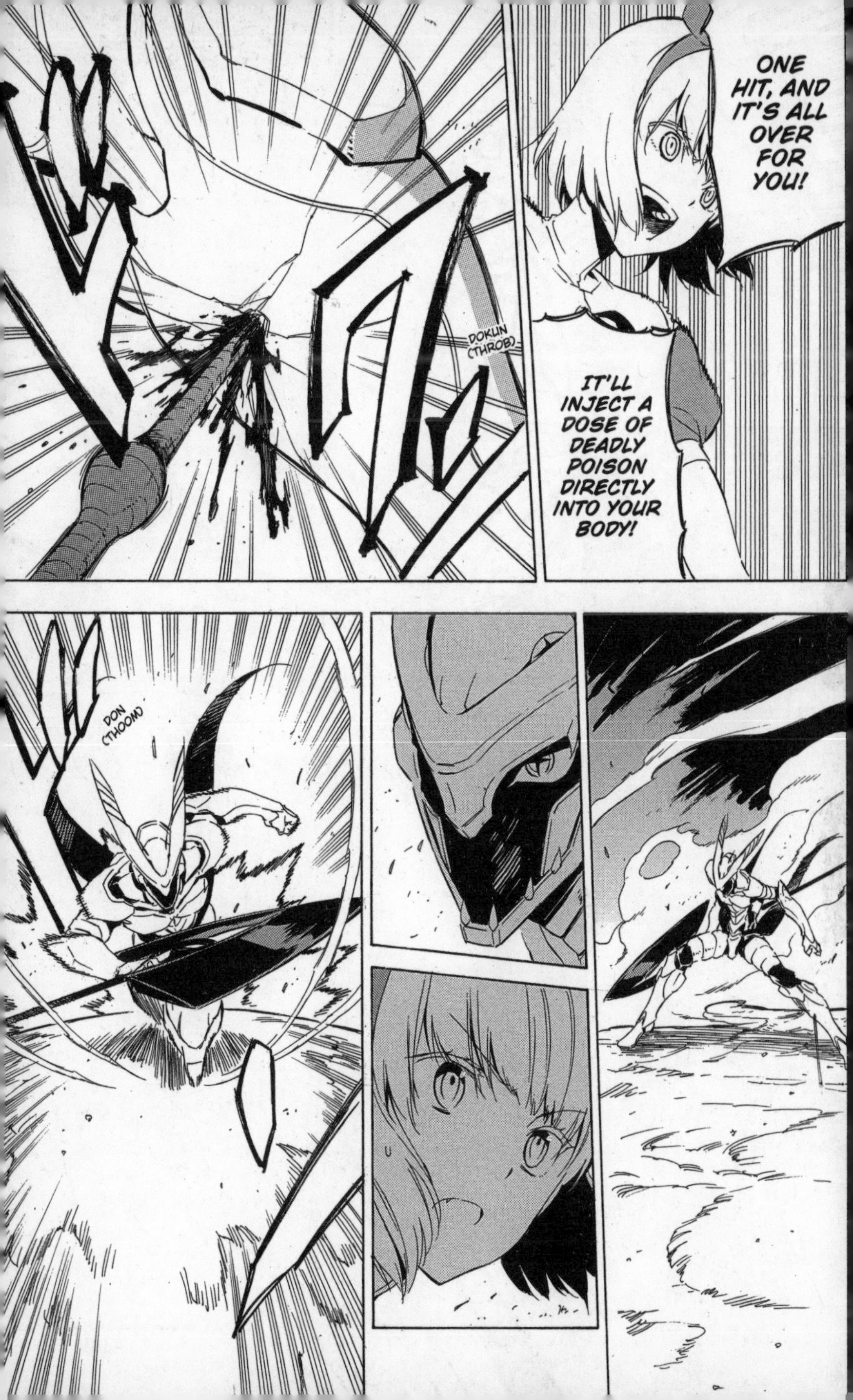
ONE HIT, AND IT'S ALL OVER FOR YOU!
IT'LL INJECT A DOSE OF DEADLY POISON DIRECTLY INTO YOUR BODY!
DOKUN (THROB)
DON (THOOM)

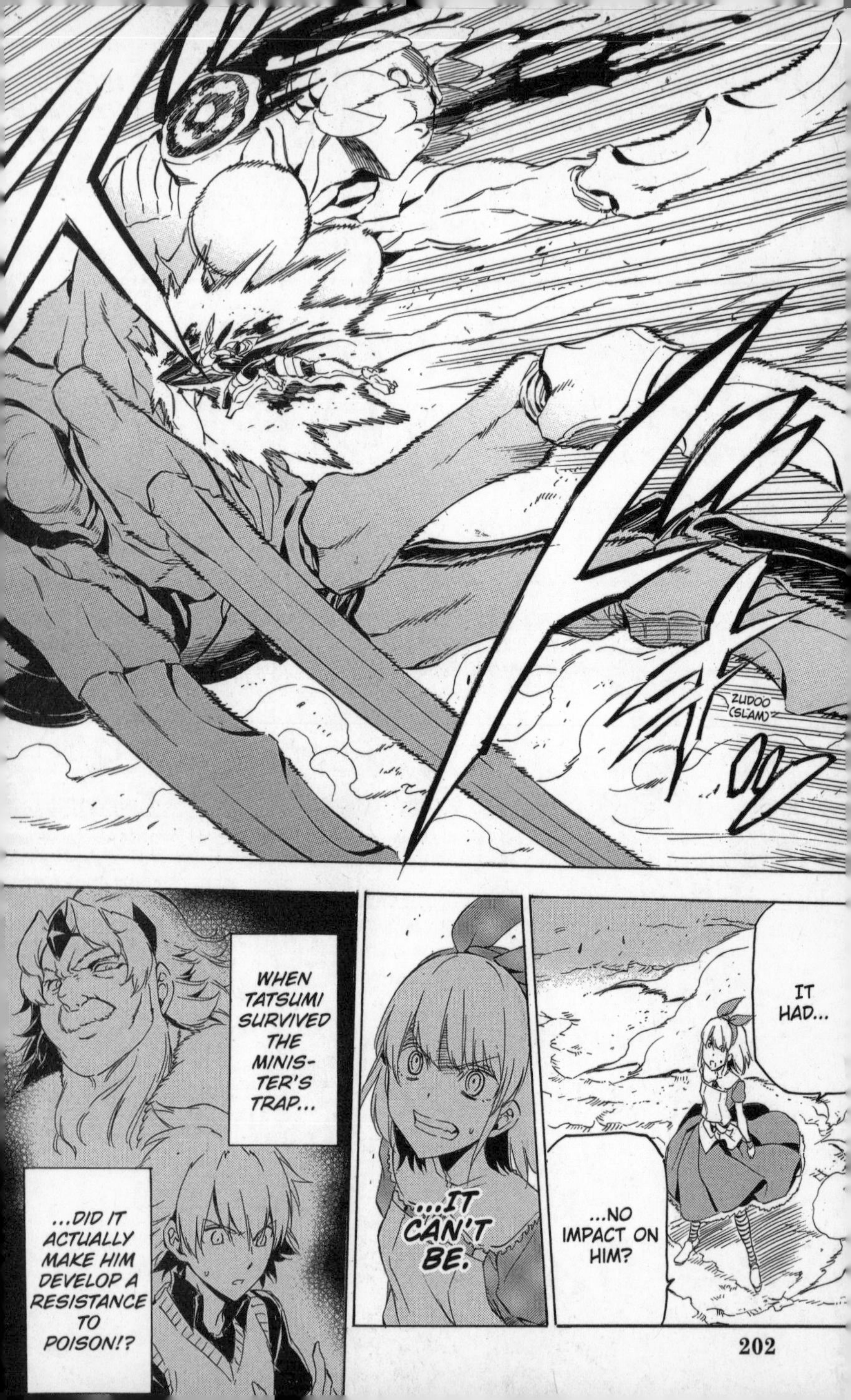

ZUDOO (SLAM)
IT HAD...
...NO IMPACT ON HIM?
...IT CAN'T BE.
WHEN TATSUMI SURVIVED THE MINIS-TER'S TRAP...
...DID IT ACTUALLY MAKE HIM DEVELOP A RESISTANCE TO POISON!?

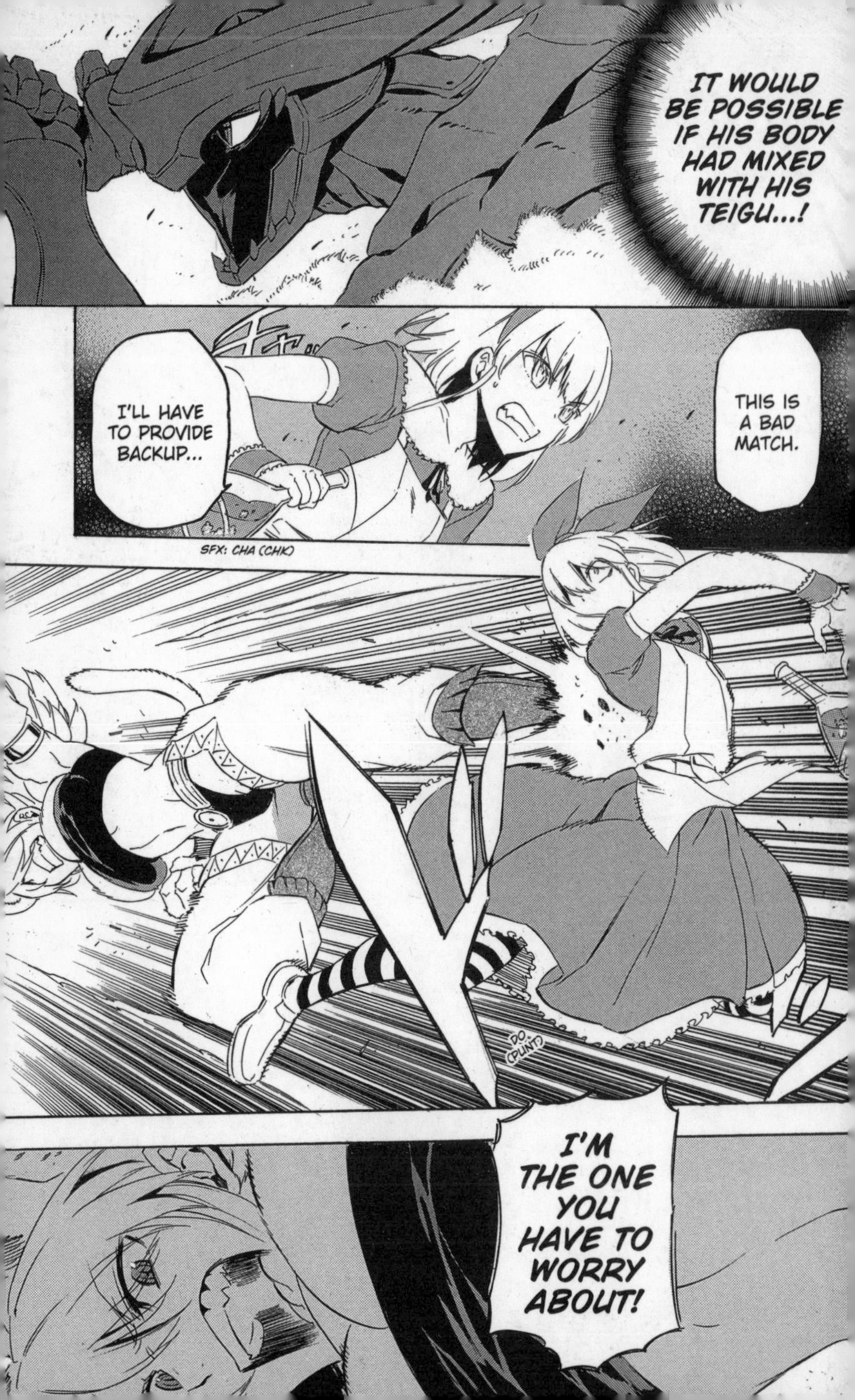
IT WOULD BE POSSIBLE IF HIS BODY HAD MIXED WITH HIS TEIGU...!
THIS IS A BAD MATCH.
I'LL HAVE TO PROVIDE BACKUP...
SFX: CHA (CHK)
DO- (PUNT)
I'M THE ONE YOU HAVE TO WORRY ABOUT!

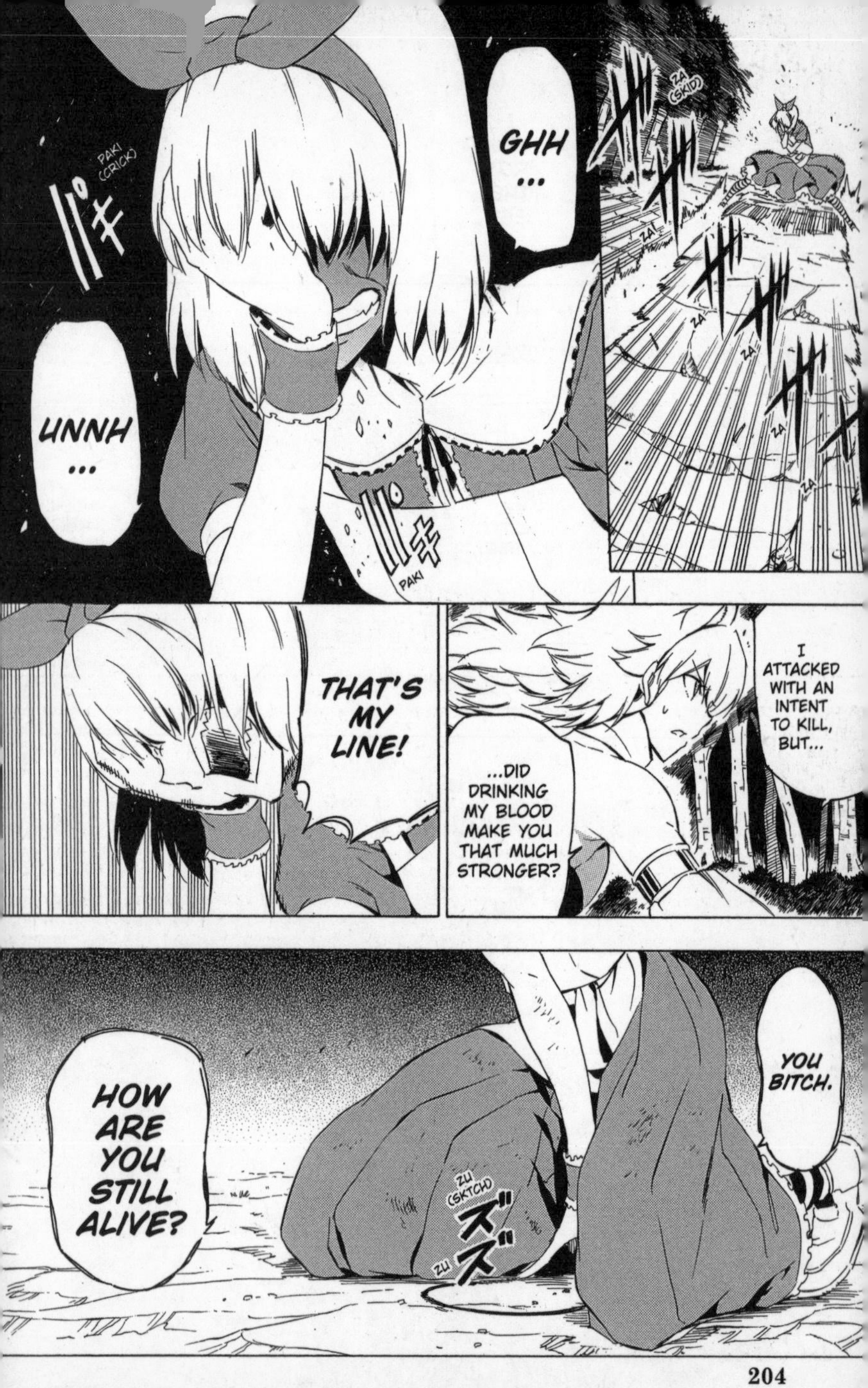
ZA (SKID)
ZA
ZA
ZA
ZA
ZA
ZA
GHH ...
PAKI (CRICK)
UNNH ...
PAKI
I ATTACKED WITH AN INTENT TO KILL, BUT...
...DID DRINKING MY BLOOD MAKE YOU THAT MUCH STRONGER?
THAT'S MY LINE!
YOU BITCH.
ZU (SKTCH)
ZU
HOW ARE YOU STILL ALIVE?

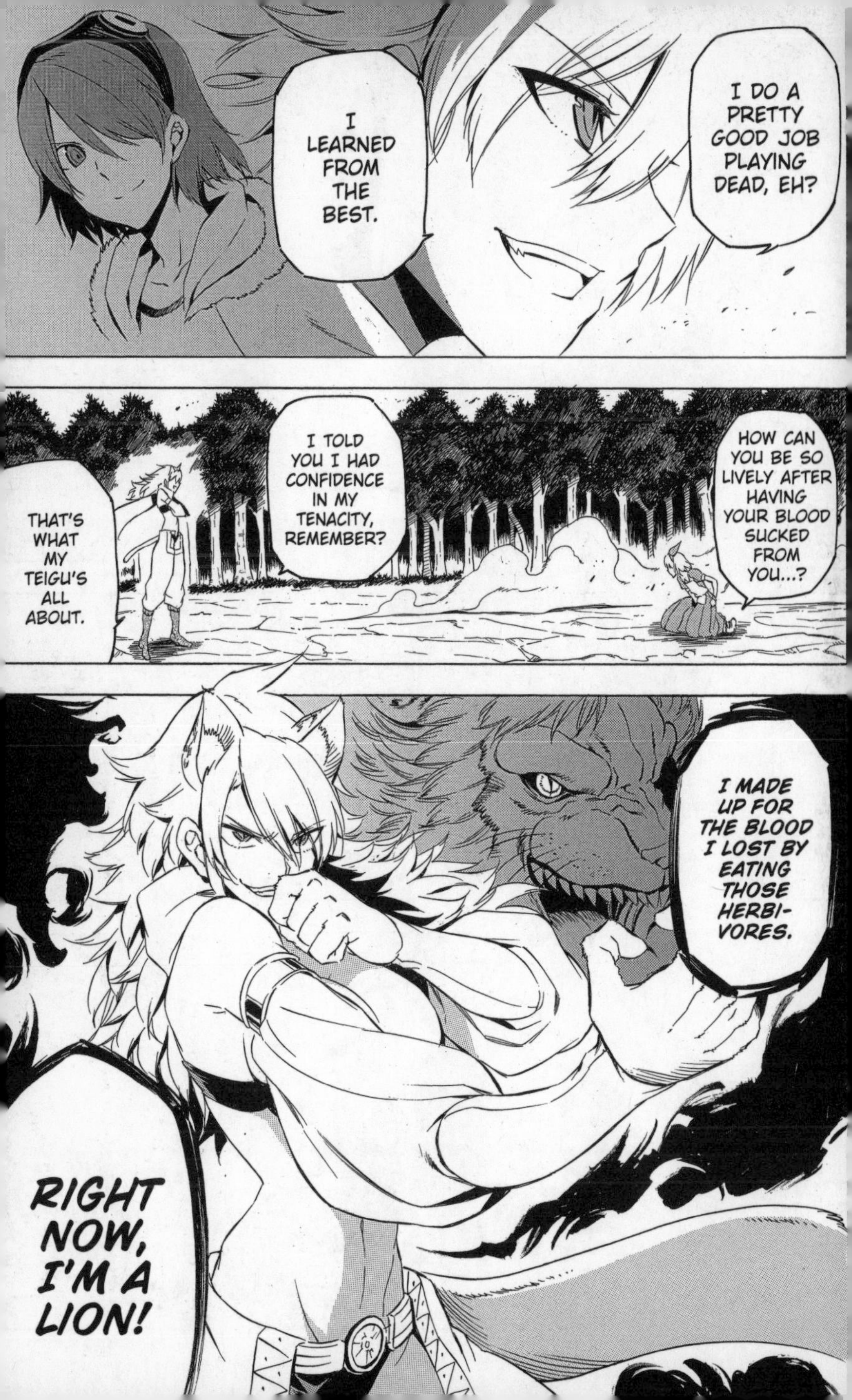
I DO A PRETTY GOOD JOB PLAYING DEAD, EH?
I LEARNED FROM THE BEST.
HOW CAN YOU BE SO LIVELY AFTER HAVING YOUR BLOOD SUCKED FROM YOU...?
I TOLD YOU I HAD CONFIDENCE IN MY TENACITY, REMEMBER?
THAT'S WHAT MY TEIGU'S ALL ABOUT.
I MADE UP FOR THE BLOOD I LOST BY EATING THOSE HERBI-VORES.
RIGHT NOW, I'M A LION!

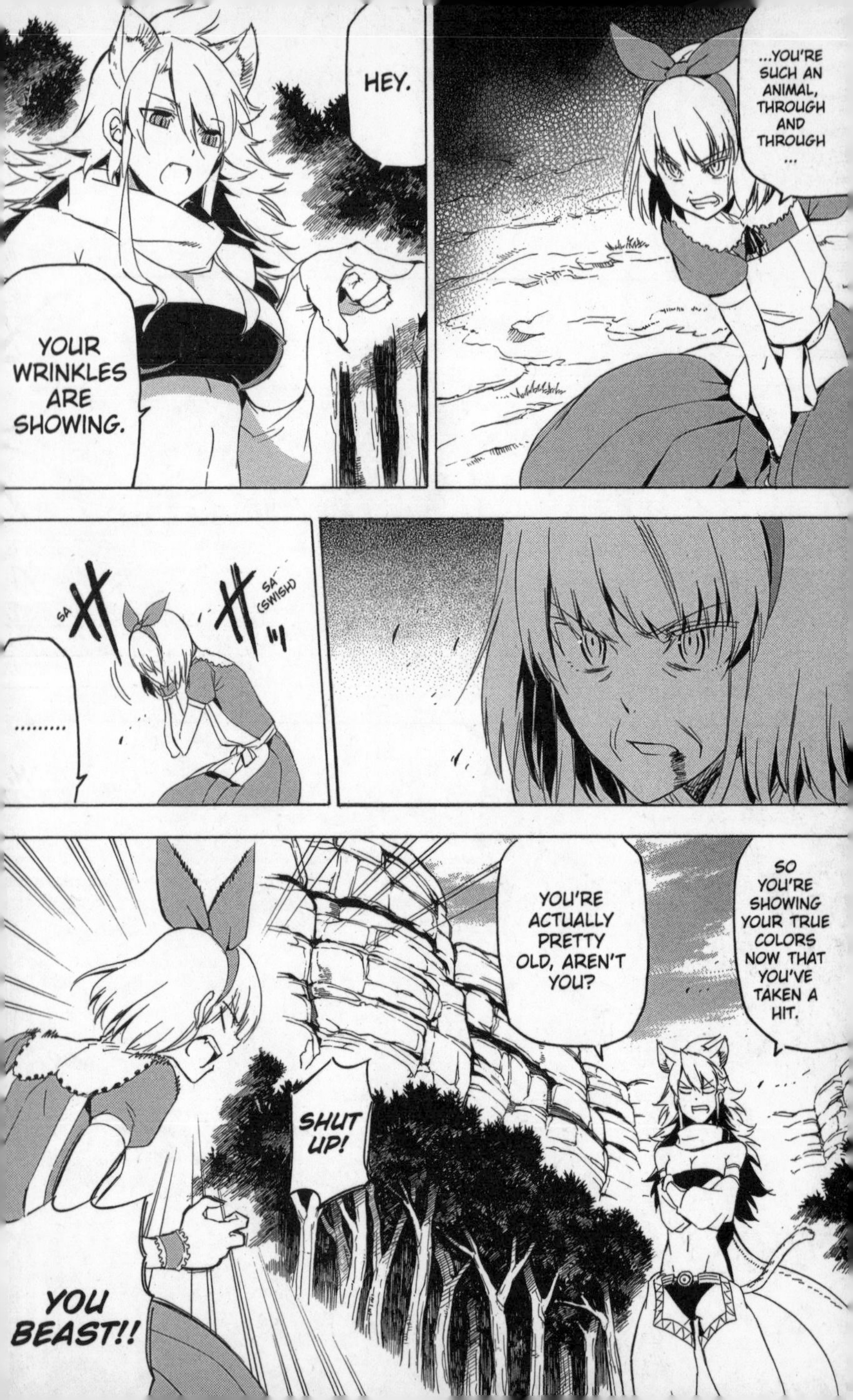
...YOU'RE SUCH AN ANIMAL, THROUGH AND THROUGH ...
HEY.
YOUR WRINKLES ARE SHOWING.
SA
SA (SWISH)
....
SO YOU'RE SHOWING YOUR TRUE COLORS NOW THAT YOU'VE TAKEN A HIT.
YOU'RE ACTUALLY PRETTY OLD, AREN'T YOU?
SHUT UP!
YOU BEAST!!

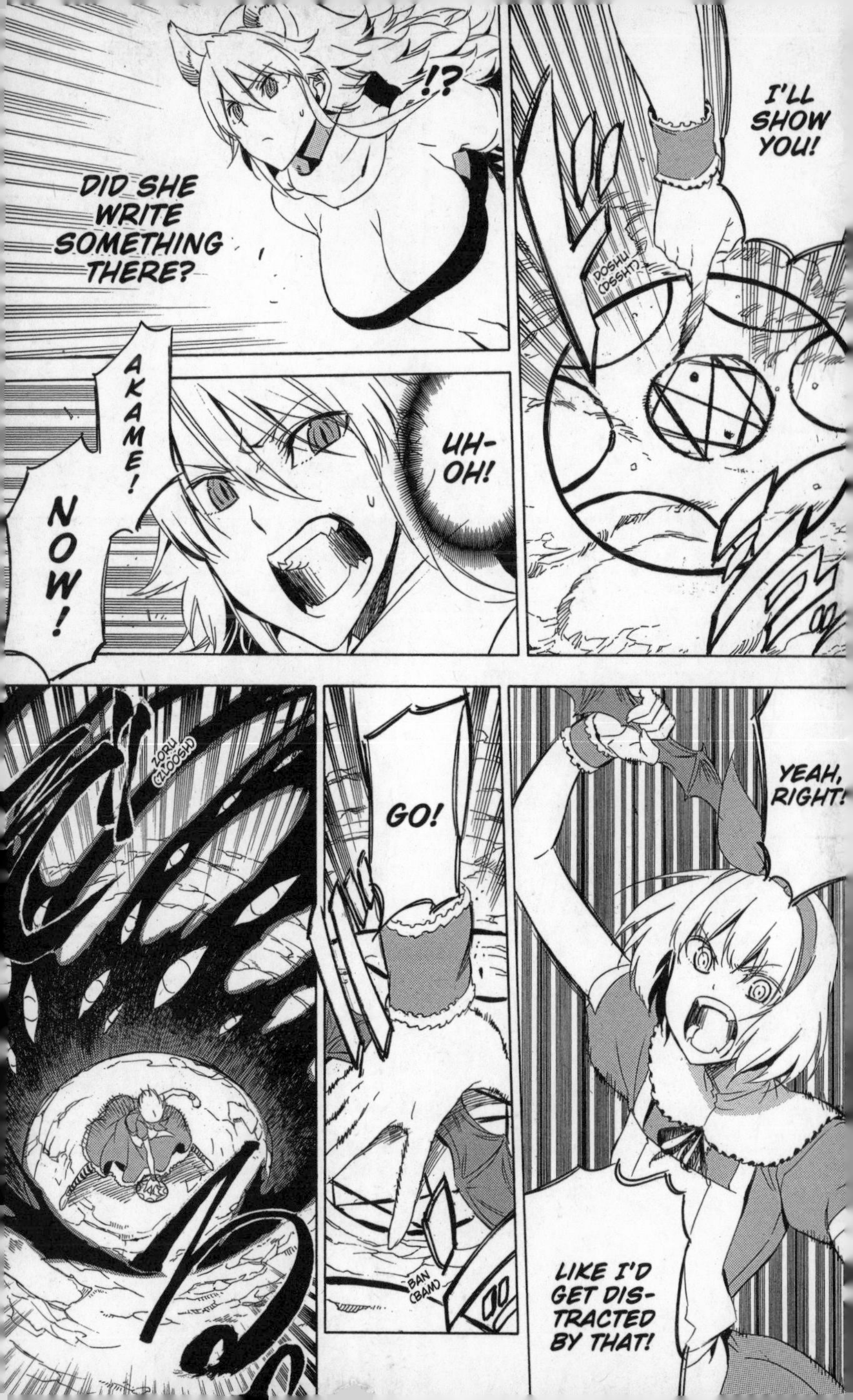
I'LL SHOW YOU!
DOSHU (DSSHT)
!?
DID SHE WRITE SOMETHING THERE?
UH-OH!
AKAME! NOW!
YEAH, RIGHT!
LIKE I'D GET DIS-TRACTED BY THAT!
GO!
BAN (BAM)
ZORU (ZLOOSH)

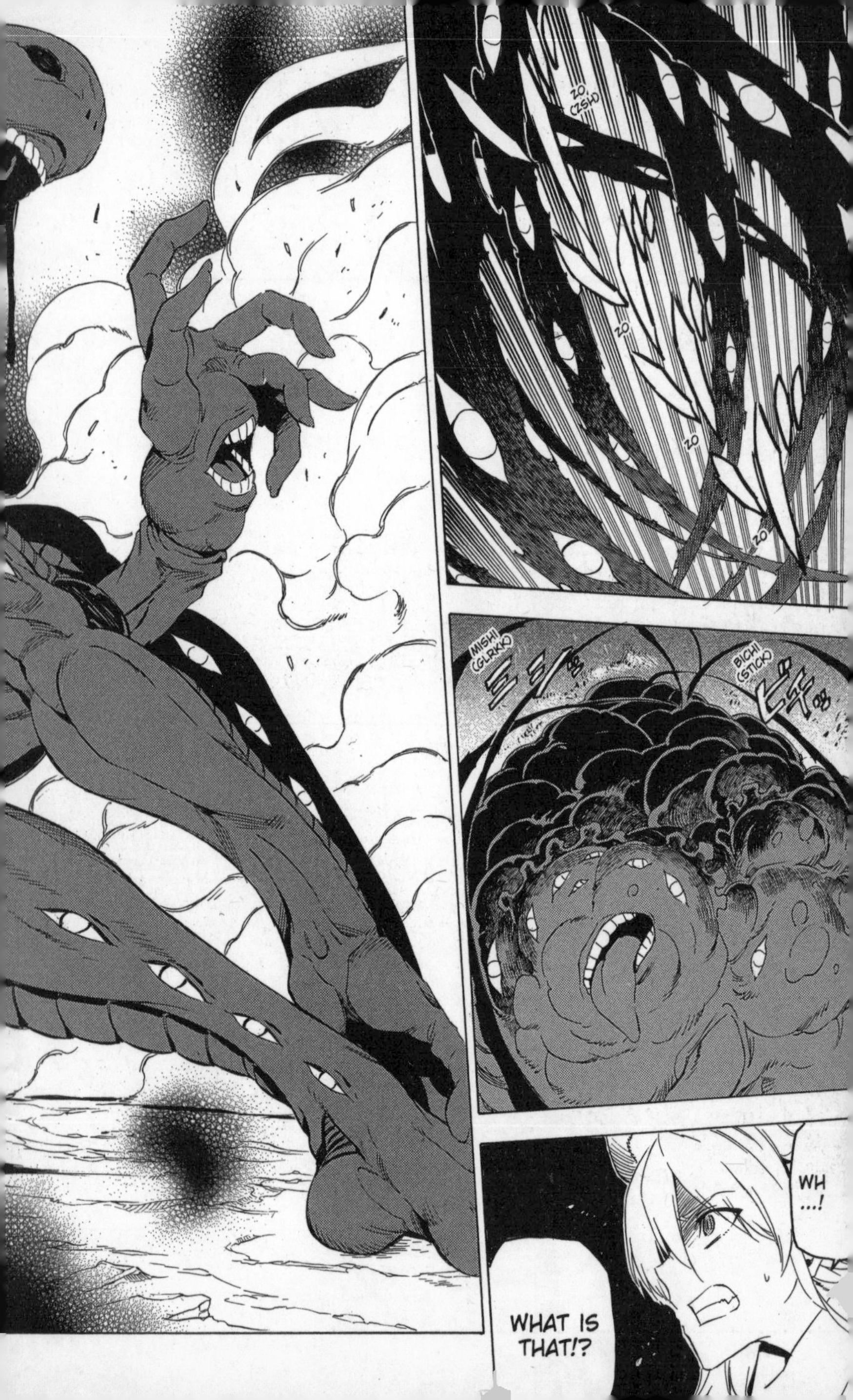
ZO (ZSHO)
ZO
ZO
ZO
MISHI (GLRKK)
BICHI (STICK)
WH ...!
WHAT IS THAT!?

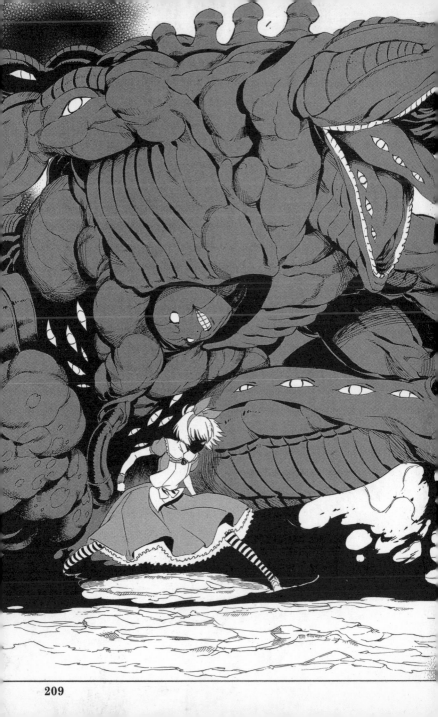

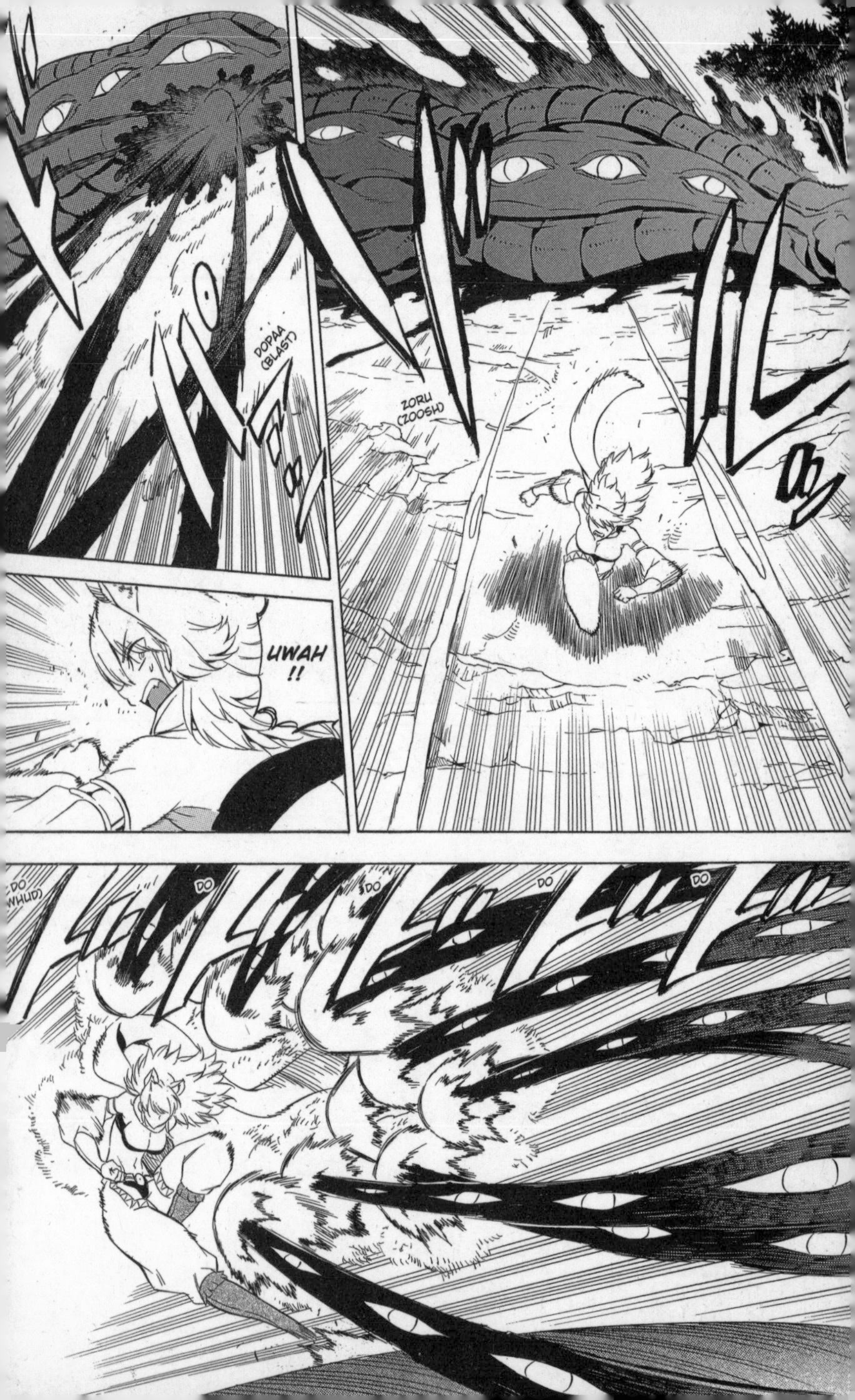
DOPAA (BLAST)
ZORU (ZOOSH)
UWAH !!
DO
DO
DO
DO
DO
WHUD)

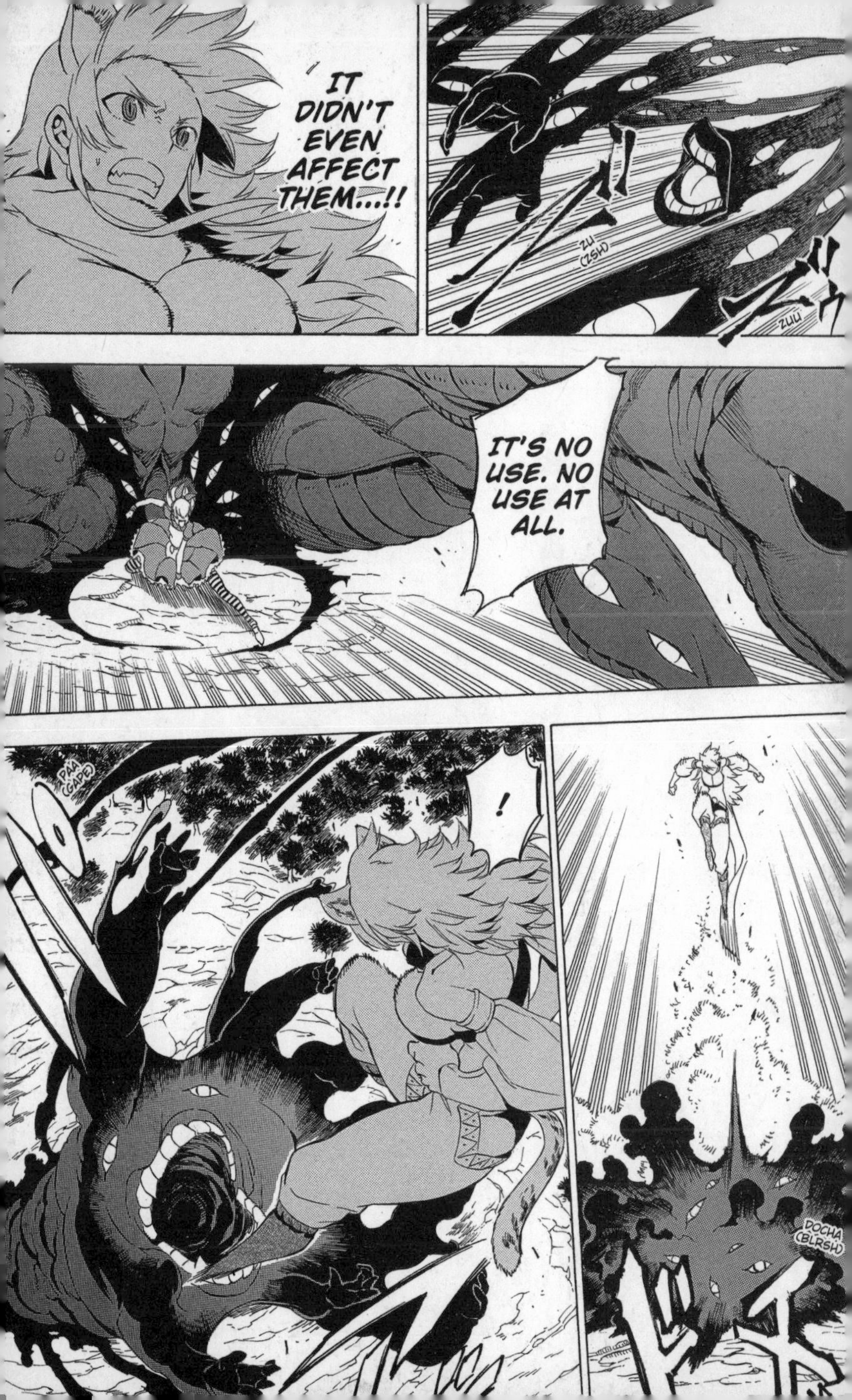
ZU (ZSH)
ZUU
IT DIDN'T EVEN AFFECT THEM...!!
IT'S NO USE. NO USE AT ALL.
DOCHA (BLRSH)
PAA (GAPE)
!

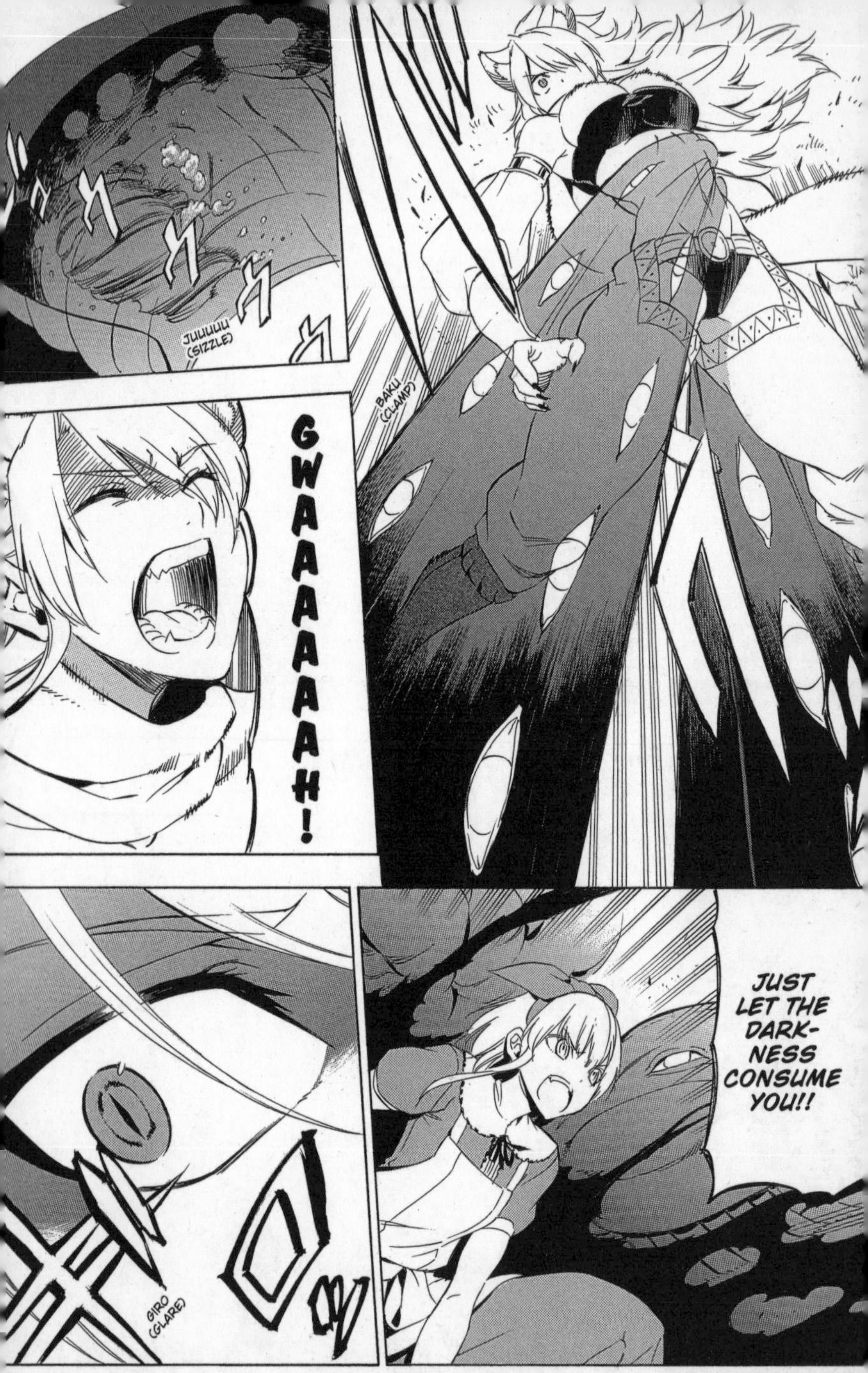

BAKU (CLAMP)
JUUUUU (SIZZLE)
GWAAAAAAAH!
JUST LET THE DARK-NESS CONSUME YOU!!
GIRO (GLARE)

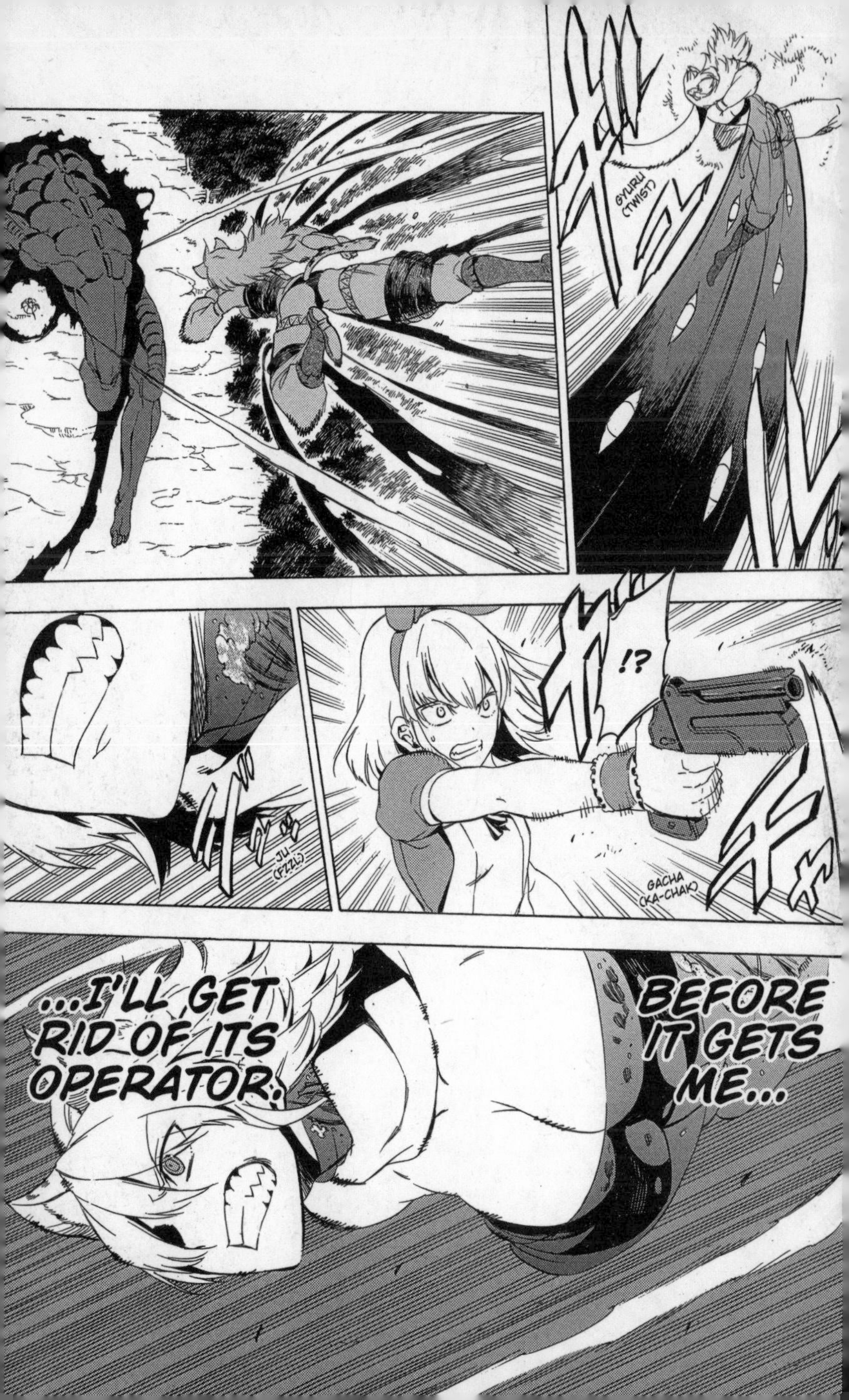
GYURU (TWIST)
!?
GACHA (KA-CHAK)
JU (FZZZ)
BEFORE IT GETS ME...
...I'LL GET RID OF ITS OPERATOR.

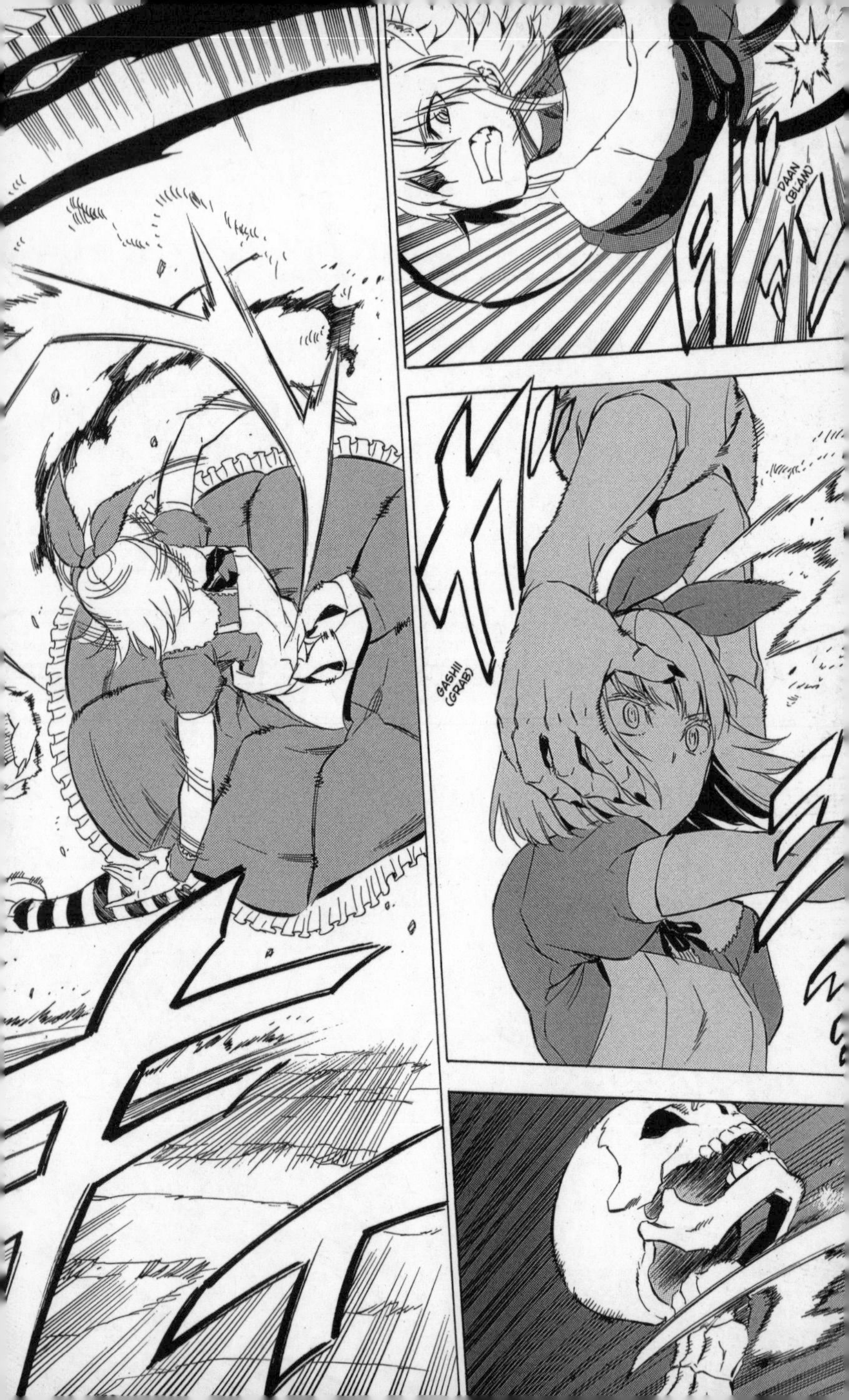
DAAN (BLAM)
GASHII (GRAB)

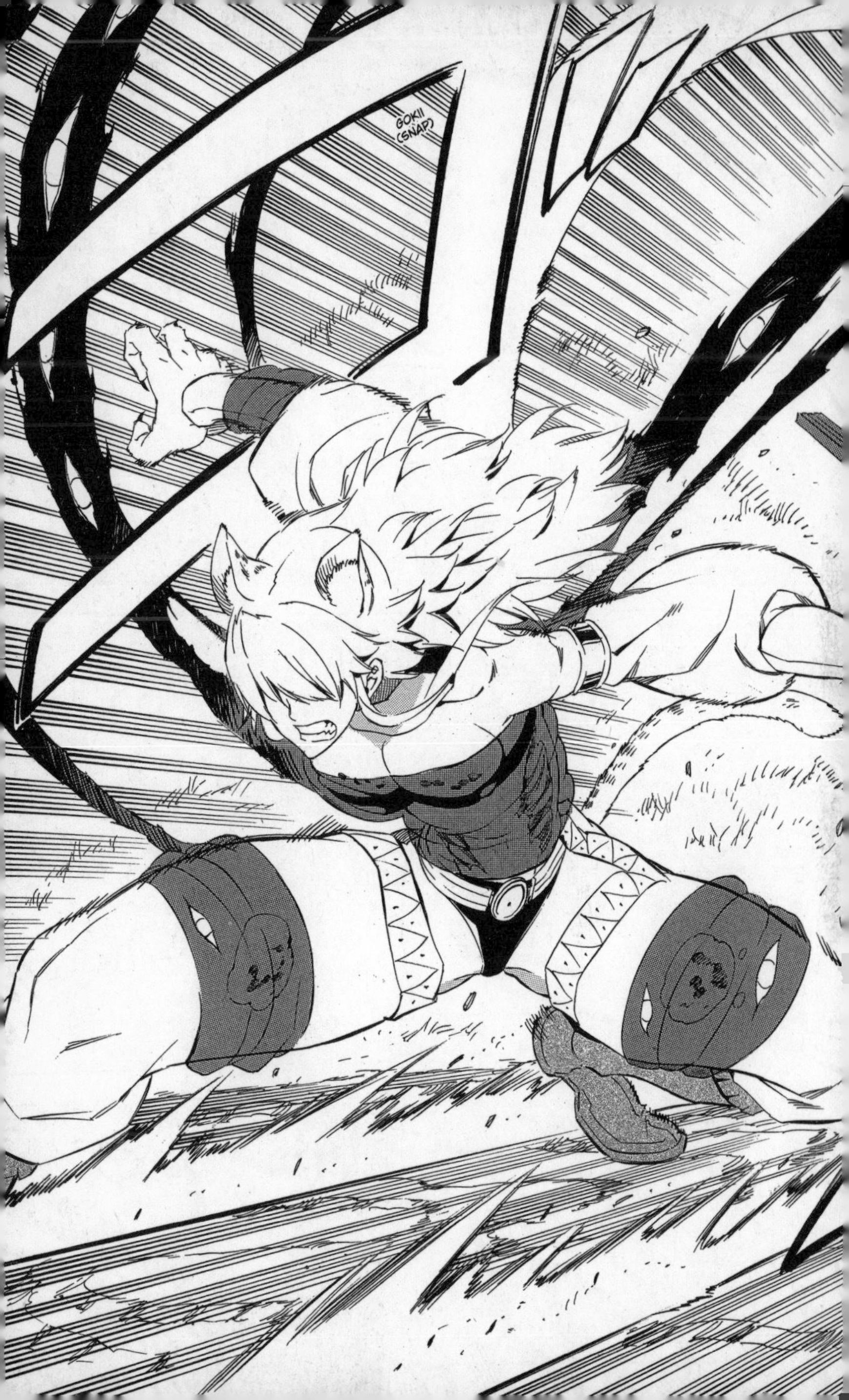
GOKII
(SNAP)

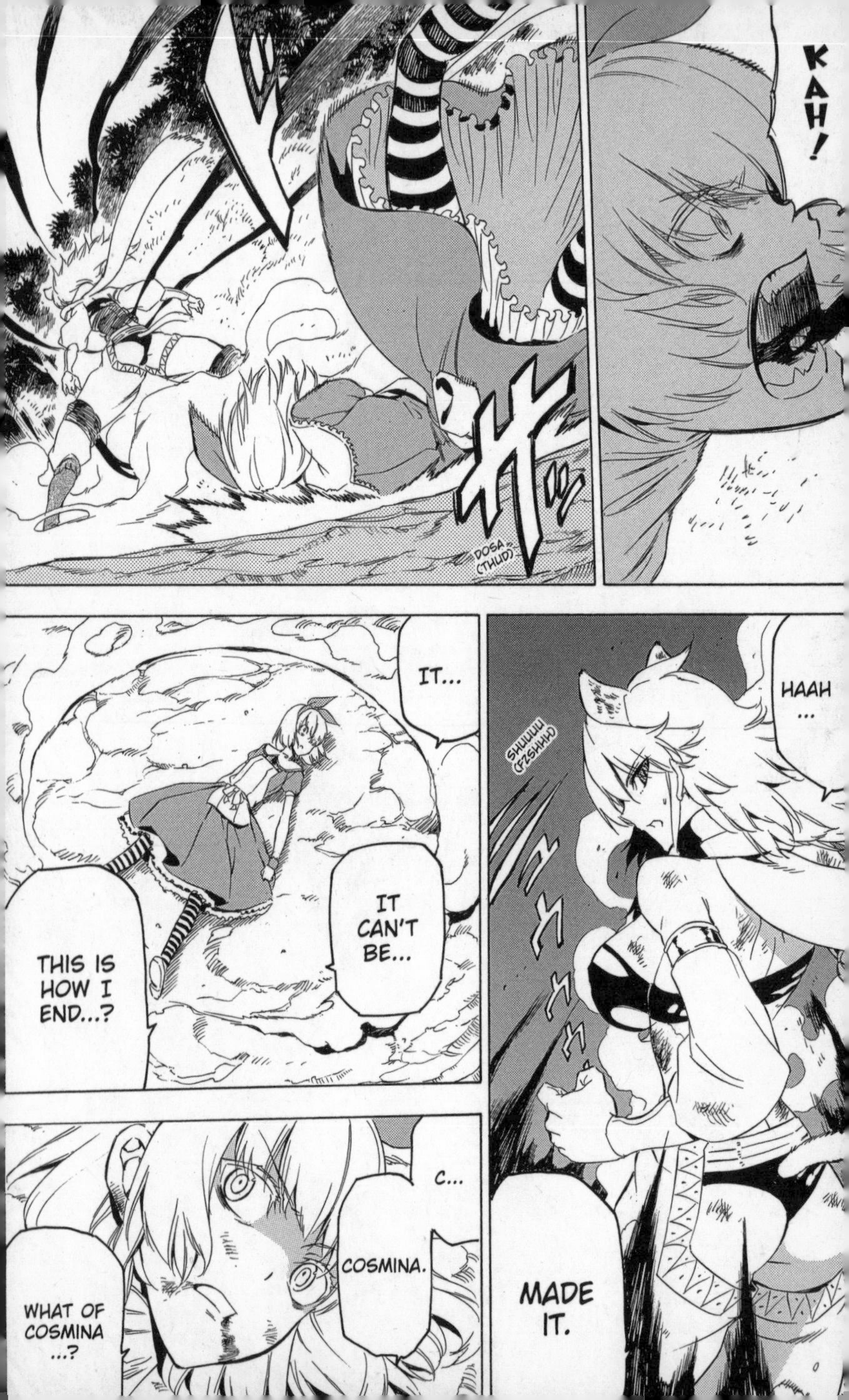
KAH!
DOSA (THUD)
HAAH ...
SHUUUUN (FZSHHH)
IT...
IT CAN'T BE...
THIS IS HOW I END...?
MADE IT.
C...
COSMINA.
WHAT OF COSMINA ...?

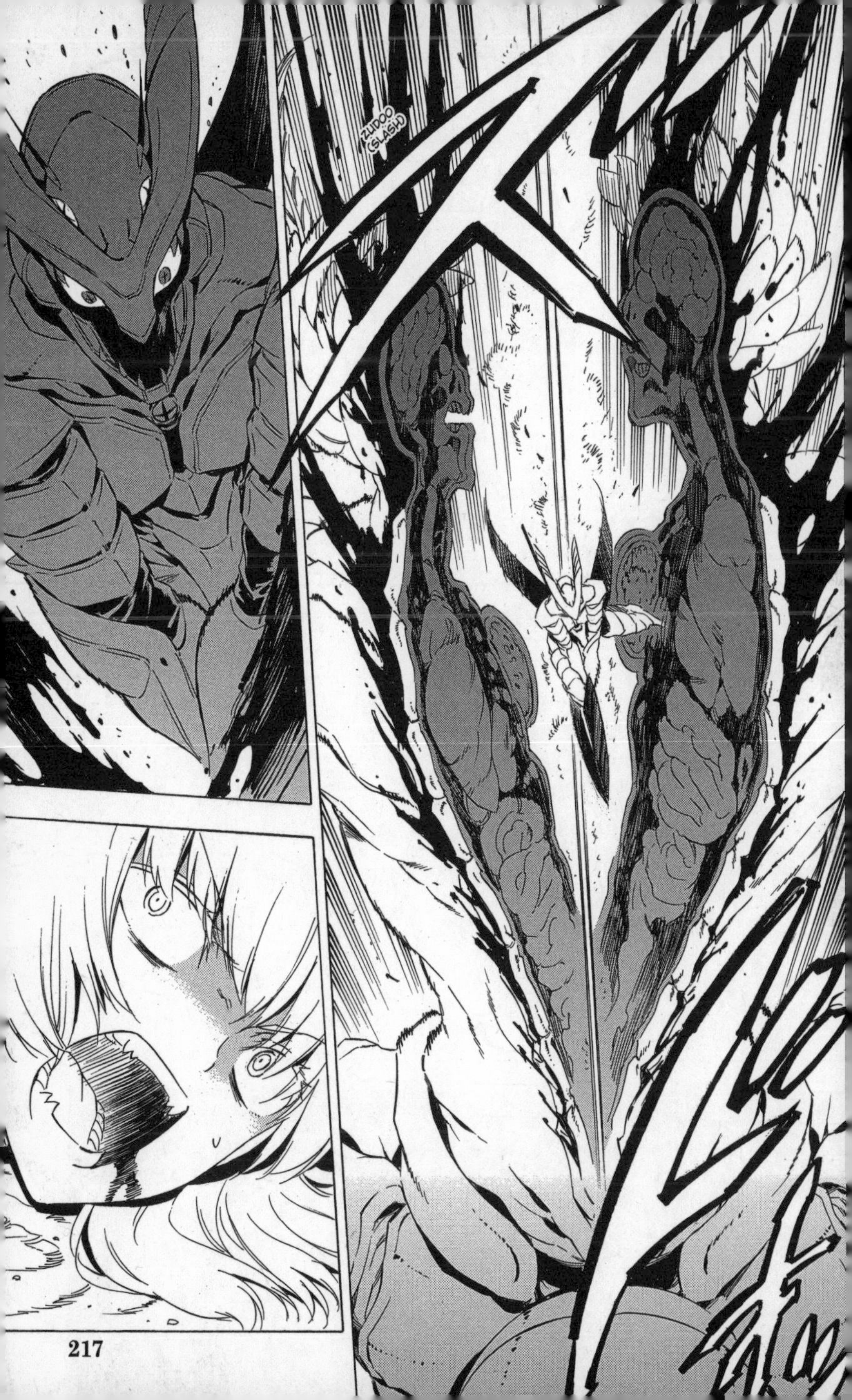
ZUDOO (SLASH)

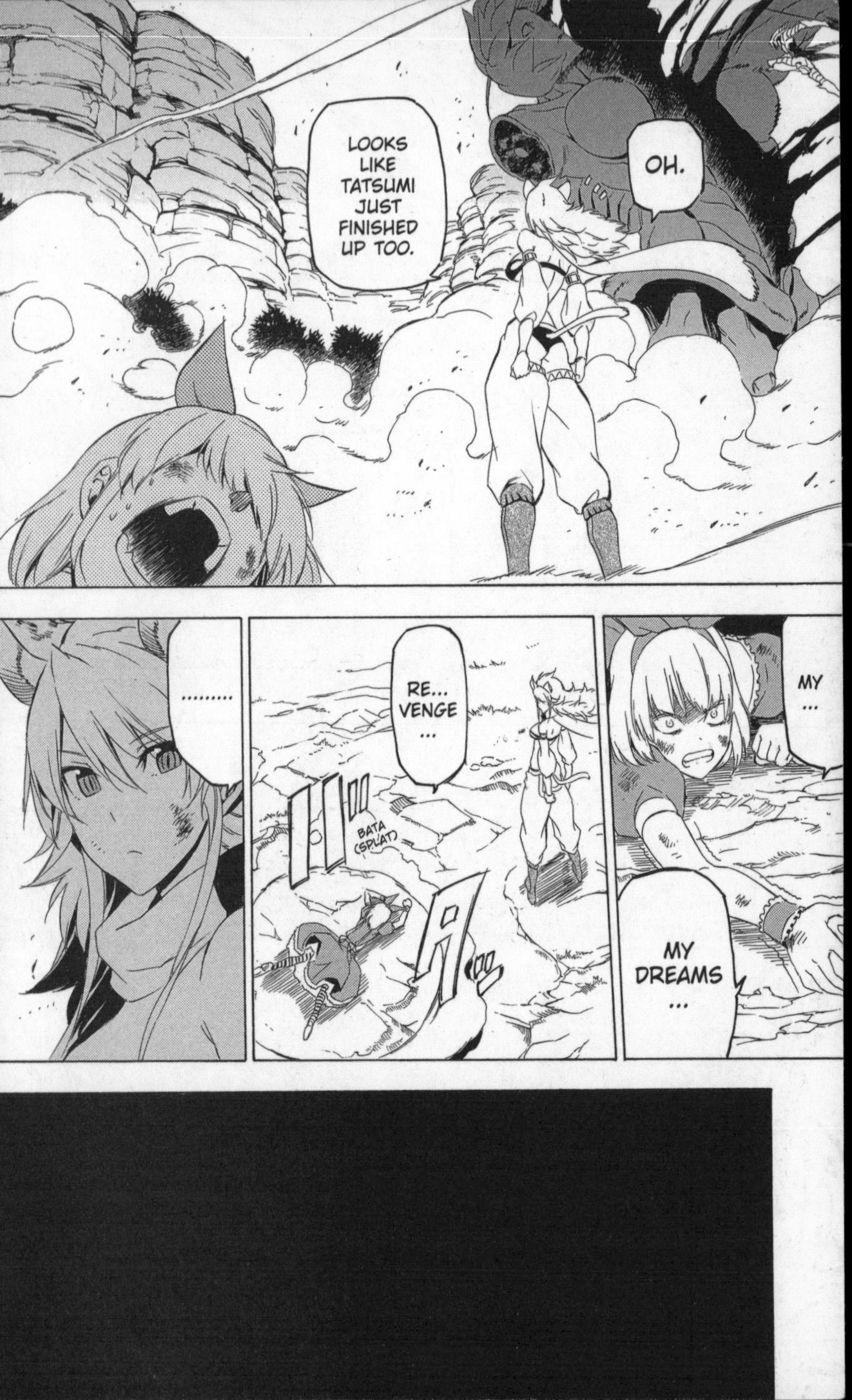
OH.
LOOKS LIKE TATSUMI JUST FINISHED UP TOO.
MY ...
MY DREAMS ...
RE... VENGE ...
BATA (SPLAT)
....

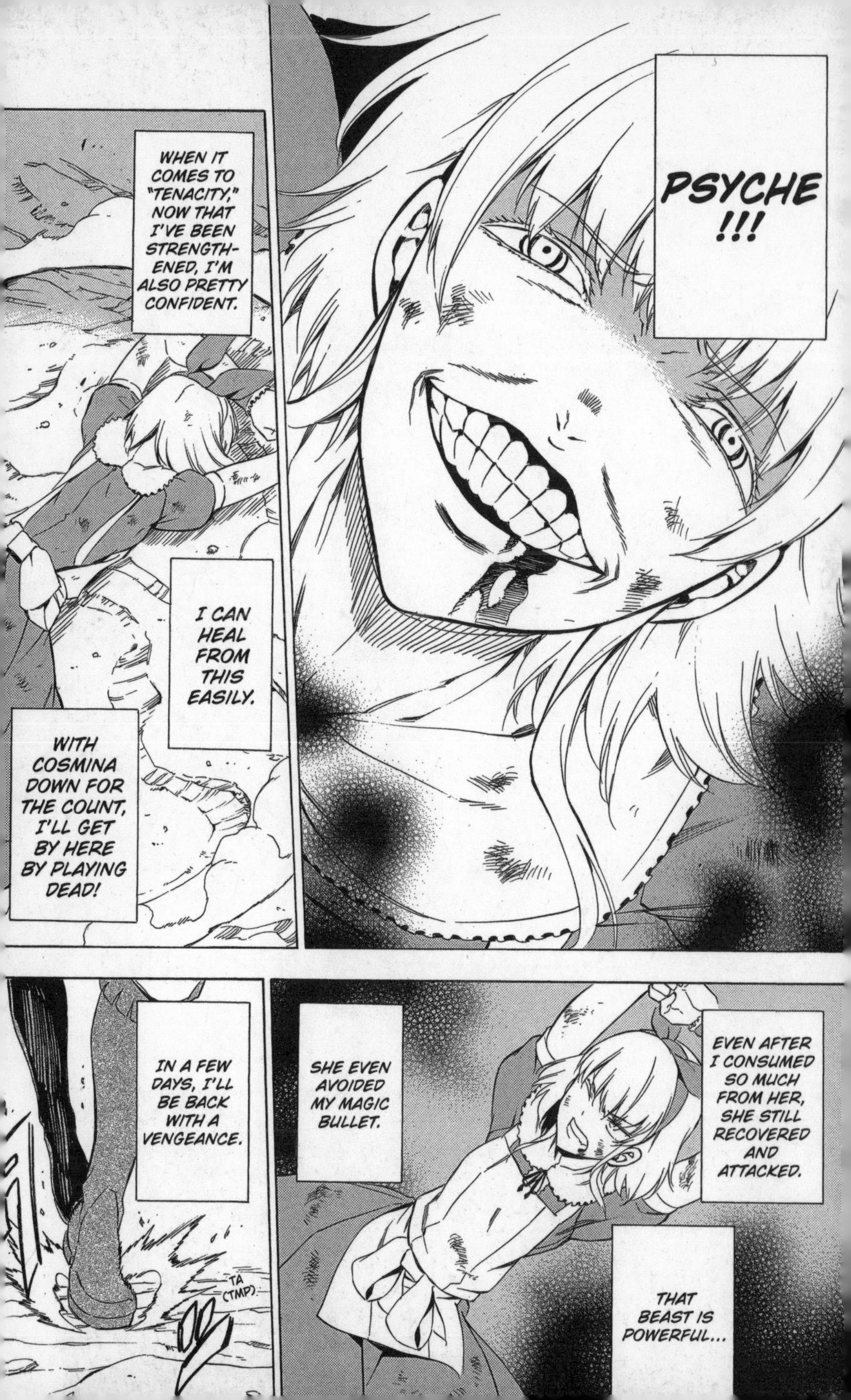
PSYCHE!!!
WHEN IT COMES TO "TENACITY," NOW THAT I'VE BEEN STRENGTHENED, I'M ALSO PRETTY CONFIDENT.
I CAN HEAL FROM THIS EASILY.
WITH COSMINA DOWN FOR THE COUNT, I'LL GET BY HERE BY PLAYING DEAD!
EVEN AFTER I CONSUMED SO MUCH FROM HER, SHE STILL RECOVERED AND ATTACKED.
SHE EVEN AVOIDED MY MAGIC BULLET.
THAT BEAST IS POWERFUL...
IN A FEW DAYS, I'LL BE BACK WITH A VENGEANCE.
TA (TMP)

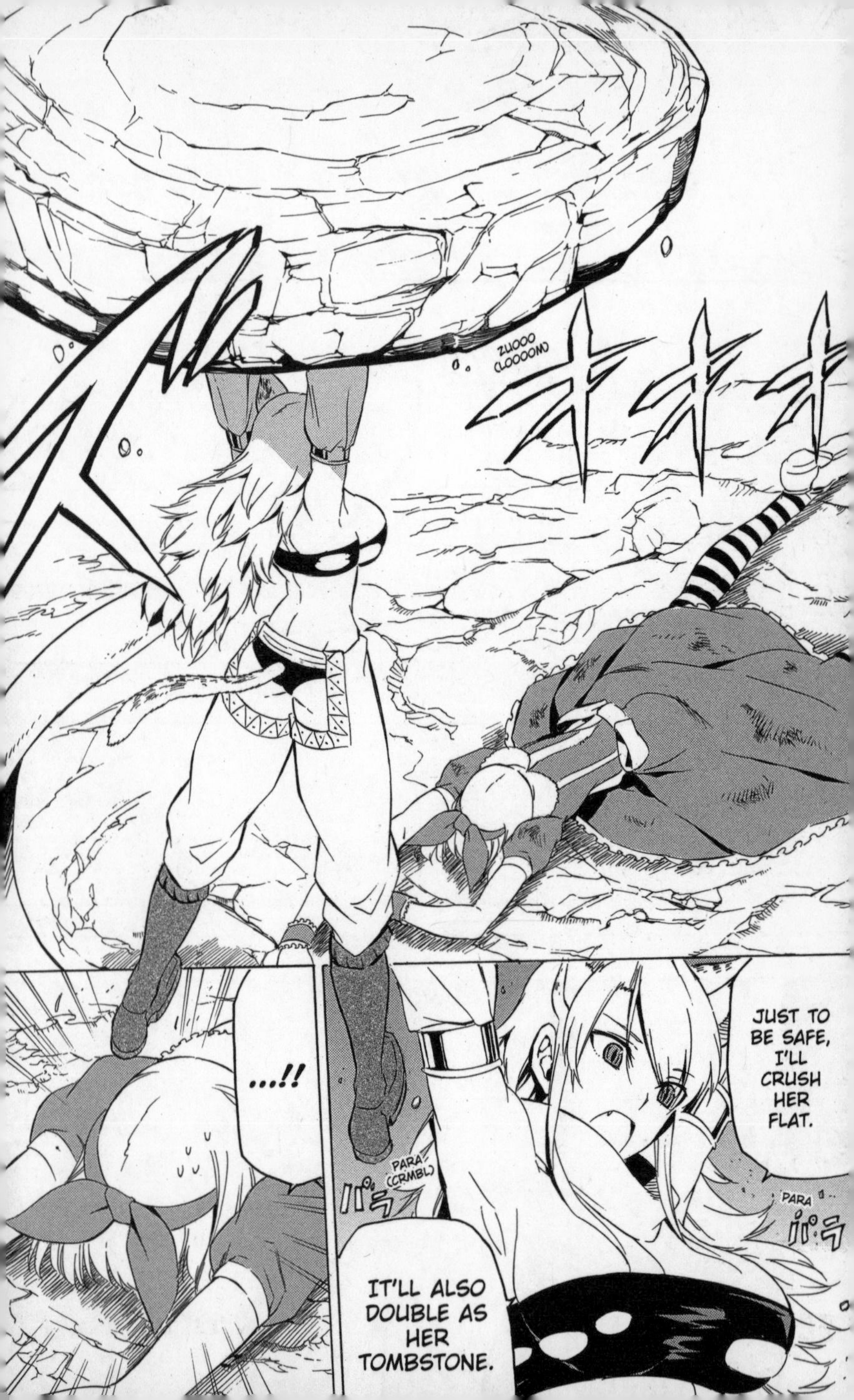

ZUOOO
(LOOOOM)
JUST TO BE SAFE, I'LL CRUSH HER FLAT.
PARA
パラ
PARA
(CRMBL)
パラ
...!!
IT'LL ALSO DOUBLE AS HER TOMBSTONE.

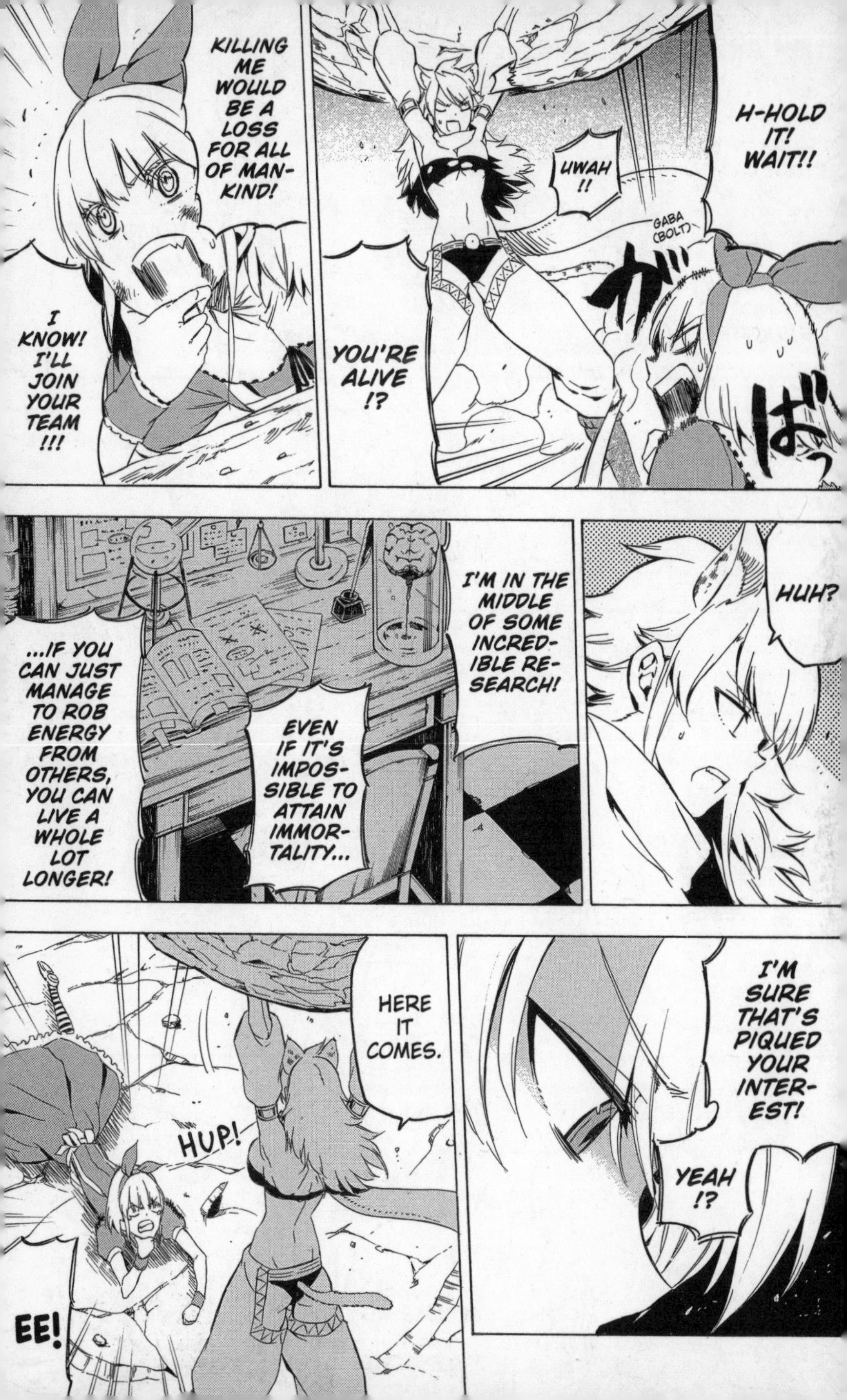
H-HOLD IT! WAIT!!
GABA (BOLT)
UWAH !!
YOU'RE ALIVE !?
KILLING ME WOULD BE A LOSS FOR ALL OF MAN-KIND!
I KNOW! I'LL JOIN YOUR TEAM !!!
HUH?
I'M IN THE MIDDLE OF SOME INCRED-IBLE RE-SEARCH!
EVEN IF IT'S IMPOS-SIBLE TO ATTAIN IMMOR-TALITY...
...IF YOU CAN JUST MANAGE TO ROB ENERGY FROM OTHERS, YOU CAN LIVE A WHOLE LOT LONGER!
I'M SURE THAT'S PIQUED YOUR INTER-EST!
YEAH !?
HERE IT COMES.
HUP!
EE!

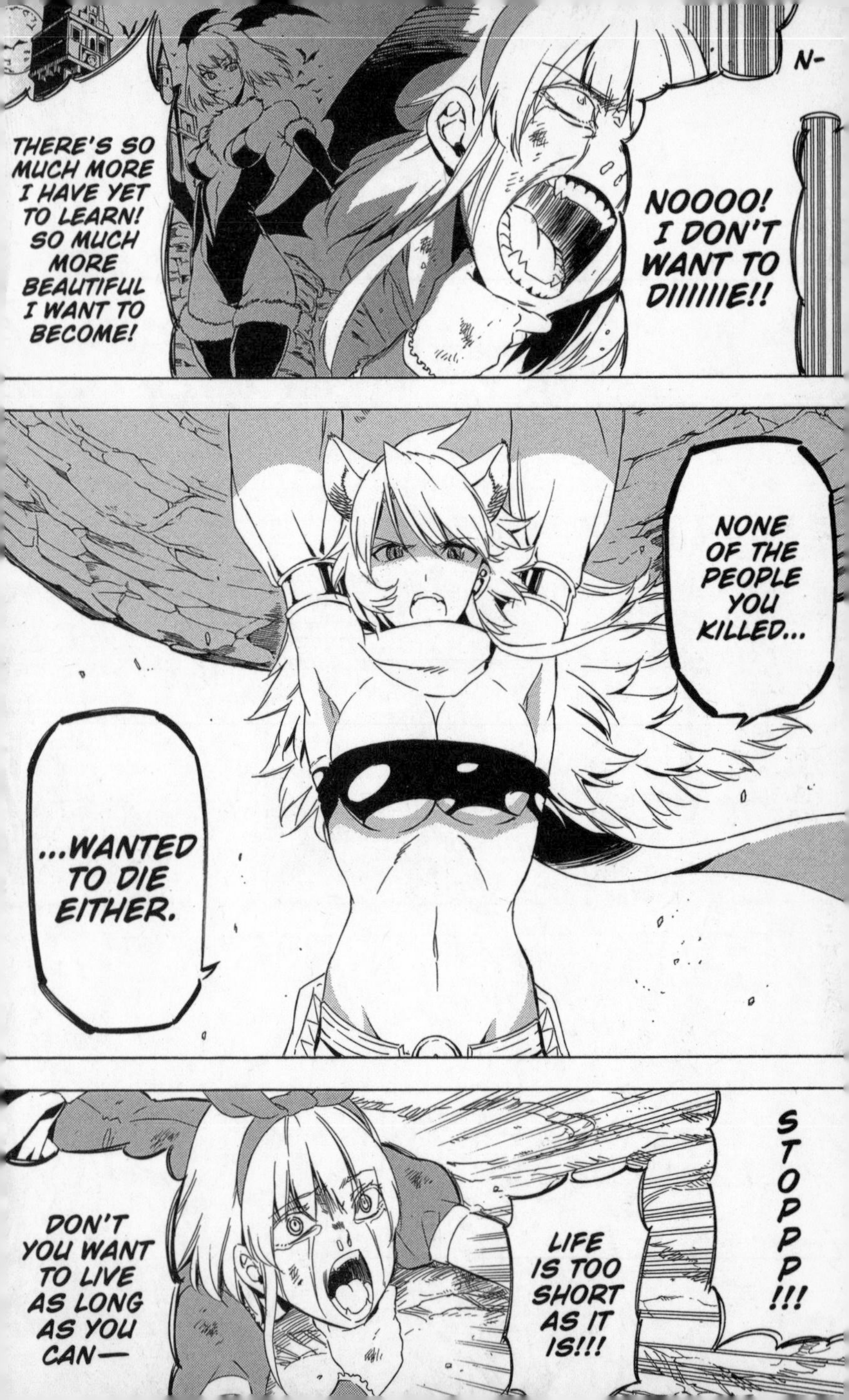
N-
NOOOO! I DON'T WANT TO DIIIIIIE!!
THERE'S SO MUCH MORE I HAVE YET TO LEARN! SO MUCH MORE BEAUTIFUL I WANT TO BECOME!
NONE OF THE PEOPLE YOU KILLED...
...WANTED TO DIE EITHER.
STOPPP!!!
LIFE IS TOO SHORT AS IT IS!!!
DON'T YOU WANT TO LIVE AS LONG AS YOU CAN—

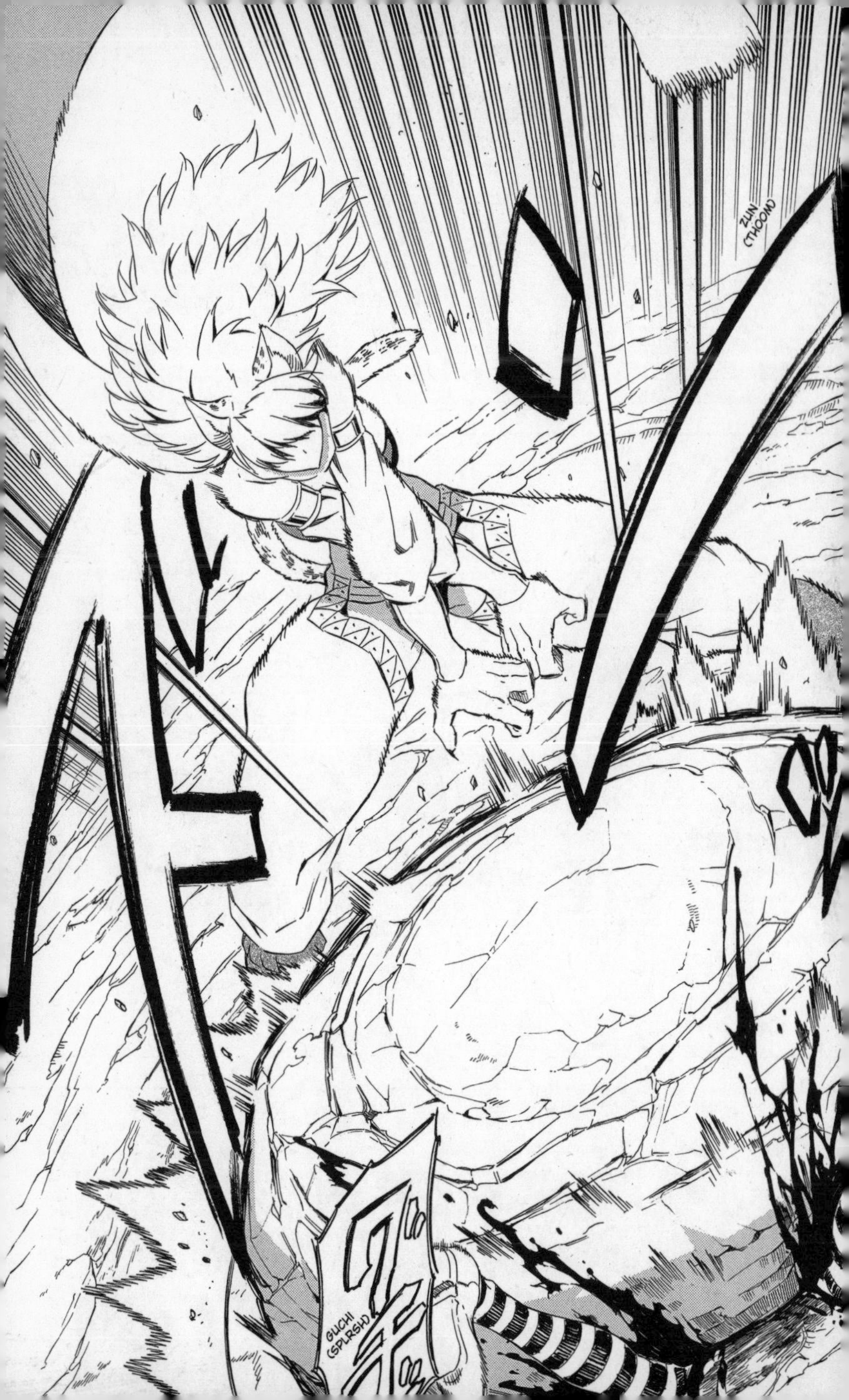
ZUN
(THOOM)
GUCHI
(SPLASH)

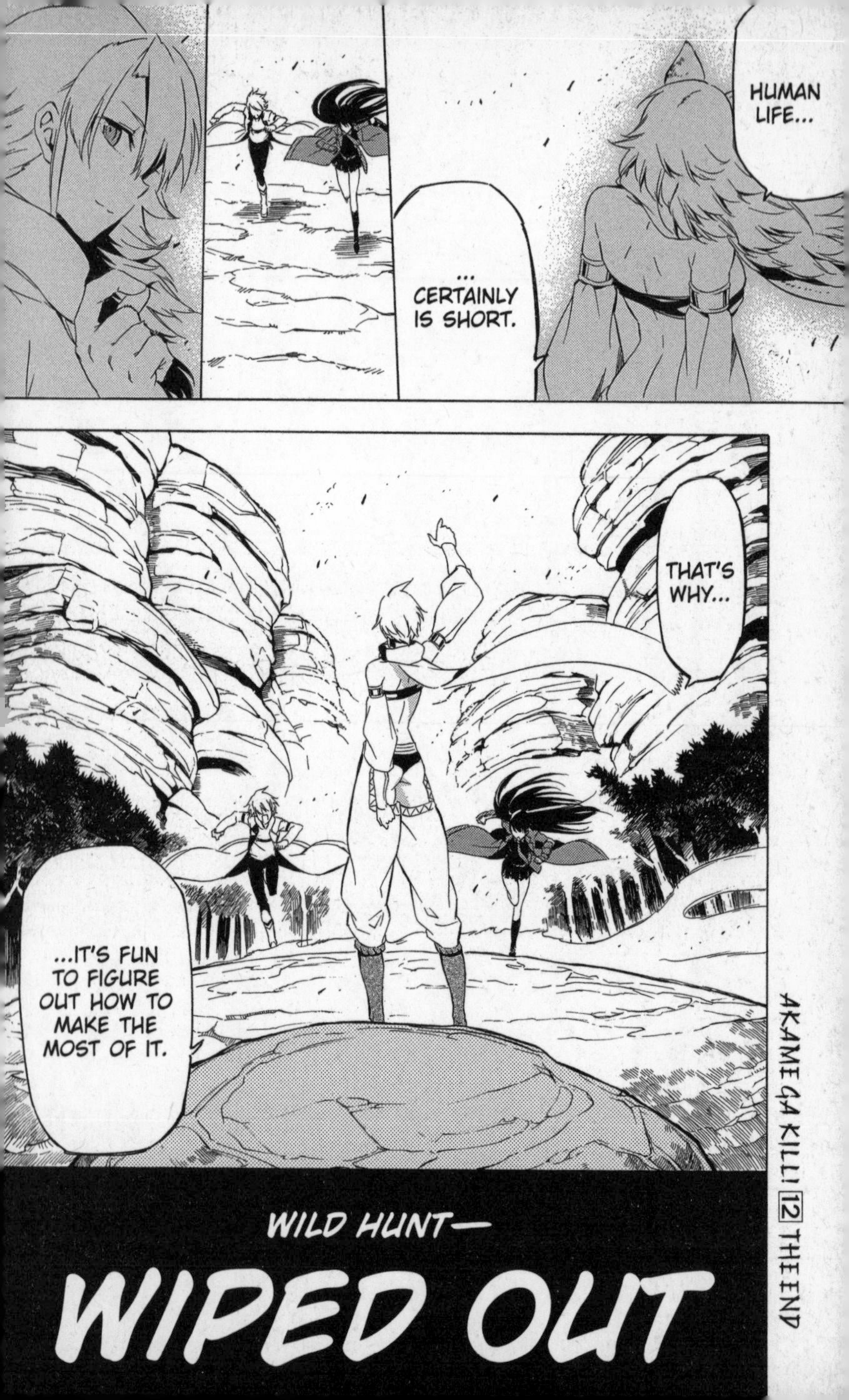
HUMAN LIFE...
...CERTAINLY IS SHORT.
THAT'S WHY...
...IT'S FUN TO FIGURE OUT HOW TO MAKE THE MOST OF IT.
WILD HUNT—
WIPED OUT
AKAME GA KILL! 12 THE END

Akame ga KILL!

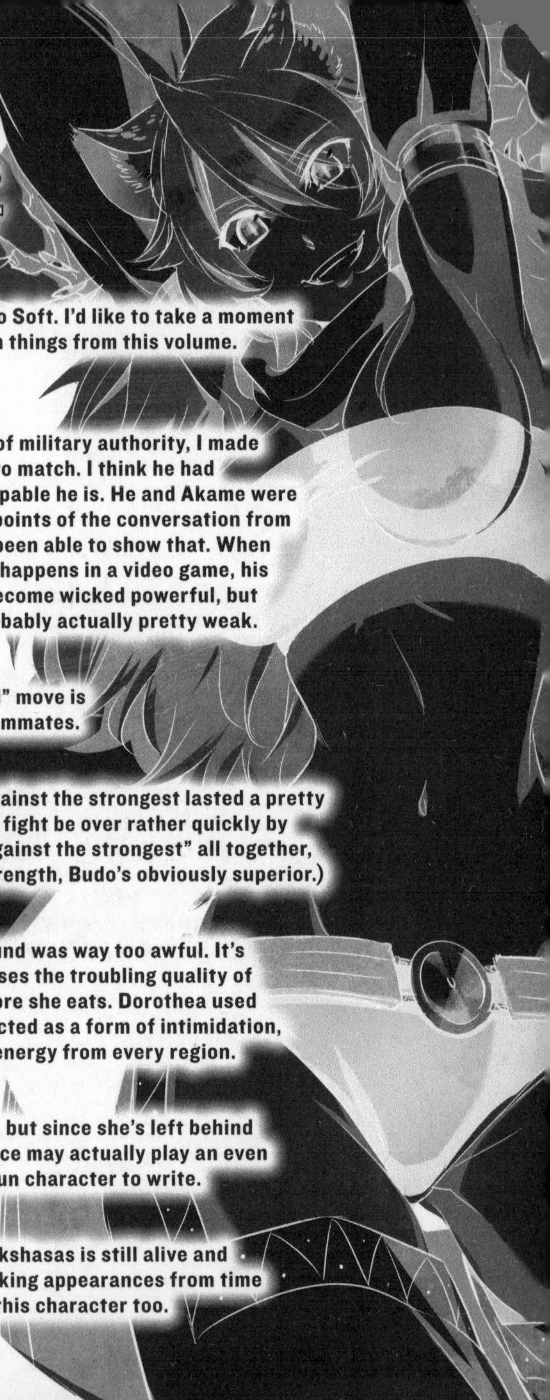

TAKAHIRO's POSTSCRIPT

Hello, this is Takahiro from Minato Soft. I'd like to take a moment to give some extra commentary on things from this volume.

●Commander in Chief Budo
Since he holds the highest office of military authority, I made sure he had a strong appearance to match. I think he had opportunity to exhibit just how capable he is. He and Akame were acquaintances in the past. Some points of the conversation from the previous volume should have been able to show that. When the parameters change, like what happens in a video game, his command and military strength become wicked powerful, but when it comes to politics, he's probably actually pretty weak.

●Lubbock
Apparently his fatal "playing dead" move is something he passed on to his teammates.

●Izou
Since Budo's fight in the battle against the strongest lasted a pretty long time, I decided to have Izou's fight be over rather quickly by comparison. (I lump the "battle against the strongest" all together, but of course when it comes to strength, Budo's obviously superior.)

●Cosmina
Tatsumi's opponent this time around was way too awful. It's just as Dorothea said: she possesses the troubling quality of growing infinitely stronger the more she eats. Dorothea used Cosmina after she'd been resurrected as a form of intimidation, as she sought to gather youthful energy from every region.

●Dorothea
Her ambitions were crushed here, but since she's left behind a terrifying parting gift, her menace may actually play an even bigger role hereafter. She was a fun character to write.

●Suzuka
This ray of hope from the Four Rakshasas is still alive and well. It looks like she'll still be making appearances from time to time. It was pretty fun writing this character too.

Akame ga Kill! 12

Staff

ITOU-SAN
HIRAIWA-SAN
FUJINO-SAN
IMAI-SAN

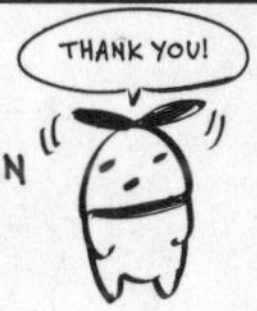
THANK YOU!

main Parther

ORIGINAL WRITER
TAKAHIRO-SAN

EDITOR
KOIZUMI-SAN

Comment

It's Volume 12. Man, time flies...! Lately, my work pace has slowly but surely been settling down. It's reached a plateau. The manga is approaching the ending, bit by bit, so I am planning to run down this final stretch while giving it my all. I hope you'll stick around to enjoy Akame ga KILL! hereafter too!
—Tashiro

SEE YOU AGAIN IN VOLUME 13.

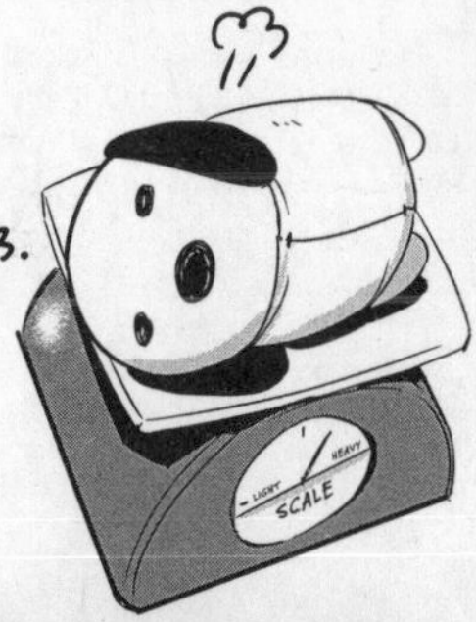
LIGHT
HEAVY
SCALE

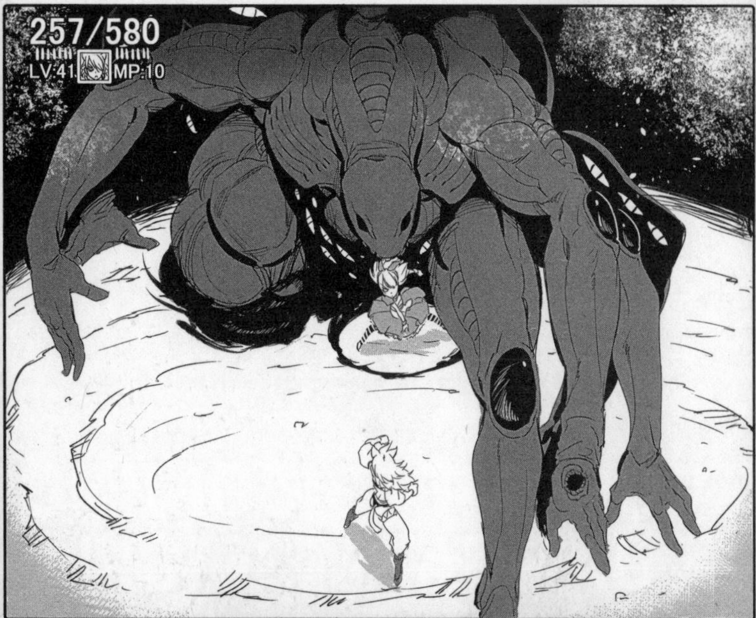
257/580
LV:41
MP:10

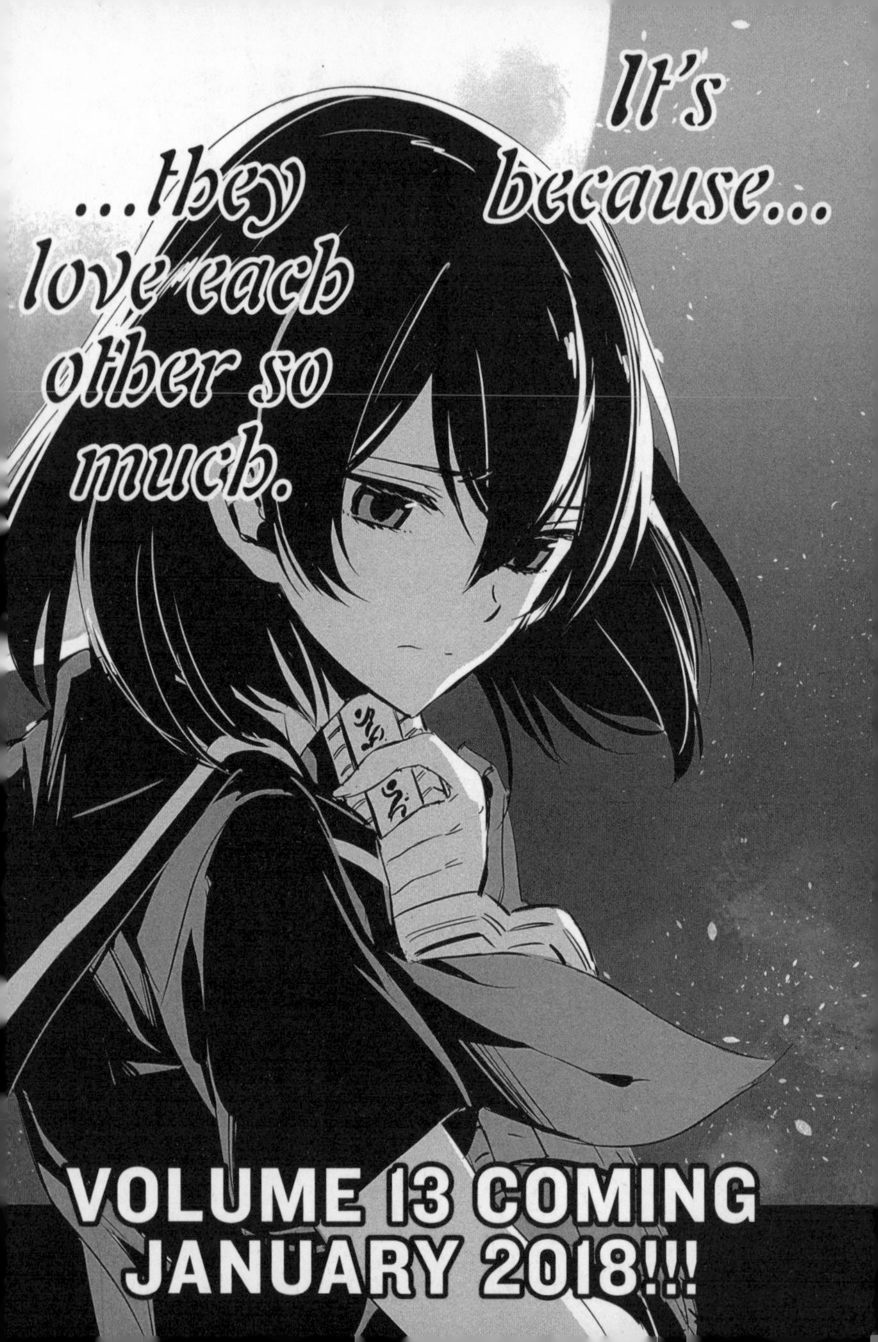

It's because...
...they love each other so much.
VOLUME 13 COMING JANUARY 2018!!!

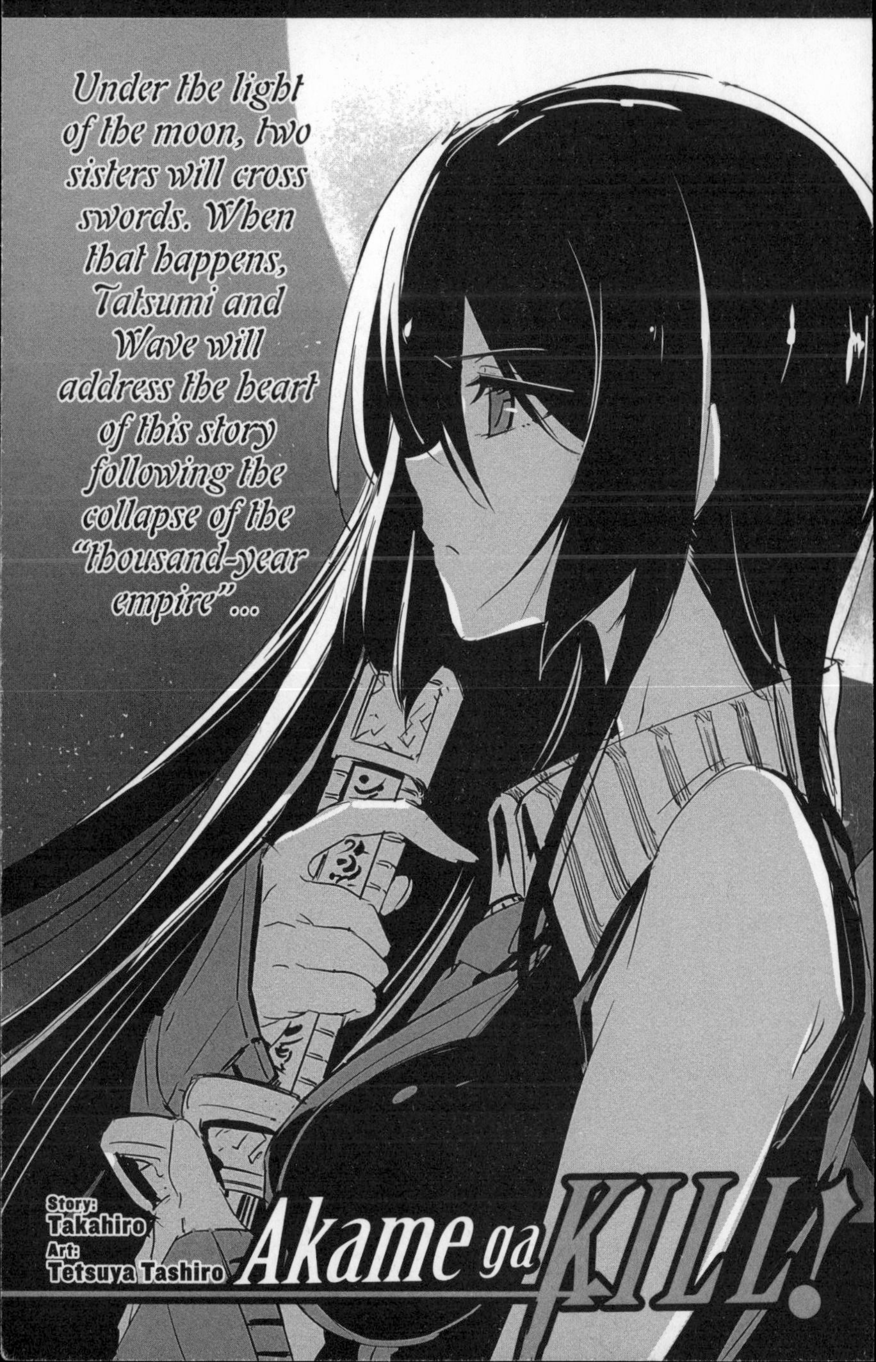
Under the light of the moon, two sisters will cross swords. When that happens, Tatsumi and Wave will address the heart of this story following the collapse of the "thousand-year empire"...
Story: Takahiro
Art: Tetsuya Tashiro
Akame ga KILL!

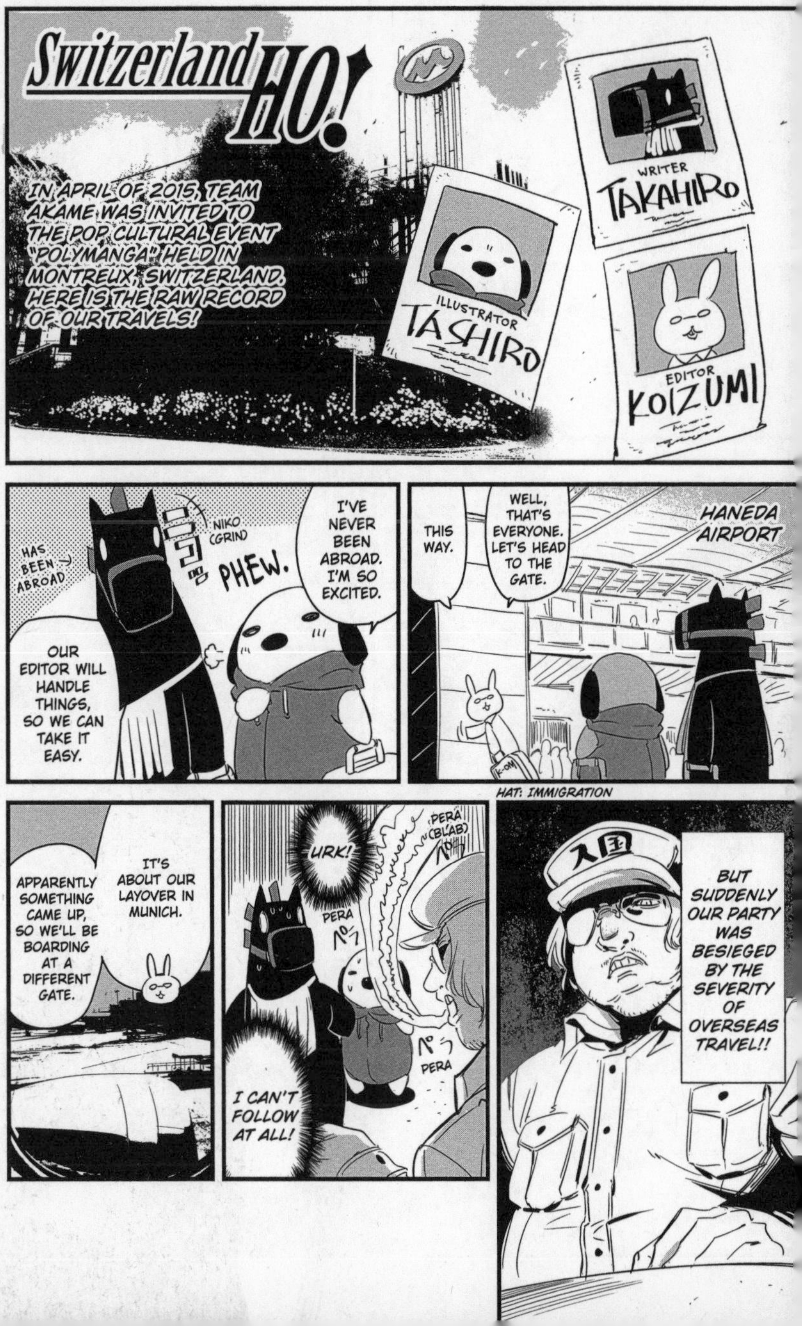

Switzerland HO!
IN APRIL OF 2015, TEAM AKAME WAS INVITED TO THE POP CULTURAL EVENT "POLYMANGA" HELD IN MONTREUX, SWITZERLAND. HERE IS THE RAW RECORD OF OUR TRAVELS!
WRITER
TAKAHIRO
ILLUSTRATOR
TASHIRO
EDITOR
KOIZUMI
HANEDA AIRPORT
WELL, THAT'S EVERYONE. LET'S HEAD TO THE GATE.
THIS WAY.
I'VE NEVER BEEN ABROAD. I'M SO EXCITED.
NIKO (GRIN)
PHEW.
HAS BEEN ABROAD
OUR EDITOR WILL HANDLE THINGS, SO WE CAN TAKE IT EASY.
HAT: IMMIGRATION
BUT SUDDENLY OUR PARTY WAS BESIEGED BY THE SEVERITY OF OVERSEAS TRAVEL!!
PERA (BLAB)
URK!
PERA
PERA
I CAN'T FOLLOW AT ALL!
IT'S ABOUT OUR LAYOVER IN MUNICH.
APPARENTLY SOMETHING CAME UP, SO WE'LL BE BOARDING AT A DIFFERENT GATE.

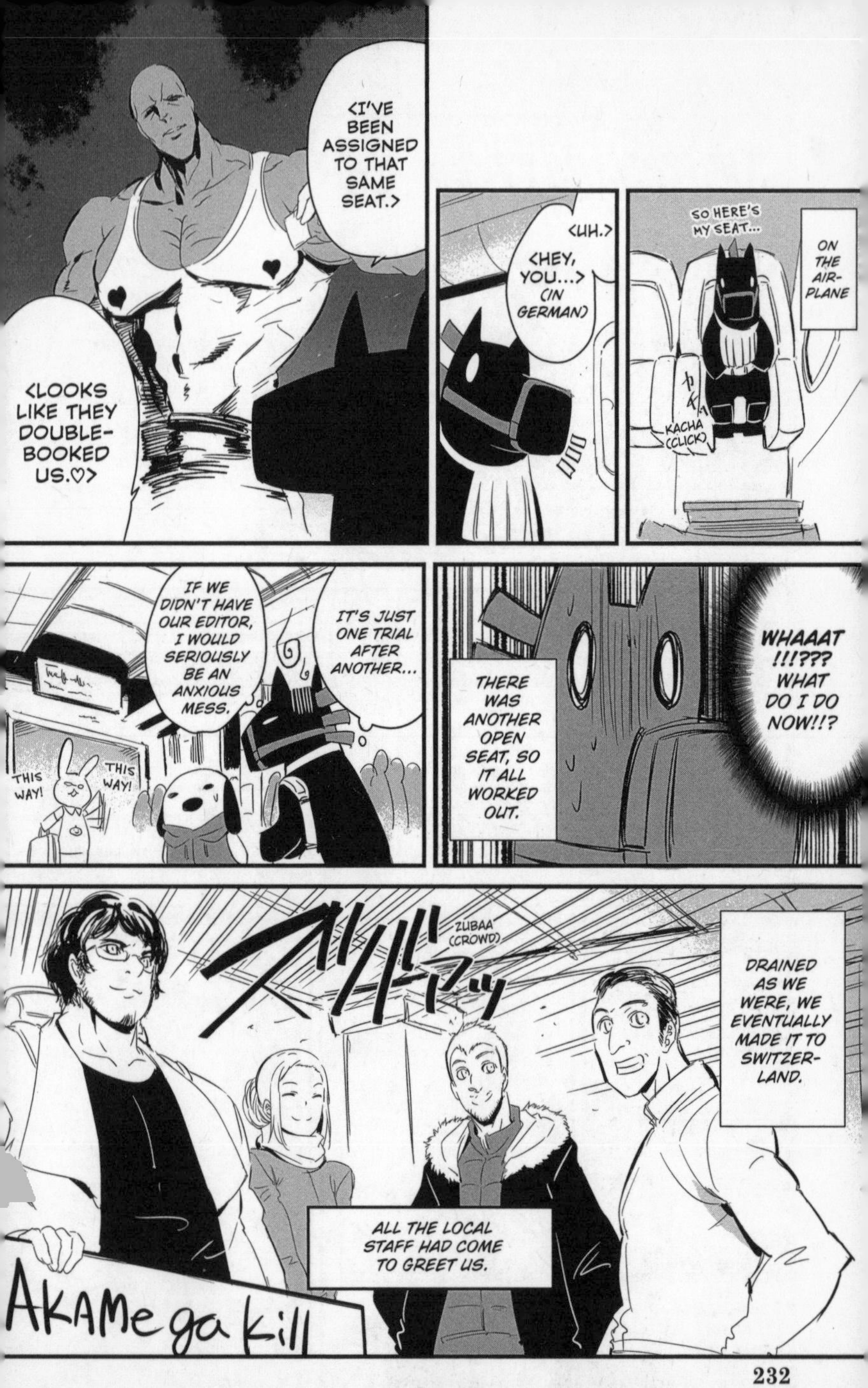

ON THE AIR-PLANE
SO HERE'S MY SEAT...
KACHA (CLICK)
<UH.>
<HEY, YOU...> (IN GERMAN)
<I'VE BEEN ASSIGNED TO THAT SAME SEAT.>
<LOOKS LIKE THEY DOUBLE-BOOKED US.♡>
WHAAAT!!!??? WHAT DO I DO NOW!!?
THERE WAS ANOTHER OPEN SEAT, SO IT ALL WORKED OUT.
IT'S JUST ONE TRIAL AFTER ANOTHER...
IF WE DIDN'T HAVE OUR EDITOR, I WOULD SERIOUSLY BE AN ANXIOUS MESS.
THIS WAY!
THIS WAY!
DRAINED AS WE WERE, WE EVENTUALLY MADE IT TO SWITZER-LAND.
ZUBAA (CROWD)
ALL THE LOCAL STAFF HAD COME TO GREET US.
AKAMe ga kill

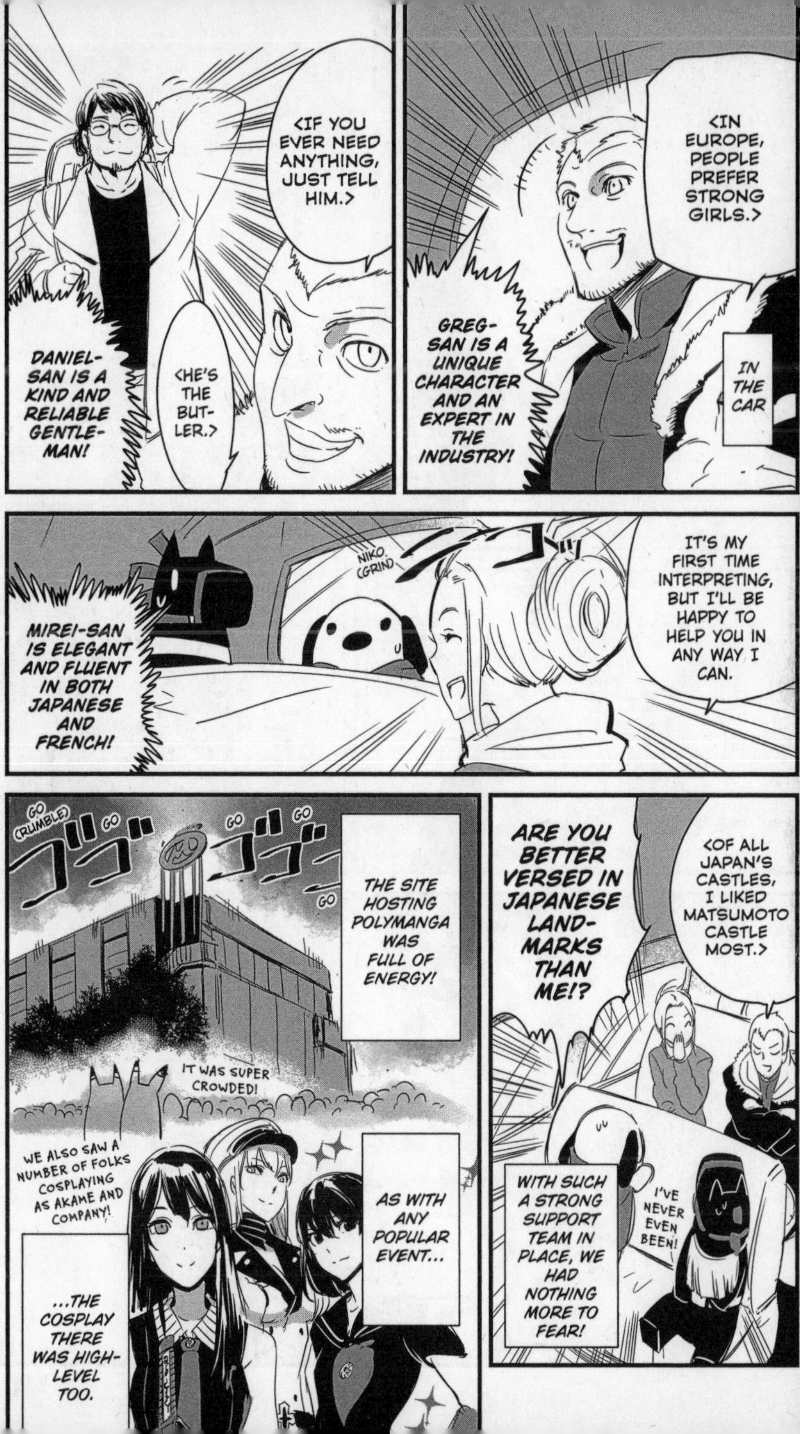
IN THE CAR
<IN EUROPE, PEOPLE PREFER STRONG GIRLS.>
GREG-SAN IS A UNIQUE CHARACTER AND AN EXPERT IN THE INDUSTRY!
<IF YOU EVER NEED ANYTHING, JUST TELL HIM.>
<HE'S THE BUTLER.>
DANIEL-SAN IS A KIND AND RELIABLE GENTLEMAN!
IT'S MY FIRST TIME INTERPRETING, BUT I'LL BE HAPPY TO HELP YOU IN ANY WAY I CAN.
NIKO (GRIN)
MIREI-SAN IS ELEGANT AND FLUENT IN BOTH JAPANESE AND FRENCH!
<OF ALL JAPAN'S CASTLES, I LIKED MATSUMOTO CASTLE MOST.>
ARE YOU BETTER VERSED IN JAPANESE LANDMARKS THAN ME!?
I'VE NEVER EVEN BEEN!
WITH SUCH A STRONG SUPPORT TEAM IN PLACE, WE HAD NOTHING MORE TO FEAR!
GO (RUMBLE) GO GO GO GO
THE SITE HOSTING POLYMANGA WAS FULL OF ENERGY!
IT WAS SUPER CROWDED!
AS WITH ANY POPULAR EVENT...
...THE COSPLAY THERE WAS HIGH-LEVEL TOO.
WE ALSO SAW A NUMBER OF FOLKS COSPLAYING AS AKAME AND COMPANY!

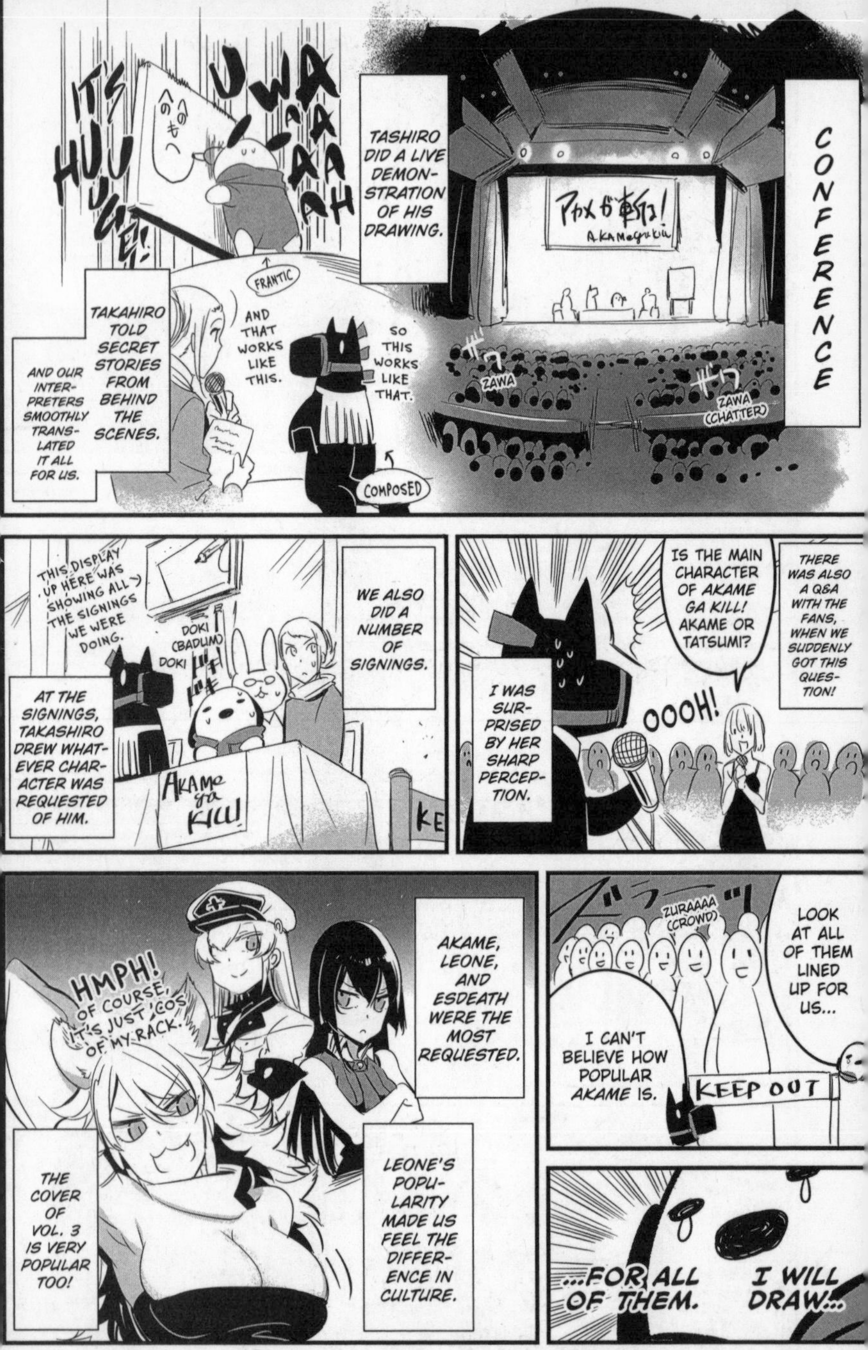
CONFERENCE
ZAWA
ZAWA (CHATTER)
TASHIRO DID A LIVE DEMONSTRATION OF HIS DRAWING.
UWAAAAAAH
IT'S HUUUUGE!
FRANTIC
SO THIS WORKS LIKE THAT.
AND THAT WORKS LIKE THIS.
COMPOSED
TAKAHIRO TOLD SECRET STORIES FROM BEHIND THE SCENES.
AND OUR INTERPRETERS SMOOTHLY TRANSLATED IT ALL FOR US.
THERE WAS ALSO A Q&A WITH THE FANS, WHEN WE SUDDENLY GOT THIS QUESTION!
IS THE MAIN CHARACTER OF AKAME GA KILL! AKAME OR TATSUMI?
OOOH!
I WAS SURPRISED BY HER SHARP PERCEPTION.
WE ALSO DID A NUMBER OF SIGNINGS.
THIS DISPLAY UP HERE WAS SHOWING ALL THE SIGNINGS WE WERE DOING.
DOKI (BADUM) DOKI
AT THE SIGNINGS, TAKASHIRO DREW WHATEVER CHARACTER WAS REQUESTED OF HIM.
Akame ga Kill!
KE
LOOK AT ALL OF THEM LINED UP FOR US...
ZURAAAA (CROWD)
I CAN'T BELIEVE HOW POPULAR AKAME IS.
KEEP OUT
I WILL DRAW...
...FOR ALL OF THEM.
AKAME, LEONE, AND ESDEATH WERE THE MOST REQUESTED.
HMPH! OF COURSE, IT'S JUST 'COS OF MY RACK.
LEONE'S POPULARITY MADE US FEEL THE DIFFERENCE IN CULTURE.
THE COVER OF VOL. 3 IS VERY POPULAR TOO!

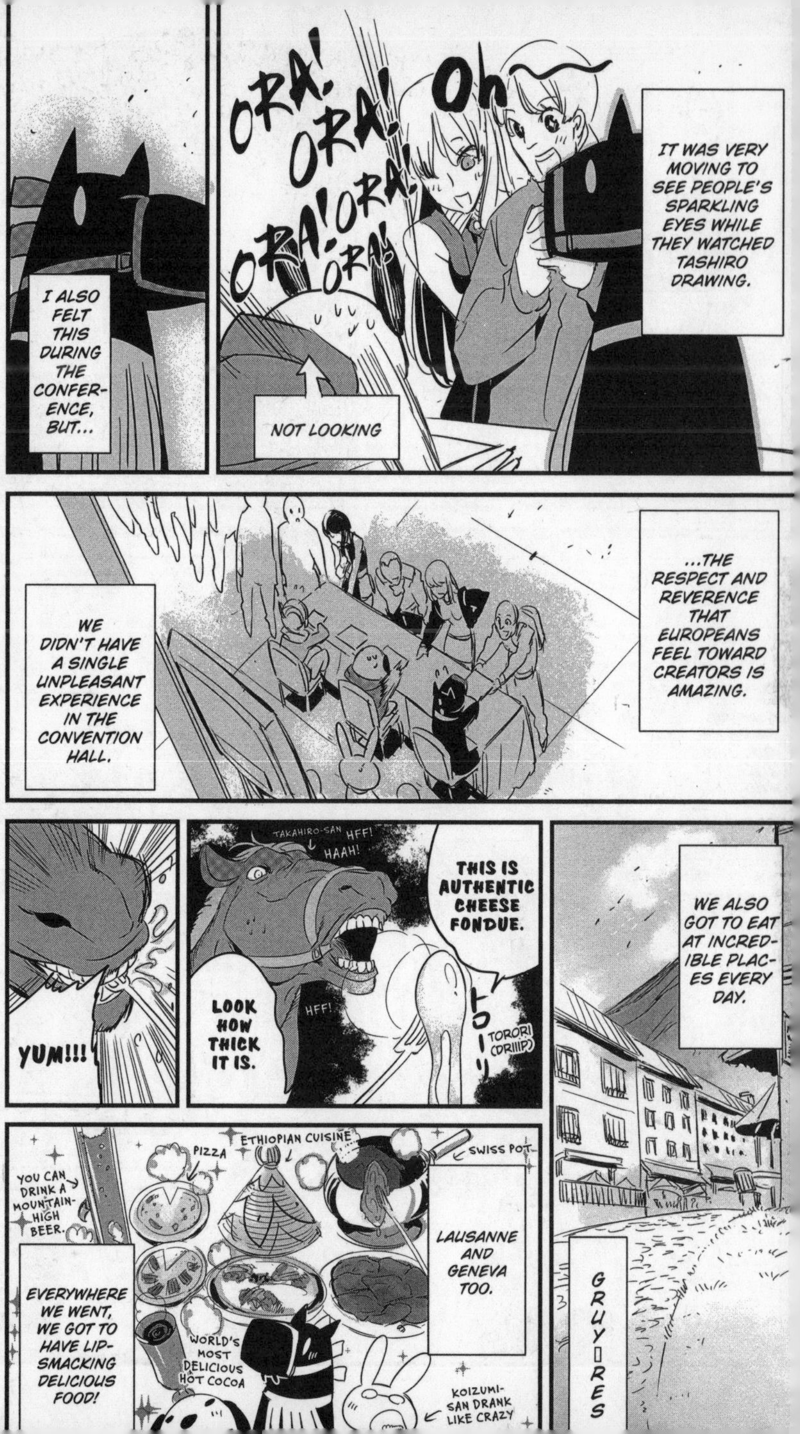
IT WAS VERY MOVING TO SEE PEOPLE'S SPARKLING EYES WHILE THEY WATCHED TASHIRO DRAWING.
Oh~
ORA! ORA! ORA! ORA! ORA! ORA!
NOT LOOKING
I ALSO FELT THIS DURING THE CONFERENCE, BUT...
...THE RESPECT AND REVERENCE THAT EUROPEANS FEEL TOWARD CREATORS IS AMAZING.
WE DIDN'T HAVE A SINGLE UNPLEASANT EXPERIENCE IN THE CONVENTION HALL.
WE ALSO GOT TO EAT AT INCREDIBLE PLACES EVERY DAY.
GRUY□RES
TAKAHIRO-SAN
HFF!
HAAH!
THIS IS AUTHENTIC CHEESE FONDUE.
HFF!
LOOK HOW THICK IT IS.
TORORI (DRIIIP)
YUM!!!
SWISS POT
ETHIOPIAN CUISINE
PIZZA
YOU CAN DRINK A MOUNTAIN-HIGH BEER.
LAUSANNE AND GENEVA TOO.
EVERYWHERE WE WENT, WE GOT TO HAVE LIP-SMACKING DELICIOUS FOOD!
WORLD'S MOST DELICIOUS HOT COCOA
KOIZUMI-SAN DRANK LIKE CRAZY

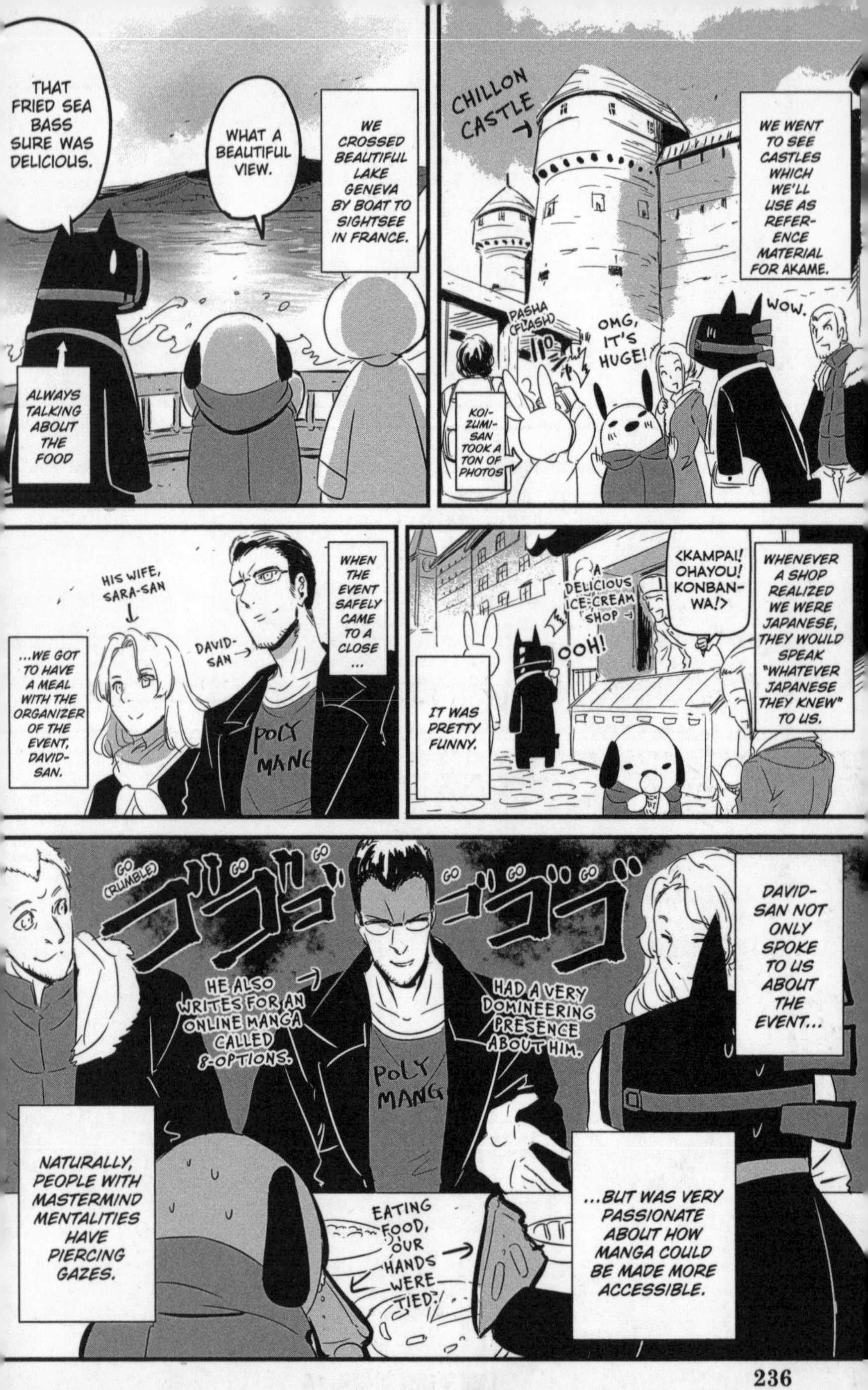
WE WENT TO SEE CASTLES WHICH WE'LL USE AS REFER-ENCE MATERIAL FOR AKAME.
CHILLON CASTLE
WOW.
OMG, IT'S HUGE!
PASHA (FLASH)
KOI-ZUMI-SAN TOOK A TON OF PHOTOS
WE CROSSED BEAUTIFUL LAKE GENEVA BY BOAT TO SIGHTSEE IN FRANCE.
WHAT A BEAUTIFUL VIEW.
THAT FRIED SEA BASS SURE WAS DELICIOUS.
ALWAYS TALKING ABOUT THE FOOD
WHENEVER A SHOP REALIZED WE WERE JAPANESE, THEY WOULD SPEAK "WHATEVER JAPANESE THEY KNEW" TO US.
<KAMPAI! OHAYOU! KONBAN-WA!>
A DELICIOUS ICE-CREAM SHOP
OOH!
IT WAS PRETTY FUNNY.
WHEN THE EVENT SAFELY CAME TO A CLOSE...
DAVID-SAN
HIS WIFE, SARA-SAN
...WE GOT TO HAVE A MEAL WITH THE ORGANIZER OF THE EVENT, DAVID-SAN.
POLY MANG
DAVID-SAN NOT ONLY SPOKE TO US ABOUT THE EVENT...
GO (RUMBLE) GO GO GO GO GO
HAD A VERY DOMINEERING PRESENCE ABOUT HIM.
HE ALSO WRITES FOR AN ONLINE MANGA CALLED 8-OPTIONS.
POLY MANG
...BUT WAS VERY PASSIONATE ABOUT HOW MANGA COULD BE MADE MORE ACCESSIBLE.
EATING FOOD, OUR HANDS WERE TIED.
NATURALLY, PEOPLE WITH MASTERMIND MENTALITIES HAVE PIERCING GAZES.

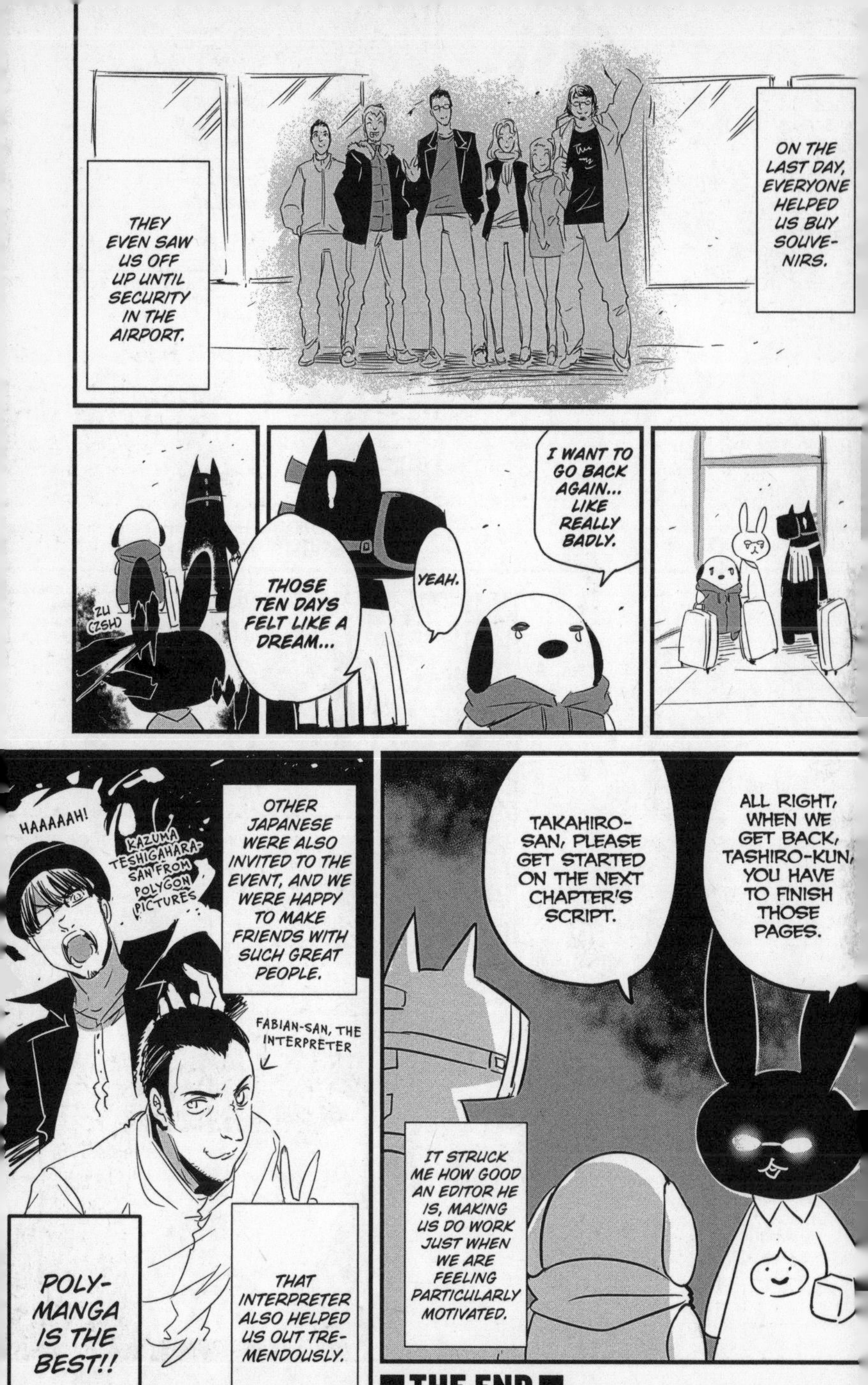
ON THE LAST DAY, EVERYONE HELPED US BUY SOUVENIRS.
THEY EVEN SAW US OFF UP UNTIL SECURITY IN THE AIRPORT.
I WANT TO GO BACK AGAIN... LIKE REALLY BADLY.
YEAH.
THOSE TEN DAYS FELT LIKE A DREAM...
ZU (ZSH)
ALL RIGHT, WHEN WE GET BACK, TASHIRO-KUN, YOU HAVE TO FINISH THOSE PAGES.
TAKAHIRO-SAN, PLEASE GET STARTED ON THE NEXT CHAPTER'S SCRIPT.
IT STRUCK ME HOW GOOD AN EDITOR HE IS, MAKING US DO WORK JUST WHEN WE ARE FEELING PARTICULARLY MOTIVATED.
OTHER JAPANESE WERE ALSO INVITED TO THE EVENT, AND WE WERE HAPPY TO MAKE FRIENDS WITH SUCH GREAT PEOPLE.
HAAAAAH!
KAZUMA TESHIGAHARA-SAN FROM POLYGON PICTURES
FABIAN-SAN, THE INTERPRETER
THAT INTERPRETER ALSO HELPED US OUT TREMENDOUSLY.
POLY-MANGA IS THE BEST!!

THE END

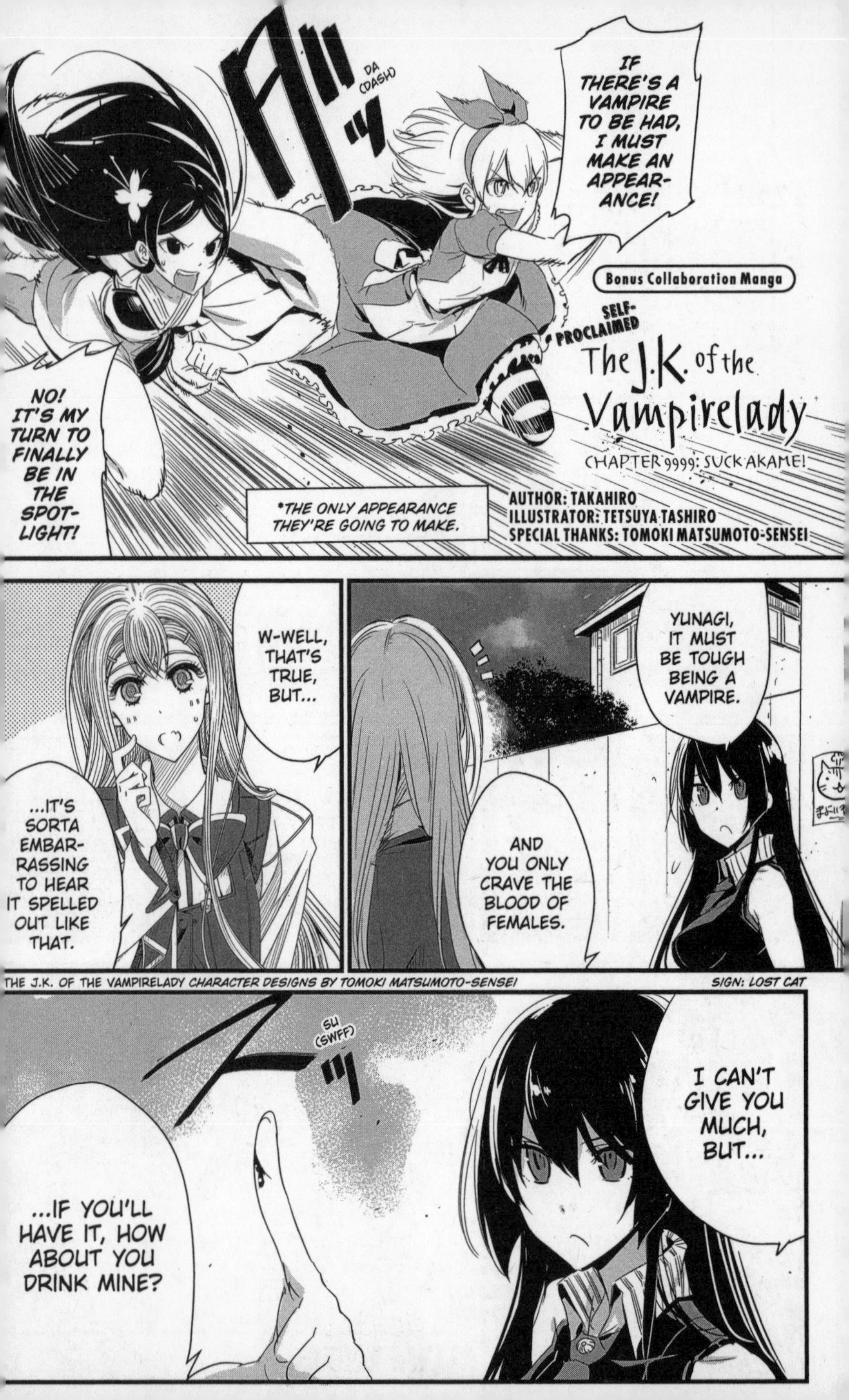
IF THERE'S A VAMPIRE TO BE HAD, I MUST MAKE AN APPEARANCE!
DA (DASH)
NO! IT'S MY TURN TO FINALLY BE IN THE SPOTLIGHT!
Bonus Collaboration Manga
SELF-PROCLAIMED
The J.K. of the Vampirelady
CHAPTER 9999: SUCK AKAME!
*THE ONLY APPEARANCE THEY'RE GOING TO MAKE.
AUTHOR: TAKAHIRO
ILLUSTRATOR: TETSUYA TASHIRO
SPECIAL THANKS: TOMOKI MATSUMOTO-SENSEI
YUNAGI, IT MUST BE TOUGH BEING A VAMPIRE.
AND YOU ONLY CRAVE THE BLOOD OF FEMALES.
W-WELL, THAT'S TRUE, BUT...
...IT'S SORTA EMBARRASSING TO HEAR IT SPELLED OUT LIKE THAT.
THE J.K. OF THE VAMPIRELADY CHARACTER DESIGNS BY TOMOKI MATSUMOTO-SENSEI
SIGN: LOST CAT
SU (SWFF)
I CAN'T GIVE YOU MUCH, BUT...
...IF YOU'LL HAVE IT, HOW ABOUT YOU DRINK MINE?

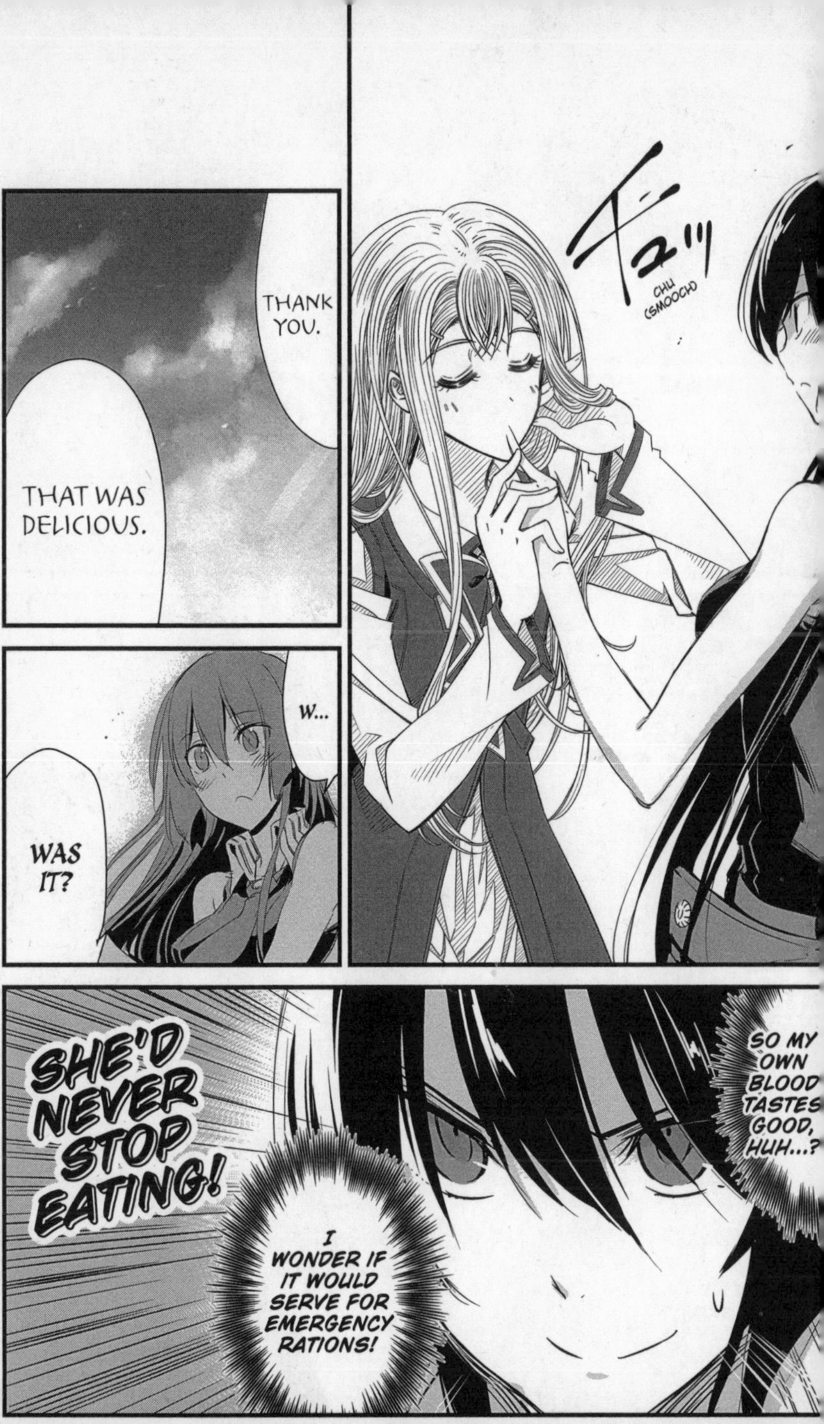
CHU (SMOOCH)
THANK YOU.
THAT WAS DELICIOUS.
W...
WAS IT?
SO MY OWN BLOOD TASTES GOOD, HUH...?
I WONDER IF IT WOULD SERVE FOR EMERGENCY RATIONS!
SHE'D NEVER STOP EATING!

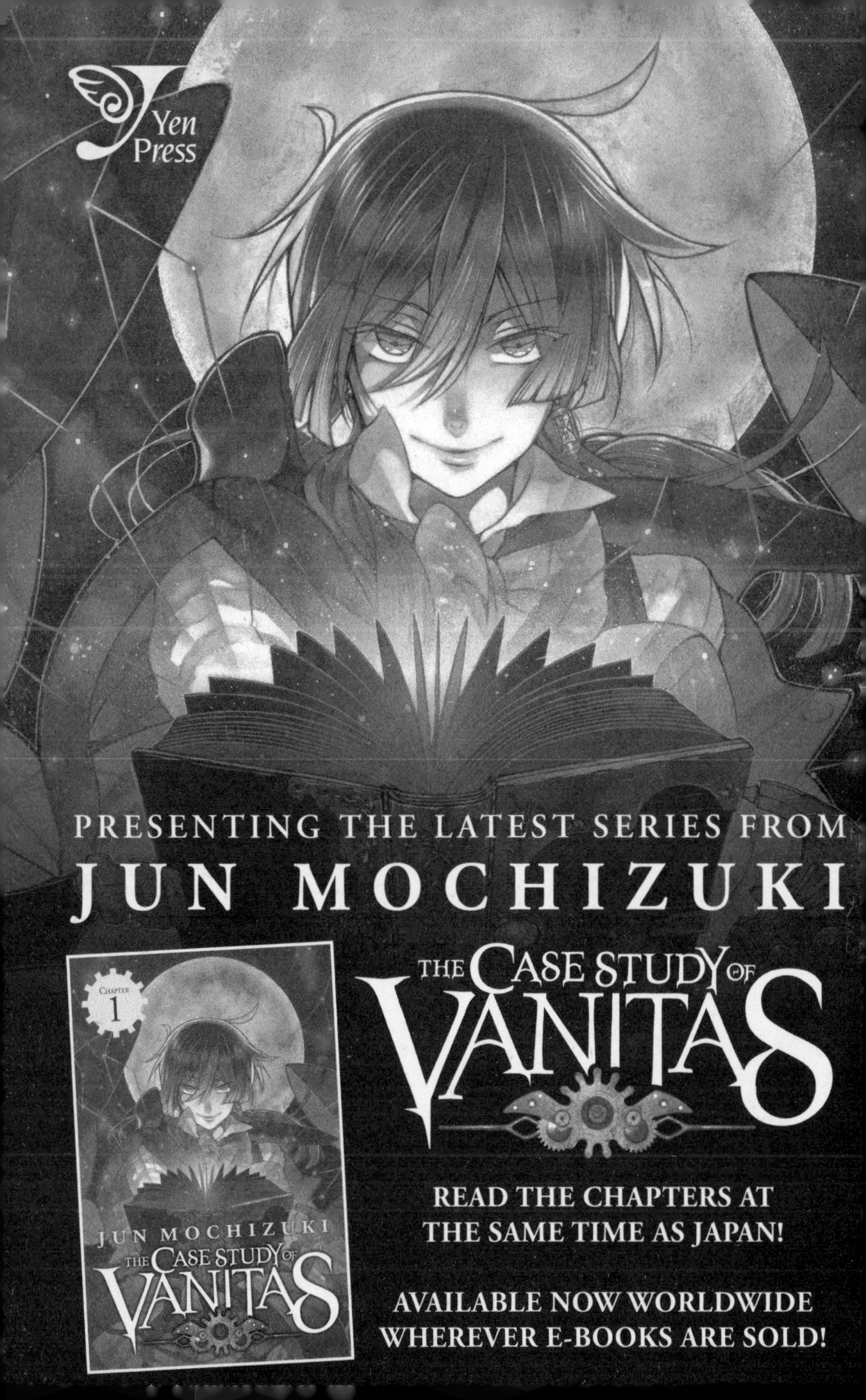
Yen Press
PRESENTING THE LATEST SERIES FROM
JUN MOCHIZUKI
THE CASE STUDY OF VANITAS
CHAPTER 1
JUN MOCHIZUKI
THE CASE STUDY OF VANITAS
READ THE CHAPTERS AT
THE SAME TIME AS JAPAN!
AVAILABLE NOW WORLDWIDE
WHEREVER E-BOOKS ARE SOLD!

AKAME GA KILL! 12

Takahiro
Tetsuya Tashiro

Translation: Christine Dashiell
Lettering: Xian Michele Lee

AKAME GA KILL! Vol. 12
© 2015 Takahiro, Tetsuya Tashiro / SQUARE ENIX CO., LTD. First published in Japan in 2015 by SQUARE ENIX CO., LTD. English translation rights arranged with SQUARE ENIX CO., LTD. and Yen Press, LLC through Tuttle-Mori Agency, Inc., Tokyo.

English translation © 2017 by SQUARE ENIX CO., LTD.

Yen Press
1290 Avenue of the Americas
New York, NY 10104

Visit us at yenpress.com
facebook.com/yenpress
twitter.com/yenpress
yenpress.tumblr.com
instagram.com/yenpress

Yen Press is an imprint of Yen Press, LLC.
The Yen Press name and logo are trademarks of Yen Press, LLC.

The publisher is not responsible for websites (or their content) that are not owned by the publisher.

Library of Congress Control Number: 2015373812

First Yen Press Edition: October 2017

ISBNs: 978-0-316-47332-3 (paperback)
        978-0-316-47334-7 (ebook)

10 9 8 7 6 5 4 3 2 1

BVG

Printed in the United States of America